The
Study
of
Philosophy

The Study of Philosophy

An Introduction

S. MORRIS ENGEL
University of Southern California

HOLT, RINEHART AND WINSTON
New York · Chicago · San Francisco · Dallas
Montreal · Toronto · London · Sydney

To the Memory of My
Mother-in-Law
ZLOTA CHISVIN
(1900–1966)
and My
Father-in-Law
ZALMON CHISVIN
With Love and Affection

The cover of this book is a rendering of a detail from a
statue of Socrates, in the British Museum.

Library of Congress Cataloging in Publication Data
Engel, S   Morris, 1931–
   The study of philosophy.

   Bibliography: p.
   Includes index.
   1. Philosophy — Introductions.   I.   Title.
BD21.E6   100   80-27458
ISBN 0-03-047511-2

1 2   3   4   5   038 9 8 7 6 5 4 3 2 1

PREFACE

A teacher of the introductory course in philosophy knows two things about his or her students: most of them will come to the course with eagerness and anticipation; most of them will avoid any second course in the subject. Obviously these students will end the course disillusioned by their introduction to philosophy, but it is questionable that their expectations were unjustified. Evidently they believed that philosophy dealt with the big questions of existence; the search for the answers to those questions — whether or not these answers were found — at least exercised the mind and provided the prerequisites for the attainment of wisdom, of an ability to recognize the nature of reality.

Because I believe that these students' expectations are — or at least could be — valid I have sought in this book to provide a text that will not disappoint our newcomers, without either oversimplifying our subject or talking down to them. To achieve this it has seemed to me that the best way would be simply to tell the story of philosophy, while at the same time attempting to recapture the older conception of philosophy.

The book thus begins at the beginning, with an account of where philosophy originated and why it did so at that particular time and place. In this first chapter I have tried to show how it was the discovery of the reality of the external world, made for the first time by these remarkable people, the so-called pre-Socratics, and their wonder and curiosity about it, that led them to propound a theory — Atomism — that in its essentials is still accepted by science today.

My next chapter is devoted to Socrates, who may be considered the father of philosophy, for he set it on the course it has followed for over two thousand years. I have tried to show that if what lies at the core of the accomplishment of the pre-Socratics is the philosophic discovery of the external world, then what lies at the core of Socrates' accomplishment is the discovery that man possesses a soul — that part of him which is most himself and which is eternal and indestructible. My account of his life, his method of philosophizing, the times in which he lived, his trial and death, is related against the background of that single, great discovery of his, and is interspersed with short quotations from the early dialogues of Plato, quotations which have been considered among the most moving and eloquent in all literature.

This first part of this text, entitled "Philosophy's Beginnings," is thus introductory and is designed to set both the tone and stage for the discussion of the main areas and problems of philosophy to follow.

Before undertaking that discussion, however, it has seemed advisable to devote a certain time to acquiring some of that skill which has always been considered inseparable from the activity of philosophy — a proficiency in the use of reason and a heightened awareness of its value. Part II of the text is thus devoted to providing the student with an increased insight into the principles of reasoning and extensive practice in its use. Avoiding formal logic, this part of the text devotes itself to a presentation of the informal fallacies — a topic that students have always found a delight to study and in which they quickly achieve mastery.

What follows after this interlude is an account of the central questions that philosophy has posed to itself over the course of the centuries. I have arranged these both in logical and in parallel chronological order. Combining the historical with a problems approach, this central part of the text shows how questions about what we ought to do (Ethics) are intimately connected with questions regarding whether the world is such that it will allow us to do it (Metaphysics), which, in turn, is connected with the question how we can know this to be so (Epistemology), which leads, finally, to the question how much faith we can place in this knowledge (Logic).

My own students have always found it stimulating to see how these four major areas of philosophy are connected and why, in the end, it is not really possible to deal with any one of them without dealing with the others. In addition, seeing this clearly enables them to recognize that at the core of philosophy lies one major fundamental goal or problem — one first raised so dramatically by Plato in his Allegory of the Cave and explored by practically all subsequent philosophers up to and including the philosopher who is regarded as probably the greatest of our century, Wittgenstein (albeit in his case it took a remarkably strange turn). It has been my experience that, if done well, such an account of philosophy (concerned with that endless search for a glimpse of the way things are) enables the student to see that there is and has been progress in philosophy: progress, not in the sense of achieving a solution to this problem of the nature of our human predicament but rather in our progressively deeper and more profound understanding of it.

Let me therefore say a few words here about these four major areas and questions of philosophy which form its core subject matter and which are taken up in Part III of this text.

The discovery of the external world and speculation about its nature by the pre-Socratic cosmologists led, in turn, to the work of Socrates. His contribution, with its focus on man's nature and vocation, set the stage for the intense investigation, in the decades and centuries that followed, of the purpose of life and the way that purpose might be achieved. These explorations culminated in one of the greatest works on ethics ever written, by one who is still regarded as among the greatest philosophers of all time, Aristotle (384–323 B. C.). The work is the *Nichomachean Ethics*. This is, therefore, the first of the four areas and problems taken up in this part of the text.

As in the previous cases, the account of that work is placed against its social and political background (for no philosophy emerges in a vacuum but is a reflection and summary of the thought and experience of its age and time). And once again, I have tried to show how it too is a product of a crucial insight — in this case the seemingly obvious yet profound truth that happiness is being able to applaud oneself, or, in words closer to Aristotle's own, that to be happy one must be good.

Were we interested in the history of philosophy and in studying its main stages, we would go on to consider how the question of human happiness, so dominant in the work of Aristotle and in his era, became transformed at the end of this period, in the hands of that strange, mystical philosopher Plotinus (A.D. 204–270), into the question of human blessedness. We would then study the main works of the Middle Ages, all largely concerned with the question of God's existence and nature. But this is not our interest here. Since, however, such questions are closely related to those raised in the area of metaphysics, the discussion of that discipline at this point has made it possible to keep to the chronological order without abandoning entirely the logical organization inherent in the material.

The next chapter is therefore devoted to metaphysics, and in choosing as the representative figure of that period Giordano Bruno (1548–1600) — whose works challenged the authority of the church and cast in doubt the world-picture it had carefully constructed and preserved — I have tried to capture something of the personal drama of philosophy, which is an intimate part of its story.

The manner in which philosophy has come to see man's condition in any particular period has very often been influenced, as we have seen, by the prevailing moral, religious, and social beliefs of the age, and as one enters the modern period (which in philosophy is considered to begin with Descartes, 1612–1665) this new factor is the rise of science. The modern period in philosophy is thus characterized by its absorption in epistemology — in the origin and validity of our knowledge — and the shunning of metaphysics (with its concern with such ultimate questions as the origin of the universe, the nature of the soul, and the existence of God).

The thinkers in this period tended to dismiss discussion of such questions because they had proven insoluble and had been for too long the occasion of interminable dispute. Following the lead of science, with its spectacular successes in the seventeenth and eighteenth centuries, philosophers turned their attention to questions that could be approached on the model of science. Epistemology thus came to dominate the period — as it still does, at least in the English-speaking world.

Although some of the most important work in the history of philosophy was done during this period, many philosophers believe that the enormous influence of science upon philosophy, and the resulting effort to model philosophy on science, was a serious blunder, one that has proven disastrous for philosophy. This "epistemological turn," as it has come to be called, has assumed the force of a fixation and has been responsible, some have argued, for the neglect of other equally important issues and questions.

However this may be, this "epistemological turn" represents an important chapter in philosophy and in what follows I have devoted more space to it than to any of the three other topics in this part of our study.

Just as the fascination with science and its spectacular successes influenced philosophy in the direction it took and the pursuits it made its own, so the preoccupation with language and meaning, characteristic of the contemporary period, is reflected in the philosophy that is presently being pursued. The last chapter in Part III of our text is thus devoted to a discussion of this area of philosophy and highlights the life and work of Ludwig Wittgenstein.

But the preoccupation with such questions as "Who are we?"; "What is there?"; "What can we know?"; and "How so?" discussed in the four main areas of philosophy (Ethics, Metaphysics, Epistemology, and Logic) does not exhaust all its concerns.

In addition to the interests that constitute the traditional core of philosophy and its specific and distinct subject matter, philosophers have also been interested in investigating the foundations of the concerns of other thinkers — artists, scientists, historians, and so on. What is it that these people do, philosophers have asked, and what is its meaning?

Part IV of this text is devoted to an account and exploration of this further reach of philosophy. I have separated this dimension of philosophy from the rest to avoid giving the beginning student the impression that philosophy is a hodgepodge of things — an endless discussion of anything and everything.

It is, of course, not that at all. Not everything is philosophy and not every discussion is philosophical. To see this clearly, however, requires that we separate (as is unfortunately rarely done) the critical investigation of such disciplines as art, history, or science (discussed under such titles as the Philosophy of Art, the Philosophy of History, and the Philosophy of Science) from the four investigations (ethics, metaphysics, epistemology, and logic) that belong to philosophy alone and that form its specific subject matter. I have found that doing so enables the beginning student to see more clearly and understand more deeply what it is that philosophers do and what its significance is.

The book thus ends with a discussion of a problem in the area of aesthetics. In choosing tragedy as the topic of discussion, I have tried to bring my account back once again to its beginnings, for what is central to this problem is the question of life's meaning and that is after all what philosophy is about.

Although what the reader has in this book was written down in its final form during the past year, it has been very long in the making. My debts are thus both many and varied. I wish to acknowledge with thanks and fondness the inspiring teachers it was my good fortune to have both as an undergraduate and graduate student: K. W. Maurer and W. M. Sibley at the University of Manitoba; and Fulton H. Anderson, Emil Fackenheim, and David Savan at the University of Toronto. If I have succeeded in writing simply and not without feeling, shunning undue complexity and remoteness, I owe the art to them. Important also have been the various distinguished teachers and scholars it has been my good fortune to come to know on their visits to our School of Philosophy here at USC during the eighteen years that I have been here, among them Lionel Ruby, Paul Weiss, and Abraham Kaplan. They too in a very real sense have been my "teachers," and much of what I have tried to achieve here has been deeply influenced by their teaching, writing, and example. Nor can I neglect here the great debt I owe to the impact of other philosophers whose writings have contributed so much to my own orientation and view of philosophy, its setting and teaching, among them John Wisdom, Walter Kaufmann, and James K. Feibleman.

Finally I would like to express my thanks to the publisher's readers for their helpful reviews of the manuscript. I am especially grateful to James L. Christian (whose kind words are still warmly remembered), Peter Angeles, and Larry Hitterdale. And many thanks too for his reading and help on the manuscript to my young colleague Doug Deaver. I would also like to express my thanks to Hoose Philosophy librarian Bridget Molloy and her assistant Ross Scimeca for help always graciously given.

Lastly a word of thanks to David P. Boynton, Philosophy Editor, for his affection and encouragement, and to Brian M. Heald, Senior Project Editor, for making this a much finer book than it would otherwise have been.

Los Angeles   S. M. E.
December 1980

CONTENTS

8 Logic: How much faith can we place in this knowledge? 279

part IV
OTHER QUESTIONS

9 Tragedy and the mystery of human suffering 311

Index

Introduction

Finding himself one day at the Olympic games and looking about him, Pythagoras, an ancient Greek thinker, observed that there were three classes of people present.

There was, first, a great mass of people who had come there to trade and barter. There was nothing wrong with that but that was their main purpose. Lovers of gain, he called them. Then there was another group of people, whose purpose was not to trade and barter but to participate in the games in the hope of winning fame and fortune for both themselves and their cities. Pythagoras called them the lovers of honor. And, finally, there was yet another group, who had come simply to watch. Pythagoras called them the lovers of the spectacle.

It then occurred to Pythagoras, the story goes, that one can find these same three classes of people everywhere. There is, first, again the vast majority of people whose main object is to try to gain as many material goods as possible. He did not think there was anything necessarily wrong with that. They were, again, lovers of gain. And then there is another, second group, smaller than the first, whose main goal is to achieve fame by distinguishing themselves in some pursuit.

They are the lovers of honor. And, finally, there is a third group, smaller even than the second group, who did not care that much for wealth or fame, but whose main hope is to gain an understanding of this spectacle called life. Pythagoras thought a good name for these lovers of the spectacle was "philosophers" — a term meaning "lovers of wisdom." Including himself in this group, he went on to remark that it would not be appropriate to call themselves wise, for only God is wise, but some people may call themselves *lovers* of wisdom. And thus the word "philosophy" was coined.

Although few since Pythagoras' time have denied that philosophy is indeed somehow connected with the love of and search for wisdom, philosophers have not found it easy to say what this thing called "wisdom" is. Although a formal definition, acceptable to all, still seems to lie beyond reach, there is nevertheless agreement on some matters.

Wisdom is not something that is achieved by discovering some new fact. In this respect philosophy is very unlike science. The failure to solve a scientific problem lies, in the great majority of cases, in our inability to get at some missing piece of information. But this is not the reason why some of our philosophical problems have continued to elude us. It is not for the lack of some fact, in other words, that a philosophic problem has escaped solution. The "facts" necessary to solve many of the most fundamental of philosophical problems, many philosophers would say, have been with us for a very long time, yet their solution continues to defy our best efforts. Discovering some further "fact" would not help at all. In many cases the trouble is that we already have too many facts.

It is like working at a massive jigsaw puzzle: one's inability to put the puzzle together does not lie in the fact that certain pieces are missing. It lies in the fact that we have before us, say, a thousand little pieces of various sizes and shapes and we do not know how they fit together. Adding another piece to the thousand would obviously be of no help at all. On the other hand, what would help would be to see how the pieces fit together, to see the thing whole.

It is the same with philosophy. As the British philosopher John Wisdom once put it: philosophy is not "knowledge of new fact" but "*new* knowledge of fact" — it is a deeper, more profound understanding of the facts we already have. It is, in short, seeing things whole, seeing how the pieces fit together. That is wisdom.

How do philosophers go about "seeing things whole"? They do so by asking, some would say, "why" sort of questions rather than "how" or "what" sort of questions; they do so, in other words, by enquiring not into the how or what of things but into their why. Let us, for example, take such a question as "Why is there evil in the world?" and note how a scientist would answer it, and how a philosopher would do so.

If one approached a geologist with this question and he tried to answer it strictly as a geologist, he might say to us: well, as far as natural evil is concerned, that is easy enough to say, for the earth has a certain mantle around it and there are various breaks in it. People — knowingly or unknowingly — build cities over or near these breaks or "faults," and when the breaks widen buildings collapse, kill their occupants, and bring death, misery, and suffering.

Such an answer, assuming it was seriously proposed, would scarcely satisfy us. And it wouldn't do so because we know well enough how evil comes about. In asking the question we were not asking for the causes of evil; we were asking the more general and basic question of why should there be evil in the world *at all*.

It is in this respect that philosophy differs significantly from science. Philosophy tries to see things whole by asking questions that are more general and fundamental than those asked by science. A scientist might be interested, to consider another brief example, in the cause (let us call it X) of a certain phenomenon. He may spend his life pursuing this problem and if fortunate may discover the cause, making in the process an important contribution to our knowledge and, more than likely, to our general welfare. The philosopher, however, as a philosopher, would not be concerned at all with the specific cause of X. The question which would, and does, concern him is whether it is the case that everything has a cause.

Philosophy tries to see things whole, however, not only by asking questions that are more general and fundamental than those asked by science, but also by asking questions that are concerned not so much with facts as with how different bodies of fact are related. Not only does the nature of the pieces of the puzzle pose a problem to the philosopher, how they fit together also poses a problem. The philosopher will thus wonder, for example, if we indeed accept, as we do, science's basic assumption that cause and effect govern all of nature, including human nature, by what right, then, can we justify holding people legally and morally responsible for what they do?

This too, like the problem of evil, is a long-standing one in philosophy, one still largely unresolved. As it exemplifies so well the structural type of question (in contrast with the strictly factual type) so typical of many of philosophy's questions, let us spend a few more moments on it.

If it is the case that everything that happens in nature (and man is part of that nature) is governed by the law of cause and effect, then it would seem that just as that stone one might throw into the air cannot help hitting the window that it shatters (as a result of the force used in sending it on its way) and finally falling to the ground, (as the result of the force of gravity), so similarly one could argue that, given a certain background and nature, so-and-so could similarly not help shattering that window in the jeweler's store and helping himself to that enticing ring or watch. Were our knowledge of human psychology as secure as our knowledge of physics, we could easily have predicted the action in question — with the result that instead of the man who helped himself to the trinkets in question being brought to trial and no doubt eventually jailed, the real culprit and the one who deserves to be punished is not the window breaker but the jeweler, for placing such enticing trinkets in the window and tempting people who are constitutionally incapable of resisting the temptation.

Another classic example of such a structural, philosophical question is the problem of evil. As in the case just noted, here too we find ourselves (those of us, at least, who are of a religious bent of mind) wanting to take two positions that seem to contradict one another. No one has expressed the problem more succinctly than the ancient philosopher Epicurus, who put it in the form of the following dilemma: Is God willing to prevent evil, he asked, but not able to do so? In that case He cannot be omnipotent. But is it perhaps the case that He is able but not willing to do so? In that case He is not a benevolent but a malevolent God. But if He is both willing and able to prevent evil, whence then comes evil?

Although this is an especially severe problem for believers who want to and do believe in a merciful and benevolent God but cannot shut their eyes to all the evil He apparently allows to exist in the world He created, one does not have to subscribe to any particular religion to find this problem of interest.

We are living through a period of intense interest in the possibility of the existence of extraterrestrial life, a period in which we are also in a position of having the means to extend our search deep into the outer reaches of space. Considering the staggering vastness of the universe, with the likelihood of planets like ours existing in the millions, the possibility of life existing elsewhere in the universe is very high. As rocket expert Dr. Wernher Von Braun remarked: "Our sun is one of 100 billion stars in our galaxy. Our galaxy is one of billions of galaxies populating the universe. It would be the height of presumption to think that we are the only living things in that enormous immensity!"

Furthermore, not only is the probability of such life very high, the likelihood of life existing elsewhere of a type superior — perhaps much superior — to ours is also very high.

This being so, one can sympathize strongly with the Jet Propulsion Laboratory scientist who on a clear evening some time ago, after scanning the sky, threw his hands up in despair and exclaimed: "Where is everybody?"

Where indeed is everybody? Some have, of course, thought that with the seemingly increasing UFO sightings, and other such inexplicable phenomena, we have been and are increasingly watched and visited.

Somewhat more skeptical people have answered this question in ways that do not compliment us very much. On our walks through the woods, they have said, we may have encountered some little colony of bugs or vermin — say, a colony apparently in the throes of some insurmountable difficulty (a boulder that has fallen in their path and crushed some of their members) or some other such disaster — one which we could so easily resolve for them by expending some little energy on our part, becoming saviors in their eyes for doing so — yet far from doing that, what we in fact do is trample them to death.

The suggestion is that there is indeed other intelligent life elsewhere in the universe, one much, much superior to anything known to us. But because we are so far down the scale of evolution compared to them, they do not bother with us and simply pass us by — if not, in fact, in their contempt for us, visiting us with the evil we all know so well. And perhaps this is what Shakespeare had in mind when he had Gloucester say in *King Lear:* "As flies to wanton boys, are we to th' Gods;/ They kill us for their sport."

But however things stand here, one need not be a devout, religious person to wonder about the existence of higher beings, perhaps even the existence of some one supreme Being. And once having entertained the possibility of the existence of such beings or Being, the old philosophical question of the existence of evil begins to acquire new force.

But when dealing with such a question one may well come to feel that not only is science not capable of throwing any light on it, but neither is philosophy, and that perhaps only religion can help us here. "A little philosophy," Bacon once said, "makes a man an atheist; a great deal turns him to religion." Maybe in the case of a problem such as this, seeing how little illumination philosophy offers, we are indeed driven back to religion for the answers we seek and the consolation we need so badly. And if religion does manage to provide answers that are satisfying, let us not look down our noses at it simply because, living in an age of science, we shall not attach much importance to the offerings of religion.

Of all the answers proposed by religion to this question, the most forceful is still the one first enunciated in the *Book of Job.* Job, having lost all his possessions, his friends, wife, and children, and now himself afflicted with a painful and odious disease, has removed himself from the city, and sitting now on a refuse heap outside the walls of that city, raises an accusing finger at God, demanding to know why this misery and agony has been visited on him.

In reply to this demand, God Himself, the *Book of Job* tells us, appeared to Job and, in turn, demanded of him: where were you when I made all this — pointing to the stars, the earth, the heavens — the implication being that if He could do all that, then surely He could easily have prevented what has happened to Job, and if He did not, there was good reason.

Although this does not make Job's suffering any more intelligible to him, it does make it more acceptable. And we can, of course, see why. If God appeared to any one of us (assuming we could be sure it was God) and gave us, as He did Job, His personal assurance that everything would be all right, our doubts too would be laid to rest and our faith restored.

And this is religion's greatest and perhaps only real answer to this problem of evil in a world presumably created and sustained by a good God. It comes up again in the New Testament. Jesus says to his disciples, trying to comfort them in their sorrow and doubts, that a sparrow could not fall to the ground without the good Father knowing about it. And when they ask him how they can be sure this is so, he replies, giving them his personal assurance, that "if it were not so, I would tell you."

To accept such an answer, to believe it and trust in it, requires, of course, enormous faith. Very few of us have that much faith or are capable of it. No doubt most of us are like the fellow who fell over the edge of a cliff but as he fell was able to catch hold of a tree. He hollered, "Hey, can somebody up there help me?" A deep voice answered, "This is God. I want you to follow My instructions. First, let go of the tree." At this the poor fellow's fear only increased and he yelled back, "Is there anybody else up there?"

That is not faith; certainly not the type religion says is necessary for understanding.

From what has been said I think we can see that philosophy differs from religion in that it bases its belief on sound reasoning and evidence and, not like religion, on appeal to tradition and sacred authority.

It is not that some religious people never do attempt to use reason and evidence to support their various beliefs. Many in the past have, and some still do. Their strongest reasons, however, are not the reasons of the mind but the reasons of the heart. Those of the mind—and philosophers have always been interested in them and have weighed them carefully—have never succeeded in withstanding close examination.

Let us take a moment to consider one or two reasons of the mind most commonly appealed to in such discussions.

Very often, in trying to justify the evil in the world, people will argue that what we see is only a small part of the total picture; were we capable of seeing it whole, we would come to see its necessity and accept it. "In the world's finale," they will sometimes say, using those eloquent words of Dostoyevski in the *Brothers Karamazov*, "at the moment of eternal harmony, something so precious will come to pass that it will suffice for all hearts, for the comforting of all resentments, for the atonement of all crimes" (Book V, Part II, Chapter 4).

But, as Dostoyevski goes on to point out in that great Russian novel, in a chapter that is the most moving and eloquent ever devoted to this problem, even if all this were true, it still does not answer our question. Coming to see the place of evil in the scheme of things does not annul the evil, and although we might come to see God's wisdom in having arranged things the way He had, where—we will still want to know—was His mercy?

Having come to that pass in the debate, a religious person, if he is still inclined to argue and not merely affirm, is very likely to go on to deny the evil and not try to justify it. What looks like evil, he may say, is not really evil but good! God's goodness, he may add, is different from human goodness.

The tempting reply to this, however, is that what this really amounts to saying is that God is not really good. For this is a sword that has a double edge and cuts both ways, because if we cannot judge evil for what it is, then we cannot judge good for what it is either. And if judgment is thus undercut, then God, it is true, cannot be blamed, but he cannot be praised either.

All this has been said not with the purpose of downgrading religion, nor of passing harsh judgment on its approach to some of the problems it shares with philosophy. We know too little about the real core of religion—especially its mystical dimension, from which it draws its greatest insights and strength—to permit ourselves to dismiss it lightly. But just as philosophy's approach to the problems it shares with science differs, so it is similarly the case with those philosophy shares with religion. Science tackles questions piecemeal, and its tool is experimentation; philosophy seeks to see things whole, but the understanding of that whole it seeks is one which must be intellectually and not simply emotionally or imaginatively satisfying. It rests its appeal on reason and not, as is the case with religion, on revelation.

Lord Balfour, British Prime Minister at the turn of the century and noted author, in a moment of deep pessimism observed the following:

> The energies of our system will decay, the glory of the sun will be dimmed, and the earth, tideless and inert, will no longer tolerate the race which has for a moment disturbed its solitude. Man will go down into the pit, and all his thoughts will perish. The uneasy consciousness which in this obscure corner has for a brief space broken the contented silence of the universe, will be at rest. Matter will know itself no longer. "Imperishable monuments" and "immortal deeds," death itself, and love stronger than death, will be as if they had not been. Nor will anything that is, be better or worse for all that the labor, genius, devotion, and suffering of man have striven through countless ages to effect.
>
> (*The Foundations of Belief*, p. 30).

It is this mood, captured so beautifully in Lord Balfour's remark, which leads some to take up science, others to turn to religion, and some few to pursue philosophy.

part one
PHILOSOPHY'S BEGINNINGS

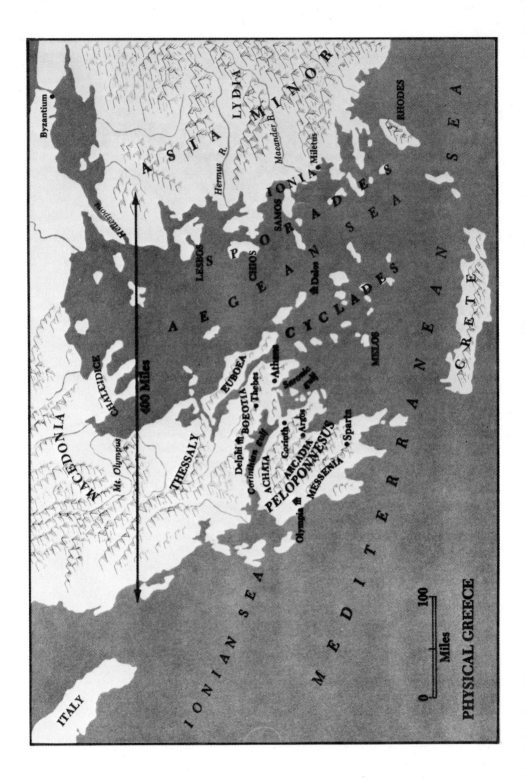

PHYSICAL GREECE

chapter 1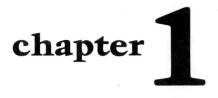

It began here . . .

It began here in this coastal city of Miletus, southeast of the Greek island of Samos, on the mainland of what is now Turkey. Miletus was a wealthy, prosperous Greek city, founded some 200 years earlier by the Athenians. What strikes one about this, and the many other famous centers of ancient Greek civilization, is the way they are all surrounded by water. Everywhere there is water and water is everywhere. The center of their world is not a mass of land but a body of water — the Aegean Sea.

On one side of this sea lay their European towns and cities; on the other side, their Asian settlements. In the middle, in the blue sea, were to be found the many islands with their now famous names: Melos, Delos, Rhodes, Samos, Chios, Lesbos.

If the waters separated these ancient Greeks within this great sea, the mountain ridges, which carved the landscape into tiny, islandlike plains, did the same for their inland centers. The paradox of diversity and unity, of isolation and community, which came to characterize these ancient Greeks, was to no small degree a result of this curious geography.

But although they occupied a rugged, isolated country, the climate was mild and hospitable, allowing its inhabitants to spend much of the year outdoors and in each other's company. In addition, the towns and cities on the coastal plains, although separated from each other, lay at the crossroads of the world, with Asia to the east, Europe to the west, and the lands of the ancient civilizations of the Near East to the south. The rational and skeptical spirit that came to characterize them was nourished by this exposure to these diverse cultures.

At first life could not have been easy for the average person. The basic occupation was farming, and both the land and the primitive methods used to cultivate it produced small if any surpluses. Most people lived a short, dismal existence, the usual life span being 35. Because of the risks and frequency of childbearing, women's life expectancy was even shorter, and those of infants shorter still.

This harsh, bitter, and uncertain life came to be reflected in their religion, a religion dominated by gods whose decrees were as arbitrary and uncertain as the lives they were thought to control; gods whose bitter conflicts with each other could not have been a source of comfort for those who worshipped them.

But with the development of industry and commerce, their situation improved greatly. By exporting such natural resources as marble, copper, iron, lead, and silver (and later such manufactured items as pottery, statuary, and textile goods), they were able to import what their own land could not produce in adequate quantities. This gave rise to an expanding population and for some a more prosperous existence. Prosperity gave birth to leisure, leisure to curiosity, and curiosity to science and philosophy.

The curiosity that gave rise to science and philosophy was, however, of a distinct sort, for other peoples had also at different times and periods achieved the leisure to pursue science and philosophy and yet had not done so. The rise of science and philosophy occurred only once and only here among these ancient Greeks. What is its explanation?

Aristotle, much closer to the event than we, although already some 300 years removed from it, tells us in a famous passage that it was their "wonder" about their world and themselves which gave birth to science and philosophy.

Aristotle speaks of wonder, and later historians have tended to agree that that was certainly part of the answer, although not the whole of it. There were, they say, two things that were contributed by these ancient Greeks, in addition to their curiosity, which were involved in the rise of philosophy and science among them. First, the Greeks asked new questions; they were curious, that is to say, about new sorts of things. In the older civilizations the questions were fundamentally of a religious kind, mainly concerned with life in the hereafter. This world and this life interested them much less. What they principally wanted to know was what the life hereafter was like and what they could do so that their journey to that other world might be a prosperous one. The ancient Greeks, on the other hand, perhaps because of their own generally humbler station in life, were interested in investigating this world and this life, not the other world and the other life. In a very real sense we might say that they were the first to discover this world.

In addition to this new interest in the things of this world, there was something else about these ancient Greeks that hastened the rise of philosophy and science. They pursued these new interests in a new way. They were the first people to see the importance not only of collecting facts and knowledge, but also of "systematizing" this knowledge. Let us take, for example, the science of geometry. Long before the Greeks, the ancient Egyptians knew many of the most important facts about geometry. The practical rules for the construction of their pyramids and temples would have been impossible without them. But in the hands of the ancient Egyptians these facts remained merely scattered "observations" or "theorems." The Greeks were the first people to hit upon the idea of trying to "prove" these theorems, of trying to find some basic and simple axioms from which they could be deduced. The concept of proof, of achieving a system, of bringing separate theorems into a single framework, was what distinguished their approach to these matters from that of their forerunners. As Herodotus, first Greek historian, put it in a striking and revealing passage: the Greeks began to study these matters "for the sake of enquiry alone."

But pursuing these questions in a new way did not mean that these early Greek thinkers were able to start afresh, with a completely clean slate. Although in the main abandoning supernaturalism for naturalism and trying to explain events as the result not of the whim of the gods but of the working of law, there were nevertheless several assumptions or "myths" these ancient Greeks inherited from the past that continued to have an impact on their thinking. This is not surprising, for no one, no matter how hard one might try, can be completely free of all past beliefs; there will always remain some that will appear indubitable, and the same was the case with these first scientists and philosophers.

It was believed, first, that the world initially was in a state of chaos, but that then some god, or gods, brought cosmos or order out of the chaos by fashioning the earth, the sun, the stars, and so forth. Second, they believed that the natural world, now so secured, was just, fair, and equitable, and would continue to be so as long as each god (who was given a different portion of the universe to rule over) refrained from upsetting the balance by overstepping the boundary of some other god's territory. But third, they believed that strife and tension were present along with order. However, this tension and conflict (as between such opposing forces as Night and Day, Winter and Summer, Love and Hatred) never went too far, with one force permanently rising triumphant over the other. Were that to happen, the balance would be upset and chaos would again set in. They were certain, however, that that would never happen again. They believed, finally, that the world, so fashioned and so sustained, was composed of four different kinds of stuff (or elements, as they were later called): earth, air, fire, and water.

Before going on to consider the boundaries to their thought which these myths posed to the first philosophers, we should take note of a much more subtle boundary, one that was no less pervasive and similarly difficult to overcome. This was the linguistic boundary.

It has become commonly accepted in our day that language and its limits vastly affect thought and its possibilities. Consider the language introduced by the rulers in Orwell's novel *1984*. This language was designed to keep people thinking in patterns preferred by the rulers. Although the Greek language was constructed for no such purpose, it had an amazingly similar effect. First, at the beginning of the pre-Socratic era Greece was still largely an oral culture. This meant that information was not written and read but spoken and heard. A problem that immediately occurs is that a book can be placed on a shelf and retrieved later, but in an oral society memory plays a singularly important role. In order to facilitate better memorization, Greek works in this period were composed almost exclusively in poetry, not prose, embodying rhythm and rhyme. The syntax also took on an interesting character: the basic unit of the Greek language became not the word but groups of recurring words. Last, much of the vocabulary that is both necessary for serious philosophical consideration and helpful in spurring such discussion was lacking. Thus, we must credit these men with fighting not only restrictive cultural frameworks but also restrictive linguistic frameworks.

The problem of being

The person who is credited with being the first philosopher and scientist was a man named Thales, who, as historians like to put it, "flourished" around 585 B.C. This is not the year of his birth but rather the year in which he predicted an eclipse of the sun would take place, and according to our modern calculations, was apparently off by only some minutes.

Although this was a remarkable feat, Thales is remembered by us not so

Thales. The Bettmann Archive, Inc.

much for it as for the question he was the first to raise and the answer he proposed to it.

If we look around us what strikes us, as indeed it must have struck Thales, is the enormous profusion and variety of things. Surely, Thales wondered, this infinite variety all around us must be different forms of the same basic and fundamental stuff. And if so, what, he asked, is the nature of that fundamental stuff out of which all of this variety arose? Having come to pose that question, and having looked around him once more, the answer he offered seemed almost inevitable — it all arose, he said, from water.

Why water? We do not know for certain why he chose it as the prime element, but it is not difficult to imagine what may have played a role in his choice. It was, first, one of the elements singled out by tradition; second, there was a lot of it around; third, it was present in all living things and was essential to life; fourth, and probably most important, it was capable of taking on the other three forms identified in the traditional fourfold classification. For water freezes and so becomes a solid ("earth"); it evaporates into a mist and becomes "air"; and it is used by the sun (which is a "fire") as a kind of fuel (when the sun "draws water to itself" or "burns off the mist"). Water was therefore a substance capable of becoming any one of the four fundamental elements out of which tradition said the world was composed.

Although still obviously much influenced by tradition, in choosing, however, a physical element as his principle of explanation, Thales was no longer bound by that tradition but was, on the contrary, already in the process of establishing a complete new tradition, one which was to profoundly affect Western civilization from that time on. Nor, it may be interesting to observe, does he seem to have been far from wrong in choosing water as the fundamental element underlying all things. If our present understanding of the universe is correct, about 90 percent of the observable universe is hydrogen, with the remaining 10 percent consisting of helium, oxygen, nitrogen, and so on. A good part of the universe is indeed, therefore, "water."

Lest we grant Thales more credit than he may deserve, let us remember that although he seems to have discarded mythological explanations, he did not yet succeed in entirely abandoning the language of mythology. In a fragment that has survived, he is quoted as having taught that "all things are full of the gods."

Thales was raising for the first time a question concerning, as it is generally referred to, the problem of Being. The second great early thinker to direct himself to this problem was a pupil of Thales by the name of Anaximander.

Anaximander (610–546 B.C.) seems to have been much bolder in his speculations than Thales. In considering what that fundamental stuff out of which everything arose might have been, he decided it could not have been any one of the four named by tradition. For had one of these four been elevated above the others, this would have involved, he reasoned, a kind of unfairness to the other three, with disastrous results. The basic element must have been, therefore, something more primitive than these four.

All this seems to be suggested in the sentence, the only one which has been preserved, from the prose treatise (the first to be written in European literature) that Anaximander wrote. Things return, that sentence runs, to their origins, "as is ordained, for they give satisfaction and reparation to one another for their injustice according to the ordering of time . . ."

The dominance of one thing over another, Anaximander seems to be saying here, is a kind of cosmic injustice for which a penalty (death) is exacted, the penalty being assessed by Time.

Such dark phrases as "ordained," "reparation," and "ordering" make us wish more of his writings had survived. But they did not.

If Anaximander seems still overly influenced by the ancient myths (in this case the idea of justice in Nature) it led him to a much more promising notion of the nature of that basic stuff than the one propounded by Thales.

Reasoning that whatever has definite qualities must in time lose them (die), and since the fundamental stuff from which everything else arose must be eternal and indestructible, it must have lacked all definite qualities. He came, therefore, to call that basic element "the *apeiron,*" meaning a kind of neutral, indeterminate stuff, boundless in amount.

Initially (and what he says here is reminiscent of the idea of chaos in the old myths) there was, he speculated, nothing but this boundless, indeterminate matter. But as a result of a certain kind of shaking process, perhaps like that of a gigantic sieve (for it was not shaking because some god or gods were shaking it) the four elements separated off. The first to do so was the solid element, the earth, which fell to the center; second was water, which covered the earth; then followed air, which formed a sphere around the water; and finally appeared a sphere of fire.

Although nothing much remains of these speculations, the essential thing is that they are of the same kind as modern science, and appeal to the same sorts of explanatory principles. They represent a kind of scientific or naturalistic account, in contrast to the mythopoetic or supernaturalistic, characteristic of previous stages of thought.

In another sphere Anaximander hit upon the very modern idea of the evolution of man and animals from lower forms of life, using a concept of natural selection to explain the extinction of some species and the survival of others.

Another distinction Anaximander enjoys is that of having been the first, as far as we know, to draw a map of the known world.

The last member of this Milesian school, a generation younger than Anaximander and possibly his pupil, was Anaximenes (585–524 B.C.). In his search for the fundamental stuff, Anaximenes reverted back to the four and chose air, a choice motivated, it seems, by his desire to strike a balance between the views of his two predecessors and preserve what was best in each. First, air, although like water present and indispensable to all life, has the advantage that it does not have as specific and defined a nature as water and is therefore more capable of transforming itself into the great variety of objects around us. And, second, air is a more likely source of this variety than Anaximander's Apeiron (Boundless), for

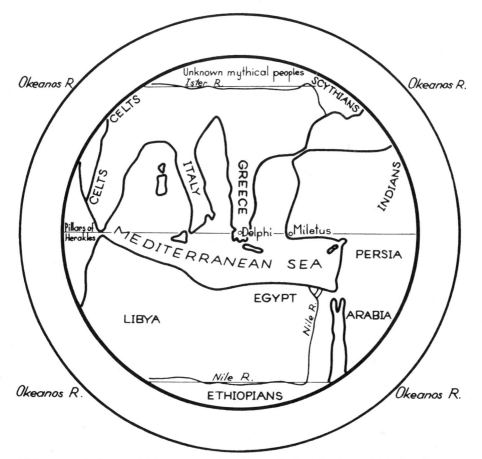

**This map of the world is a reconstruction of what is thought to be the first
geographical map ever drawn. Its center is Delphi, where a stone—the
omphalos, or "navel"—marked the exact center of the earth. The
cartographer was Anaximander, a Greek philosopher and practical
scientist who lived in Miletus from about 611 to 547 B.C. Early maps were all
circular. Half a century later, Herodotus commented: "I laugh to see how
many before now have drawn maps of the earth, not one of them showing
the matter reasonably; for they draw the earth round, as if fashioned by
compasses, encircled by the river of Ocean ..."** (Drafted by Nina Thiel; coastlines
are based on W. H. Heidel, *The Frame of Ancient Greek Maps*, Plate I, by permission of the
American Geographical Society.)

the Boundless seems too empty and vacuous a stuff to be capable of giving rise to
that variety and profusion. Air, having none of the heaviness or solidity of water
and being as infinite, as all-pervading, and as supple as the Boundless, must have
been, Anaximenes concluded, the source of it all.

His efforts to explain how air could become any one of the other three elements led Anaximenes to hit upon the notion of condensation and rarefaction, a

notion that will become indispensable in later speculations. He argued that when particles of air get tightly packed together the result is a fluid, and when they become still more tightly packed we get a solid. On the other hand, when the particles become rarefied, separated, the solid turns to a fluid, the fluid to a mist, and the mist (or air) to fire.

Seeing, apparently, that the thinner or rarer air is, the hotter it becomes; and the thicker it is, the colder it gets, Anaximenes conducted the first recorded experiment. Blow on your hand hard through compressed lips, he said, and you'll find the "thick" air feels cold. Now open your mouth wide and blow gently, the "thin" air is warm.

Although Anaximenes' physical explanation of the process whereby one fundamental substance gets transformed into another is superior to the moral explanation entailed in Anaximander's theory (the giving of satisfaction for some injustice), like Anaximander and Thales before him, his overall view is still not entirely free of anthropomorphism — the assignment of human characteristics to nonhuman beings. Air, he thought, was the more fundamental element, because "just as our soul, being air, holds us together, so do breath and air encompass the whole world" which is its soul.

With Anaximenes the Milesian school comes to an end. Its speculations, which mark the beginning of science and with it the beginning of Western culture, were conducted in the shadows of the rise in the east of the great Persian empire. Founded by Cyrus the Great in 550 B.C. with his conquest of the Near East, it spread to Lydia, ruled by its famous king Croesus, and then to the Greek cities on the east coast of the Aegean Sea. When, in 499 B.C., these Greek city-states revolted, the Persians put down the revolt and as a further warning and punishment destroyed its greatest city, Miletus.

Although the Persians subsequently succeeded in extending their rule into Europe along the north coast of the Aegean as far as Macedonia, their attempts to extend it farther into Old Greece resulted in the great Athenian victories at Marathon (490 B.C.) and Salamis (480 B.C.), victories that marked the beginning of the Golden Age of Greece.

The problem of becoming

The first question raised by these early thinkers soon gave rise to a second, for the first question asked essentially "What is it that is constantly changing or becoming?" and it was soon realized that change or becoming was itself a puzzling thing.

There is indeed something very curious about the idea of change once we begin to think about it. When something changes it ceases to be what it was and becomes something else. But if this is so, what becomes of that original thing? Has it vanished from existence? And if it has, what sort of reality or being could it have had, seeing it could lose it so completely and swiftly? Surely not real Being.

Furthermore, if we are to grant that things change, as our senses tell us is obviously the case, then we must assume there is something permanent continuing throughout the process, for otherwise we would not have change but first one thing then something else — something totally different from it. But to assume that there is something permanent in change is to embrace a contradiction, for the permanent, by definition, is that which does not change.

Such thoughts about being and change led one famous ancient philosopher and his followers to the very odd position of maintaining that change is really an impossibility. This was Parmenides, who was born in 515 B.C. in Elea, a city founded by Ionian refugees in southern Italy.

Parmenides had to agree, of course, that things do seem to change, but he held that logic could show that in reality they did not. And Parmenides' logic was simple and seemingly irrefutable. He reasoned that if Being came to be, it must have come from Being or from Not-Being. If it came from Not-Being it has come from nothing, which is impossible (for nothing comes from nothing); and if it came from Being, it has come from itself, which means that it always was and so has not changed after all. Although our senses tell us, he concluded, that things change, reason and logic show us that this is impossible.

Following reason and logic led Parmenides to the view that ultimate reality was an unchanging, unitary Being. Nothing determinate, of course, could be said of Being, and he himself spoke of it simply as *It*. "One path only is left for us to speak of, namely that *It* is. In this path are very many tokens that what is, is uncreated and indestructible, for it is complete, immovable and without end."

About the same time as Parmenides, there lived another famous thinker named Heraclitus (540–480 B.C.), who took a diametrically opposite view from that of Parmenides.

So impressed was he by the universality of change that he compared reality to a river. You cannot step into the same river twice, he asserted — to which one of his disciples soon added that you cannot even step into it once (for both you and the river are constantly changing). Defying logic, Heraclitus therefore went on to assert that "there is nothing permanent except change."

Concerning the nature of the underlying substance that is constantly in flux, Heraclitus thought it was fire. In doing so, Heraclitus was approaching more closely to our modern understanding of these matters than his predecessors. Of this view, the physicist Werner Heisenberg has written that:

> ... modern physics is in some way extremely near to the doctrines of Heraclitus. If we replace the word "fire" by the word "energy" we can almost repeat his statements word for word from our modern point of view. Energy is in fact that substance from which all elementary particles, all atoms and therefore all things are made, and energy is that which moves. Energy is a substance, since its total amount does not change, and the elementary particles can actually be made from this substance as is seen from many experiments on the creation of elementary

particles. Energy can be changed into motion, into heat, into light and into tension. Energy may be called the fundamental cause for all change in the world.

(*Physics and Philosophy.* New York: Harper Torchbook, 1962, p. 63).

Heraclitus' view that nothing is constant and unchanging is more in agreement with our sense-experience than is Parmenides', for our senses tell us that things do change. Yet from the point of view of reason it is not satisfactory, for unless, as we clearly see with our minds, there is something permanent and unchanging, we cannot speak of change at all. We may not be able to step into the river twice (or once) but if there were no banks, there would be no river to begin with.

Change obviously involves permanence and the difficulty is to see how they are related. Parmenides retained the permanent and this forced him to rule out change; Heraclitus attempts to get along without the idea of the permanent but this seems to fail too.

In addition to being a brilliant thinker, Heraclitus was also a brilliant stylist and aphorist, many of whose sayings have survived. Among the briefer and more memorable ones are the following:

"A man's character is his destiny."
"Every beast is driven to the pasture with a blow."
"The way up and the way down is one and the same."

It was no doubt on account of remarks like the last which led antiquity to refer to him as "The Dark." In view of the nature of the substance he had picked as underlying reality, the surname strikes one as ironic.

The Theory of Atomism: a synthesis

In the next 50 years attempts were made to deduce change without resorting to the paradoxically extreme positions of either Heraclitus or Parmenides. The eventual outcome was an extremely ingenious answer, which, as far as the physical world is concerned, is still in its essentials accepted by science today.

This is the Theory of Atomism, propounded by Leucippus (490–430 B.C.) in a work entitled *The Great World System*, and improved and developed by Democritus (460–370 B.C.) in a work entitled *The Small World System*. This theory proved to be an excellent solution to both problems, Being and Becoming.

There is an interesting story about Democritus that illustrates very clearly what was characteristic of these new thinkers. Considerable interest, it runs, had been aroused by the strange death of a prominent man. While strolling along the beach an eagle dropped a turtle on his head and killed him. It was recalled that an oracle had once predicted that the man would die by a "bolt from Zeus," and although this was thought to mean that he would die by lightening, it was never-

Democritus. The Bettmann Archive, Inc.

theless felt that the prediction had been fulfilled since the eagle was a bird sacred to Zeus. This explanation, however, did not satisfy Democritus, who went out to the beach to observe the eagles. He noticed that they would swoop down and seize a turtle with their talons and then fly up with it and drop it on a rock in order to crack the shell of its stomach to get at its meat. When Democritus recalled that the deceased had been bald, the solution immediately unfolded itself to him. There was obviously no need to appeal to the designs of unseen beings in order to solve the mystery; ordinary natural principles sufficed.

Leucippus began by criticizing Parmenides' conception of space. For Parmenides the notion of space presented a problem because he rejected the existence of Not-Being. Not-Being, he said, cannot be; it cannot even be thought of, for to think of Not-Being is to think of nothing (and to think of nothing is not to think). But space, being a part of the total *It*, could not be nothing, and, therefore, with no void between things, motion, as movement in empty space (and with it change or becoming) must be impossible. And if it appears to take place this must be an illusion.

But Leucippus, admitting that in a sense the void or space was "what is not," a kind of nothing, nevertheless decided to go ahead and defy the logic of Parmenides and claim that in this case, "What is not, is." If we could think of space as a kind of receptacle, full in some parts and empty in others, Parmenides' difficulties about change and motion would not arise, he thought.

Leucippus' first assumption was therefore that space is real. His second assumption was that within this space, which he believed was infinite in extent, there moved originally an infinite number of tiny particles, which he called "atoms" — meaning "uncuttables."

How did he come to this notion? Matter, he reasoned, was obviously divisible into parts, and those parts into lesser and lesser parts. Such division, however, must lead eventually to particles so tiny that, because they would be absolutely solid and have no space within them, would resist further division. These would be the uncuttables or "atoms." Leucippus thought that like space, there must be an infinite number of these particles, moving randomly about in infinite space.

These atoms were not thought of by Leucippus and Democritus as being regular in shape, like the tiny round billiard balls envisioned by modern science. On the contrary, they thought of them as having irregular surfaces, and some as being endowed with little hooks. Originally these tiny atoms flew in random directions through empty space, motion being natural to them. How often two such little particles would collide, only to bounce off and continue on their separate paths, no one, of course, could say. Sooner or later, however, two such atoms were bound to get entangled. Now hooked together they would soon be joined by another tiny atom, with others then quickly following. As a large mass thus formed, a vortex was created which swept more and more matter into its orbit. And out of these larger masses there eventually arose a universe of stars, sun, moon, and planets.

On this view, then, every tangible and visible body that we find is simply an agglomeration, or collection, of atoms, all things of whatever kind being ultimately made of the same particles. But if so, why do things appear different? They appear different, these atomists explained — invoking here Anaximenes' theory of condensation and rarefaction — because of the different ways in which these particles or atoms are joined together. If they are loosely joined, we have a liquid; if tightly joined we have a solid, and so on. Differences are also due, they explained, to the different patterns (or "atomic structure" as we would now put it) of the same particles.

Without a scientific tradition to draw on and no scientific instruments to aid them but with only their senses and reason, these first atomists succeeded not only in solving the first two major problems bequeathed to them by their predecessors but also did so in a way that is still astonishing.

It was an ingenious answer to the first problem concerning Being and it was an extremely satisfying solution to the problem of Becoming or Change. Parmenides, it showed, was right in maintaining that what is real does not change, for atoms are indeed real and they do not change; and Heraclitus was right in insisting on the existence of change, for change too is real, but it occurs only to complex bodies. Each, the theory indicated, was correct in what he asserted but wrong in what he denied — with both saying more than they knew.

Democritus, who expanded and developed this atomic theory first propounded by Leucippus, also went on to make explicit the theory's mechanistic-materialist implications for religious orthodoxy, especially the fears, superstitions, and terrors such orthodoxy tended to generate. Fears and superstitions, he announced, need no longer plague us; all phenomena are easily explainable as being the product of the generation and dissolution of atoms. There is no place remaining in such a world for demonic forces and powers and the tortures and torments of hell.

Worlds come into being through the coming together of large collections of atoms isolated in a large patch of void. There are probably, therefore, an infinite number of worlds such as ours, worlds in the process either of formation or of dissolution through the generation or destruction of their mass. And the same is the case with us, who are collections of smaller numbers of atoms.

This dimension of Democritus' atomic theory was later to be used by another ancient Greek, Epicurus of Samos (342–270 B.C.), as the basis of his famous moral philosophy, and later still, to inspire the Roman poet and author Lucretius (94–55 B.C.) to write his *De Rerum Natura*—a long poem devoted to explaining "the nature of things" in terms of atomic and Epicurean science and ethics.

The achievements of these first philosophers and scientists must be measured not by the empirical validity of their specific findings (remarkable as these sometimes were) but rather by their choice of methods and assumptions. They tried to answer questions about nature without resorting to divine revelation, by speculating in a rational way about the natural world and its possible origins. They replaced the older concept of a world governed by gods with the concept of nature as obedient to law, one intelligible to reason and amenable to its methods of investigation. That they achieved all this without the aid of scientific instruments and in the face of an opposing tradition is all the more remarkable.

But they were remarkable men living in a remarkable period of history. The sixth century B.C., when all this began, was a century unlike any other either before or after it. The last prophecies of Jeremiah (c. 645–580 B.C.) date from this period; the period marks the rise of the Buddha in India (563–483 B.C.); of Confucius in China (551–479 B.C.); and of Zarathustra or Zoroaster (627–551 B.C.) in Persia, the founder and prophet of a religion that had an enormous impact on both Judaism and Christianity.

It will be the fate of these two great traditions, the religious and scientific, with their separate rallying calls of faith and reason, to run headlong into each other in subsequent centuries as each grows in strength and followers.

Summary

1. Philosophy and science arose in the sixth century B.C. in the ancient city of Miletus in Asia Minor.

2. It was the wonder and curiosity of the Greeks about this world, which they were the first to *see*, rather than concern about the next, that led to the rise of philosophy and science.

3. Discovering the world for the first time not only led these first thinkers to raise new questions about it but also led them to pursue these new questions in a new way. They sought natural rather than supernatural knowledge about the world, and their goal was

the achievement of a system of unified knowledge rather than a collection of facts.

4. The first philosophers and scientists, however, did not succeed in seeing the world entirely anew. There were a number of beliefs (concerning the genesis, government, and composition of the world) that they inherited from the past, which continued to influence their thinking on the new questions they raised.

5. The first philosopher and scientist was Thales, who flourished around 585 B.C. This was the year in which Thales predicted that an eclipse of the sun would take place, a prediction which proved remarkably accurate.

6. The first question raised by Thales and his successors concerned the nature of "Being." The great variety and profusion of things surrounding us must all have arisen, Thales and his successors speculated, from some one fundamental substance. Picking one of the four elements mentioned by tradition, Thales said that it must all have come from water. Anaximander, believing that it would have been unjust (and a threat to the harmony of the cosmos) for one of the elements to be elevated above the others, speculated that it could not have been any one of the four but something more primitive and prior to them. He identified it as the Boundless — some neutral, indeterminate, and infinite stuff. Anaximenes, the last member of this school, trying to preserve and synthesize what seemed best in the thought of his two predecessors, suggested that the fundamental stuff was air — a substance not quite so definite as water and not so indefinite and empty as Anaximander's Boundless. The other three elements, he further suggested, arose from it by way of the principle of condensation and rarefaction.

7. Thinkers soon realized that the first question raised and discussed: "What is the nature of that stuff which seems constantly to be changing or becoming something else?" entailed another, even more fundamental question: "What is change itself?" and they turned their attention to it.

8. The first to do so was Parmenides, who argued that change or becoming, if we use reason as our guide and are not deceived by what our senses tell us, must be an illusion. Since space, logically, is Nothing, and since Nothing is not, it does not exist. If there is no space, there cannot be motion in which it can take place, and without motion there cannot be change. Furthermore, since for there to be many things there must be space between them, and since there is no space, all there can be is just one thing. Parmenides called that unitary, unchanging being the *It*. Heraclitus, a

thinker living at about the same time as Parmenides, adopted a diametrically opposite view. Far from change being unreal, it is, he argued, the most real thing there is. "Everything flows — nothing abides," he said. Concerning the nature of that which is in constant flux, he said it was fire.

9. The effort on the part of subsequent thinkers to preserve what was correct in each extreme finally resulted in the theory of Atomism, a theory that proved to be an ingenious solution not only to the problem of Becoming but also to the problem of Being. The atomists suggested that the basic stuff out of which everything arises are atoms — tiny, indestructible particles, infinite in number. Bodies, large and small, are collections of atoms, and arise and disappear as a result of their generation or dissolution. Parmenides was correct in maintaining the real was unchanging, for the real are atoms and they do not change; and Heraclitus was correct in insisting on change, for change too is real but it only happens to complexes of atoms. And the Milesians too were correct in seeking a unitary source of Being. Atoms are that source.

10. Although it is remarkable that thinkers living in the fifth century B.C. should succeed in arriving at a physical theory that in its essentials is still accepted by science today, what is even more noteworthy about both them and their predecessors is the new spirit that guided their investigations. In them, for the first time, supernaturalism gave way to naturalism, making possible the birth of science and philosophy.

For further study

1. The standard collection of ancient texts relating to the Pre-Socratic philosophers is Herman Diels's *Die Fragmente der Vorsokratiker,* first published in 1903. Later editions of the work were revised and edited by W. Kranz, and the work is usually referred to as "Diels-Kranz" or "DK." There is an English translation by Kathleen Freeman, entitled *Ancilla to the Presocratic Philosophers* (Cambridge: Harvard University Press, 1948). A selection of the more important fragments is contained in another English translation by G. S. Kirk and J. E. Raven, entitled *The Presocratic Philosophers* (New York: Cambridge University Press, 1957). Two other works that will be found valuable on this period are: Philip Wheelwright, *The Presocratics* (New York: Odyssey, 1966) and J. M. Robinson, *An Introduction to Early Greek Philosophy* (Boston: Houghton Mifflin, 1968).

2. Concerning the influence of ancient Greek myth and religion on the thought of the first philosophers, see the following two works by the great classical scholar F. M. Cornford:
   a. *From Religion to Philosophy* (New York: Harper Torchbooks, 1957).
   b. *Principium Sapientiae* (New York: Cambridge University Press, 1952). Reprinted as *Origins of Greek Philosophical Thought* (Philadelphia: University of Pennsylvania Press, 1973).

3. Look up some detailed account of the history and events of this period. For some suggested works see:
   a. J. B. Bury, *A History of Greece* (3rd edition revised by R. Meiggs, London, Macmillan 1959).
   b. A. Andrewes, *The Greek Tyrants* (London: Hutchinson, 1966).
   c. T. J. Dunbabin, *The Greeks and Their Eastern Neighbours* (London: Oxford University Press, 1957).

4. Still one of the most readable and insightful accounts of both the philosophers in question and the times in which they lived is B. A. G. Fuller's *History of Greek Philosophy: Thales to Democritus* (New York: Holt, 1923).

5. There are full-length studies of each of the ancient philosophers discussed in this chapter. Look up one concerning a philosopher you have found especially interesting. The following are some recent studies:
   a. C. H. Kahn, *Anaximander and the Origins of Greek Cosmology* (New York: Columbia University Press, 1960).
   b. A. P. D. Mourelatos, *The Route of Parmenides* (New Haven: Yale University Press, 1970).
   c. Philip Wheelwright, *Heraclitus* (New York: Atheneum, 1964).
   d. A. T. Cole, *Democritus and the Sources of Greek Anthropology* (Cleveland: The Press of Case Western Reserve University, 1967).

6. For a collection of recent critical essays on the pre-Socratics see A. P. D. Mourelatos, *The Pre-Socratics* (New York; Anchor Books, 1974).

Socrates. The British Museum.

chapter 2

"And so I go about the world . . ."

Introduction

The man who is the subject of this chapter wrote not a single book, left not a scrap of written information for posterity, and is known only at second hand through the writings of his contemporaries. Yet he was one of the most remarkable people who ever lived and was part of an age and culture whose profound and overwhelming effect on the Western world helped determine the form our civilization has taken. His name was Socrates.

In an absorbing series entitled "The Miracle of Greece" that appeared in *Life Magazine*, this age and this people were described in its opening lines:

> It was sudden. It was miraculous. Nobody knows why it happened. But on a small rock-bound Mediterranean peninsula 2,500 years ago a handful of people called Greeks roused the human race to a new ambition and sense of purpose and launched it into history (January 4, 1963, p. 28).

That the modern world still feels the impact of that awakening is in great part due to Socrates, who set Western thought on its course and gave it the tone and character it still bears.

The editors of *Life* go on to say that on the surface these ancient Greeks seem unlikely candidates for this momentous mission:

> They were always fighting among themselves. They were garrulous and monstrously egocentric. They were often treacherous. They were so eager that they had to mount the slogan "Nothing to Excess" in big letters at Delphi to remind them to be less excessive. But they did have one idea, so novel and profound that a whole new age dawned in its light. It was simply that man's nature, even in its mortality, is the glory of creation, and that man has a noble purpose: to live at the highest possible pitch of human perfection — physically, morally and intellectually (p. 29).

To Socrates, who understood that idea probably better than anyone else, and who may even be credited with being the first to articulate it, it consisted in the belief that man possessed a *psyche*, a soul, that part of him which is most truly his self. That was in fact his single greatest discovery — perhaps the single greatest discovery in the whole of philosophy — a discovery which more than anything else accounts for the obsessive urgency, gradually assuming the force of a compulsion, with which he went about trying to reveal it to others.

Socrates was not, of course, the first to speak of the soul. Among the pre-Socratics both Democritus and Heraclitus had in fact a good deal to say about it. Democritus, for example, maintained that the soul was composed of "finer" atoms, and Heraclitus that the most reasonable soul was the dry one, the one closest to that ultimate stuff, fire. Heraclitus added, as evidence, that imbibing liquor moistens the soul and that the results were, of course, obvious. Socrates' conception, however, went beyond these materialistic metaphors to what was genuinely important — the *excellence* of the soul and how to attain it. It is this attempt to discover what is truly unique about human beings and how we can preserve it that has led such classical scholars and historians as F. M. Cornford to say that whereas "Pre-Socratic philosophy begins with the discovery of Nature; Socratic philosophy begins with the discovery of man's soul" (*Before and After Socrates*, p. 4; Cambridge University Press, 1950), and A. E. Taylor to remark that "it was Socrates who, as far as can be seen, created the conception of the *soul*" (*Socrates*, p. 132; Oxford University Press, 1933).

It was this new conception of the soul and the use he made of it, which in the end cost him his life. Why should people take the life of such a man?

As we will see, it was in part because of the increasing hostility engendered by the kind of activity he engaged in, and partly because of the tragic social and political events of the final 30 years or so of the fifth century, events ending in the defeat of Athens by Sparta and in the death of this great civilization.

Before turning to consider these activities of Socrates, it will be useful to look for a few moments at a group of other thinkers — called Sophists — circulating in Athens at this time, and with whom, unfortunately, Socrates tended to be confused.

The Sophists

It is ironic and sad that Socrates, who believed that man's soul was the only thing worth caring about, should be confused in the public mind with these people, whose main concern was not the salvation of man's soul but the secret of worldly success.

Who were these Sophists? They were itinerant teachers who began to gravitate to Athens around the fifth century B.C. The Greek term that referred to them, expressive of the respect in which they were initially held, meant "expert" or "wise one."

They did not, however, succeed in retaining this good name for very long. Becoming masters of the arts of political success, they offered to teach these skills to anyone able to afford their fees. Athens was now a democracy and such skills were important tools for anyone wishing to get ahead. Understandably, the demand for their services increased and the Sophists grew wealthy from the large fees they received. The poor, who could not afford to pay their high fees but who needed these skills as much as anyone, if not more, came to despise them.

But others were soon to follow suit, for although confining themselves at first to teaching only practical subjects, they began to explore and raise questions about matters of much wider implication and concern, regarding the state and its justification, traditional religion, and orthodox morality.

As they became more and more radical, their attacks upon the established system of political, social, and religious life became more and more severe. Might it not be the case, they began to ask their listeners, that our notions of law, conduct, and religion were merely a matter of custom and convention; and if so, by what right can one say one way is better than another? And if we have indeed merely agreed to adopt certain ways of conducting and governing ourselves, what stops us, should we be so inclined, from abandoning these ways, or overthrowing them?

The result of the extreme subjectivism adopted by the Sophists is perhaps best epitomized in the famous line of Protagoras that "Man is the measure of all things."

Going on from teaching how to win, by fair means or foul, they went on to enquire whether there was such a thing as fair or foul, right or wrong, to begin with, and finally to wonder whether perhaps winning is not all. The public, scandalized by the expression of such views and questions, came to regard them with increasing suspicion and alarm.

Opposed to these Sophists, although no less critical than they, stood Socrates, who showered both them and the state with abuse for neglecting what he believed was man's chief and proper concern: knowledge of oneself and of the right way to live. For he believed there was a right way and that it was not all simply relative. Yet he was also certain it had not yet been found, at least in Athens.

The details of Socrates' life are unremarkable. He came of a middle-class Athenian family. His father was a bricklayer and his mother a midwife. Socrates himself seems to have been trained in his father's craft. Physically, he was by all accounts rather odd-looking: short, ugly, pop-eyed, pot-bellied, pug-nosed, walking with a shambling gait. But he was also obviously a man of considerable courage and vigor, well-known for his courageous behavior in battle. Intellectually, needless to say, he was brilliant.

But he does not seem to have worked very hard, if at all, at his trade, nor does he seem to have spent much time with his family, preferring to spend it in following his profession of philosophy, which took the form of questioning people concerning their beliefs and way of life.

Most of the accounts that have come down to us depict him as engaged in this sort of investigation of his fellow Athenians. He believed they were occupied with all sorts of trivial pursuits and were neglecting the one thing that was really important, which for him was the pursuit of virtue and knowledge. He thought it was not possible to acquire virtue, to act rightly, without knowledge. This was why clear thinking about right conduct and the need to achieve exact definitions were of such importance to him. This was a necessary first step.

To this, however, he added a view that looks paradoxical to us: that if you do have this kind of knowledge, you cannot fail to *be* good and act as a good man should, regardless of the circumstances in which you may find yourself or the stresses you may be subjected to. Such, he believed and taught, was the power of knowledge — and deep within his fellows' hearts, he insisted, they knew he was right.

In maintaining all this Socrates was really addressing two very different but related questions. The first concerned the role that learning performs in making a person good. Most of us would probably agree that learning does indeed play such a role. We believe, for instance, in trying to incorporate a "moral education" in our children's upbringing. Further, we tend to value a literary work more if it incorporates a moral tale. Also we seem to believe that by example of those around us we can assimilate some good traits. So, for most of us the answer to the question cast at this level would be that learning is a necessary condition for becoming good. This would amount to the rather moderate claim that in order to become a person of good character, we must at some time have learned about what kinds of acts are right and what makes them right.

Socrates was, however, also making the much more ambitious claim that learning about such things was not only a necessary but a sufficient condition for becoming a good person. This amounts to saying that should we come to such knowledge of good and bad, right and wrong, we could not help becoming a virtuous person. It also means that the morally undeveloped, and indeed the vicious, necessarily lack such knowledge and are as they are because they lack it. This position would seem to be very difficult to defend against empirical evidence. We hear of people daily doing vicious and barbarous acts and admitting that they knew they were wrong. We do not think, typically, of the murderer or rapist as one who is unfortunately short of knowledge of right or wrong, but rather as a person who perpetrates the crime knowing full well that his deed is heinous.

However that may be, Socrates himself believed he still lacked this knowledge that would make him truly good and was hoping to find it with the help of others who might be, as he would add — perhaps ironically — "more gifted than himself."

Obviously Socrates could not have run into very many, if indeed any, who were more gifted than he was, and very few no doubt could have been expected to respond kindly to this appeal to their better selves, if indeed they were not angered by it. So there were reasons enough for his own growing personal unpopularity with many of his fellow citizens.

Thus it could not have been entirely unexpected either of him or of them that when he was finally brought to trial he took the opportunity to dwell again on their failures and past mistakes and to explain to them the real source of their animosity toward him. This stemmed, he told them, from his "philosopher's mission of searching into myself and other people," from his having been a gadfly to the state, urging its citizens to self-improvement, and from his search for wisdom, having exposed their ignorance.His true enemies are not his present prosecutors, but all those who oppose the life of reason and virtue and who shrink before his conviction that "the unexamined life is not worth living."

Although these factors no doubt played a role in the decision to bring him to trial, there were other factors, not unrelated to them, that seem to have played an even more decisive role. These concerned the social and political events of the last 30 or so years of this fifth century B.C.

Athens reached her peak development under the great democratic statesman Pericles (495–429 B.C.). She was a great naval and military power, had built an empire and possessed great wealth; and had advanced to a democratic form of government. It was the most brilliant society ancient times produced.

If you will think of a small city of about 130,000 inhabitants producing in a short span of time buildings unsurpassed in beauty to this day, two of the greatest historians of all time, some of the greatest dramatists the world has ever known, to say nothing of achievements in philosophy, sculpture, and music, you will have some idea of the splendor of the age. Pericles himself was not unaware of the greatness of the period over which he presided. "Future ages," he said, "will wonder at us, for our adventurous spirit has taken us to every sea and country, and everywhere we have left behind us everlasting monuments" (Thucydides, *The Peloponnesian War*, Book II).

But this high point of Athenian development was no sooner reached than its decline began. As is so often the case, the cause was war: here it was the Peloponnesian War (431–404 B.C.). Socrates was 38 when this long, exhausting war began, which ended in the defeat of Athens by Sparta and her allies.

In order to understand these events a bit better and grasp what it might have felt like to wake up one morning and realize that you, a member of this great,

The Parthenon. The Greek Tourist Office.

magnificient civilization, had been defeated by a state like Sparta, we must look for a moment at the sort of city-state Sparta was.

Located about 150 miles by land from Athens, Sparta occupied the southeast part of the Peloponnesus. The Spartans conquered the country at the time of the Dorian invasion and reduced the population to the condition of serfs. The serfs, called helots, were forced to work the land for their new masters. Being Greeks, like the Spartans, the helots bitterly resented their condition and when they could rebelled. The Spartans had a body of secret police to deal with this danger. In addition, once a year they would declare war on the helots so that their young men could legally kill any helot who seemed insubordinate.

Freed from labor, which they regarded as degrading, the Spartans devoted themselves, from birth, to becoming invincible warriors. Sickly children would be killed by exposure and only those judged vigorous were allowed to live. Those so selected were then, to the age of 20, trained in one big school. The object of the training was to make them hardy, indifferent to pain, and submissive to authority.

At 20 actual military service began. Although marriage was permitted to anyone over 20, all men (including those who were married), had to live in the "men's house" until the age of 30. Homosexuality was encouraged, in the belief that fighting next to one's lover would make one braver and more heroic. It was also the theory of the state that no Spartan should be poor or rich. No one was therefore allowed to own gold or silver, and their money was made of iron. Spartan simplicity became proverbial.

Women were also treated differently in Sparta than they were anywhere else in Greece. Not secluded as elsewhere, they were given the same training as were the boys, with the same design in mind—to turn them into wholly devoted citizens of the state. They were not allowed to show grief if their newborn child was condemned to death, or if their son was killed in battle. If childless, they were trained to raise no objection if the state ordered them to see whether another man might be more successful than their husband in begetting children for the state. Such children, once begotten, reared, trained, and sent off to battle, would be told by such mothers to come back *with* their shields or *on* them.

It was these people, who neither tried to make nor made any contribution to civilization but sacrificed everything to success in war, who finally, in the year 404 B.C., managed to defeat Athens. Driving out its whole population—men, women, and children—the Spartans forced the Athenians to submit to the final humiliation of tearing down the wall surrounding the city. That marked the end of that great Greek civilization.

But that empire and greatness, as glorious and inspiring as it might appear to us, was nevertheless secured at a very high price. As we noted in the last chapter, Greece's Golden Age began with the victories at Marathon (490 B.C.) and Salamis (480 B.C.). After these Persian invasions had been repulsed, the Greeks, under the leadership of Athens, formed a league whose aim was to protect the Aegean from fresh Persian attacks. In time, however, the Athenians, by threat and deception, converted this voluntary league into an empire, an empire that exacted with growing ruthlessness huge sums of money from its subject states, money which it used to increase its military might, beautify the city, and finance the expensive projects on the Acropolis, the statue of Athena in the Parthenon alone costing the equivalent of some 10 million dollars. All this occurred while some 20,000 slaves, many of them Greeks, were worked to death in Athens and its silver mines, and many thousands of other Greeks led a dismal existence.

There was, then, much to criticize. Democracy with its glorious achievements was financed by imperialism abroad and exploitation at home, an imperialism and exploitation growing more oppressive and ruthless with each year. Dreams of world conquest and the good life corrupted them, proving that the democracy they had achieved—for the elite—was only skin deep after all. On the stage their dramatists portrayed and taught how a surfeit of goods leads to pride, rashness and ruin, and their audiences proved them right.

But however comforting it might be to believe that they knew the truth, recognized that they did not deserve to keep what they so ignobly obtained, and desired Socrates' life because of the guilt he aroused in their hearts, it is probable that this is not the way the the ordinary citizen of Athens and those in authority saw it. They undoubtedly regarded those who, like the Sophists, asked too many questions, or those who, like Socrates, raised doubts even if only to the extent of wondering how it might profit a man if he gain the whole world and lose his own soul, as subversives, busy undermining the loyalties of those, and especially the youth, on whom the city's continued happiness depended.

And so in 399 B.C., after the Thirty Tyrants, who had been installed to rule Athens by the Spartans, had been overthrown and the democrats returned to power, Socrates was indicted on the charge of "corrupting the minds of the young and introducing strange gods."

Although the charges strike us as ridiculous, they would not necessarily have appeared so to his fellow citizens: after all Socrates did profess to be guided by a "voice," and there had been in the recent past the case of Alcibiades, the gifted, charismatic leader of Athens, who had turned traitor in the course of the war, and more recently still, Critias, the cruelest of the Thirty Tyrants, both of whom had attended on Socrates when they were young.

The "voice" in question here is one that Socrates, we will see later, claimed to receive direction from. He understood it to be of divine origin and as such always unquestionably correct. "I am subject," he said of it at his trial, "to a divine or supernatural experience, which Meletus saw fit to travesty in his indictment."

Socrates was obviously not unaware of these undercurrents of suspicion, but at his trial he seemed less interested in exposing them than in using the occasion to once again explain to his fellow citizens what their mission in life should be.

Was he unaware of the more serious factors in the case against him and their dangerous potentials? No. Did he care? No. Did he seek martyrdom? Possibly.

Socrates' Trial and Death

Plato. Mary Evans Picture Library, London.

The person who immortalized Socrates was his young pupil Plato. He was born in 427 B.C. — in the early years of the Peloponnesian War. He was a young man when Athens was finally defeated by Sparta and he may even have fought in the war.

Plato belonged to one of the best families in Athens, a family both wealthy and politically influential. On his mother's side he could claim descent from Solon, the great Athenian statesman and reformer; on his father's side he could claim descent from the last kings of Athens.

The normal career for Plato would have been in politics. But as we have seen, the political life of Athens had degenerated greatly in the last 30 years of the century. The Peloponnesian War had exhausted the city's resources, and Plato, after fulfilling his military service, steered clear of politics. He decided instead to develop a sound political philosophy. This remained a leading interest with him all his life; it is in the forefront of his speculations. He began by writing dialogues to commemorate the memory of his teacher and mentor, Socrates, in whose company (he was 28 when Socrates was executed) he had spent over ten years.

His lifelong passion, acquiring the thrust it did as a result of the unjust and tragic death suffered by his beloved teacher, was to arrive at a conception of a state in which such an injustice could not be perpetrated. Justice, or the just state, is thus the subject of many of his works, including the greatest and best-known of these, the *Republic*. It is in this work that he arrives at the solution that the just state will be achieved only when either philosophers become kings or kings become philosophers.

It is interesting that Plato's conception of justice, which leads to this conclusion, is reminiscent of one of the mythopoetic beliefs we explored in the previous chapter in connection with the thought of the first Greek thinkers. Justice is a kind of disposition existing in each member of the just state (rulers, soldiers, workers) to mind their own proper business and not meddle in the affairs of the others, affairs in which, by their nature, they lack competence. Put in contemporary terminology it is to resist the Peter Principle — that is, to resist the temptation to rise to your level of incompetence. If your nature has provided you with the abilities to be a first-rate shoemaker, you and others should resist the temptation to accept the reward of promotion to a higher office for which you may lack any competence (for example, the management of the entire shoe factory or president of the union). A just society is a society where everything has its proper place and everyone does what is proper for him (what his nature or talents prepared him best for).

Plato had an opportunity to put his theories into practice. About 11 years after Socrates' death, Plato was invited by the tyrant of Syracuse, Dionysius I, to visit his court. He disliked the dissolute life there and Dionysius did not care much for Plato either. The result of the unfortunate encounter ended, if we can trust tradition, in Plato being sold into slavery. Friends, however, managed to ransom him. On his return to Athens they refused to take back the money used in gaining his freedom and Plato used it to found the Academy. This school, of which he remained the leader until his death in 347 B.C., was in effect the first

......rsity in the Western world. He gathered around him a group of scholars and pupils. The scholars organized research projects and quite soon made brilliant contributions in such fields as mathematics and astronomy. The Academy continued in existence for over 900 years before it was finally closed by the Roman Emperor Justinian in A.D. 529 — a record for unbroken existence never exceeded by any other university.

Plato was the first philosopher whose literary output is largely (but not wholly) preserved. All his writings are in the form of dialogues, initiated as a means of paying tribute to Socrates. These writings are among the most brilliant and eloquent we possess, although toward the end of his life Plato's style became more prosaic and scientific. Socrates is the main speaker in all but a few and he is represented as being present in all save one.

Scholars have generally divided Plato's work into three periods.

The Early or Socratic Period includes a dozen or so dialogues, of which the *Euthyphro* and the *Apology* are good examples. These dialogues analyze the chief virtues and are characterized generally by Socratic irony, although the real answers to the questions raised are indicated rather clearly.

The Middle Period consists of somewhat longer works, and it is here that Plato reaches the height of his dramatic power. *The Republic,* to which we have already referred, and the *Phaedo,* which we will be looking at later, are good examples of the works of this period.

Finally, there are the works of the *Late Period* or the later works. These are drier in style and more technical. Plato is getting into questions here that Socrates probably did not discuss. The *Theaetetus* (a long dialogue about knowledge in which Plato attempts to demolish the views, ascribed to Protagoras, that knowledge is based on sense perception and is relative to the individual perceiver) and the *Timaeus* (a similarly long work dealing with cosmology) are typical of this period.

Finally there is the *Laws,* his last work, which is also concerned with the problem of constructing an ideal state. The deeply conservative view that Plato takes in this longest of all his works has been a source of great puzzlement to its readers, leading some to regard him as one of the major Western proponents of totalitarianism.

Of Plato's achievement, the great British-American philosopher Alfred North Whitehead once said: "The safest general characterization of the European philosophical tradition is that it consists in a series of footnotes to Plato." In short, Plato said it all — everything else is simply commentary.

Although Plato was obviously the deepest and most profound student of Socrates to write about him, he was not the only one. We have, in fact, two further main sources of information regarding Socrates: Aristophanes and Xenophon.

Of the three, Aristophanes was the only one to have written about Socrates while he was still alive. The other two wrote about Socrates only after his death: Plato soon after; Xenophon some 15 years later. Scholars do not generally attach too much significance to Aristophanes' picture of Socrates as contained in his comic drama *The Clouds,* for it was intended as a farce and Socrates is caricatured in it neither as a moral reformer nor a political subversive but a kind of crack-brained scientist, running a shabby establishment called a Thinkery. The play was first performed in 426 B.C., about 25 years before Socrates' trial, when Socrates was 46 and the playwright 23. On the other hand, some 25,000 spectators viewed it when it was first performed, and although it failed to win a prize, coming in third, it is difficult to say what role this depiction of Socrates as a type of Sophist may have played in some people's minds — even at that much later date of 399 B.C. Plato himself hints at some such connection.

Nor do scholars generally attach a great deal of significance to the much more voluminous body of writings devoted to Socrates by Xenophon, concerning whose intellectual abilities they appear to have many reservations. The 10,000 Greeks who had been in service to the Persians and then found themselves stranded in enemy territory apparently had a higher opinion of Xenophon, choosing him as one of the generals to lead them back to their homeland; a feat of some magnitude that he successfully accomplished and later wrote about in a work called the *Anabasis*. Although Xenophon is undoubtedly not a Plato, what he has to tell us about Socrates very often has a very strong ring of truth about it.

Nevertheless we will follow tradition here and complete our account of the life and thought of Socrates by basing it on Plato's portrait of him as contained in the *Euthyphro*, the *Apology*, the *Crito*, and the *Phaedo*, all of which form a single story and were written to perpetuate and vindicate Socrates' memory.

Although the *Euthyphro* precedes the *Apology* and the *Crito* in the drama unfolded in these dialogues, it is generally regarded as having been written after them. The *Apology* is not really written in dialogue form: it is the speech (or series of speeches) delivered by Socrates at his trial. There can be little doubt that it is in substance a faithful record of what was said, for the dialogue was written soon after the event and was meant to be read to and by groups of people (some of whom had been present at the trial), and Plato would therefore not have tried to misrepresent facts that were familiar to large numbers of the Athenian people.

The same may be said of the *Crito*, which depicts him in prison, although the conversations it contains may well be a dramatic summary of arguments with several friends on different occasions. The object of the dialogue is to explain and justify Socrates' attitude towards escape, for the benefit of those friends who felt that he was sacrificing himself too easily. It also has the aim of displaying Socrates' loyal obedience to constitutional authority. The guilt for his condemnation is attached not to the state or its laws, but to those enemies of the state who have perverted justice. The *Euthyphro* is the prologue of this drama. It shows us Socrates awaiting his trial, and informs us of the charges preferred against him. The story of Euthyphro prosecuting his father for manslaughter is probably fictional. The dialogue illustrates Socrates' methods and suggests some ground for his unpopularity. Finally, the *Phaedo*, whose theme is the immortality of the soul (not an inappropriate theme for the occasion), carries the story to its conclusion by narrating, through the mouth of an eyewitness, Phaedo of Elis, the events and discussions of the last day in Socrates' life and the manner of his death.

Let us turn now to the first of these four dialogues.

Outside the courtyard where he is shortly to stand his trial, Socrates meets Euthyphro, a seer and religious expert, who says that he is going to charge his own father with manslaughter. Socrates is startled, and inquires how Euthryphro can be sure that such conduct is consistent with his religious duty. There seems to be here an extreme clash of pieties; a kind of absurdity in itself. The result is a discussion of the true nature of piety or holiness.

Euthyphro is obviously sympathetic to Socrates. But he is also, obviously, just the kind of person to whom Socrates likes to apply his curative treatment, for Euthyphro claims to be an expert and feels supremely confident in his ability. Socrates is going to clear his mind of some of these false assumptions and thus enable it to receive real knowledge. Poor Euthyphro is now his victim. The dialogue is only some 20 pages in length.

Euthyphro is surprised to find Socrates before the religious courthouse and asks him why he is there and not, as is usual with him, at the Lyceum — the recreation grounds. "I don't suppose," he says, "that you have actually got a case before this court as I have." This gives both of them a chance to bring before us the two themes or lines of the dialogue: Euthyphro's prosecution of his father, and the coming trial of Socrates. Socrates replies to Euthyphro's question.

Socrates: No Euthyphro; the official name for it is not a private case but a public action.

Euthyphro: Really? I suppose that someone has brought an action against you; I won't insult you by suggesting that you have done it to somebody else.*

As you see, the dialogue is packed with irony. Euthyphro won't think so badly of Socrates as to suppose that he would initiate such a thing himself, yet he himself is now on his way to do just that — and to his own father!

Socrates tells Euthyphro that Meletus has brought charges against him and that these charges are rather serious. When Euthyphro complains that no one takes his predictions seriously; in fact, that they laugh at him even though his predictions generally come true, Socrates replies that he should consider himself lucky. For if that is all they intended to do with him and planned no other harm, he wouldn't mind at all. In fact it "wouldn't be at all unpleasant," he says, "to spend our time in the lawcourt joking and laughing. But if they are going to be serious, then there's no knowing how the case will turn out — except for you prophets."

The last remark is, of course, a dig at Euthyphro (who as a seer should know the future) but Euthyphro is undaunted and replies: "I dare say that it will come to nothing, Socrates, and you will conduct your case satisfactorily, as I expect to conduct mine." This last remark is a reminder to Socrates that he wants to talk

*The translation here is from Hugh Tredennick, *Plato: The Last Days of Socrates* (Harmondsworth, England: Penguin Books, 1954). Reproduced by permission.

about himself. Socrates gets the message and replies: "Oh, yes, Euthyphro, what is this lawsuit of yours? Are you defending yourself or prosecuting? The next few interchanges are quite amusing as Euthyphro hesitates to reveal to Socrates what his lawsuit is about and against whom.

Socrates:	Oh, yes, Euthyphro, what is this lawsuit of yours? Are you defending yourself or prosecuting?
Euthyphro:	Prosecuting.
Socrates:	Whom?
Euthyphro:	Someone by prosecuting whom I am increasing my reputation for craziness.
Socrates:	Why, is he such a nimble opponent? [*Notice the double play on the word "nimble."*]*
Euthyphro:	Not at all nimble; actually he's quite an old gentleman.
Socrates:	Who is this person?
Euthyphro:	My father.
Socrates:	My good man! Your own father?
Euthyphro:	Yes, indeed.
Socrates:	What is the charge? What is the trial for?
Euthyphro:	Manslaughter, Socrates.
Socrates:	Good heavens!

When Socrates gets over the shock, he says to Euthyphro, with his tongue in his cheek: "Of course, most people have no idea, Euthyphro, what the rights of such a case are. I imagine that it isn't everyone that may take such a course, but only one who is far advanced in wisdom." To this Euthyphro replies: "Far indeed, Socrates." (A far-out fellow!)

Well, what happened? Euthyphro tells his story:

We were farming in Naxos and the deceased was working for us there. Well, he got drunk, lost his temper with one of our servants, and knifed him. So my father bound him hand and foot and threw him into a ditch; and then sent a man over here to ask the proper authority what has to be done. In the meantime he not only troubled himself very little about the prisoner but neglected him altogether, considering that he was a murderer, and it would not matter if he died. And that was just what happened; what with starvation and exposure and confinement, he died before the messenger came back from consulting the expert. That is why both my father and my other relatives are angry with me; because on the murderer's account I am prosecuting my father for manslaughter,

*All matter in brackets and in italics, appearing from now on in the selections quoted, are editorial comment and not part of the text.

whereas in the first place (as they maintain) he did not kill the man, and in the second, even supposing that he did kill him, since the dead man was a murderer, one ought not to concern one's self in defense of such a person, because it is an act of impiety for a son to prosecute his father for manslaughter. They have a poor comprehension, Socrates, of how the divine law stands with regard to piety and impiety.

But this leads Socrates to ask Euthyphro: "But tell me, Euthyphro, do you really believe that you understand the ruling of the divine law, and what makes actions pious and impious, so accurately that in the circumstances that you describe you have no misgivings; aren't you afraid that in taking your father into court you may turn out to be committing an act of impiety yourself?"

When Euthyphro assures Socrates that he indeed knows what piety and impiety are, Socrates remarks that in that case it might be a good idea for him to become Euthyphro's student, and before Meletus has a chance to bring charges against him, he will tell him that he has now become a student of Euthyphro; and if he still thinks that he is guilty, then instead of bringing charges against him for corrupting the young, he had better bring charges against Euthyphro for corrupting the elderly! Although this would probably be enough to discomfort anyone, it does not disturb Euthyphro. He seems ready to take on anyone.

Socrates is ready to be instructed and asks Euthyphro to tell him what he was just insisting piety was. Euthyphro's first definition of piety is that it is "prosecuting a wrongdoer, whether the offender happens to be your father or anybody else." (In other words, it is what he is now in fact doing.) And Euthyphro supports his case by reminding Socrates that that is what the children of the gods do. And it is therefore absurd, as he adds with overweaning vanity (to say nothing of impiety), to criticize him for doing the same. In taking him to task, his family contradict themselves "by laying down one rule for the gods and another for me."

What Euthyphro has in mind here are such tales of the gods as that of Uranus (Heaven), who imprisoned his children, the Titans, deep in the body of his consort Gaia (Earth). She encouraged them to assert themselves, and Cronos, the youngest but most formidable of them, attacked Uranus and castrated him. To avoid such a fate for himself, he swallowed his own children as they were born. But his wife Rhea smuggled the infant Zeus away to Crete and put his baby-clothes on a stone, which Cronos swallowed. It acted as an emetic and made him vomit up the other children. Zeus later led a revolt against him and put him in chains. These are some of the doings of the gods Euthyphro is referring to here.

Socrates is, of course, not very happy with this definition of piety offered by Euthyphro. In fact, as he points out to him, it is not so much a definition of piety as an example of it. Surely, Socrates tells him, there are other things that are pious in addition to bringing a wrongdoer to trial, and what is it that is common to all of them? To this new demand, Euthyphro offer this new definition: "Piety is what the gods love." To this Socrates replies that it is an excellent answer. Whether it is true or not is something they will have to see.

Socrates now goes on to cross-examine Euthyphro. Haven't we said a few moments ago, he asks him, that the gods are divided and disagree with one another, and feel enmity toward one another? The question is: What sort of disagreement are the gods involved in?

There can be two sorts of disagreements: we can disagree about such things as the length or weight or number of things, in which case (these being matters of fact) we can settle our disputes by measuring, or weighing, or counting. This sort of disagreement wouldn't make us hostile and angry with one another. But since the gods apparently do disagree with one another, it must be about something else — about such things as right and wrong, good and bad. Disagreement over these sorts of things does make us hostile and angry. Well, seeing that the gods are hostile to one another, they must be in disagreement over what is right and wrong, and if they disagree over this, what sort of authority are they on these matters? We cannot appeal to them. For if you ask Uranus he might say "Yes, it is right"; but if you ask Cronos he might say "No, it is wrong!"

For a moment, Euthyphro feels beaten and does not know what to reply. He hesitates and then gets a brilliant idea. He says, "I imagine, Socrates, that none of the gods disagree with one another on this point, at any rate: that whoever kills without justification should be brought to justice" — in short, that the guilty should be punished!

At first this might look like a very good reply, for surely the gods indeed could not be in disagreement on this point. But if we look at this answer carefully we will see that it really says nothing. And that, indeed, is what Socrates points out to Euthyphro. Of course, he says to him, the gods are not in disagreement over that! No one would dispute that the guilty should be punished. But what is in dispute on such occasions is whether the person is indeed guilty. Can Euthyphro prove that all the gods regard what his father has done as being wrong and reprehensible? In short, in saying that the guilty should be punished Euthyphro had simply begged the question of his father's guilt.

"Come," says Socrates, "try to give me some definite proof that in these circumstances and beyond all doubt, all the gods regard this action as right; and if you prove it to my satisfaction, I shall never stop singing the praises of your wisdom."

But Socrates does not want to push this point too far. On the contrary, he realizes that even if it could be proven that all the gods find what Euthyphro is doing wrong or right, this still would leave unanswered what piety or impiety are — the answer would only supply us with some information about some particular action, but will tell us nothing, in general, about the meaning of these terms — unless, of course, we generalize and say that "Piety is what *all* the gods love." And so Socrates is willing to concede the point and willing to assume, for the sake of the argument, that all the gods regard this sort of homicide as wrong and detest it. Is Euthyphro willing to use this as his model for piety? In short, what this will mean is that whenever we find that all the gods love or approve of a certain thing, it is a sign that the thing or action in question is good or right, and when they are all agreed that it is wrong then this will be proof of its wrongness. (Of course when the gods are in disagreement, then we will simply be in the dark about the things or actions in question.) Euthyphro agrees to adopt this as his position. This is what he had in mind all along, he says.

Very well, then, replies Socrates. Let us see now what this means, what the implications are of this. And so he asks Euthyphro: "Is what is pious [*and here follows the most difficult part of the dialogue*] loved by the gods because it is pious, or is it pious because it is loved by them?"

This question is one that occupied philosophers and religious thinkers a great deal during the Middle Ages. It then took the form: Is something good because God wills it; or does God will it because it is good?"

At first sight this may seem to be an unimportant and quibbling question. One who does not take such matters very seriously may be tempted to say, "If God's will and the good coincide, what does it matter?" To this the believer may retort, "A great deal!" for one's answer really affects and reflects how we conceive of God. If our answer is that they are indeed the same, then we commit ourselves to the belief in the absolute omnipotence of God. This God not only can create and order a world, but those acts that are right and wrong are so because he makes them. Indeed, such a believer might criticize someone maintaining the opposite by saying that such a view imposes a standard upon God, one that is prior to and above him and that governs his will. There is, however, something to be said for this line of thought. For instance, we do seem to have faith in a certain order to those acts we deem right and wrong. Saving an innocent life is typically right, whereas willfully killing an innocent is typically wrong. Yet if God willed just the opposite, would it then be so? Many, of course, would say "No, it would not." But how would they justify this?

And there is, of course, the further difficulty of finding out what exactly God wills. There are many conflicting claims here and no very obvious way of mediating between them. Thus, we can see that much rides on the answer the believer may give to such a question.

The reply Euthyphro gives to the question is that "The gods love the pious thing because it is pious; it is not pious merely because they love it." Hearing this, Socrates is somewhat taken aback and says: "But if it is something else and not their *loving it* which makes it pious, then what is that something else about piety that makes the gods love it so? What then, indeed, is piety? Aren't we back where we began — now saying again that piety is what the gods love?" (And we are still in the dark, as before, as to *why* they love it.)

Becoming understandably demoralized at this turn in the argument, Euthyphro says to Socrates: "But, Socrates, I don't know how to convey to you what I have in mind. Whatever we put forward somehow keeps on shifting its position and refuses to stay where we laid it down."

Socrates tries to come to his rescue again, but the solution continues to elude them. The dialogue finally ends with the following exchange between Socrates and Euthyphro:

Socrates: We shall then have to start our inquiry about piety all over again from the beginning; because I shall never give up of my own accord until I have learnt the answer. Only don't refuse to take me seriously, but do your best to give me your closest attention, and tell me the truth, because you know it if any man does. If you didn't know all about piety and impiety you would never have attempted to prosecute your aged father for manslaughter; you would have been too much afraid of the gods, and too much ashamed of what men might think, to run such a risk, in case you should be wrong in doing so. As it is, I am sure that you think you know [*note the qualification*] all about what is pious and what is not. So tell me your opinion, my most worthy Euthyphro, and don't conceal it. [*Socrates pretends Euthyphro knows the answer but just won't tell it!*]

Euthyphro: Another time, Socrates; at the moment I have an urgent engagement somewhere, and it's time for me to be off. [*The universal excuse!*]

Socrates: What a way to treat me, my friend! Fancy you going off like this and dashing me from my great hope! I thought that if I learnt from you about piety and impiety I should both escape from Meletus' indictment (by demonstrating to him that I had now become instructed by Euthyphro in religion, and no longer in my ignorance expressed independent and unorthodox views) and also live better for the rest of my life.

And this is the way this dialogue ends. It shows how people's actions, which often have serious and even tragic consequences, are all-too-often based on ignorance. Here is Euthyphro about to prosecute his own father for impiety, and when asked what impiety is, he very soon becomes confused and must admit his ignorance. And similarly with Socrates: he is about to be prosecuted on the same charge by people who are probably as confused and ignorant as Euthyphro is regarding this matter. But in his case, of course, it will lead to his condemnation and execution.

Let us now turn to the *Apology*. The title comes from the Greek word *apologia*, which was the technical term for a defendant's speech. What the dialogue contains is not an apology in our sense of the word. It is Socrates' defense of himself.

There are two persons in this dialogue: Socrates and Meletus. The charges against Socrates, however, were formally brought by three Athenians: Meletus, Anytus, and Lycon. The charges against Socrates were that he was, first, guilty of heresy or impiety, and, second, guilty of corrupting the minds of the young by his teaching. These were standing charges, not invented for just this occasion.

The procedure in court was for the litigants to state their own cases. The prosecution spoke first and the defendant replied. The jury (consisting of 501 representative citizens) would then give its verdict by a majority vote. If the plaintiff received less than one-fifth of the total number he was fined. If the verdict was guilty and, as in the present case, there was no penalty fixed by law, the plaintiff proposed one, the defendant another, and the jury voted between them.

The *Apology* consists of three separate speeches: Socrates' defense; his counter-proposal for the penalty; and a final address to the court.

We do not have the prosecutor's speech, but Socrates' sarcastic and ironic opening remarks tell us a good deal about its tone. The dialogue begins with these words of Socrates:

> I do not know what effect my accusers have had upon you, gentlemen, but for my own part I was almost carried away by them; their arguments were so convincing. On the other hand, scarcely a word of what they said was true. I was especially astonished at one of their many misrepresentations: I mean when they told you that you must be careful not to let me deceive you — the implication being that I am a skillful speaker. I thought that it was peculiarly brazen of them to tell you this without a blush, since they must know that they will soon be effectively confuted, when it becomes obvious that I have not the slightest skill as a speaker — unless, of course, by a skillful speaker they mean one who speaks the truth. If that is what they mean, I would agree that I am an orator, though not after their pattern.

Socrates now goes on to deal with his earliest accusers, those not present in court but who have been spreading false rumors about him for many years. This is his big task — to rid his listeners of these ancient prejudices and charges against him, prejudices and charges which are customarily made against all philosophers. He pretends to read out the affidavit his ancient critics would have drawn up had they brought him to trial: "Socrates is guilty of criminal meddling in that he inquires into things below the earth and in the sky, and teaches people to disbelieve in the gods." The accusation is, in other words, that Socrates is a student of natural philosophy or science and as such must be an atheist. To this he replies:

> I mean no disrespect for such knowledge, if anyone really is versed in it — I do not want any more lawsuits brought against me by Meletus — but the fact is, gentlemen, that I take no interest in it. What is more, I call upon the greater part of you as witnesses to my statement, and I appeal to all of you who have ever listened to me talking (and there are a great many to whom this applies) to clear your neighbours' minds on this point. Tell one another whether any one of you has ever heard me discuss such questions briefly or at length; and then you will realize that the other popular reports about me are equally unreliable. The fact is that there is nothing in any of these charges. But here perhaps one of you might interrupt me and say "But what is it that you *do*, Socrates?

How is it that you have been misrepresented like this? Surely all this talk and gossip about you would never have arisen if you had confined yourself to ordinary activities, but only if your behavior was abnormal. Tell us the explanation, if you do not want us to invent it for ourselves." This seems to be a reasonable request, and I will try to explain to you what it is that has given me this false notoriety; so please give me your attention. Perhaps some of you will think that I am not being serious; but I assure you that I am going to tell you the whole truth.

At this point he tells them of his friend's visit to the oracle at Delphi. Here follows a rather long section, but it is one of the most eloquent in all of Western literature and deserves to be quoted in full.

When I heard about the oracle's answer, I said to myself "What does the god mean? Why does he not use plain language? I am only too conscious that I have no claim to wisdom, great or small; so what can he mean by asserting that I am the wisest man in the world? He cannot be telling a lie; that would not be right for him.

After puzzling about it for some time, I set myself at last with considerable reluctance to check the truth of it in the following way. I went to interview a man with a high reputation for wisdom, because I felt that here if anywhere I should succeed in disproving the oracle and pointing out to my divine authority: "You said that I was the wisest of men, but here is a man who is wiser than I am."

Well, I gave a thorough examination to this person — one of our politicians — and in conversation with him I formed the impression that although in many people's opinions, and especially in his own, he appeared to be wise, in fact he was not. Then when I began to try to show him that he only thought he was wise and was not really so, my efforts were resented both by him and by many of the other people present. However, I reflected as I walked away: "Well, I am certainly wiser than this man. It is only too likely that neither of us has any knowledge to boast of; but he thinks that he knows something which he does not know, whereas I am quite conscious of my ignorance. At any rate it seems that I am wiser than he is to this small extent, that I do not think that I know what I do not know."

After this I went on to interview a man with an even greater reputation for wisdom, and I formed the same impression again; and here too I incurred the resentment of the man himself and a number of others.

From that time on I interviewed one person after another. I realized with distress and alarm that I was making myself unpopular, but I felt compelled to put my religious duty first. Since I was trying to find out the meaning of the Oracle, I was bound to interview everyone who had a reputation for knowledge. And by Dog, gentlemen! (For I must be frank with you) my honest impression was this: it seemed to me, as I pursued my investigation at the god's command, that the people with the greatest reputations were almost entirely deficient, while others who were supposed to be their inferiors were much better qualified in practical intelligence.

I want you to think of my adventures as a sort of pilgrimage undertaken to establish the truth of the oracle once for all. After I had finished with the politicians I turned to the poets, dramatic, lyric, and all the rest, in the belief that here I should expose myself as a comparative ignoramus. I used to pick up what I thought were some of their most perfect works and question them closely about the meaning of what they had written, in the hope of incidentally enlarging my own knowledge. Well, gentlemen, I hesitate to tell you the truth, but it must be told. It is hardly as exaggeration to say that any of the by-standers could have explained those poems better than their actual authors. So I soon made up my mind about the poets too: I decided that it was not wisdom that enables them to write their poetry, but a kind of instinct or inspiration, such as you find in seers and prophets who deliver their sublime messages without knowing in the least what they mean. It seemed clear to me that the poets were in much the same case; and I also observed that the very fact that they were poets made them think that they had a perfect understanding of all other subjects, of which they were totally ignorant. So I left that line of inquiry too with the same sense of advantage that I had felt in the case of the politicians.

Last of all I turned to the skilled craftsmen. I knew quite well that I had practically no technical qualifications myself, and I was sure that I should find them full of impressive knowledge. In this I was not disappointed; they understood things which I did not, and to that extent they were wiser than I was. But, gentlemen, these professional experts seemed to share the same failing which I had noticed in the poets; I mean that on the strength of their technical proficiency they claimed a perfect understanding of every other subject, however important; and I felt that this error more than outweighed their positive wisdom. So I made myself spokesman for the Oracle, and asked myself whether I would rather be as I was — neither wise with their wisdom nor stupid with their stupidity — or possess both qualities as they did. I replied through myself to the Oracle that it was best for me to be as I was.

The effect of these investigations of mine, gentlemen, has been to arouse against me a great deal of hostility, and hostility of a particularly bitter and persistent kind, which has resulted in various malicious suggestions, including the description of me as a professor of wisdom. This is due to the fact that whenever I succeed in disproving another person's claim to wisdom in a given subject, the bystanders assume that I know everything about that subject myself. But the truth of the matter, gentlemen, is pretty certainly this: that real wisdom is the property of God, and this is the Oracle's way of telling us that human wisdom has little or no value. It seems to me that he is not referring literally to Socrates, but has merely taken my name as an example, as if he would say to us "The wisest of you men is he who has realized, like Socrates, that in respect of wisdom he is really worthless".

And so I go about the world, obedient to the god, and search and make enquiry into the wisdom of any one, whether citizen or stranger, who appears to be wise; and if he is not wise, then in vindication of the Oracle I show him that he is not wise.

With these remarks Socrates ends his defense against the charges brought by the first class of his accusers, and turns to his present prosecutors — in particular to Meletus ("high-principled and patriotic as he claims to be"). He questions Meletus on the new charges and in a very short time shows him to be as confused about these questions as Euthyphro was, if not, indeed, more so. So he leaves off questioning him.

Knowing, however, there are still many questions troubling the jury, he turns and addresses himself directly to them.

But perhaps someone will say, "Do you feel no compunction Socrates, at having followed a line of action which puts you in danger of the death penalty?" I might fairly reply to him, "You are mistaken, my friend, if you think that a man who is worth anything ought to spend his time weighing up the prospects of life and death. He has only one thing to consider in performing any action; that is, whether he is acting rightly or wrongly, like a good man or a bad one. The truth of the matter is this, gentlemen. Where a man has once taken up his stand, either because it seems best to him or in obedience to his orders, there I believe he is bound to remain and face the danger, taking no account of death or anything else before dishonor."

This being so, Socrates, who has faced death in battle, will not make any concessions in order to save his own life; for he does not know whether death is a good or an evil. Then he goes on to raise, on their behalf, another question:

Suppose you said to me "Socrates, on this occasion we shall disregard Anytus and acquit you, but only on one condition, that you give up spending your time on this quest and stop philosophizing. If we catch you going on in the same way, you shall be put to death." Well, supposing, as I said, that you should offer to acquit me on these terms, I should reply, "Gentlemen, I am your very grateful and devoted servant, but I owe a greater obedience to God than to you; and so long as I draw breath and have my faculties, I shall never stop practicing philosophy and exhorting you and elucidating the truth for everyone that I meet. I shall go on saying, in my usual say, 'My very good friend, you are an Athenian and belong to a city which is the greatest and most famous in the world for its wisdom and strength. Are you not ashamed that you give your attention to acquiring as much money as possible, and similarly with reputation and honor, and give no attention or thought to truth and understanding and the perfection of your soul?' It is my belief that no greater good has ever befallen you in this city than my service to my God; for I spend all my time going about trying to persuade you, young and old, to make your first and chief concern not for your bodies nor for your possessions, but for the highest welfare of your souls, proclaiming as I go 'Wealth does not bring goodness, but goodness brings wealth and every other blessing, both to the individual and to the State.' Now if I corrupt the young by this message, the message would seem to be harmful; but if anyone says that my message is different from this, he is talking nonsense. And so, Gentlemen, I would say: "You can please yourselves whether you listen to Anytus or not, and whether you acquit me or not; you know that I am not going to alter my conduct, not even I have to die a hundred deaths."

He throws out a challenge to them. If he has indeed corrupted anyone, then surely they will rise and say so. A good many of his listeners are here in court. And if they won't speak up, perhaps their brothers, uncles, or kinsmen will do so. These are the people Meletus should have produced as his witnesses. "If he forgot to do so then," he says with sarcasm, "let him do it now." He will not appeal to the pity of his judges or make a scene in court such as he has often witnessed. The judge should not be influenced by his feelings, but convinced by his reason.

A vote is taken and the verdict is "Guilty": 281 against Socrates, 220 for. Since, as we saw, there was no penalty fixed by law, each side had the option of proposing one. The prosecution proposed the death penalty. Socrates, arguing that since he has really been a benefactor of the state, the only just penalty would be to pension him off, like the Olympic heroes, in one of the fancy "hotels" of Athens, for he has done more for them than they and besides he needs the money more than they do. His friends — Plato among them — become alarmed and urge him to propose a fine, which he does: first a ridiculously low one (arguing that he cannot afford more) and then, at the urging of Plato and others who will guarantee it, a larger one.

A vote is taken and Socrates is condemned to death, this time by an even larger majority: 301 against, 200 for him.

The dialogue ends with a short closing address by Socrates in which he prophecies that they will be accused of killing a wise man. And why could they not wait a few more years? He is an old man and certainly has not much longer to live. They are about to kill him because he has been their accuser, but other accusers will rise up and denounce them even more vehemently. He believes that what is happening to him will be good because that inner voice, which always restrains him when he is about to do something that he should not, gives no sign of opposition. Death, he finally argues, is either good or is nothing; it is either a profound sleep, or if not a profound sleep but a prelude to another life, then how wonderful it would be to rejoin and converse with Homer and Hesiod, to see the heroes of Troy, and to continue the search after knowledge in another world. As he adds: nothing can harm a good man either in life or in death, and his fortunes are not a matter of indifference to the gods.

He has, finally, only one wish to make: he says to them — do to my sons as I have done to you.

In Xenophon's account we are told that as Socrates stepped off the platform on his way to prison, he passed one of his young disciples, Apollodorus, who was weeping bitterly. "Why are you crying, Apollodorus?" Socrates is said to have asked him. "I am crying, Socrates," Apollodorus replied, "because they have condemned you unjustly." To this Socrates is said to have responded: "Would you have been happier had they condemned me justly?"

It was for this reason that the author, watching a movie based on Socrates' life made by famed Italian movie director Roberto Rossellini, who used Plato as the major source, found himself greatly relieved and impressed to see the court-room scene done without this episode. But the relief was short-lived, for when Rossellini came to the scene where Socrates and his wife, who was weeping bitterly, were about to take their final leave of each other, he had Socrates put his arm around her and say: "Why are you crying, Xanthippe?" And Xanthippe replied . . . well, the reader knows the rest of it. The transfer of the exchange (assuming it ever took place to begin with) to this much more moving and tragic moment, if not against nature, is certainly against good taste.

The trial is over and Socrates is now in prison awaiting execution.

In Athens, sentence of execution was normally carried out at once. But the day before Socrates' trial was also the first day of the annual mission to Delos (Apollo's birthplace). This was a state holiday, during which no executions were permitted in commemoration of the legendary deliverance of the city from the Minotaur by Theseus, Prince of Athens.

Because of bad weather the mission to Delos in 399 B.C. took so long that Socrates remained in prison for a month. (This delay in the execution, some scholars have argued, must have been forseen, with the hope, they have suggested, that Socrates would use the occasion to escape.)

The ship, however, has now been sighted and is about to reach Athens. Crito, who has not been able to sleep, has been watching for the ship's return and has now come to tell Socrates the bad news. It is ironic that while Crito is wakeful and in distress, he finds Socrates soundly and peacefully asleep.

Crito is a wealthy Athenian. He is an old man and Socrates' oldest and closest friend. He has come now to beseech Socrates to let them save him.

Friends are ready with money and a refuge can easily be found. There is plenty of money to buy off the guards and Crito knows men who will take Socrates out of the country where friends will take good care of him. He musn't worry about the risks involved. They are willing and ready to take them. They are prepared to risk a large fine, loss of property, or other punishment. He must come and do so quickly, for time is running out.

By submitting to the sentence imposed by the Athenian court, Crito tells Socrates, he is playing into the hands of his enemies, deserting his children, and allowing the world to believe his friends were deficient in courage. "Look here, Socrates," Crito tells him, "it is still not too late to take my advice and escape."

> Your death means a double calamity for me. I shall not only lose a friend whom I can never possibly replace, but besides a great many people who don't know you and me very well will be sure to think that I let you down, because I could have saved you if I had been willing to spend the money; and what could be more contemptible than to get a name for thinking more of money than of your friends? Most people will never believe that it was you who refused to leave this place although we tried our hardest to persuade you.

To this Socrates replies: "My dear Crito, I appreciate your warm feelings very much — that is, assuming that they have some justification. Very well, then, we must consider whether we ought to follow your advice or not."

With characteristic irony, Socrates adds that since Crito is in no danger of death, he will be more likely to be impartial and objective in such a discussion than he himself!

Crito has argued that Socrates should consider the *consequences* of his staying, but what Socrates wants to consider are only the *principles* on which he has always acted — whatever the consequences. These two positions have acquired separate names in philosophy: the former is called "teleological," the latter "deontological." If you are a teleologist you evaluate the rightness or wrongness of proposed actions by the kind of results you think will issue from them. If the results are good, the proposed action, in your view, is good. On the other hand, if you are a deontologist you tend to evaluate the rightness or wrongness of proposed actions in accordance with whether or not they conform to certain principles you feel bound to obey or follow regardless of their consequences.

Thus to Crito's remark: "See now, Socrates, how sad and discreditable are the consequences, both to us and to you," by your staying, Socrates replies: "The principles which I have hitherto honored and revered I still honor, and unless we can at once find other and better principles, I am certain not to agree with you."

The sole question we have to consider, he goes on to say, is not reputation, or expense, or the bringing up of children, but:

Shall we be acting rightly in paying money and showing gratitude to these people who are going to rescue me, and in escaping or arranging the escape ourselves; or shall we really be acting wrongly in doing all this? If it becomes clear that such conduct is wrong, I cannot help thinking that the question whether we are sure to die, or to suffer any other ill effect for that matter, if we stand our ground and take no action, ought not to weigh with us at all in comparison with the risk of doing what is wrong.

We have no right, he goes on to say, to return evil for evil — "whatever the provocation." For it is "never right to do a wrong or return a wrong or defend one's self against injury by retaliation. . . . I know," he adds, "that there are and always will be few people who think like this; and consequently between those who do think so and those who do not there can be no agreement on principles; they must always feel contempt when they observe one another's decisions."

For him to try to escape now would be to reverse the whole conduct of his past life, to say nothing of making a hypocrisy of his statement at the trial that he would prefer death to exile. For although he has been a critic of the state, he recognizes the authority of law as well as of his own conscience. The trial may have been unjust and the charges false, but the sentence was pronounced by the law of Athens, and it is therefore his duty to submit.

Going on to reinforce his point, Socrates explains to Crito that when a man is legally but wrongly convicted of an offense he has not committed, the wrong is inflicted not by the law, but by the persons who have misused the law; Anytus, not the law, has done him a wrong. The prison-breaker, however, in doing what he does, is doing all he can to make the whole social system ineffective. *His* conduct is a direct challenge to the authority of law itself.

"Compared with your mother and father and all the rest of your ancestors, your country, "Plato has Socrates exclaim, "is something far more precious, more venerable, more sacred, and held in greater honor both among gods and among all reasonable men."

This remark (as well as a few others that Plato reports Socrates as expressing) has occasioned much discussion. In fact it embodies one side of a debate that has been carried on in political philosophy for centuries. Among those holding the view expressed here perhaps the greatest and best known was the German philosopher of the nineteenth century, Hegel. Proponents of this view tend to revere the state as something holy and magnificent, regarding it as a creation separate from and higher than any individuals that compose it. As such it is much more worthy than the persons who make it up, whose good must always be subordinate and rightly sacrificed when required for the good of the state. Nazi Germany was able to exploit this idea to the extreme, with well-known, devastating results for all concerned.

The other side of the debate has been represented by those who have taken what we might call an institutionalist approach — a much less romantic and heroic view, one typified by historical and contemporary "libertarian" movements. According to this view, the state is nothing more than a human institution. It is an instrument designed to do the necessary jobs of offering services to a populace and protecting its citizens from each other. Indeed, it maintains that it might be better if there were no need for this instrument at all. But, as there is a need, we must do our best to see to it that it does not get out of hand. Under this view the state is obviously no entity at all and merely serves to enhance the liberty and protect the rights of individuals. To revere it, then, even in the form of superpatriotism, is not only dangerous but a form of madness — dangerous, perhaps, because irrational.

Socrates' further argument here, however, is that if he did not like the law of Athens he was free to go to another city or state. By staying, as the laws themselves seem to be saying to him now, he had entered into a kind of pact with them which he is not at liberty to break at his pleasure. If he does, he will only harm his friends and disgrace himself. He must think of justice first, and of life and children afterwards — so that when he enters the next world he may have all this to plead in his defense before the Authorities there.

"That, my dear Crito," Socrates tells him in the dialogue that bears Crito's name, "I do assure you, is what I seem to hear them saying. And the sound of their arguments rings so loudly in my head that I cannot hear the other side. However, if you think you will do any good by it, say what you like."

"Socrates," Crito replies, "I have nothing to say." "Then, Crito, let us follow this course, since God points out the way."

And so with sadness and resignation, Crito gives in.

The last hours of Socrates' life are described in Plato's dialogue, the *Phaedo*. Unlike the dialogue just outlined, the *Phaedo* is very long and very difficult. It has two themes: the death of Socrates and the immortality of the soul. These two themes are tied together, for it is Socrates' firm belief in the latter that enables him to meet his death so courageously and hopefully.

The scene is Socrates' prison room on the day set by the Athenian court for his death. His friends have come to take their leave of him. He uses the occasion to talk to them about the nature of the soul. Towards the evening, the jailor brings in the fatal cup of hemlock.

All this is told by an eyewitness, Phaedo of Elis, to a group of fellow-philosophers, only one of whom is named and speaks. Plato, we are told, was not present at the execution; he is at home ill (an illness brought on, no doubt, by the event about to happen to his teacher and master).

The friends gathered round Socrates in these last few hours of his life express surprise that he remains as calm and reasonable as ever in the face of approaching death, but he argues that the philosopher has nothing to fear: philosophy, which is always trying to release the soul from the limitations of the body, is, in effect, the study of death.

What Socrates means by this seemingly paradoxical definition of philosophy is that it is only at death, when the soul is freed from the body, that it is at long last able to see things as they really are. For so long as our soul is embedded in the body, it must view reality only through the distortions of our bodily organs. At death, however, the soul is finally released from its prison, the human body, and at long last is able to see things as they are in themselves.

This idea of the soul imprisoned in the body and the ideal that can be reached only at death is one whose echoes can be heard later in the works of other authors. Shakespeare, for example, uses it in one of the love scenes in the *Merchant of Venice*. Lorenzo is outside in the garden with Jessica. They sit down, and pointing to the sky, Lorenzo remarks how beautiful it all is. It would be even more beautiful were we able to hear the music the various planets of the heaven make as they move about in their orbits, but our souls, which would be able to hear this music, are imprisoned in our bodies—the "muddy vesture of decay" as Shakespeare here describes it—and therefore we cannot hear it. In Shakespeare's own words:

> *Lorenzo:* Sit, Jessica. Look how the floor of heaven
> Is thick inlaid with patines of bright gold:
> There's not the smallest orb which thou behold'st
> But in his motion like an angel sings,
> Still quiring to the young-eyed cherubins.
> Such harmony is in immortal souls;
> But whilst this muddy vesture of decay
> Doth grossly close it in, we cannot hear it.

And this same thought—of being able to reach the ideal only at death—will sometimes be found in sadder, more tragic contexts. On Martin Luther King's tomb, for example, are inscribed these deeply moving and tragic words, perhaps taken from some old Negro spiritual:

> Free at last. Free at last. Thank God Almighty
> I'm free at last.

And this paradoxical use of the term "free" always recalls to this writer's mind the grim Nazi joke that greeted the millions of unfortunate victims who were sent to the infamous death camp Auschwitz. Over the entrance there hung the sign: *Arbeit Macht Frei*—Work Brings Freedom. And of course it did: if you worked hard and used up the little strength remaining to you, you were no longer useful to them and were immediately sent to the gas chamber—"freed."

The arguments in support of immortality that Socrates proposes and discusses in this dialogue are very difficult. Involved in one of the main arguments is the idea, a popular one of Plato's, that "our birth is but a sleep and a forgetting"; that to learn is in part to remember knowledge which must have been gained in another life. Another argument involves the idea that the soul is immortal because it can perceive and have a share in Truth, Beauty, and Goodness, which are immortal and eternal. Man can know God, the Eternal, because he has something in him that is Godlike.

At death, Socrates goes on to argue, the soul retires into another world. In the beautiful Myth of the Earthly Paradise and the Myth of the Destination of Souls, he makes some attempts to describe the other world. The description, he ends by saying, provides ground enough "for leaving nothing undone to attain during life some measure of goodness and wisdom; for the prize is glorious and the hope great."

It is typical of Plato and his works that where he reaches a certain point in his thought at which he can only guess and speculate, where he is no longer certain of himself, he chooses to present his account in the form of a story or a myth. It is as if he were saying to us that what you are about to hear is only a story; here is where philosophy ends and fiction begins. But, of course, it is not mere fiction for him. It is certainly a product of his imagination but there may be, for all we know, much truth in the account.

These myths from the *Phaedo* should be read together with the account of similar matters given in Plato's *Republic* — especially the Myth of Er towards the end of the work. Er, having died before his time was really up, and having already seen part of what lies ahead on this journey, was sent back to tell his fellowmen what awaits them. After telling his tale, Plato adds these concluding words:

And so Glaucon, the tale was saved from perishing; and if we will listen, it may save us, and all will be well when we cross the River of Lethe. Also we shall not defile our souls; but, if you will believe with me that the soul is immortal and able to endure all good and ill, we shall keep always to the upward way and in all things pursue justice with the help of wisdom. Then we shall be at peace with heaven and with ourselves, both during our sojourn here and when, like victors in the Games collecting gifts from their friends, we receive the prize of justice; and so, not here only, but in the journey of a thousand years of which I have told you, we shall fare well.

"Of course", Socrates says here in the *Phaedo*, "no reasonable man ought to insist that the facts are exactly as I have described them."

But that either this or something very like it is a true account of our souls and their future habitations — since we have clear evidence that the soul is immortal — this, I think, is both a reasonable contention and a belief worth risking; for the risk is a noble one. We should use such accounts to inspire ourselves with confidence; and that is why I have already drawn out my tale so long.

The last few pages of the *Phaedo*, describing Socrates' death, are among the most moving in Western literature; they are written with a plainness and simplicity that is always the mark of great writing. There is, however, a certain allusion made toward the end of the passages about to be quoted that needs explaining to a contemporary reader. To Crito's question whether he has any last requests to make, Socrates replies that he is to make sure to offer a sacrifice of a cock to Asclepius. Asclepius was the God of Healing. People who had been through a serious illness would offer a sacrifice to him in gratefulness. And so what this means is that now that he, Socrates, is about to enter a greater life (death releasing him from the "fitful fever" of this one) he wants to thank the God of Healing by offering a sacrifice to him. It is Socrates' final irony: he has been accused of impiety; is about to die because of it; yet his last deed is one of deep piety.

Now, the conclusion:

When he had finished speaking, Crito said, "Very well, Socrates. But have you no directions for the others or myself about your children or anything else? What can we do to please you best?"

"Nothing new, Crito," said Socrates, "just what I am always telling you. Look after yourselves and follow the line of life as I have laid it down now and in the past."

"We shall try our best to do as you say," said Crito. "But how shall we bury you?"

"Any way you like," replied Socrates, "that is, if you can catch me and I don't slip through your fingers." He laughed gently as he spoke, and turning to us went on: "I can't persuade Crito that I am this Socrates here who is talking to you now and marshalling all the arguments; he thinks that I am the one whom he will see presently lying dead; and he asks how he is to bury me! As for my long and elaborate explanation that I shall depart to a state of heavenly happiness, this attempt to console both you and myself seems to be wasted on him. You must assure him that when I am dead I shall not stay, but depart and be gone. That will help Crito to bear it more easily, and keep him from being distressed on my account when he sees my body being burned or buried, as if something dreadful were happening to me; or from saying at the funeral that it is Socrates whom he is laying out or carrying to the grave or burying. No, you must keep up your spirits and say that it is only my body that you are burying; and you can bury it as you please, in whatever way you think is most proper."

With these words he got up and went into another room to bathe; and Crito went after him, but told us to wait. So we waited, discussing and reviewing what had been said, or else dwelling upon the greatness of the calamity which had befallen us; for we felt just as though we were losing a father and should be orphans for the rest of our lives. Meanwhile when Socrates had taken his bath, his children were brought to see him — he had two little sons and one big boy — and the women of his household — you know — arrived. He talked to them in Crito's presence and gave them directions about carrying out his wishes; then he told the women and children to go away, and came back himself to join us.

It was now nearly sunset, because he had spent a long time inside. He came and sat down, fresh from the bath; and he had only been talking for a few minutes when the prison officer came in, and walked up to him. "Socrates," he said, "at any rate I shall not have to find fault with you, as I do with others, for getting angry with me and cursing when I tell them to drink the poison — carrying out Government orders. I have come to know during this time that you are the noblest and the gentlest and the bravest of all the men that have ever come here, and now especially I am sure that you are not angry with me, but with them; because you know who are responsible. So now — you know what I have come to say; try to bear what must be as easily as you can." As he spoke he burst into tears, and turning around, went away.

Socrates looked up at him and said: "We will do as you say." Then addressing us he went on "What a charming person! All the time I have been here he has visited me, and sometimes had discussions with me, and shown me the greatest kindness; and how generous of him now to shed tears for me at parting! But come, Crito, let us do as he says. Someone had better bring in the poison, if it is ready prepared; if not, tell the man to prepare it."

"But surely, Socrates," said Crito, "the sun is still upon the mountains; it has not gone down yet. Besides, I know that in other cases people have dinner and enjoy their wine, and sometimes the company of those

Jacques Louis David (1748–1825), *The Death of Socrates.* The Metropolitan Museum of Art.

whom they love, long after they receive the warning; and only drink the poison quite late at night. No need to hurry; there is still plenty of time."

"It is natural that these people whom you speak of should act in that way, Crito," said Socrates, "because they think that they gain by it. And it is also natural that I should not; because I believe that I should gain nothing by drinking the poison a little later — I should only make myself ridiculous in my own eyes if I clung to life and hugged it when it has no more to offer. Come, do as I say and don't make difficulties."

At this Crito made a sign to his servant, who was standing near. The servant went out and after spending a considerable time returned with the man who was to administer the poison; he was carrying it ready prepared in a cup. When Socrates saw him he said "Well, my good fellow, you understand these things, what ought I to do?"

"Just drink it," he said, "and then walk about until you feel a weight in your legs, and then lie down. Then it will act of its own accord."

As he spoke he handed the cup to Socrates, who received it quite cheerfully, without a tremor, without any change of color or expression, and said, looking up under his brows with his usual steady gaze, "What do you say about pouring a libation from this drink? Is it permitted, or not?"

"We only prepare what we regard as the normal dose, Socrates," he replied.

"I see," said Socrates. "But I suppose I am allowed, or rather bound, to pray the gods that my removal from this world to the other may be prosperous. This is my prayer, then; and I hope that it may be granted." With these words, quite calmly and with no sign of distaste, he drained the cup in one breath.

Up till this time most of us had been fairly successful in keeping back our tears; but when we saw that he was drinking, that he had actually drunk it, we could do so no longer; in spite of myself the tears came pouring out, so that I covered my face and wept brokenheartedly — not for him, but for my own calamity in losing such a friend. Crito had given up even before me, and had gone out when he could not restrain his tears. But Apollodorus, who had never stopped crying even before, now broke out into such a storm of passionate weeping that he made everyone in the room break down, except Socrates himself, who said:

"Really, my friends, what a way to behave! Why, that was my main reason for sending away the women, to prevent this sort of disturbance; because I am told that one should make one's end in a tranquil frame of mind. Calm yourselves and try to be brave."

This made us feel ashamed, and we controlled our tears. Socrates walked about, and presently, saying that his legs were heavy, lay down on his back — that was what the man recommended. The man kept his hand upon Socrates, and after a little while examined his feet and legs;

then pinched his foot hard and asked if he felt it. Socrates said no. Then he did the same to his legs; and moving gradually upwards in this way let us see that he was getting cold and numb. Presently he felt him again and said that when it reached the heart, Socrates would be gone.

The coldness was spreading about as far as his waist when Socrates uncovered his face — for he had covered it up — and said (They were his last words): "Crito, we ought to offer a cock to Asclepius. See to it, and don't forget."

"No, it shall be done," said Crito. "Are you sure there is nothing else?"

Socrates made no reply to this question, but after a little while he stirred; and when the man uncovered him, his eyes were fixed. When Crito saw this, he closed the mouth and eyes.

Such was the end of our comrade, who was, we may fairly say, of all those whom we knew in our time, the bravest and also the wisest and most upright man.

It will not be until some 400 years later that we will be left with another equally deeply moving account of a martyrdom, one strangely similar to it in so many ways.

Summary

1. Socrates differs from the philosophers studied in the previous chapter in being concerned not with the external world but with the inner world of man and his nature.

2. Believing that the most precious thing about man is his psyche or soul, he went about Athens trying to persuade others of its care and value. It was unworthy of them, he insisted, to devote themselves to pursuing wealth and glory and to neglect what really mattered most.

3. The hostility this activity aroused against him was, however, also due to the public confusing him with other kinds of critics, itinerant teachers circulating at Athens at this time, called Sophists. Although at first highly respected, these "experts" or "wise men" gradually lost their good name as a result of their increasingly severe attacks on the established system of law, ethics, and religion. The hostility was, in addition, aggravated as the result of the disastrous social and political events surrounding the Peloponnesian War and its aftermath.

4. Although Socrates might have gotten off with a fine or by apologizing, he used the opportunity of the trial to speak instead about his "philosopher's mission to search into myself and others."

5. The person who immortalized the name of Socrates was his young
    pupil Plato, whose works were all written in the form of dialogues
    and feature Socrates (with whom he had been associated for over
    ten years) as the main speaker. Of these, the four dialogues—the
    Euthyphro, the *Apology*, the *Crito*, and the *Phaedo*—form a unit,
    and are devoted to describing Socrates' thought, trial, and death.

6. After some good-natured banter, Socrates' discussion with Euthy-
    phro turns to the question of the nature of piety. To Euthyphro's
    first definition—that piety is "prosecuting a wrongdoer"—Socrates
    remarks that although this may be an example of piety, it is not a
    definition of it. Euthyphro's second definition of piety—that it is
    "what is pleasing to the gods"—also proves unsatisfactory because,
    as Socrates reminds him, the same things please some gods and dis-
    please others. To Euthyphro's rejoinder here that the gods surely do
    not disagree with each other on this point at any rate—that the
    guilty should be punished, Socrates replies that of course no one
    would dispute that. But what is disputed at such occasions is
    whether the person in question is guilty. But, as Socrates himself
    recognizes, even if Euthyphro could prove that all the gods agree
    that what his father did was wrong and that what he, Euthyphro,
    is doing is right or pious, this still would not tell us what piety in
    general is—unless we could generalize here and say that "Piety is
    what all the gods love." Euthyphro accepts this as his new defini-
    tion. The question that now emerges, however, is this: "Is what is
    pious loved by the gods *because it is pious;* or is it pious *because it
    is loved by them?*"When Euthyphro replies that the gods love a
    thing because it is pious (and not the other way around), Socrates
    replies in surprise: "If that is so, then what is it about such things
    which make the gods love them? Aren't we back at the beginning,
    wondering what is piety and saying, as you did then, that it is what
    is pleasing to the gods!" Despite Socrates' plea that he try again,
    Euthyphro declines, saying he has an urgent engagement and must
    be off. The dialogue shows us how people's actions are often based
    on ignorance, actions which nevertheless have serious, even tragic,
    consequences.

7. Socrates begins his defense against the charges of "corrupting the
    minds of the young and not worshipping the gods the state wor-
    ships" by saying that he wants to deal first with his earliest accusers,
    those not in court now but who nevertheless have been spreading
    false rumors about him for many years. These rumors accuse him
    of speculating about the earth and the stars in the tradition of his
    predecessors, and assert that he is, like them, no doubt, an atheist.
    Socrates argues that these accusations are simply false; that he has
    never had any interest in these matters. But if he has not been
    spending his time doing that, what is it that he does? In answer to

this question he relates the story of his friend's visit to the Oracle; the Oracle's pronouncement that Socrates is the wisest man in the world; what he did to determine the meaning of the pronouncement; and how this aroused hostility against him. These investigations, he tells them, led to the discovery that the Oracle was indeed right: he is the wisest of them all, for unlike everyone else, he knows that he knows nothing; whereas they are equally ignorant but do not know it. Sensing that the jury might think he has failed to recognize the seriousness of his position, he assures them he is fully aware of the implications of the charges. It is simply that having faced death before he is not afraid to die now; nor is he about to give up the one thing that is more precious to him than life itself: the pursuit of wisdom. If he has corrupted anyone as a result of this pursuit, let that person (or his kin) rise and say so. What he will most certainly not do is appeal to their pity. This, he says, would be unbecoming for all of them, for a judge should not allow himself to be influenced by his feelings. The jury votes and finds him guilty. Condemned to die, his last request is that they "do to my sons as I have done to you."

8. Socrates is now in prison awaiting execution. Crito, a wealthy Athenian and Socrates' oldest friend, has come to plead that he escape. Socrates, while appreciating Crito's warm feelings, wants to consider the matter only on its merits. Crito urges Socrates to consider all the bad consequences that would result from his staying, but Socrates wants to consider only what his duty is, regardless of the consequences. The question we should always ask, he tells Crito, is whether we are acting rightly or wrongly, risking doing something wrong or not, not forgetting that it is never right to do a wrong, or to return evil for evil. He is not, of course, guilty, but nevertheless when a person is legally but wrongly convicted of an offence he has not committed, the wrong is inflicted not by the law but by those who have misused the law; the prison-breaker, however, in doing what he does, challenges the whole fabric of law. Besides, if he did not like living in Athens he was free to go; by staying (as the laws themselves seem to be saying to him now) he had entered into a pact with them he is not now at liberty to break at his pleasure. When Crito is at a loss to reply, Socrates says to him: "Then, Crito, let us follow this course, since God points the way."

9. The *Phaedo*'s two main themes are the death of Socrates and the question of the immortality of the soul. The scene is Socrates' prison-room on the day set by the Athenian court for his death. The friends who have come to bid farewell to Socrates are surprised to find him calm and cheerful at this hour. In reply Socrates explains

why the philosopher does not fear death (living, as he does, constantly with it). Several arguments for the soul's immortality are examined, and through the medium of myth an attempt is made to explore the nature of the soul's destination. The dialogue ends with a detailed and profoundly moving account of Socrates' last moments and death.

For further study

1. Look up Socrates' debate with Thrasymachus in Plato's *Republic* concerning the latter's claim that "injustice" is more profitable than "justice."

2. In Plato's *Gorgias* Callicles, in addition to arguing the view that might is right, tries to persuade Socrates to give up philosophy, which, he says, is all right for a "lad" but ridiculous when still engaged in by an "adult" and a "gentleman." Look up both this scene in the dialogue as well as Socrates' later striking remarks about the fate he expects awaits him should he ever be arraigned. [W. C. Helmbold's translation of this dialogue (published in paperback by Bobbs-Merrill Co., in the Library of Liberal Arts series) is especially readable].

3. The animosity aroused by the Sophists among those in power is graphically conveyed in a scene featuring Socrates, Anytus, and Meno in Plato's dialogue, the *Meno*. Look this scene up and compare Socrates' attitude to the Sophists with those of Anytus. (The text of this dialogue and several outstanding essays devoted to its explication and analysis can be found in *Plato's Meno: Text and Criticism*, edited by Alexander Sesonske and Noel Fleming. Belmont, Calif.: Wadsworth, 1965.)

4. Another important source of information regarding Socrates' life comes to us from Plato's dialogue, the *Symposium*, which deals with the nature of love. It is regarded by many scholars as Plato's most polished and finished dialogue. A good deal of the new information conveyed in it comes from Alcibiades, who, somewhat tipsy, crashes the party (which is the occasion of the discussion) and insists on speaking on the topic. Love to him, he tells the company, is what he feels for Socrates, and so what we get are some very personal and intimate glimpses of Socrates that help complete Plato's picture of him for posterity. (Fulton H. Anderson's Introduction to the Liberal Arts Press edition of this dialogue will be found especially helpful.)

5. Read Aristophanes' comedy *The Clouds* and compare the picture drawn of Socrates in it with that depicted by Plato in the four dialogues discussed in this chapter. (William Arrowsmith's modern translation of this play [New American Library, 1962] makes delightful reading.)

6. Look up Xenophon's *Memorabilia* (recollections of Socrates) and *Defence of Socrates.* Compare the latter work with Plato's *Apology.* Two works on Xenophon that will be found informative and helpful are Anton-Hermann Chroust's *Socrates, Man and Myth: The Two Socratic Apologies of Xenophon* (Notre Dame: University of Notre Dame Press, 1957); and Leo Strauss' *Xenophon's Socrates* (Ithaca: Cornell University Press, 1972).

7. There are many translations and treatments of the four dialogues of Plato (the *Euthyphro*, the *Apology*, the *Crito*, and the *Phaedo*) that describe Socrates' life and death. Hugh Tredennick's translation of these four dialogues published under the general title *Plato: The Last Days of Socrates* (Harmondsworth, England: Penguin Books, 1954) is especially readable. And helpful too is Romano Guardini's book *The Death of Socrates* (Cleveland: World, 1962), which is a paragraph-by-paragraph commentary on these four dialogues.

8. Among the various fictional treatments of the life of Socrates some might find interesting are: Maxwell Anderson, *Barefoot in Athens: A Play in Two Acts* (New York: Sloane, 1951); Babette Deutsch, *Mask of Silenus: A Novel about Socrates* (New York: Simon and Schuster, 1933); and Mary Renault, *The Last of the Wine* (New York: Pantheon, 1956).

9. Those interested in exploring the parallels between the lives of Socrates and Jesus might begin by consulting Robert M. Wenley, *Socrates and Christ: A Study in the Philosophy of Religion* (Edinburgh: Blackwood, 1889).

10. For an account of the schools developed from Socrates' thought, see Eduard Zeller, *Socrates and the Socratic Schools*, translated by Oswald J. Reichel (London: Longmans, Green, 1877). Concerning Socrates' impact on various figures in subsequent centuries see Herbert Spiegelberg, *The Socratic Enigma: A Collection of Testimonies through Twenty-Four Centuries* (New York: Bobbs-Merrill, 1964).

11. For a recent collection of studies of Socrates see Gregory Vlastos (Ed.), *The Philosophy of Socrates: A Collection of Critical Essays* (New York: Doubleday, 1971).

part two
ITS METHOD

Raphael, detail from the *School of Athens*; Plato and Aristotle. The Bettmann
Archive, Inc.

chapter 3

Aristotle and the art of thinking

Introduction

There is no greater skill that one can acquire in life than the ability to think. Contrary to what many believe, this is not a skill that comes naturally to us, nor is it one we exercise a great deal. As George Bernard Shaw once remarked, few people think more than two or three times a year. He had managed to achieve an international reputation by thinking as often as once a week.

Although this is not a natural skill, it is one, as we have had occasion to see, that has been integral to the activity of philosophy from its very beginning — so much so, in fact, that to philosophize and to think have come to be regarded as almost synonymous.

But although this is so, thinking did not assume the importance that it came to possess and its study did not achieve the rank of a separate and distinct discipline until the arrival of Aristotle, whose investigation of it transformed it into the important discipline it has become.

Who was Aristotle and how did this happen?

Aristotle (384–322 B.C.) was born at Stagira, a Macedonian city some 200 miles to the north of Athens. In the year of his birth Plato was 43 and Socrates had been dead 15 years.

Aristotle's father was court-physician to the King of Macedonia. His parents, however, died while he was still young and he was given a home and an education by a friend of the family.

At the age of 18 he was sent to Plato's Academy in Athens, where he remained for the next 20 years, first as a pupil and then as a colleague of Plato's. When Plato died in 347 B.C. and the leadership of the Academy passed to Plato's nephew, Aristotle left. He went to Assos, a town on the coast of Asia Minor opposite the island of Lesbos. There was a regular school there, established by its philosophically sympathetic ruler, Hermias. Aristotle taught at this school for the next three years. He married Hermias' daughter and they had two children, a son, Nicomachus, and a daughter, Pythias, named after her mother.

After spending another two years on the neighboring island of Lesbos, Aristotle was invited by Philip of Macedonia to superintend the education of Alexander the Great, then a boy of 13.

Aristotle spent seven years as a tutor to the young prince. His assignment came to an end when on the death of Philip in 336 B.C. Alexander ascended to the throne of Macedonia, which by then dominated all Greece, and began his spectacular career as the conquerer of Persia.

Aristotle returned to Athens and founded his own school. It was called the Lyceum, and his system of philosophy came to be known as the Peripatetic Philosophy — apparently from his habit of teaching while walking up and down its covered walk. Aristotle spent the next 12 years at the Lyceum, where he started a library (the first in history), made vast collections of scientific data (much of the material coming to him from Alexander's expeditions), and built residential halls to accommodate the growing number of students. The Lyceum very quickly outstripped the Academy in fame. The two schools were very different in their orientation, each tending to reflect the temperament of its founder: the Academy was devoted to the study of the rational sciences — mathematics and astronomy; the Lyceum to the study of the empirical sciences, especially biology.

Aristotle's work at the Lyceum came to an end in 323 B.C. with Alexander's sudden death. In a wave of anti-Macedonian feeling, he was marked down as an associate of Alexander by the rebellious Athenians and they drew up a charge against him — one very similar to the accusation that had been brought against Socrates in 399 B.C. Not wanting, as he said, "to give the Athenians a second chance of sinning against philosophy," he returned to his country estate, where he died a few months later at the age of 63.

Aristotle's ability was recognized by Plato, who called him the *nous* (the "brain" or "mind") of the school. And Aristotle also always spoke highly of Plato. He said of him that he was a man "whom bad men have not even the right to praise and who showed in his life and teachings how to be happy and good at the same time."

Aristotle is known variously as the "Stagirite," after his birthplace; the "Peripatetic," from his habit of teaching; and as "The Philosopher" — the name given to him by St. Thomas Aquinas to indicate that there was no other.

The study of logic, or thinking — which, as we have said, has come to be considered so integral a part of philosophy — can be said to have begun at that moment, some 2,000 years ago, when Aristotle, a student at Plato's Academy and following Plato around as the latter engaged in discussion with the still ubiquitous Sophists, found himself baffled and challenged by their ability to outwit and outsmart all comers. He decided to examine what it was that enabled these "experts," as they were called, to accomplish these feats.

The result was a work on logic (one of six he was to devote to the study of thinking) entitled *Of Sophistical Refutations.* The title hints at its contents, for what we have here is a manual in which Aristotle sets out to expose the strategy and tactics the Sophists often resorted to in order to gain their verbal victories.

To call someone a sophist nowadays is not, of course, to pay them a compliment. As the dictionary tells us, a "sophist" is someone who is clever and tricky, who engages in fallacious reasoning, and who tries to outmaneuver and take advantage of an opponent in every possible way. But, as we have already observed, the meaning was not always so.

Aristotle's teacher Plato has left us some memorable and graphic descriptions of these "experts" in action. Probably the most memorable of these, although it is the least subtle of them and hardly does them justice, is in the dialogue entitled the *Euthydemus.* Since it contains the kind of logical points in argumentation that formed part of the basis of Aristotle's work in logic — work which will occupy us for some time here — let us spend some moments with it.

The dialogue opens with Socrates relating his encounter with two recent arrivals in Athens: the Sophists Euthydemus and Dionysodorous. In this particular encounter they have encountered a young boy, Cleinias, and are busy questioning him. Socrates is there and so is Cleinias' close friend, a youth called Ctessippus, who will later get clobbered when he tries to come to his friend's rescue. The Sophists always attracted a large crowd and there is one here too.

The questioning begins with Euthydemus asking Cleinias who learn things best — the wise or the unwise? The boy, understanding the word "wise" to mean "intelligent," naturally replies that it is the wise who learn best and not the unwise.

However by playing fast and loose with the meaning of the word, quickly shifting from one meaning of it to another, the Sophists soon get Cleinias to deny what he has just affirmed, subsequently to affirm it once again, then to deny it, until he is naturally completely befuddled — to the great amusement of the crowd which has gathered to watch the spectacle.

Having finished off Cleinias, they turn next to Socrates.

Socrates: Then once more the admirers of the two heroes, in an ecstasy at their wisdom, gave vent to another peal of laughter. Turning to me Dionysodorous said:

Dionysodorous:	Reflect Socrates: you may have to deny your words.
Socrates:	I have reflected, and I shall never deny my words.
Dionysodorous:	Well, and so you say that you wish Cleinias to become wise?
Socrates:	Undoubtedly.
Dionysodorous:	And he is not wise as yet?
Socrates:	At least his modesty will not allow him to say that he is.
Dionysodorous:	You wish him to become wise and not to be ignorant? You wish him to be what he is not, and no longer to be what he is? . . . You wish him no longer to be what he is? Which can only mean that you wish him to perish! Pretty lovers and friends they must be who want their favorite not to be, that is, to perish!
Socrates:	I was thrown into consternation at this and quite baffled. While in this state, a friend of Cleinias', Ctessippus, intervened and the Sophists turned to him.
Dionysodorous:	If you will answer my questions, I will soon extract the same admissions from you, Ctessippus. You say you have a dog.
Ctessippus:	Yes, a villain of a one.
Dionysodorous:	And he has puppies?
Ctessippus:	Yes, and they are very like himself.
Dionysodorous:	And the dog is the father of them?
Ctessippus:	Yes, I certainly saw him and the mother of the puppies come together.
Dionysodorous:	And he is not yours?
Ctessippus:	To be sure he is.
Dionysodorous:	Then he is a father, and he is yours; ergo, he is your father, and the Puppies are your brothers.
Euthydemus:	Ctessippus: Let *me* ask you one little question: you beat this dog?
Ctessippus:	(Laughing). Indeed I do; and I only wish I could beat *you* instead of him.
Euthydemus:	Then you beat your father!

Of course Plato is engaging in broad humor. Not all Sophists were as easy to ridicule, nor were the fallacies committed by them always as easy to track down as those represented here. Nevertheless, this was the task Aristotle set himself.

Aristotle's little work on *Sophistical Refutations* led to a whole new type of investigation, one that continued to be pursued by other philosophers after him. They recognized, like him, that these errors in logic, although often very funny and enjoyable, nevertheless can cause serious problems—for individuals, for groups, and for nations. The tradition of beginning the study of philosophy with the investigation of reasoning, motivated by these considerations, is one that arose early and has continued to this day.

There is, of course, more to the study of logic than an investigation of common fallacies, as those who go further in the study of philosophy will soon enough discover, but the investigation of the forms of fallacious reasoning is the peculiar province of reasoning and it is to this that our attention in this part of our study will be directed.

Fallacy, Wit, and Madness

Aristotle, who was the first to explore these common errors of reasoning, divided them into two groups: those that have their source in language (*in dictione*) and those whose source lies outside language (*extra dictionem*). Although many writers have tended to follow Aristotle's classification, neither the list of fallacies he compiled nor their treatment has remained fixed. Thus, some writers, while still maintaining the classification, have tended to depart from it by their treatment of several of the fallacies, or have gone to increase the list by adding types not identified by him. On the other hand, some writers have argued that no satisfactory classification of the fallacies is possible. The ways to error, they have argued (probably with justice) are too numerous and complex to admit of any neat division. Finally, still others have tended to take the position that since logic is the study of the correct forms of reasoning, the fallacies should be entirely omitted. But this argument is itself probably a fallacy, since there is perhaps no better way of illustrating, explaining and coming to know the correct ways of reasoning than by contrasting them with the incorrect ones.

In departing from Aristotle's twofold classification here an attempt has been made to stress the fact that all the fallacies have their source in some dimension of language. What distinguishes them cannot therefore be the fact that some have their source *in dictione* while others have their source *extra dictionem*. But although all have their source in language, they differ in that different aspects of language are responsible for the three large groups we will be distinguishing.

Thus, in one group of fallacies — we will call them fallacies of Ambiguity — it is the ambiguity of the words used that proves deceiving; in another group — fallacies of Presumption — what deceives is their similitude to the valid argument forms; and finally in still another group — fallacies of Relevance — it is the emotional appeal of the language used that does this.

We might also mention here that whereas in ordinary speech "fallacy" refers to any false belief that happens to be widely held, in logic a fallacy is an argument which appears sound to us but for various reasons is not. Very often the very thing which is responsible for the fallacy is that which makes the argument appealing to us. That is why we are so often deceived by them. Fallacies, in other words, although unsound are psychologically persuasive. And this is so not only because they evoke such attitudes as pity, fear, reverence, disapproval, and enthusiasm (which tends to blind us to the purely logical merits of the case being argued), but also because they are often extremely subtle and complex.

In order to learn how to deal more easily with these more complex and subtle cases, it will sometimes be helpful to use somewhat absurd examples. These should not be misunderstood as meaning that the reader or anyone else is ever likely to commit these fallacies in these extreme and absurd guises. Such absurd examples serve rather the same purpose in logic as the telescope and microscope serve in their respective fields: they magnify the structure and nature of the difficulty under examination so that we may see it more clearly.

Let us consider, for example, the following absurd argument: "Everything that runs has feet; the river runs; therefore the river has feet." This argument may appear sound because we do say such things as "the river *runs*." Of course, when we do so we do not mean that it has feet on which it runs. We mean that it *flows*. That is, of course, an absurd and obvious example, but the persuasiveness of even the most subtle examples depends on this very same device: a key term switches its meaning at a critical point in an argument.

Consider, for example, the case of the fellow with a Bible tract under his arm who comes knocking at our door and says to us: "If you believe in the miracles of science how come you don't believe in the miracles of the Bible? As a student of science and logic you ought to be consistent."

If he truly believes in this argument, he has come to do so by failing to see that the word "miracle," as used in the context of the remark about science, is quite different in meaning from its standard, Biblical use. Used in the Biblical and literal sense, a miracle is any occurrence that goes against, or interrupts, or breaks, the laws of nature. But as used metaphorically in the context of "miracles of science" that term means "great discovery" or "outstanding achievement." We are so impressed and grateful for the remarkable achievement or breakthrough that we try to give expression to that feeling by attaching the label "miracle" to it. This being so, as we might therefore reply, we are not being inconsistent in believing in the so-called "miracles of science" and not in the miracles of the Bible.

Unlike the example of the river running, this one is more subtle and more difficult. The absurd example, however, will be found useful in learning how to deal with the more difficult ones we will ordinarily run into.

It may be interesting to observe that the same devices which are responsible for these logical traps can be used by us, if we have our wits about us, for the expression of our sense of humor. "Good steaks are rare these days, so don't order yours well done"; "Diamonds are seldom found in this country, so be careful not to mislay your engagement ring"; "Your argument is sound, nothing but sound." In these cases we are not equivocating with the words "rare," "found," and "sound"; we are punning with them. Sometimes the pun can be very pointed, as in Benjamin Franklin's famous quip: "We must all hang together, or assuredly we shall all hang separately."

What may be even more interesting is that the same devices which are responsible for logical fallacies and can be exploited for the expression of our wit will sometimes, in addition, be found to lie at the root of various psychological disturbances.

A typical case would be the following, taken from a work by British psychiatrist R. D. Laing (*Interpersonal Perception: A Theory and a Method of Research.* New York: Springer, 1966, pp. 41–42.) Jack and Jill's marriage is coming apart and they seek help. Each claims the other does not love them, neglects them, and is in the process of destroying them, while they, on the contrary, always have and probably always will love the other. How is this possible? When we look into the background of this couple, we find, says Laing, that what lies at the root of their troubles is their differing and contradictory conceptions of "love": One discovers that Jack's father treated his mother very differently from the way Jill's father treated her mother. Jack's father was too poor to have brought home enough money to make his family feel secure against the possibility of being evicted or not having enough food. Jack remembers vividly how his mother complained to this father about his inadequate income. From this Jack developed the viewpoint that if his father had simply made enough money his mother would have been eternally grateful. Since he is now successful financially, he expects Jill to be eternally grateful to him for providing her with a security that his mother never had. On the other hand, Jill has come from a wealthy family in which there was never any comparable issue of financial security. In Jill's family, consideration, love, and kindness were expressed through the giving of gifts, the remembering of anniversaries, and so on. She had learned to take it for granted that the man will provide her with an economically secure home. What she looks for are the little niceties which she feels indicate true considerateness, kindness, and love. For Jack these niceties are irrelevant; they are minor details, trivia by comparison to the other things he does for the family. However, if each can discover his or her own and the other's value system and thereby see the conjunctions and discrepancies between them, it becomes possible for each to explain himself or herself to the other. It is now, for the first time, feasible for Jack to say: "Well, if it really is that important to you that I remember your birthday, I'll do my darndest to try." It is now possible for Jill to "appreciate" Jack more as a provider in the family. If bitterness and revenge (I am going to hurt you for the hurt you have done to me) have not intensified too much, it may still be relatively simple for each to satisfy the other's expectations according to their idiosyncratic value systems. Such an incredibly simple move can sometimes produce very powerful effects, particularly, early in a relationship. Once a history of pain and misery has been developed, the matter becomes correspondently more complex and difficult to reorient.

Although we are here mainly interested in coming to understand and to deal with logical fallacies, it is nevertheless interesting to reflect upon the possible connections between these three seemingly different phenomena of fallacy, wit, and madness. What is it about language or ourselves, one cannot help wondering, that enables us to put these same devices to such strangely different uses? What common, inner principle allows these forms to undergo, under the pressure of changing circumstances, such startling transformations?

A clue to the solution to this problem may be found, perhaps, in a justly

Henri Bergson. Mary Evans Picture Library, London.

famous little book on *Laughter* by the great French philosopher Henri Bergson (1859–1941).

Bergson was born in Paris in 1859. In 1889, when he was 30, he published his first major work, *Time and Free Will*, in which he argued the novel thesis that it was intuition and not our intellect which provides our most trustworthy perception of the world. For unlike the intellect, which only distorts and falsifies reality by analyzing and cutting it up, intuition grasps experience and reality as it is.

Seven quiet years intervened before the appearance of his next and most difficult book, *Matter and Memory* (1896). Here Bergson began to explore in detail an idea central in all his works: that life is a struggle between the material and the vital, in which the life force tries to overcome the obstacles put in its way by inert matter, and although it often succeeds in this, the material world does mold and determine life's possibilities.

That there is, nevertheless, a great amount of freedom and openness in this process, Bergson detailed in yet another work, *Creative Evolution* (1907)—a work that won him international fame. It was recognized as a masterpiece. As a result of it, he became almost overnight the most popular figure in the philosophic world. He was already by this time a Professor at the College de France—famous as a great teacher and lecturer, in addition, of course, to his fame as a noted author. In 1914 he was elected to the French Academy and in 1927 won the Nobel Prize.

Bergson's international fame was so great that after the collapse of France in 1940, the Vichy government, which collaborated with the Nazis, offered him exemption from the Jewish racial laws, which were patterned after the infamous Nuremberg Laws. Bergson, however, now very old and frail, declined the exemption and insisted on registering at the police station with all the others. He died soon after in 1941.

As Bergson shows in his beautifully written essay on laughter, humor results when human beings assume the character of things and respond and act in a mechanical, inflexible, machinelike fashion. That is why we find the stiff and artificial dance of the clown funny; laugh at the poor fool who trips over some object in his path which, had he been less absentminded, he might have avoided; and find amusing all sorts of other blunders that result from our lifeless, rigid, and attentionless propensities. As Bergson argues convincingly, what calls forth laughter in all such cases is our absentmindedness, our lack of suppleness, which makes our activities appear to be mechanical and those who perform them more like things or objects than human beings. Our laughter at such mindlessness, Bergson adds, is a form of social criticism, designed to correct such behavior in order to preserve both life and society.

Bergson's book does not concern itself with the analysis of fallacies, but its main thesis fits fallacies extremely well. It is, in fact, surprising how many fallacies are illustrations, on the conceptual plane, of that same inflexible, mechanical, mindlessness which, Bergson has shown, is the source of laughter. On the other hand, it should not perhaps be that surprising, for it is just as easy, after all, to trip over a word or concept, if we are distracted and proceed mechanically along the lines laid down by the words spoken, as it is to trip over a log lying in our path.

Of course, in an example such as the one about miracles the lapse is unintentional; it is also subtle enough for its essential absurdity to escape us. This is not the case, of course, with the example of the river running; the absurdity is pretty plain there and so we laugh. Here the lapse, if not entirely deliberate, is certainly almost so. And, of course, in the case of Benjamin Franklin's quip about hanging together, we have a true case of a witticism. For Benjamin Franklin sets out here to exploit the device that in other circumstances often exploits us. We laugh at its cleverness, realizing full well how such things generally master us and not we them.

But not only do fallacy and wit have much in common; both also have a good deal in common with various forms of madness. According to Bergson, as we have just seen, what makes us smile in the case of certain amusing anecdotes or laugh at certain jokes is the mindlessness exemplified by the subject of the joke or person of the anecdote. Interestingly enough, it is this same absence of mind, as Freud discovered, this temporary lack of watchfulness on the part of our consciousness, that allows repressed material from our unconscious to momentarily surface and become the stuff of psychoanalysis.

That this mindlessness and the symptomatology which sometimes ensues is not a feature of behavior characteristic only of those who have gone mad, but can be characteristic of all of us in our everyday activities, was shown by Freud in *The Psychopathology of Everyday Life*. In this remarkable book — addressed to the general public — Freud analyzes the unconscious sources of ordinary errors and lapses and shows that such "mistakes" are not accidents but stem rather from disturbances in our personalities, some of which may be buried so deep that we ourselves are barely aware of them.

A case in point is the common phenomenon of forgetting. As Freud points out, we forget names of people or places, or just ordinary words and phrases, because they become connected in our minds, often in a most superficial way, with something painful that we wish to repress or have already repressed. Freud gives an example of a woman who, having been preoccupied with thoughts of no longer being young, could not remember the name of Freud's colleague, the famous psychoanalyst Carl Jung. As in this case, what happens in forgetting is

Sigmund Freud. Mary Evans Picture Library, London.

that the disturbing thought ("no longer young") becomes connected with the neutral word ("Jung") by way of a "verbal bridge," as Freud called it.

There are, of course, other ordinary day-to-day mishaps: slips of the tongue or pen, misreadings, breaking objects, falling and injuring oneself, and so on. In many ways, these are even more revealing than ordinary forgetting, for the repressed things use such moments to break out and reveal themselves — betraying in this way, on occasion, our deepest feelings. Freud gives an example of the disappointed guest who, having expected something more in the way of a repast from his host, remarked in the course of a political conversation (Theodore Roosevelt was then running for president for the second time under the slogan "He gave us a square deal"): "You may say what you please about Teddy, but there is one thing you can't deny — he gave us a square meal." Of course he had meant to say "square deal."

Another example mentioned by Freud is the woman who, waiting for Freud to write out her prescription, said to him: "Please, Dr. Freud, don't give me big bills. I can't swallow them."

Our tendency to read into a text what we have an unconscious wish to see there is often similarly amusing and revealing. One of Freud's examples is of a woman who, very anxious to have children, always reads "storks" instead of "stocks." As in ordinary cases of forgetting, here too, obviously, the most superficial verbal resemblance is used by our unconscious. Needless to say, such errors are not always so irreproachable; in misreading names, as Freud points out, the psychological motive at work may very well be unconscious hostility.

Freud calls such mishaps as dropping and breaking things, mislaying or losing them, and so on, "symptomatic actions." Such actions, in his view, are not only psychically determined but are also revelations arising from the most intimate and deepest parts of our psyche. These mishaps, he argues, are executions of unconscious intentions; intentions, that is, which we have not entirely succeeded in repressing. Although these intentions are, strictly speaking, unknown to consciousness, they are nevertheless "intended" by us, and are therefore in a very profound sense valid for us. This is true of such an unconscious and seemingly "accidental" (although not uncommon) act as dropping a wedding ring that one has unconsciously removed while distracted in a conversation; and it is true of such "accidents" as breaking some personal (but unconsciously unwanted) possession or even injuring oneself.

Freud sees confirmation of the essential meaningfulness of such errors and symptomatic actions in the fact that such blunders are often met with knowing smiles and laughter, and occasionally with derision. Also revealing is the fact that those who commit these "mistakes" and "accidents" will often indignantly deny having done so, and are intensely offended if one (correctly of course) insists that they have. Obviously they are ashamed of what they have done, even if they do not consciously know it. And similarly revealing is our own anger at our inability to recall a forgotten word or name. We are not, apparently, in the habit of treating such blunders as mere "mistakes" or "accidents" but, whether bystanders or victims, tend to regard them as deeply motivated, although unwittingly so.

Freud leaves it an open question whether the basically intentional nature of such blunders or mistakes cannot be applied to the more important errors of judgement made by us in our other, more serious, activities. How "accidental," for example, is the unfortunate, but none too rare, administration of the wrong drug to a patient either by the physician or by the nurse? It is not clear Freud thinks that all such errors are avoidable, but it is obvious he thinks many are.

In an age of great psychological ferment and interest, as ours is, it is hardly likely that anyone needs to be reminded that the harm others do to us comes nowhere near what we do to ourselves. Although we can prevent a good deal of such harm to ourselves by becoming more "logical" and "rational," we are likely to be more successful in doing this by trying to learn as much as possible about the kinds of tactics and strategies used by the enemy. Such strategies are now called "games," and the most dangerous are the kind we play with ourselves.

Nor are these games, ironically and perversely, without their amusing aspect. Freud's famous Rat Man Case is typical. The man had many other symptoms and problems in addition to the one which brings him to mind here. One summer, while on holiday in the mountains, this man suddenly got the idea that he was too fat and that he needed to reduce. He subjected himself to the severest regimen: running furiously along the roads in the heat of August, climbing mountainsides, and so on — all in an effort to lose weight. The origin and nature of his compulsion did not become clear until in one session a chain of associations led from the word *dick* (meaning "fat" in German) to the name of the Rat Man's American cousin, Richard, known as Dick. When it emerged that the Rat Man was jealous of this cousin and felt threatened by him because of the attentions he was paying to the girl with whom the Rat Man was in love, it became clear that his furious efforts to get rid of his fat was really a disguised and symbolic way of disposing of his cousin Richard.

The Rat Man was, of course, neither punning (as Benjamin Franklin was) nor equivocating (as the man with his argument about miracles was). The Rat Man was in the grip of a delusion. He had become the slave and tool of a master (his own unconscious) who, as we have seen, makes no distinctions, takes account of no degrees, and for whom the most superficial resemblances suffice to forge binding links.

The striking unity that seems to underlie fallacy, humor, and the operations of the unconscious can on occasion help us unravel and understand somewhat more serious conditions. Consider for a moment the catatonic schizophrenic — the poor wretch who, in a fit of rage, takes, say, the life of his girl friend, or of his wife and children, or perhaps of all of them. Overcome by the horror of the deed, he lapses into madness and for hours or even days stands there in a rigid posture. Why this immobilized posture? If we would see him standing that way on the street corner we would find him amusing. We would laugh at him, probably because, as Bergson has helped us see, he has turned himself into a thing or object. But why? Not, of course in order to make us laugh but very likely in the hope either of preventing a repetition of the horrible deed or of denying responsibility for it — for if he is a mindless thing he could not possibly have done it, and if he did it, it was not really him but this mindless thing. And so he stands there like a thing.

Rigidity and mindlessness — these are are the things which make us laugh; they are also, as we will see, the stuff of fallacy, the things that trip us up so that we commit all sorts of logical blunders; and they are also, apparently, the condition, at times, we lapse into when that fragile balance called life is upset.

Looking Ahead

In the chapter that follows we are going to explore in detail some of these major logical fallacies. Although Aristotle, as we have mentioned, divided these fallacies into two major groups — fallacies originating *in dictione* and those originating *extra dictionem* — we shall follow here the later tradition of regarding them as somehow all arising from an aspect of the language, and we shall discuss them under three headings: Ambiguity, Presumption, and Relevance.

It is not clear who first proposed and used this threefold division. It nevertheless fits the subject very well. For logic is the study of argument and before giving our assent to an argument we should always make sure we are clear about the following three things:

1.   Is what the argument asserts clear?

2.   Are the facts in the argument correctly represented?

3.   Is the reasoning in the argument valid?

The three traditional categories are tied to these three aspects of argument. The first set (the fallacies of Ambiguity) deals with arguments that fail to meet the challenge of the first question (Is the argument *clear?*); the second (the fallacies of Presumption) deals with arguments that fail to meet the challenge of the second question (Is what the argument asserts *true?*); and the third (the fallacies of Relevance) deals with arguments that fail to meet the challenge of the third question (Is the argument *valid?*)

The fallacies generally discussed under the category of ambiguity are, as traditionally identified, Amphiboly, Accent, Hypostatization, Equivocation, Composition, and Division. What tends to deceive us, as we will see, in these fallacies is the confusing nature of the language in which the argument is expressed. Each type of confusion, in addition, centers within an important aspect of the nature of sentences. Thus:

1.   *Amphiboly* explores the consequences of not taking sufficient care with the way we structure our statements.

2.   *Accent* explores what can go wrong when we mistake the context of a sentence or statement, and as a result fail to understand it in the way it was intended to be understood.

3. *Hypostatization* explores what is entailed when we mistake the reference of a sentence or statement, as a result of confusing concrete with abstract terms.

4. *Equivocation* explores the errors we are prone to commit when we fail to recognize that many of our words have multiple meanings.

5. *Composition and Division* explore the mistakes we make as a result of confusing the collective with the distributive senses of terms.

One of the benefits of the study of these six fallacies is that they help us develop our ability to express ourselves with greater clarity and precision. One's first efforts at this are usually surprisingly weak.

In dealing with these fallacies one's goal, therefore, should not be simply to identify the fallacy in question (tag it with some appropriate label) but rather to develop the skill of explaining with clarity and precision why this or that particular argument is less than sound.

Let us take, for instance, the following typical example of the fallacy of amphiboly:

> The concert held in Good Templars' Hall was a great success. Special thanks are due the Vicar's daughter, who labored the whole evening at the piano, which, as usual, fell upon her.

Its analysis may take the following form:

> From the somewhat careless way the second sentence of the argument is constructed, it could be interpreted to mean either that the piano itself fell on the Vicar's daughter, or, more likely, that the labor of playing it fell on her. What confuses here is the term "which," whose antecedent is ambiguous.

Normally you will not need more than two or three such sentences in order to explain the example and expose its fallacy. The object is to develop the skill to do so with economy and clarity.

Just as it is confusing language that deceives in the case of the fallacies of Ambiguity, so it is the misleading resemblance to valid argument forms (achieving this deception by misrepresenting the facts disclosed in the argument) that deceives in the case of the fallacies under the category of Presumption. The argument, for example, "Exercise is good; Jones therefore should do more of it, for it will be good for him" looks deceptively like the classic argument "All men are mortal; Socrates is a man; therefore Socrates is mortal" but, unfortunately, differs from it in that the statement "Exercise is good" is an unqualified generalization which may not apply to Jones, who may suffer from a heart condition and has been told specifically by his doctor not to exercise.

What is most characteristic of the fallacies of Presumption is that facts relevant to the argument have not been represented correctly in the premises. This inappropriate treatment of the facts may take the form of "overlooking," "evading," or "distorting" them. These are the three subheadings under which the ten fallacies of Presumption will be discussed in the next chapter.

Finally, fallacies of Relevance can be confusing because of the emotional storm raised by the speaker. As those who make use of these devices know, when feelings run high almost anything will pass for argument. The six fallacies traditionally discussed in this connection cover a very wide spectrum of emotion: our susceptibility to prejudice in the fallacy of *ad Hominem*, flattery and envy in the fallacy of *ad Populum*, sympathy in the fallacy of *ad Misericordiam*, vanity in the fallacy of *ad Verecundiam*, pride in the fallacy of *ad Ignorantiam*, and intimidation in the fallacy of *ad Baculum*.

A word, finally, about examples that have the appearance of statements rather than arguments, and would therefore seem to be out of place here. These statements, however, are in reality highly abbreviated arguments, and are included here because that is the way we do in fact, often argue (for time is short and thought is quick and we therefore feel free to omit much that seems unnecessary to state explicitly).

Thus pointing a finger at someone and shouting the epithet "Liar!" can be considered an argument, for in essence what is being asserted (not that anyone would ever take the trouble to do so explicitly) is the following:

All people who try to deceive others by uttering what they know to be
   false are liars.
You are such a person.
Therefore you are a liar.

Of course, establishing the full text of the intended argument (which is another important and useful skill to develop) does not make the argument sound; it does, however, place us in a better position to determine whether it is or is not.

Summary

1. Aristotle, Greek philosopher of the fourth century B.C., founded the science of logic.

2. Among Aristotle's works on logic was one entitled *Of Sophistical Refutations*, which dealt with what has come to be known as the common fallacies — arguments that appear sound but for one reason or another are not.

3. What seems especially remarkable about fallacies is that the linguistic devices responsible for the confusions in question are the very same that, if we have our wits about us, can be used to express our sense of humor and, more strangely, are what sometimes lie at

the foundation of various mental disturbances. Thus the ordinary pun is the humorous equivalent of the fallacy of equivocation, and the same appears to be true of various psychological confusions (as in Freud's famous Rat Man Case).

4.   Logical fallacies have been divided traditionally into three main categories: those in which the error is due to the confusing nature of the language in which the argument is expressed (fallacies of Ambiguity); those that achieve their deception by misrepresenting the facts disclosed in the argument (fallacies of Presumption); and those that confuse by stirring up powerful feelings (fallacies of Relevance).

For further study

1.   For a detailed account of Aristotle's work on informal logic — *Of Sophistical Refutations* — and its influence on later thought see C. L. Hamblin, *Fallacies* (London: Methuen, 1972).

2.   Those who may wish to consult the original works discussed in this chapter will find the following editions readily available: Plato, *Euthydemus*, translated with an Introduction by Rosamond Kent Sprague (New York: Bobbs-Merrill, 1965). Henri Bergson, *Laughter: An Essay on the Meaning of the Comic*, translated by Cloudesley Brereton and Fred Rothwell (New York: Macmillan, 1928). Sigmund Freud, *The Psychopathology of Everyday Life*, translated by A. A. Brill (New York: Mentor, 1970).

François Auguste René Rodin, *Le Penseur.* The Bettmann Archive, Inc.

chapter 4

The fallacies

section one
AMBIGUITY

1. Amphiboly

We have seen that the first thing we have to watch out for when confronted with an argument is that we are not taken in by any ambiguity it may contain. Let us now look at how such ambiguity misleads or deceives.

Language admits of different sorts of ambiguity and each major kind has come to receive its own name. Amphiboly is the term which we attach to the fallacies or deceptions that result from faulty or careless sentence structure.

The carelessness may be intentional, as in the case of the title of the record "Best of the Beatles," which misled many people to buy it thinking they were getting a record featuring the "best songs of the Beatles" when in fact they had purchased a record featuring Mr. Peter Best, who had been "a member of the Beatles" early in their career.

Shakespeare loved to exploit this particular ambiguity of language — in his case not, of course, for gain but simply for dramatic effect.

In *Henry VI* (Part II, scene iv) a witch prophesies that "The Duke yet lives that Henry shall depose," which leaves it unclear whether the Duke will depose Henry, or Henry will depose the Duke. To make it clear which is which the word "that" would have to be replaced either with "who" or "whom."

A more striking use of this kind of ambiguity by Shakespeare occurs in the play *Macbeth*. The witch there tells Macbeth:

> Be bloody, bold, and resolute; laugh to scorn
> The power of man, for none of woman born
> Shall harm Macbeth.

The phrase "none of woman born" turns out to be a ghastly deception when Macbeth discovers, all too late, that Macduff had been "untimely ripped from his mother's womb" and thus, although torn of woman not literally born of her.

It is interesting to observe that it is because of such inherent ambiguity that when we are asked to swear an oath, we promise not only to tell the truth (for we might then only tell part of it), and not only to tell the whole truth (for we might then throw in a few lies as well), but "to tell the truth, the whole truth, and nothing but the truth," which takes care of all contingencies. Had the witches taken such a vow they would not have been able to tell Macbeth what they did.

Exercises

Directions: In this and each of the subsequent exercises explain in two or three sentences how the examples given illustrate the fallacy discussed.

1. It would be a great help toward keeping the churchyard in good order if others would follow the example of those who clip the grass on their own graves.

2. Mrs. Manning's are the finest pork and beans you ever ate. So when you order pork and beans, be sure Mrs. Manning is on the can.

3. Sign on window: Wanted Smart Young Man for Butcher. Able to Cut, Skewer, and Serve a Customer.

4. Headline: Nude Patrol OK'd for Muir Beach

5. Report of Social Worker: Woman still owes $45 for a funeral she had recently.

6. Announcement: Dr. W. T. Jones read an interesting paper on "Idiots from Birth." There were over 200 present.

2. Accent

Accent is the name logicians have come to attach to those fallacies or deceptions that arise from ambiguity or confusion as to emphasis.

The fallacy can take three forms: (1) It can result from confusion concerning the *tone of voice* a certain statement was meant to be spoken in. (2) It can result from confusion concerning where the *stress* was meant to be placed in a remark. (3) And it can arise when a passage is torn out of context and thus given an emphasis it was not meant to have.

Let us consider the first of these three forms.

In one of the transcripts of the Watergate tapes, John Dean warns Richard Nixon against getting involved in a coverup, and the President replies: "No—it is wrong, that's for sure." But what inflection was in Nixon's voice when he made this remark? Was it said in a serious and straightforward tone of voice, or was it said ironically? If it was uttered ironically this remark would represent additional evidence of his involvement.

It is because tone of voice adds a further dimension to language that Clerks of Court usually read testimony in a deliberate monotone, trying in this way to keep out any inadvertent indications of their own feelings about the matter read.

The following are somewhat more mundane examples of the fallacy in this first form. "I cannot praise this book too highly" (Meaning what? That it is impossible to praise it at all or enough?) "You never looked better" (Meaning what? That you always look that way—namely, bad; or that you were never more beautiful?) "I wish you all the good fortune you deserve." (Meaning what?)

What has been said of tone of voice applies to stress as well. Thus, to consider a somewhat artificial example, if we were to emphasize the word "friends" in the statement: "We should not speak ill of our friends" we might succeed in conveying the thought that it is all right to speak ill of our enemies; or if we emphasize

"I asked for the *Peking* duck!" © 1971 by *Playboy*.

the word "speak" we might convey the idea that is all right to *think* ill of them, and so on. The same applies to such a remark as: "men were created equal." If we stressed "men" we might thereby imply that women were not created equal; and if we stressed "were created" we might suggest that although that is the way they started out, they are no longer so.

As these examples indicate, the fallacy of Accent arises either when a wrong or unintended stress is placed upon some word or phrase in a statement, or when a statement is read in a tone of voice different from the one that was intended for it. As such the fallacy is unlike Amphiboly, whose ambiguity is due not to misplaced emphasis or intonation, but to misplaced words or faulty sentence structure.

How can one avoid the fallacy? Sometimes it will simply be unavoidable. We cannot foretell how our words will be used or abused, understood or misunderstood on some future occasion. We can, however, take some precautions. We can provide a background or context that will be difficult to distort. And this need not be anything very elaborate. The addition of another emphatic word will sometimes do it.

Sometimes in order to avoid misunderstanding we must avoid using terms which tend in that context to call too much of the wrong sort of attention to themselves, as in the following two examples, both involving the word "hope": "They will be married Sunday. Then they will spend a few weeks in a cottage by the sea, and by the time the honeymoon is over the groom hopes to be in the army." (The word "expects" would be much more advisable here.) Inscription on a tombstone: "Sacred to the Memory of ———. After living with her husband for 55 years she departed in hope of a better life." (Simply "she departed to a better life" would be kinder here.)

As with the fallacy of Amphiboly, Accent can be exploited for humorous purposes as well. A notable example is the poor worker in Charlie Chaplin's film *The Great Dictator*, who growled "This is a fine country to live in" and was promptly arrested by the dictator's police. He managed to get himself off, however, by pleading that all he said was "This is a fine country to live in" — meaning that it was a lovely, wonderful place.

The ambiguity is not always so innocuous, however. The command given at the institution of the Eucharist is a case in point. Does the command "Drink ye all of it" mean (a) "Drink *ye all* of it" — meaning everyone should drink it or does it mean (b) "Drink ye *all of it*" — that is, some of you drink it, but drink it all up. Doubt regarding its meaning was the cause of a good deal of heated dispute. The modern translation, opting for the former interpretation, reads "Drink it, all of you."

Accent is obviously more a reader's than a writer's fallacy. The author of a particular remark or statement presumably knows what emphasis he wishes to give to it or how he wishes it to be understood, and were he present to translate it into spoken words he would be able to make that meaning clear to us. In his absence, some doubt is always possible.

The fallacy of Accent can be found in one further form. This occurs whenever the meaning of a statement or the content of a book, a speech, or a review is distorted by removing or quoting (not merely a word or a phrase, as in the ordinary case of Accent) sentences or portions of sentences out of context. This is a favorite device not only of propagandists but also of blurb-writers and newspapermen. Since very few people ever bother or have the time to read everything in their newspapers or other reports, the damage and misinformation conveyed by such dishonest captions, misleading headlines, and misquotations are probably enormous. The same applies to advertisements. How many of us have not at one time or another been misled into buying a certain book or seeing a certain movie as a result of misleading blurbs and quotations?

A drama critic might write that he "Liked all of the play except the lines, the acting, and the scenery," only to find himself quoted the next morning that he "liked all of the play . . ." Or, to take another rather sadder example, a schoolteacher might tell her civics class that "Communism is the best type of government if you care nothing for your liberty or your material welfare," only to discover that Johnny had quoted her at home as saying that "Communism is the best type of government."

There is probably no way to be sure what Johnny will take back from school with him, but responsible writers who make a direct quotation should always indicate any omission of words or phrases by the use of dots. Not to do so is to tell only half the story and with it only half the truth. In addition they should make a sincere effort to capture both the tone and flavor of the original in their paraphrase, providing as well the proper context of the remark in question.

Exercises

1. Only Hollywood could produce a film like this.

2. Member of audience after sitting through a five-hour performance of Wagner's opera *Parsifal*: "I can't believe I heard the whole thing!"

3. Question: What are you doing this weekend? The usual?

4. Thou shalt not bear false witness against thy neighbor.

5. Be courteous to strangers.

6. Federal regulation: Warning: Under Title 18 US Code: It Is a Federal Offense to Assault a Postal Employee While on Duty.

7. School Sign: Slow Children Crossing.

8. Speaker: Lincoln could not have been such a fine man, for didn't he say that "You can fool some of the people all of the time"?

3. Hypostatization

Everyone will remember that delightful encounter between Alice and the cat in *Alice in Wonderland.* On taking her leave, the cat begins to vanish slowly, "beginning," as Alice tells us, "with the end of the tail, and ending with the grin, which remained some time after the rest of it had gone." Alice is led to remark in astonishment: "Well! I've often seen a cat without a grin; but a grin without a cat! It's the most curious thing I ever saw in all my life!"

If we were properly trained in logic we would feel this same sense of astonishment that Alice felt whenever anyone spoke of such things as "redness" or "roundness" or "truth," "beauty," and "virtue," as if these things could exist by themselves and in their own right and were not merely abstractions, which (like the cat's grin) depend on some concrete entity for their existence. Imitating Alice, we would express our astonishment by remarking that we have certainly seen "red" *apples* or "round" *balls* and "truthful, beautiful, and virtuous" *people,* but never "roundness" or "redness," or "truth, beauty, and virtue" as such.

To think that we have seen or could see "redness" and "roundness" and "truth" independently of red or round things or truthful people or statements is to commit the fallacy of Hypostatization. It is to treat abstract terms or concepts as if they were real beings or things having an existence all their own.

The fallacy of Hypostatization obviously has much in common with such familiar phenomena as personification. And in the case of personification, it has much in common with the so-called "pathetic fallacy," as that term is used in the context of literary criticism. To personify and to be guilty of the pathetic fallacy is to ascribe properties that only human beings can possess to things or animals. It is to turn things or creatures, which are not persons, into persons and to speak of their condition in terms appropriate, strictly speaking, only of persons. For example, it is to complain of the "cruelty of weasels" when, of course, weasels, being innocent creatures, cannot be considered to be either kind or cruel. For to be cruel is to intend and plan some harm on someone, knowing that this would cause them pain and suffering, and weasels are not capable, as far as we know, of entertaining such designs. They simply are what they are and do what they do. The same applies, of course, to such expressions as "the cruel sea." If understood literally that expression is simply false.

Hypostatization is doing this sort of thing to concepts: in other words, Hypostatization is to concepts what personification is to things and animals. It is to speak of abstract entities or concepts as if they had a life of their own. It is to say such things as: "Economics dictated what we were to do" — as if economics were some live, thinking, designing being, when what we really mean is that economic *considerations* were what led us to do whatever it was we did.

There is another interesting phenomenon anthropologists have made us aware of that is also closely related to Hypostatization. This is animism. Animism ascribes a soul or spirit to such inanimate objects as stones or plants, or to such natural phenomena as thunderstorms and earthquakes. It is to animate what is inanimate — a practice found widely in so-called primitive societies. We, of

"For God's sake, can't you just take down the data it feeds us without exclaiming 'You're *so* right!'?" © 1965 by *Playboy*.

course, feel very superior to such societies and think ourselves incapable of such foolishness. But hypostatization is a matter of perpetrating the same error — except that in our case what we animate are not thunderstorms and earthquakes, or trees and stones, but such more sophisticated and abstract entities as "Beauty," "Justice," "Law," and "Nature."

In its grossest form, then, to hypostatize is to treat abstract terms as if they were living, breathing beings capable of things that only human beings are capable of. The following is a typical example: "Today's big and complicated government has one hand in everybody's business and another in every person's pocket." What we need to note here is that "government" as such does not literally have a "hand" and so from a strictly literal point of view the statement makes no sense. Of course, people in government do have hands and minds and certain plans, and they may very well be responsible for what the statement complains about. Understood in this way, then the statement is not, of course, a fallacy but merely a figurative way of speaking, and harmless.

A more revealing example of the dangers involved in this use of language is the following: Nature produces all improvements in a race by eliminating the unfit and preventing them from polluting the fit." By hypostatizing the concept

"Nature" its author is led to speak of it as if it were capable of recognizing what is an "improvement" and what is not, of distinguishing what is "fit" from what is "unfit"—he is led to look on nature, that is, as if it were some humanlike agency, capable of intention and design. To be led to say this sort of thing about nature, and to believe it, is only a short step from embracing a whole world view regarding man, politics, and ethics, a world view for which, in this case, we have paid dearly in the very recent past. This is not to say, of course, that all this has come about, or always does come about, as a result of the hypostatization of a word; it is merely to point out that this is certainly one way in which such views become frozen in the language and widely embraced and respected.

In the case of "Nature" (which is especially favored and abused in this way) the appeal doubtlessly also involves the belief that Nature was created by God and is therefore somehow basic and unquestionable—part of the divinely ordained order of things. Although ancient, this notion, as we have already had occasion to see, is the source of some of our own relatively more recent and related doctrines of "natural rights," "natural law," and so on. But if what is meant by "Nature" is really "God," the speaker should say so. This would certainly change the tone and the direction of any discussion that might follow.

Whenever such terms appear suspicious try to trace them back to their referents. Sometimes this can be done simply by using the abstract term as an adjective instead of a noun. Thus, replace "truth"(as in "the truth will make you free") with "truthful statements will make you free"; the "state" (as in "the state can do no wrong") with "people in government can do no wrong"; "nature (as in "Love Nature") with "love sticks and stones"; and so on. Under this treatment statements that seem significant and even profound will often be seen to be pure nonsense.

Exercises

1. What Americans need is patience. A water well goes dry. Nature replenishes it by sending a good rain. Nature will replenish the great oil reservoirs. Scientists say it takes a few million years. All we need is patience.

2. The world will no longer laugh.

3. Nelson: "England expects every man will do his duty."

4. President Kennedy: "And so, my fellow Americans, ask not what your country can do for you; ask what you can do for your country."

5. Letter to the editor: "The Secret Army Drug Experiments were shocking. It seems that our government 'of the people, by the people and for the people' is doing it to the people. Our bureaucratic sys-

tem is one big cover-up leaving the American people in the dark. It's like the old dog's body that grew too big for his legs. He couldn't scratch all the fleas."

6. Because the dumping ground was so far out to sea, the city believed it would never hear from its sludge again, but the city was wrong. The mass of goo slowly grew, and sometime around 1970 it began to move, oozing back to haunt New York and the beaches of Long Island.

7. Headline: Industry Struggles in the Pincers of Inflation

8. Speaker: Science has not produced the general happiness that people expected, and now it has fallen under the sway of greed and power.

9. Bumper sticker: Freedom is not only worth fighting for; it is also worth dying for.

4. Equivocation

We saw how ambiguity of sentence structure gives rise to the fallacy of Amphiboly; we saw how ambiguity concerning emphasis gives rise to the fallacy of Accent; and we saw how ambiguity of reference gives rise to the fallacy of Hypostatization. Now we want to note how confusion arises from the ambiguity of the words and phrases themselves.

The fallacy of Equivocation consists in using a word with two or more meanings during the course of an argument, while conducting the argument as if the meaning of the word was being held constant. If the change in meaning is subtle, the conclusion of such an argument will seem to follow from the premises and the argument will appear a good deal more convincing than it deserves to be.

A rather obvious and absurd example of the term "man" used equivocally for purposes of constructing a seemingly sound argument would be the following: "Only man is rational; no woman is a man; therefore no woman is rational." This argument would be valid if the term "man" had the same meaning each time it occurred. However, for the first premise to be true, "man" must mean "human being," whereas for the second premise to be true, "man" must mean "male." Thus, if the premises are to have any plausibility, the term "man" must shift its meaning.

A good test to apply to arguments you suspect turn on the fallacy of Equivocation is to make them stick to the original meanings of their terms and see whether by so doing the argument still makes sense. If it turns on equivocation, it will not. Let us try it with our last example. Let us make the term "man" mean "male" throughout the argument. It will then read: "Only males are rational. . . ." We need not go further because we would immediately reject this as either false or a matter of assuming the very point to be proven. On the other hand, if we made the term "man" mean "human being" throughout the argument, we would get the following result: "Only human beings are rational; no woman is a human being. . . ." Here again, we need not go further, for we have already committed an absurdity.

The fallacy of Equivocation is especially easy to commit when the key term happens to be a figure of speech or a metaphor. By interpreting the metaphor literally, we can sometimes persuade ourselves that our argument is sounder than it really is. Consider the following example:

> It is the clear duty of the press to publish such news as it shall be in the public interest to have published. There can be no doubt about the public interest taken in the brutal murder of the Countess and concerning the details of her private life that led up to the murder. The press would have failed in their duty if they had refrained from publishing these matters.

The arguer here apparently does not seem to realize that what is "in the public interest" is not quite the same thing as what the public is interested in. The former is a metaphorical expression meaning "what is for the public good," the latter simply means what the public is curious about.

The warning against being misled by figures of speech should not be mistaken to imply a warning against their use. Language is shot through with figures of speech (including the one just used) and it is not possible to avoid them entirely. Nor should we try to. Our speech and writing would be much poorer without them. Not only do they make for pungent expression, economy, and tact, but very often a figure of speech is the only way yet devised of saying precisely what we wish to say.

Equivocation, however, is not confined to figurative expressions. On the contrary, since the vast majority of our words have more than one meaning, any one of them (and not merely those that are figures of speech) can occasion the fallacy. An absurd example would be the following: "Some birds are domesticated; my parrot is domesticated; my parrot, therefore, is some bird!" As this example shows, even such a common and simple word as "some" can lend itself to Equivocation. Here "some" is used first in a quantitative sense, meaning "a number of," and in the conclusion it is used in a qualitative sense, meaning "a magnificent bird." Although probably no one would ever become confused over such a word as "some," the example brings out the important point that almost any word in our language can either be exploited for its ambiguity or be itself ambiguous, so that it occasions various mistakes in our thinking.

Ironically, as we have already had occasion to note, this inherent ambiguity of language is not really a defect we should wish to remedy. It is one of the major vehicles for the expression of our wit and would be sorely missed were it possible to eliminate it from language.

Exercises

1. There are laws of nature. Law implies a lawgiver. Therefore, there must be a cosmic lawgiver.

2. I have the right to publish my opinions concerning the present administration. What is right for me to do I ought to do. Hence I ought to publish them.

3. *Jane:* That old copper kettle isn't worth anything. You can't even boil water in it.
   Mary: It is worth something. It's an antique.

4. Birth control is race suicide, for when no children are born, as happens when you practice birth control, the human race must die out.

5. Anyone who is considered old enough to go into the army and fight for his country is a mature person, and anyone old enough to vote is a mature person too. Hence, anyone old enough to fight is old enough to vote.

6. I do not believe in the possibility of eliminating the desire to fight from humankind because an organism without fight is dead or moribund. Life consists of tensions. There must be a balance of opposite polarities to make a personality, a nation, a world, or a cosmic system.

7. In our democracy all men are equal. The Declaration of Independence states this clearly and unequivocally. But we tend to forget this great truth. Our society accepts the principle of competition. And competition implies that some men are better than others. But this implication is false. The private is just as good as the general; the file clerk is just as good as the corporation executive; the scholar is no better than the dunce; the philosopher is no better than the fool. We are all born equal.

5. Composition and division

I can obviously break this stick here, and I can break the next one, and the one there. Does that mean I can break the bundle of sticks as a whole? Probably not.

I can tear this page from the telephone book, and I can tear the next one, and the one after that. Does that mean I can rip the whole telephone book? Again, obviously not.

What is true of the part is not necessarily true of the whole. To think so is to commit the logical fallacy called Composition. It is to try to compose the whole out of its parts. The whole, as the old saying has it, is more than the sum of its parts.

We can reverse the order of the argument and arrive at the fallacy of Division. Thus, obviously I cannot break this bundle of sticks, therefore I cannot break any one of them individually? Of course I can.

I cannot tear the telephone book apart, I therefore cannot tear page 781? Again, I obviously can.

What is true of the whole is not necessarily true of its parts. To think so is to commit the logical fallacy of Division. It is to try to divide what is true of the whole among its parts.

What is true here of parts and wholes is also true of groups and their members. Thus, Jones may be the best quarterback in the country, and Smith the best halfback, and Davis the best receiver — but putting them and other outstanding players together into one team will not (as we have seen only too often) necessarily give us the best team in the country.

Or, to use another example, the Chicago Symphony Orchestra may be the best orchestra in the country but that does not necessarily mean that the first violinist in the orchestra is the best violinist in the country.

Why, one might ask, is it not the case that what is true of the parts is not necessarily true of the whole? Or why is it not the case that what is true of the whole is not necessarily true of the parts? Or, similarly, why is it not the case that what is true of the members of some particular group or team is not necessarily true of the group or team — and vice versa? The reason is because a whole or a group is something functional and organic and therefore has properties just in virtue of being such a whole or a group.

Another example will make this clearer: I look at a flower and I say to myself: "Oh, what a very pretty flower!" I look at the next one and feel the same about it, and the same about the next. But does this mean that if I put them all together I will therefore have a pretty bouquet of flowers? Perhaps not, and the reason I may not is because when I put them together something new arises: will all these different flowers blend together properly? And that was not a question at all pertinent when each flower was considered by itself. The same would apply to a group of players or a group of singers, and so on. Although each, when considered by himself or herself, might be outstanding, whether they will be outstanding as a group will depend upon a new factor that arises only with the formation of the group: how well they will work together or how well their different voices will blend together? These are questions that had no meaning when each was considered individually.

Although obviously not a very difficult nor subtle kind of fallacy, taking essentially these two forms — confusing parts with wholes, and members with their classes — it is a fallacy we tend to commit rather frequently. Often the reason lies in our tendency to confuse the collective with the distributive sense of certain key terms that figure in these arguments. By a "collective" term we mean a term that refers to a collection or a whole; by a "distributive" term we mean a term that applies only to individuals or parts. The word "all" is probably the best example of such a potentially ambiguous term. When we say, for example, "All donors have contributed $1,000" do we mean that each and every one of them has contributed this amount (using the word "all" distributively): or do we mean that all together have done so (understanding the word "all" now collectively)? Understanding the nature of these fallacies of Composition and Division enables us to understand better such curious phenomena as:

1. The behavior of people in crowds. A group of intelligent people does not always act intelligently, nor does a group of civilized people always act in a civilized manner. A mob, as we all know, is not simply a large group of individuals. Something happens to people when they become parts of crowds. To forget this is to commit the fallacy of composition — to think the whole is merely the sum of its parts.

2. The belief many foreigners have about America, that because America is a rich country, every American must therefore be rich. It would be nice if it were so! To think it is is to commit the fallacy of division — to apply to each part or member the quality or property the whole possesses.

Exercises

Composition

1. No one on this committee is especially outstanding in ability. It is impossible for the committee, therefore, to bring in an able report.

2. Jones can run the half mile in two minutes. Therefore he can run the mile in four minutes.

3. Each manufacturer is perfectly free to set his own price on the product he produces, so there can be nothing wrong with all manufacturers getting together to fix the prices of the articles made by all of them.

4. You need have no fear of the patient's life; he has received many injuries but none of them is serious when considered individually.

5. Since every member of the club has paid his bills, the club must be out of debt.

6. It is not going to help the energy crisis to have people ride buses instead of cars. Buses use more gas than cars.

Division

7. It is predicted that the cost-of-living index will rise again next month. Consequently you can expect to pay more for butter and eggs next month.

8. I am interested in hiring only the kind of man who will be efficient. Jones simply does not deserve to be classed as such a man. He worked for the civil service five years, and everybody knows the civil service is a notoriously inefficient organization.

9. The instructor in our physics class told us that all things are made of very small particles or waves. Headaches, dreams, doubts, thoughts, and the like, must also therefore be made up of small particles and waves.

10. Carrier pigeons are practically extinct. This bird is a carrier pigeon and is therefore practically extinct.

11. Since every third child in New York is a Catholic, Protestant families there should have no more than two children.

12. Salt is not poisonous, so neither of the elements of which it is composed — sodium and chlorine — is poisonous either.

section **two**
PRESUMPTION

Overlooking the facts

1. Sweeping and hasty generalization

Fallacies of Presumption get their power to deceive because they resemble, often very closely, correct or valid argument forms. The first two discussed under this category — Sweeping Generalization and Hasty Generalization — go together in that (like Division and Composition) one is the reverse of the other.

Although Sweeping and Hasty Generalization superficially resemble Division and Composition, they should not be confused with them. As we have seen, Division and Composition are essentially whole–part and group–member fallacies. They arise from our failure to realize that a whole is not merely the sum of its parts (and similarly with groups and their members); on the contrary, being an organized entity, a whole has properties it does not share with its parts.

In the case of Sweeping Generalization and Hasty Generalization (or Accident and Converse Accident, as these fallacies are sometimes called) we are not dealing with the physical relation between parts and wholes (or members and their classes) but rather with the application and misuse of rules and generalizations and with our tendency to engage in sweeping generalizations and to come to snap decisions.

Thus we would be guilty of the fallacy of Sweeping Generalization if we were to argue that "Since encyclopedias are heavy, the one about to be published by the Jones Publishing Company will be heavy too," but guilty of the fallacy of

"Everybody complains about overpopulation, but we get damned little gratitude for trying to do something about it." © 1972 by *Playboy*.

Division if we argue that "Since encyclopedias are heavy, therefore page 625 of volume 3 must be heavy too." In the first case our error would be due to our failure to note that perhaps the new encyclopedia will be an exception and not so heavy as the general run of encyclopedias; in the second case it would be due to our failure to remember that parts cannot possess all the properties the whole possesses.

To argue, therefore, that "since horseback riding and mountain climbing are healthful exercises, Harry Smith ought to do more of it because it will be good for his heart trouble" would be to commit this fallacy, for what is good for a person's health normally is not good where special conditions prevail. And the same is true of the following argument: "It is my duty to do unto others as I would have them do unto me. If I were puzzled by a question in an examination, I would like my neighbor to help me out. So it is my duty to help this man beside me who is stuck." Here our reply should be that to try to do one's duty in such circumstances would not be to help the person. This is an examination and the point of it is to find out what each one knows by himself.

Arguments of the kind we are examining here have two parts to them: a rule and a case. If the argument in question is invalid, it is because the case to which the rule is being applied is exceptional and therefore does not fall under the given rule. To expose them, therefore, all one needs to do is to isolate the rule and show that, understood properly, it cannot be applied to the case in question.

Exercises

1. I don't care if he did weigh three times as much as you. A good scout always tries to help. You should have jumped in and tried to save him.

2. Narcotics are habit-forming. Therefore if you allow your physician to ease your pain with an opiate you will become a hopeless drug addict.

3. No man who lives on terms of intimate friendship and confidence with another is justified in killing him. Brutus, therefore, did wrong in assassinating Caesar.

4. The president should get rid of his advisors and run the government by himself. After all, too many cooks spoil the broth.

5. American Secretary of State, refusing to grant asylum to refugees on the ship the *St. Louis*, whose forced return to Germany meant certain death: "I took an oath to protect the flag and obey the laws of my country and you are asking me to break those laws."

The fallacy of Hasty Generalization (or Converse Accident) is the reverse of the fallacy we have just examined.

This fallacy is committed whenever some isolated or exceptional case or event is used as the basis for a general conclusion.

Let us look at some examples. A woman argues: "I had a bad time with my ex-husband. From that experience I learned that men were no good." And someone else complains: "I've only known one union representative and he was a louse. I wouldn't trust any of them." The arguments in both cases are invalid because they assume that what is true under certain conditions is true under all conditions. At most, the evidence (if one may call it that) presented here warrants only a specific, not a general, conclusion. And this is typical of the fallacy: unlike Sweeping Generalization, which results when a rule or a generalization is misapplied, the fallacy of Hasty Generalization results when a particular case is misused.

Of course, in generalizing we should remember that it is not possible (or necessary) to consider all the cases involved. Nevertheless, unless a sufficiently large number is examined, the conclusion cannot be relied upon. A small sample may not be at all representative. On the contrary, it may be quite "exceptional."

"See what I mean? Nobody gives a damn anymore!" Drawing by Claude; © 1960 The New Yorker Magazine, Inc.

The following would be an absurd example: "They just don't care about traffic law enforcement in this town, for they let ambulances go at any speed they like, and let them run red lights too." This is absurd, of course, because there are good reasons for permitting these vehicles to do these things. No such conclusion can therefore be built on the basis of such unrepresentative examples of supposed law-violation.

The fallacy of Hasty Generalization also is committed when we select and consider only the evidence that favors our position and ignore all the evidence that would tend to throw doubt on it. The following would be a typical example: "State-owned industries encourage featherbedding and absenteeism. All state-owned industries should therefore be abolished." Even if it were true that state-owned industries encourage featherbedding and absenteeism, this is hardly a sufficient basis for the kind of drastic action recommended. To try to get rid of these abuses by abolishing the industries in which they tend to flourish would be like throwing out the baby with the bathwater.

Exercises

1. The clerks in Mason's Department Store are incompetent. They got two of my orders mixed up during the last Christmas rush season.

2. Doctors are all alike. They really don't know any more than you or I do. This is the third case of faulty diagnosis I have heard of in the last month.

3. She is very fond of children and so will undoubtedly make a fine kindergarten teacher.

4. He speaks so beautifully that anyone can see he must have studied acting.

5. High tariffs enable our industries to grow strong; they assure high wages to the workers and they increase federal revenues. High tariffs, therefore, are a benefit to the nation.

2. Bifurcation

The term *Bifurcation* refers to a fallacy that presumes a certain distinction or classification is exhaustive and exclusive when other alternatives are possible. The fallacy is sometimes referred to as the "Either/Or Fallacy" or the "Black or White Fallacy." All these names, as we will see, are appropriate.

In some cases of "either/or" the situation is such that there is no middle course between the two extremes noted. The two poles of the proposition exhaust all the possibilities and therefore if one of them is true, the other must be false and vice versa. "Either the man is dead or he is alive"; "Either it is your birthday today or it is not" are typical examples of such propositions.

However, polar terms that usually go into the formation of such propositions or arguments do not exhaust all the possibilities and are therefore not logical contradictories (but rather contraries). These result in the fallacy of Bifurcation. The debates in 1948 over the atomic bomb, in which the great British philosopher Bertrand Russell figured prominently, gave rise to many examples of the fallacy. In this debate Russell argued that either we must have war against Russia before she has the atom bomb, or we will have to lie down and let them govern us. In other words, what he was saying was, as the position came to be tagged, "Better Dead than Red." Others who disagreed with him retorted, "Better Red than Dead"; both parties were overlooking, as still others added, "Better Pink than Extinct." That would be the middle course between the two extremes.

In the same vein we have all seen the bumper stickers that read "America: Love It or Leave It" and the reply to it "America: Change It or Lose It". Or perhaps even the sign near an Indian reservation "America: Love It or Give It Back."

As our vocabulary is replete with such terms, the tendency to bifurcate is all too common. We are thus prone to people the world with the *rich* and the *poor*, the *have* and the *have-nots*, the *good* and the *bad*, the *normal* and the *abnormal*, the *heroes* and the *villains*, forgetting that between these extremes are to be found numerous gradations which lead from one to the other — any one of which could be further alternatives to the either/or proposed.

Thus we frequently hear people say such things as: "Only the rich and the poor need be of any concern to the government: the rich because they will try to influence our legislatures through the power of their wealth; the poor because they must be cared for by the state." Of course, since most people are neither rich nor poor, their voice is as important, if not more so, than these two groups.

From a logical point of view what is objectionable about these arguments is that there is no necessary connection between the two alternatives proposed in them. The fact that we do not want our soup cold does not mean, nor does it logically follow, that we want it hot; it is not necessarily the case that if something is not good it must be bad. It could be neither good nor bad, but a bit of both.

It is, however, in the context of political debate that the fallacy will be most often committed. It is typical in such debates for opponents to adopt extreme positions. Extreme positions, unfortunately, seem more attractive than the saner middle-of-the-road positions. But the middle of the road is not an exciting area, and one meets few fascinating creatures there in comparison with the gutter and the ditch. On the other hand, one can get along faster there and arrive at one's destination more quickly.

Exercises

1. There are only two kinds of people in the world: winners and losers.

2. Either he knew everything that was going on, in which case he's a liar, or, alternatively, he's a fool.

3. God doesn't tolerate fence-riders in the cosmic sense. You must be either committed to Christ or fall in with the Devil. There are only two places to spend eternity: Heaven and Hell. You can't be somewhere in between.

4. It seems to me that now more than ever before in our history, one is either for law enforcement or against it. He is either for mob rule or he is for the law. He either loves a cop or he hates him.

5. We can become independent of Arab oil only by ruining our environment.

Evading the facts

In this second category of the fallacies of Presumption, the error lies not in overlooking facts as in the first category, but in seeming to deal with all relevant facts without actually doing so. Such arguments deceive by inviting us to assume that the facts are as they have been stated in the argument when they are quite otherwise.

Four fallacies commit this error. The fallacy of Begging the Question tries to settle a question by simply reasserting it. Question-begging epithets avoid a reasonable conclusion by prejudging the facts. Complex Question evades the facts by arguing a question different from the one at issue. And, finally, special pleading invites us to view the argument from a biased position.

3. Begging the question

In its rudimentary form, the fallacy of Begging the Question is committed when instead of providing proof for our assertion we simply repeat it. If the statement or argument is brief, not many will be taken in by it. Thus, if we should argue that "The belief in God is universal, because everybody believes in God," it would be apparent to almost everyone that since "universal" means "everybody," all we have done is reaffirm that the belief in God is universal without having confirmed or proved it. The same would be true if we argued that "Honesty is praiseworthy, because it deserves the approval of all." Again, since "praiseworthy" means "deserving of approval" we have merely repeated in our premise (which should contain our evidence) the very conclusion ("Honesty is praiseworthy") to be established. The argument, therefore, lacks evidence and is no real argument. The same would be true if, finally, we argued that "Miracles are impossible, for they cannot happen." Here, too, all we have done is reassert the very point we began with.

Of course, to assert, or even reassert, something is not in itself objectionable. What makes arguments of this sort objectionable is that they suggest they have done more than this; they imply that by reasserting the point they have somehow established or confirmed it. It is this that makes them fallacious.

As obvious as this error may seem, it is a surprisingly common one. Nor does it spare the mighty. It was one of President Coolidge's misfortunes to provide logicians with a rather classic example of it. He once remarked "When large numbers of people are out of work, unemployment results." Perhaps we should not think too harshly of Coolidge for this absurdity; arguments of this sort are fallacious, we should remember, not because they argue a point invalidly, but because they do not argue it at all.

Although this is essentially all one can and need say regarding the logic of such an argument as Begging the Question, this hardly exhausts the uses, both sound and unsound, to which this form is often put. Politics provides us with a rich source of further uses of the fallacy. Thus, in reply to a reporter's question as to why Hubert Humphrey lost Illinois in the 1968 elections, Mayor Richard Daley of Chicago replied that "He lost it because he didn't get enough votes." Although it may appear as if Mayor Daley is guilty here of the same fallacy as President Coolidge, this is not at all the case, for far from falling victim to the fallacy, Mayor Daley, unlike President Coolidge, is rather cleverly using it as a humorous dodge in order to avoid an embarrassing question.

It may seem strange that the same structure should lend itself to such widely divergent uses, but obviously fallacy and wit (and madness, as we have seen) have much in common. Mayor Daley's reply is amusing and meant to be so. That is why it is not a fallacy, for to feign an error is not to commit it. The mechanism exploited for its humor by him here is found in numerous witty remarks — including Joe E. Lewis' memorable quip "I don't want to be a millionaire; I just want to live like one."

Often quite flagrant examples of this fallacy will escape detection if the statements involved are somewhat drawn out. Our memories, not always very good, fail to make the repetition immediately apparent to us. Consider the following example:

> Free trade will be good for this country. The reason for this is patently clear. Is it not obvious that unrestricted commercial relations would bestow upon all sections of this community the advantages and benefits which result when there is an unimpeded flow of goods between nations?

Since "unrestricted commercial relations" is simply a more verbose way of saying "free trade," and "would bestow upon all sections of this community the advantages and benefits" is a more verbose way of saying "good for this country," the argument merely says, in effect, that "free trade will be good for this country, because free trade will be good for this country." Unfortunately, a good many of our arguments often consist of such restatements. Language hides this from us and makes it easy for us to forget that this is so because of the numerous synonyms it contains. Although the existence of this large body of words makes it possible to make our speech seem less dull, it also makes it seem more cogent that it often really is.

To see even more clearly why these arguments are fallacious, we might note a further form in which they sometimes appear. A person will occasionally try to establish a particular proposition by subsuming it under a generalization. Should the generalization itself be questionable, then the argument is fallacious. Consider the following argument: "Communism is the best form of government, because it alone takes care of the interests of the common people." Here the conclusion ("Communism is the best form of government") is made to rest upon a principle ("it alone takes care . . ."), which is much wider and much more questionable than the conclusion itself! What we might say here is: obviously, if the conclusion needs proving, how much more so does the premise. For after all who will grant that "communism *alone* takes care of the interests," and so forth.

Exercises

1. School isn't worthwhile because book learning doesn't pay off.

2. Death for traitors is properly justified, because it is right to put to death those who betray our country.

3. To allow every man an unbounded freedom of speech must always be, on the whole, advantageous to the state. You ask why? Well, it is highly conducive to the interest of the community that each individual should enjoy a liberty, perfectly unlimited, of expressing his sentiments.

4. He talks with angels.
   How do you know?
   He said he did.
   But suppose that he lied!
   O, perish the thought! How could any man lie who is capable of talking with angels?

5. Smith cannot have told you a lie when he said he was my cousin, for no cousin of mine would ever tell a lie.

6. Moral beliefs are unjustified because they are not verifiable in sense-experience.

4. Question-begging epithets

As we just noted, to beg the question is to assume the point in dispute. We want now to observe that it is possible to do this with a single word. A word begs the question when its meaning conveys the assumption that some point in dispute has already been settled when there may still be some doubt or question about it. Since a good many of our words have both a descriptive and an evaluative dimension, the possibilities for begging the question in this form are endless. (Another term we may use for "descriptive" is "factual"; and another term for "evaluative" is "judgmental." So we really want to consider the difference between stating a fact and making a judgment about it.)

Let us consider an obvious example. To call a certain act "stealing" is obviously not merely to describe it, but also to make a judgment about it, since the term not only conveys the idea that a certain action has been done, but also conveys the thought that the action is wrong. However, if this were a case of a man "stealing" to save his children from starving to death, he would no doubt regard calling it so a matter of begging the question, since in the light of the circumstances, he would not consider what he has done as wrong.

Many of our most severe disputes and misunderstandings — among individuals and among nations — can be traced to this failure to distinguish the evaluative from the descriptive dimension of words. As in our example about the man who took something that did not belong to him, such misunderstandings arise as a result of using words that not only describe a certain action, but at the same time also judge or prejudge it — often without us being aware of this.

The misunderstandings the Western world has had with the Soviet Union are a classic case of this.

Both the Russians and the Western nations seem to be agreed as to the factual or descriptive meaning of the word "totalitarian," and when both use that word, both seem to be describing the same thing. But to us, the word "totalitarian" is a mixed word, carrying with it an element of disapproval, whereas to the Russians it has no such implication. To them it is simply a neutral, descriptive term. Their failure to feel moral indignation at being accused of "totalitarianism" is therefore not to be taken by us (as we may be tempted to) as a sign of their moral depravity. It should instead be seen to be what it really is: a failure to understand each other.

Another case in point is the word "aggression." While both parties or nations seem to agree on the evaluative meaning of the word — it is a "bad" word for

"COON!"   "HONKIE!"

both — they apparently do not agree regarding its descriptive meaning. Thus for the Russians it does not seem to include propaganda; sending military equipment or intelligence into another country; providing foreign armies with a body of instructing officers; and so on. In Western eyes, however, all such acts (at one time, anyway) have been considered acts of "aggression." And here again to accuse the Russians of hypocrisy (as many were inclined to) when they denied being guilty of "aggression" was to be blind to the underlying semantic problems that lay at the root of our misunderstandings.

We saw the way the term "totalitarian" has tended to cause confusion and irritation, but the term "democracy" is an even more instructive example of such a misunderstanding. For the communists to call their system democratic was at one time regarded (and by many still is so regarded) as either comical or perverse. But we have come to be a little more tolerant and see that it was neither perverse nor hypocritical, for in calling it democratic, what they had mainly in mind were such things as the elimination of class antagonism; the removal of economic classes; universal education — in short it was, for them, chiefly a social notion whose value was to be judged by the ends achieved, and not by the means used to achieve them. For us, on the other hand, it has always been a political notion, standing for a certain form of government and a certain way of arriving at political decisions. Without freedom of speech, parliamentary procedures, majority vote, and civil liberties, you can have no "democracy," we have tended to think. Since the term was being used by both sides to stand for such vastly different things, it is little wonder that each came to accuse the other of bad faith.

We must remember, however, that realizing what the term is actually used to refer to by each side does not mean that we have somehow magically changed the things referred to so that suddenly we have come to agree the Russians do have democracy (in our sense of the word) after all! Obviously, despite such clarification, the communist system is still what it is, and ours is what it is. What such clarification does achieve is a clearing of the air, better understanding, and more tolerance.

As we have seen, confusion can arise here in two separate ways: first, when, as in the case of "aggression" or "democracy," both parties, although sharing the same emotional or evaluative dimension of the word, differ in their understanding of its descriptive dimension; and, second, when, as in the case of "totalitarianism," both parties, although in agreement in their understanding of the descriptive dimension of the word, have entirely different responses regarding its emotional or evaluative dimension.

On a more mundane level this fallacy is committed when people say such things as "This criminal is charged with the most vicious crime known to man." Our objection here should be that if he is going to be called a "criminal" then they may as well not bother having a trial. They have already, apparently, decided he is guilty. And the same would be true of such a remark as "The scoundrel hounded his wife to the grave." Here again, to call the person a "scoundrel" is already to condemn him. Merely to tag him with this label is not to prove that the label fits or that he deserves it.

Exercises

1. Milton Gross, writing in the *Chicago Sun Times*: "James Simon Kunen, a young heavily haired dissident, has become a wealthy post-adolescent as author of the best selling "The Strawberry Statement," a report on . . ."

2. A man should find it degrading to live on a dole or any payment made to him without his being required to render some service in return. But how many of them do feel degraded by it? From an economic standpoint such loafers are simply parasites and should be dealt with accordingly.

3. Senator Charles H. Percy (R., Ill.) should be lauded for submitting legislation to repeal the no-knock statute of the Drug Abuse Prevention and Control Act of 1970. Unannounced destructive raids perpetrated by government agents rabid for the "bust" are at best the antithesis of law, order, and democracy. Drug trafficking has been and continues to be a menace to the welfare of America's youth; yet Gestapo tactics that encroach upon the innocent cannot be condoned.

4. This is the same cynical, rotten, misleading bull-roar that the oil companies have been handing us all along. Why should we continue to listen to these selfish bastions of entrenched interest and misbegotten wealth? How can we be so shortsighted? Critical oil shortage, my asthma! Miasma is what it is — a poisonous foul-smelling vapor of smog and oil company propaganda.

5. Complex question

It is told of King Charles II of England that he once asked the members of the Royal Society to determine for him why it is that if you place a dead fish in a bowl of water it makes the water overflow, while a live one does not. Some of the members thought about this a very long time and offered ingenious but unconvincing explanations, until one of them finally decided to test the question. He discovered, of course, that it did not make a bit of difference whether one placed a dead fish or a live one in the bowl of water — in either case, the water either flowed over or did not.

Whether the story is true or not, it conveys a rather important lesson, namely, that before jumping in to answer a question, it is best to question the question. For every question necessarily brings along with it a set of assumptions that determine the lines along which it is to be answered. These may not lead to the required solution. To find such a solution, an investigator may often have to struggle long and hard to liberate himself from the misleading influence of the question.

It is good to remember that the fallacy of Complex Question can have such serious and far-reaching consequences, for this may not always be evident from the type of example sometimes used to illustrate the fallacy. The most popular is the question: "Have you stopped beating your wife?" Of course, one cannot answer such a question without incriminating oneself. To say that one has not stopped is, of course, bad, for that means one is still beating her; and to say one has stopped is to admit that one did it at one time.

What is wrong with all such questions is that they assume a particular answer to a prior question — one that had neither been asked nor answered in the way required by the subsequent question. Such questions, for example, as: "Why is it that girls are more interested in religion than boys?" assumes that girls *are* more interested in religion than boys. Until, however, the question whether girls are indeed more interested has been asked and answered in the affirmative, it does not make sense, and it is fallacious, to inquire *why*.

Complex Question can also take the form of asking for an explanation for "facts" that are either untrue or not yet established. An example here would be this: "What is the explanation of mental telepathy?" What is assumed here is an affirmative answer to a prior question: the assertion that there is such a thing as "mental telepathy." (Of course, if there is no such thing, then it is absurd to inquire about its explanation, for there would be nothing to explain.)

To deal with complex questions, what we need to do is, as we say, divide the question: that is, separate the part we can answer with a "Yes" from the part or question we can or wish to answer with a "No". For example, if someone should ask us: "Is Smith an unthinking conservative?" we might wish to answer by saying: "Yes, Smith is a conservative, all right, but not an unthinking one."

A complex question may often be combined with question-begging epithets, as in the following example: "Was it through stupidity or through deliberate dishonesty that the Administration has hopelessly botched its foreign policy?" Questions such as these must not only be divided before being answered, but the evaluative dimension must be separated from the descriptive dimension before dealing further with them. Depending upon the facts of the case, we might respond to the last question by saying either that the Administration has not botched its foreign policy at all; or if it has, that it has done so neither through "stupidity" nor "deliberate dishonesty," nor, finally, "hopelessly."

Exercises

1. Could the reason for the unexcelled superiority of American optical goods be this: they have been made under a competitive system?

2. You say we ought to discuss whether or not to buy a new car now. All right, I agree. Let's discuss the matter. Which should we get, a Ford or a Chevy?

3. Should government rob its citizens?

4. How much longer are you going to waste your time in school when you might be doing a man's work in the world, and contributing to society? If you had any sense of social responsibility, you would leave immediately.

5. What is the biggest number?

6. Advertisement: "Can we know our past lives?"

7. Beet-growers' advertisement: If sugar is so fattening, how come so many kids are thin?

6. Special pleading

To engage in Special Pleading is to apply a double standard — one standard for ourselves (because we are special) and another (a stricter and stiffer one) for everyone else. Bertrand Russell once illustrated this characteristic by showing how we "conjugate" certain words — "firmness," for example. If we display a certain characteristic, we would describe it as a matter of being firm. Should our friend display the same characteristic, we may very likely describe it as a case of his being stubborn; and should someone we don't like give evidence of having this characteristic, we doubtlessly will say that he is pigheaded. So, as Russell put it: "I am firm; you are stubborn; he is pigheaded."

The fallacy can obviously be exploited for its humorous effects. Thus, when asked some years ago what she thought of on-stage nudity, the actress Shelley Winters (who was 46 years old then) replied — with tongue in cheek: "I think it is disgusting, shameful, and damaging to all things American. But if I were 22 with a great body, it would be artistic, tasteful, patriotic, and a progressive, religious experience."

Even as this example illustrates, Special Pleading (in one sense of that label, anyway) is a matter of being inconsistent and partial; of favoring ourselves and being prejudiced against others. It is to reserve the nice words for ourselves and the bad ones for everyone else. It is to regard one's own situation as privileged and special and so to fail to apply to ourselves those standards we are willing to apply to others. It is to speak, for example, of the heroism of our troops, of their devotion and self-sacrifice in battle, and then change our tone and describe the enemy as savage, fanatical, and suicidal.

It is important to keep in mind that the abuses we are speaking about are very frequently unconscious ones. Those who use language in this way or put words to these uses are often unaware of it. If you should ask them why, for example, they call someone of a certain mixed heritage a "half-breed," they might well answer with sincerity, "Well, isn't he a half-breed?" — But even if all this is unconscious it is not, as Freud taught us, completely unmotivated.

Exercises

1. I might be a little overweight but the rest of the girls in my house are a lot fatter than me.

2. Speaking of not trusting people, it's no wonder you can't trust anyone nowadays. I was looking through the desk of one of my roomers, and you won't believe what I found.

3. Woman (indignantly denying the charge of hoarding): "I'm not hoarding. I'm only stocking up before the hoarders get everything."

4. Sultan Khaled Hethelem, Crown Prince of the Ujman tribe of Saudi Arabia:

   Interviewer: Some people criticize the Arabs for using oil to blackmail; how do you feel about this?

   Sultan: We are not trying to blackmail Western Europe or Japan; we are just trying to convince them to help us.

   (Quoted in RUFII, International Relations Newsletter, USC, Vol. 11, No. 2).

5. From a speech by Andrei Y. Vishinsky delivered in the UN General Assembly, September 20, 1950:

   While in those countries which have entered the North Atlantic alliance a mad armament race is taking place and an unbridled war propaganda is being broadcast, and while the war psychosis is being incited more and more, the Soviet Union is the scene of peaceful, creative work. All the forces of our country are directed to the fostering of our national economy and to improve the standard of living and the welfare of the Soviet people.

Distorting the facts

In this third and final part of the fallacies of presumption we shall consider fallacies that, rather than overlooking or evading relevant facts, actually distort them. In the fallacy of False Analogy, certain cases are made to appear more similar than they really are. The fallacy of False Cause makes it appear that two events are causally connected in a way they are not. And the fallacy of Irrelevant Thesis distorts by concentrating on an issue that is irrelevant to the argument.

7. False Analogy

Perhaps no other technique of reasoning has been more helpful or harmful than reasoning by analogy.

Analogy is a method of reasoning whereby we attempt to explain facts that are obscure or difficult by comparing them to facts that are already known or better understood and to which they bear some likeness. It is to argue that because two things or situations are similar in certain respects, they must therefore be similar in other respects. Now, to be able to draw attention to such similarities can be extremely useful, so long as we are careful that the two things being compared resemble each other in important respects and differ only in trifling ones. If, on the contrary, they resemble each other in unimportant ways and differ from each other in important ones, then there is no analogy between them. Merely to seize upon some slight similarity between two things and then to conclude on that basis that what is true of one is also true of the other is an almost certain way of going astray.

Consider the following extreme but not necessarily absurd example:

It is praiseworthy to force people to accept the gospel for their own good, just as force must be used to prevent a delirious person from throwing himself over the edge of a steep cliff.

Although it might be tempting to try to refute the argument by pointing out that it has yet to be proven that there is an afterworld, actually this is not much of an argument — even for those for whom the existence of an afterworld is not a matter of doubt. In the one case it is a matter of saving a delirious person from doing away with himself, and in the other, the person involved presumably is not delirious. In other words, even if we were to grant that just as we are obligated to do all we can to save people for this life, so we are similarly obligated to do all we can to save them for the afterlife, it still would not follow that just as force is allowed in the case of the delirious person and where this life is concerned, so force should be permitted in the case of other people and the other life. In the one case we are dealing with a person who has lost his reason, and in the other we are dealing, presumably, with people who have not lost their reason and should be allowed, therefore, to make up their own minds about such things.

Incidentally, if someone should say in reply to this that surely anyone who did not believe in the gospel must be out of his mind (must be delirious), then that would be a matter of committing the fallacy of Begging the Question. (The mere fact that he says so is no proof that it is so.)

As in all cases of imperfect or false analogy, the one we have just examined is faulty because the two things that are compared in it resemble each other only in trifling ways and differ in significant ones.

To expose imperfect analogy, all it is necessary to do is simply to point this out. In the case of some analogies this is not at all difficult. Consider the following example:

Why should we sentimentalize over a few thousand people who were cheated or ruined when our great industrial enterprises, railroads, and pipelines were being built? It may be that they suffered an injustice, but, after all, you can't make an omelet without breaking a few eggs.

Here one might point out that even if it were true that it is just as impossible to build great industrial enterprises without causing pain and suffering as it is to make an omelet without breaking a few eggs, the two cases are not comparable, for to break eggs is not to cause them any pain, while to build great empires by destroying people's lives is.

It should be noted that not every analogy is an argument by analogy. Often analogies will be constructed, not with the purpose of advancing an argument, but merely for illustrative purposes or to lend color to a position supported in other ways. Such analogies may still mislead, of course, but no more weight should be placed on them than their authors intended them to carry. The following passage from Karl Marx is a case in point:

> As the heavenly bodies, once thrown into a certain definite motion, always repeat this, so it is with social production as soon as it is once thrown into this movement of alternate expansion and contraction.

Unlike the examples we have been looking at thus far, the cyclic and periodic behavior of the heavenly bodies is used here merely as an illustration of economic cycles and not as the reason for their occurrence.

For the sake of completeness, we should add here that it is not really possible to argue by analogy at all. Two things may be similar in a half-dozen different ways, and these similarities may make possible a number of interesting metaphors, but the similarities noted cannot form the basis for assuming that they will resemble each other in some further property. Analogy may help us see that it is likely that they will, but it cannot establish it.

It is this capacity of language to do double service that enables so many of our arguments by analogy to appear more forceful than they frequently really are; often, no doubt, deceiving their own authors into thinking so. It was obviously a Misleading Analogy, due to the use of a misleading metaphor, which led King James I to argue that:

> If you cut off the head of a body, the other organs cannot function, and the body dies. Similarly, if you cut off the head of the State, the State may flop around awhile, but it is due to perish in time or become easy prey to its neighbors.

King James apparently overlooked the fact that while a body certainly cannot grow a new head, a State easily can — by appointing another ruler.

Exercises

1. President Truman: "We should never have stopped it [atmospheric testing of nuclear weapons]. Where would we be today if Thomas Edison had been forced to stop his experiments with the electric bulb?"

2. Why should we criticize and punish human beings for their actions? Whatever they do is an expression of their nature, and they cannot help it. Are we angry with the stone for falling, and the flame for rising?

3. Philosopher Sidney Hook: "A philosopher in his own life need be no more wise than a physician needs to be healthy."

4. Advertisement for skin lotion: "You've seen land crack and dry when it loses its essential moisture, the same thing can happen to your skin when it loses its moisture."

5. If we find it necessary to tip waiters and other hotel servants, why should we not similarly reward the bus driver, the saleslady, or the doctor. Either they should be included, or hotel tipping should be abolished.

8. False cause

Although formerly the most widespread of fallacies, false cause has tended to slip in prominence because of the impact of education on the general public. This is not to say that we are no longer inclined to commit it. We are, but the tendency to do so does not reveal itself any longer in the crude forms in which it once did. Thus, we no longer take the trouble to walk around a ladder rather than under it, but a hotel management will seldom risk giving the thirteenth floor that number, for fear it would never get anyone to sleep there.

To give some further illustrations. We have no doubt become too sophisticated to argue as the nineteenth-century English reformer did who, because he noted that every sober and industrious farmer owned at least one or two cows and that those who had none were usually lazy and drunken, recommended giving a cow to any farmer who had none in order to make him sober and industrious.

On the other hand, students will be found who will tell their professors that since those who get A's study hard, the best way to get *them* to study hard is to give them A's.

Finally, we will often find persuasive the following argument: More and more the government is originating welfare legislation designed to free our citizens from the slavery of economic necessity. At the same time, however, we are seeing an increase in immorality, alcoholism, and suicide. This makes it clear that to get rid of this upsurge in immorality, alcoholism, and suicide we must stop the government from instituting welfare measures.

Although the fallacy of false cause can assume a variety of different forms, all are essentially a matter of mistakenly believing that because something occurred just prior to something else, it was therefore its cause. Much more knowledge is required in order for us to be able to identify the cause than the mere fact that it occurred a second, or even a split second, before the given event. In short, sequence alone is no proof of consequence.

"I can see why they made February the shortest month of the year."
Drawing by Drucker; © 1971 The New Yorker Magazine, Inc.

Failure to give due weight to this simple point is what lies behind the following example of the fallacy:

Sociologists have shown beyond doubt that in 1965 the number of television programs depicting crimes of violence increased 12% as compared with the figures of 1964. Subsequently, the Department of Justice index of juvenile delinquency showed a corresponding increase. Hence, the evidence shows that a stricter control of television crime programs would result in a lowering of the juvenile crime rate.

What we might say in response to this argument is that the fact that a rise in the crime rate followed a rise in the number of crime programs is not sufficient to establish a causal connection. The rise in crime might have been due to any number of different factors — for example, the rise in population, or change in economic conditions.

In addition, it is important to remember that two events may be causally related though neither is the cause of the other but both are effects of a third event. An interesting historical example concerns the ibis. The ancient Egyptians worshipped this bird because at a certain time each year, shortly after these birds migrated to the banks of the Nile, the river would overflow its banks and irrigate the land. The birds were credited with magical powers, when in fact both their migration and the overflow of the river were effects of a common cause, the change in seasons.

Let us consider another somewhat more difficult example. Twenty-five years after graduation, alumni of Harvard College have an average income five times that of men of the same age who have no college education. If one wants to be wealthy, he should enroll at Harvard.

Although, of course, going to a school such as Harvard no doubt contributes to the kind of income one is likely to make, one must remember that since Harvard attracts or takes only the most outstanding students or students who already come from wealthy homes, they would probably make that kind of income regardless where they went to college, or whether they went at all. Going to Harvard is no guarantee, therefore, that anyone would do as well. The causes at work here are again somewhat more complicated than is assumed by the author of this argument. Harvard is not the sole, simple, immediate, or direct cause of higher income.

If immediate temporal succession is an insufficient basis for establishing causal connection, it goes without saying, of course, that somewhat more remote temporal succession gives even less warrant of assuming this. Thus, the fact, to take some very broad examples, that man follows the ape in the succession of primates, is no proof at all that he is descended from the ape; nor is the fact that because the Roman Empire declined and fell after the appearance of Christianity, proof that Christianity was the cause of its decline and fall.

Exercises

1. No sooner did they start to fluorinate the water but my friends began dying of heart disease. It just doesn't pay to tamper with nature.

2. *Parent:* Illegitimate, you know.
    Parent: Oh, *that* explains it.

3. From early Greek physics: Night is the cause of the extinction of the sun, for as evening comes on, the shadows arise from the valleys and blot out the sunlight.

4. If strong law enforcement really prevented crime, then those areas where police patrols are most frequent would be the safest and the best protected. Actually, the very reverse is true, for in such areas even one's life is in danger, and crimes of all kinds are more common than in other areas where police patrols are infrequent.

5. The president of the Women's Christian Temperance Union said Sunday that people were turning to drink to escape the worries of the troubled national economy. "Liquor dealers admit that since the

energy crisis began, the consumption of alcoholic beverages has greatly increased," said Mrs. Fred Tooze, head of the national anti-alcohol group. Mrs. Tooze said the need to conserve gasoline would cause people to stay home and drink more, creating broken homes and harming the mental capacity of the nation's work force.

9. Irrelevant thesis

Of all the fallacies studied so far none is potentially more deceptive or — for that matter, more interesting — than irrelevant thesis. The fallacy goes by a variety of names. First, there are two more or less technical names: Irrelevant Thesis and Irrelevant Conclusion; then there are other names: Ignoring the Issue, Befogging the Issue, Diversion, Red Herring. As we will see, all these names are appropriate.

"Red herring" may be a puzzling name. Its appropriateness derives from the fact that escapees will sometimes smear themselves with a herring (which turns brown or red when it spoils) in order to throw dogs off their track. To sway a red herring in an argument is, similarly, to try to throw those concerned off the right track and onto something not relevant to the issue at hand. The fallacy derives its persuasive power from the fact that it often does prove *that* conclusion or thesis, and it is this which tends to throw us off our guard. An example will make this clear.

"The advocate of laissez-faire contends that if we adopted his principles, we would be better off than under any other system. But he is mistaken for it is easy to show that laissez-faire will not produce a social Utopia." Two different questions are obviously at issue here: one, whether laissez-faire is better than any other economic system and, two, whether laissez-faire can bring about a social Utopia. What obviously had been maintained was not that by adopting laissez-faire we would achieve Utopia, but simply that we would be better off by so doing than we would if we adopted some other system. The refutation above seems persuasive because, by pointing out what is obviously true, namely, that laissez-faire is unlikely to bring about a social Utopia, we are tempted to reject out-of-hand any suggestion that contends that it will. This may make us blind to the fact that no suggestion of the kind had, after all, been made.

A maneuver that is frequent in debates and arguments consists essentially in imputing to one's adversary opinions a good deal more extreme than those he himself has set out and is willing to defend. By extending, exaggerating, or distorting them, the opinions are either made to appear ridiculous and thus easily overthrown (that is, he sets up a straw man") or one is tricked into defending (if one is not careful) a position that is much more extreme than the original one — a position one in all likelihood never intended to defend. No doubt you can recall some such experience in debate or discussion. Although this is a popular trick in debating, it is a dishonest one.

Irrelevant Thesis is a fallacy that is, unfortunately, all too easy to commit.

To decide at all times what is relevant and what is not is not at all easy. Pressed for time, or lacking distance, we may regard certain factors relevant when with more time and distance their irrelevance would stare us in the face. Thus certainly no dishonesty or bad faith is involved, for example, in the remark with which Descartes opens his *Discourse on Method*. On the contrary, it is designed to encourage and stimulate us to exert our best efforts, for what has enabled him to make the discoveries he succeeded in making was not, he is here trying to tell us, that he is wiser than the rest of mankind but simply because he had found the right method. Now that this method is available to others, they too can expect to share in the many discoveries yet to be made. Still, as stated in the opening lines of his book, the argument is a case of irrelevant thesis. It runs as follows:

> Good sense is of all things the most equally distributed among men. For everybody thinks himself so abundantly provided with it that even the most difficult to please in all other aspects do not commonly desire more of it than they already possess.

From a logical point of view this argument is fallacious because although it may very well be true that everybody is pleased with the amount of good sense he has, this is no proof at all, and is irrelevant to the question whether in fact he has as much of it as everyone else.

But to return to the fallacy of Irrelevant Thesis. As in the example from Descartes's book the fallacy of irrelevant thesis is one we sometimes commit innocently. The same, perhaps, may be said of the following argument, which was probably not meant to divert our attention away from the central issue by drawing a red herring across our trail, but is one which many of us may quite innocently regard as relevant and persuasive:

> I fail to see why hunting should be so desperately cruel when it gives a tremendous amount of employment to a lot of people and a lot of pleasure.

At a little distance, however, we cannot fail to see that here, too, whether hunting gives a lot of employment or a lot of pleasure to people is completely irrelevant to whether it is cruel to animals. The question is, do animals find it fun? And if it is irrelevant, then the argument that it is cruel has yet to be challenged. Not to do so is simply to evade the issue.

Not all cases of irrelevant thesis are as innocent as we might consider this last example to be. Just as some people, when faced with a problem, simply get up and run away, so in argument or debate some people, when faced with a difficult or unpleasant line of reasoning, will simply try to take cover under a piece of irrelevance. Typical here is the case of the prosecutor who will try to persuade a jury of the guilt of a defendant by arguing at length that murder is a horrible crime; or the politician who, instead of facing up to his responsibilities, will try to evade them by playing on our sense of loyalty and our passions.

Exercises

1. It is silly to say that modern killer-diller comic books hurt young-sters; they are just the modern version of the dime novel.

2. *Guest:* I maintain that the government should increase its welfare benefits.

   Host: Ladies and Gentlemen! Mr. Jones would recommend that the country go communist!

3. *Child:* Do you love me?

   Mother: What is love?

4. Vegetarianism is an injurious and unhealthy practice. For if all peo-ple were vegetarians, the economy would be seriously affected and many people would be thrown out of work.

5. George Meany, AFL President: "To these people who constantly say you have got to listen to these younger people, they have got some-thing to say, I just don't buy that at all. They smoke more pot than we do and if the younger generation are the hundred thousand kids that lay around a field up in Woodstock, N.Y. I am not going to trust the destiny of the country to that group."

section three
RELEVANCE

What tends to confuse us in the case of the fallacies of Relevance is the emotional storm raised by the speaker. Powerfully aroused, we fail to see the essential invalidity of the argument advanced. In studying these fallacies, there-fore, our focus is upon how emotion very often plays havoc with our thought.

The six fallacies selected for examination here are far from exhaustive. They probably represent only a small fraction of the types of irrelevance often appealed to. The Latin names which the fallacies carry go back some centuries and have become part of our language.

Argumentum ad Hominem
Argumentum ad Populum
Argumentum ad Misericordiam

Argumentum ad Verecundiam
Argumentum ad Ignorantiam
Argumentum ad Baculum

1. Argumentum ad Hominem

In *Argumentum ad Hominem* an attempt is made to divert attention from the question argued by focusing the argument on those arguing it. This can take a number of forms, depending upon the kind of irrelevance appealed to. In its strictly abusive form (which we might designate as the *Abusive ad Hominem*), it casts aspersions on the character of one's opponent. The following would be a typical example: "This theory was introduced by a man known for his Communist sympathies. There can't be much to it."

Turning attention from the facts in the argument to the people participating in it, as is done in this example, is characteristic not only of a good many of the discussions and debates among ordinary people; it is, unfortunately, all too characteristic of our political debates. Rather than discuss political issues, rivals will often find it easier to discuss personalities and engage in "mudslinging." Not only does this tend to be effective — for once a suspicion is raised it is difficult to put it to rest — it also tends to have more lasting effects, remaining in people's minds longer. It is not surprising, therefore, that Argumentum ad Hominem is such a common dodge.

Not all appeals of this kind are irrelevant, however. In a court of law, for example, it would not be irrelevant to point out that a witness is a chronic liar. If the assertion is true, the information is not irrelevant. On the other hand, although this would tend to reduce the credibility of his testimony, it would not in itself prove that testimony false, for even chronic liars have been known to tell the truth. On the contrary, we ourselves would be guilty of a breach of logic were we to argue that what a man says is a lie because he is a liar.

Let us now look at an example or two where an attempt is made to lower whatever value we would have been inclined to place on a person's utterance by insulting the person who utters it.

The president of the bank maintains that personal income taxes for the wealthy should be reduced. It is just what you would expect from him. He has a big income and is greedy for more.

Here again abuse is involved — we are calling him "greedy" and money-hungry. Very few will therefore place any importance on what he says. By lowering him in people's eyes, one lowers, in their eyes, whatever he may have to say.

There is another way in which we can abuse our opponent and destroy his "credibility," as we now put it: by accusing him of being changeable, inconsistent, and even, perhaps, erratic. The following would be a typical example:

> In reply to the gentleman's argument, I need only say that two years ago he advocated the very measure he now opposes.

Here we are saying that the man is not to be trusted (so don't pay any attention to what he says) for he is erratic. Last year it was this; this year it is this, and only God knows what it will be next year.

In cases of such accusations we must realize, first, that if there is a true inconsistency, then of course one of the views must be incorrect, for if one's views contradict one another, they cannot both be true. So in this sense it is not irrelevant to point out to an opponent that he is inconsistent. But simply to charge one with an inconsistency is not to say which of the two views is the true one. Obviously, it need not be the one upheld by you! Nor does it necessarily follow that if one is inconsistent, both views are incorrect and should be rejected. This would still need to be shown to be the case. It is in this sense that the charge of inconsistency should by itself not be allowed to carry much weight. Nor should the charge of having changed one's mind. Here the implication is that the person who does this is erratic. But why not consider such a person as being, instead, flexible and even perhaps courageous — having the courage to admit having been mistaken and the flexibility to perceive and do something about it.

Closely related to this variant of the *Ad Hominem* argument is one sometimes described by the name "genetic fallacy." It is an attempt to prove an idea or contention false or unsound by condemning its source or genesis, its origin. Such arguments, again, are fallacious, for the source of a view, or what led one to it, is entirely irrelevant to whether or not the view is true. Thus it would be fallacious to argue that: "Religion began with magic and animism. Religion is, therefore, nothing but pure nonsense."

Accounts of the way in which the views in question were arrived at may very well be true; they may even be highly illuminating, but they are irrelevant to whether or not the views in question are true.

This variant differs from the ordinary Argumentum ad Hominem in that no abuse is involved. We merely point out that that source, being what it is, affects adversely the thing it gave rise to. But to consider the example we looked at a moment ago, the fact — assuming it is a fact — that religion began in the way described, does not mean that that is what it means to us today. This is, indeed, how the idea of religion and God may have first occurred to man, but this is not what that idea means to him now.

The spread of psychoanalysis has tended, unfortunately, to make this kind of appeal especially popular and persuasive. By inventing, as is only too easy, some unfavorable account of how or why the advocate of a certain view came to hold it, it is possible to refute any argument whatever. The following would be an example of an argument which exploits this kind of stratagem:

> We must take Schopenhauer's famous essay denouncing and belittling women with a grain of salt. Any psychiatrist would at once explain this

"Do you mind if I make the little chap's suit blue? I seem to be out of vermillion." © 1966 by *Playboy*.

essay by reference to the strained relationship between Schopenhauer and his mother.

Here, again, one must keep in mind that while it may be true that certain motives may weaken our credibility, they are entirely irrelevant to whether the argument is credible. For arguments are sound, not because of the kinds of people who happen to propose them, but in virtue of the kind of internal support they possess. If the premises of an argument prove the conclusion, they do so no matter by whom they happen to be stated. If they do not, not even an Einstein can make them sound. The reasons that may have led certain people to be especially interested in a particular theory, or the ways in which they have arrived at the particular view (although this often makes fascinating reading and sometimes makes the meaning of the view clearer to us) are not at all relevant to the soundness or truth of the views in question.

It will occasionally happen that, instead of directly abusing an opponent, an attempt will be made to undercut his position by suggesting that in advancing the views in question he is merely serving his own personal interests. A person making use of the circumstantial form, as it is known, of the Ad Hominem argument will point out, for example, that a manufacturer's argument in favor of tariff protection should be rejected on the grounds that as a manufacturer he is naturally in favor of such a protective tariff. In all such cases, an attempt is made to discredit the arguments of those with whom we disagree by fixing on the fact that their special interests are involved. Rather than offering reasons why the conclusions in question are true or false, what is offered are simply reasons why one's opponent might be expected to believe or disbelieve, as the case may be, those conclusions.

Although to charge an opponent with having certain vested interests in a matter may be regarded as a kind of reproach or abuse, these arguments differ from the ordinary abusive Ad Hominem in that the abuse is only incidental. The following would be a typical example:

> Congress shouldn't bother to consult the Joint Chiefs of Staff about military appropriations. As members of the armed forces, they will naturally want as much money for military purposes as they think they can get.

This argument does look as if it could easily fit under the category of abusive Ad Hominem for there is a certain amount of abuse implied in it. It does suggest that the people in question are self-interested and perhaps even greedy, and certainly irresponsible. On the other hand, being able to see that it is a case of circumstantial Ad Hominem is to see more clearly the tactic exploited and thus to be in a better position to deal with it. For, after all, who else could really tell us so well the needs they have and what they believe would be required to meet them?

In addition to these three forms of the Ad Hominem, there are two others. The first of these goes under the Latin label, *tu quoque*. It does not have a very neat English translation but it can be rendered roughly either as "This from you?" or, more colloquially, as "Hey! Look who's talking!"

Suppose someone says, "Smoking is unhealthy! You should quit!" If we replied by saying, "Hey! Look who's talking! You smoke!" we would be guilty of the fallacy. For obviously the fact that he smokes does not make his statement that smoking is unhealthy false. It still might very well be true. In any case, we could not possibly find out whether it is by seeing whether he himself smokes.

Therefore, when a person, charged with a wrong replies that the one bringing the charge is himself guilty of the same practice, he commits the fallacy of *tu quoque*. As we have seen from the smoking example, the fallacy consists in trying to show that an opponent's argument against an action is worthless because the opponent has himself done the same thing. But, as we might reply here, the fact that one's opponent is himself guilty of some particular fault does not make the act right. Two wrongs do not make a right. Unfortunately, those who resort to this kind of attack often draw courage from another popular maxim, that "Peo-

"Furthermore, all the storks I know are against liberalized abortion laws."
© 1973 by *Playboy*.

ple in glass houses should not throw stones." But, as has sometimes been pointed out, there is no reason why a stone thrown from a glass house should not find its mark.

Another common form of the Ad Hominem fallacy, which is called Poisoning the Well, is illustrated by the following remark:

"Don't listen to him; he's a liar."

This may seem, at first, simply a case of the abusive Ad Hominem. But it is a little more complicated than that, for it is not merely a matter of "putting your opponent down," as we now say it; it is an attempt to make it impossible for him to defend himself. A position is assumed in which nothing can count as evidence against it. Everyone having been told that he is a liar, what can he possibly do to defend himself, for every attempt at defense will be discredited in advance as a further case of lying.

This form of the fallacy was given its name of "poisoning the well" by Cardinal Newman (1801–1890). The occasion was a famous debate between himself and Charles Kingsley (1819–1875) regarding evolution. During the course of this debate, Kingsley suggested that truth did not possess the highest value for a Roman Catholic priest. Newman protested that such an accusation made it impossible for him, or for any other Catholic, to state his case. For how could he prove to Kingsley that he did have more regard for truth than for anything else if Kingsley simply presupposed, and wished everyone to believe, that he did not? By saying what he did, Kingsley automatically ruled out anything that Newman might offer in defense. Kingsley, in other words, had "poisoned the well, making it impossible for anyone to drink from it."

Exercises

1. Present economic policies are rapidly placing this country in a bad condition. This is mainly due to some of the ex-White House advisers connected with the former Administration, plus some of the eggheads still in power. These people are evidently very egotistical and smug, entirely out of contact with the American people and Congress.

2. Humans are made of nothing but atoms and since atoms have no free will, therefore, humans don't either.

3. *Smith:* Of course you would be in favor of reduced real estate taxes because you would benefit personally by such a reduction.

   Jones: Of course you are against such a reduction because you own no real estate.

4. A top Soviet authority on U.S. Affairs showed irritation at Americans over the humanitarian issue. "What moral right do they have to act as preachers of freedom and democracy, especially in the light of events which occurred in America itself?" asked Georgy Arbatov, listing Watergate and Wounded Knee.

5. *She:* I don't think I really matter to you.
   He: Now why are you saying that? I'm doing the best I can.
   She: Well, I just feel taken for granted.
   He: I think you are insatiable. There is never enough.
   She: See, this is proof of what I just said. I don't really matter to you. If I did you wouldn't talk this way to me.

2. Argumentum ad populum

Literally, "an argument addressed to the people," this fallacy is an attempt to sway public opinion by appealing to people's emotions and passions. Instead of arguing the point at issue, it is an attempt to gain assent by arousing people's prejudices. Its main tool is the use of violent language. It is a very effective tool indeed. Another name under which this fallacy is frequently discussed is "mob appeal."

Mark Antony's funeral oration over the body of Caesar in Shakespeare's *Julius Caesar* is not only a famous but also an excellent example of mob appeal. This oration repays study, for the techniques it makes use of are still the stock-in-trade of all propagandists and hate-merchants.

As the reader will recall, after having aroused the Roman mob to fury, Antony stays behind and mutters to himself:

Now let it work. Mischief thou art afoot.
Take thou what course thou wilt!

These two lines are very significant, for this reason: it wouldn't be so bad if people who set out to win over a mob, to arouse and move them, were themselves caught up in the emotions they were trying to evoke. But often such people are very much out of it. They do not at all feel the emotions and passions they are generating. On the contrary, they are calculating and cool. Of course, the outburst of passion appears as if it arose spontaneously; but we know, as Shakespeare obviously did, that it is the result of the most careful artifice. That is what is so evil about it. They are using the crowd for their own purposes. For people like that, language is a weapon they have learned to use with great skill and ingenuity.

On a more subtle level, such people will sometimes resort to subliminal suggestion by exploiting the well-known psychological principle of association. Let us examine the use of this device by Westbrook Pegler, who was one of America's most notorious propagandists and hate-merchants:

Mayor LaGuardia, who himself is a very noisy member of the crowd known as the labor movement, certainly must know that the worst parasites, thieves, and bread robbers now in active practice in the United States, and specifically in the city of New York, are the union racketeers. The waterfront is crawling with them; they are even preying on men employed to produce entertainments for troops under the auspices of the USO and thus filching from the fighters for whose benefits the USO funds are raised. Throughout the country, they are reaching their dirty hands into the homes of the poor and stealing bread and shoes from children of the helpless American toiler. LaGuardia has never said a word against such robbery and, by his association with the union movement, he has given approval of this predatory system.

Although this passage reads as if it came about spontaneously, it is the result of careful artifice. It is remarkable how well-chosen its terms are, and how well-adapted for the effect they are designed to bring about. For example, Mayor LaGuardia is described as a noisy member of the labor movement, not simply a busy one. The labor movement is a crowd of racketeers. And these racketeers, we are told, are busy at work, stealing not from the American worker but from the American toiler; and not from him but from his children; and not merely such things as toys or playthings but bread and shoes. And what kind of racketeers would steal so indiscriminately? Apparently, only those who, like rats, crawl about the waterfront. And so, even though not a single word has been said about rats, the image is very much there and the entire passage trades on it and exploits it.

From the opposite end of the political spectrum, we might consider the following passage, which was directed against Winston Churchill and is taken from the Communist publication *New Masses* (March 19, 1946). The editorial was in response to Churchill's famous "Iron Curtain" speech at Westminster College in Missouri.

> Winston Churchill, the archbishop of torydom, came to tell us how we shall live. And what is the life he maps for us? An Anglo-American tyranny to ride roughshod over the globe. He said that it was against Communism that he wanted the armies and navies combined. The words are Churchill's but the plan is Hitler's. Churchill's own domain of plunder is ripping at the seams and he asks Americans to save it for him. We are to be the trigger men, we are to provide him billions in money to regain what the robber barons are losing.

Like the former passage, such suggestive phrases as "archbishop of torydom," "domain of plunder," "trigger men," "robber barons," are directed to our subconscious minds, where by their means the writer hopes certain images will be built up and the appropriate associations made. Whether he succeeds here or not, his design seems to be to associate Churchill in our minds with the typical gangster, trying to get us to join his gang.

We call such appeals as are involved in the Ad Populum fallacious, because strong feelings do not constitute evidence for the truth of a proposition. Certitude is no proof of certainty. The fact that one feels strongly about something is no proof that one is therefore right.

Exercises

1.   Advertisement: Great American Soup. About as close as you can get to homemade without making it yourself.

2.   Advertisement by Licensed Beverage Industries, Inc.: One American custom that has never changed: a friendly social drink.

3.   Speaker: "No one in this room wants to deny any child a decent education. But let's remember that this is our school and it belongs to our children."

4.   In answer to Mr. Parker who states we should send our troops overseas to capture Arab oil fields and that he, for one, is "ready to go." It seems the war-hungry are now developing an unholy thirst for oil. To him and others of his ilk, let me say, your thirsts will never be quenched — nor your gas tanks filled — with my sons' blood.

5.   National Socialist White People's Party Poster: "Had enough, 'Pig'? Had enough of being called 'Pig' by scum not fit to wipe your feet

on? Are you sick and tired of hearing about "police brutality" from the swarms of degenerates in the streets—and from City Hall and Congress too? . . . What you've seen up till now is just the beginning of the hell that's going to break loose in the next few years. Let's begin doing something about it—NOW. Join us today!"

3. Argumentum ad misericordiam

The fallacy of *Argumentum ad Misericordiam*—appeal to pity—is a special form of the *Argumentum ad Populum*. Like it, it is an attempt to sway people by playing on their emotions. It differs from the Ad Populum only in that one particular emotion is appealed to: pity or sympathy.

This is a very common appeal. It is also a very ancient one, as may perhaps be gathered from Socrates' reference to it in his own trial, as recorded in Plato's Apology.

> Perhaps there may be some one who is offended at me, when he calls to mind how he, himself, on a similar or even less serious occasion, prayed and entreated the judges with many tears, and how he produced his children in court, which was a moving spectacle, together with a host of relations and friends; whereas I, who am probably in danger of my life, will do none of these things.

In spite of Socrates's refusal to employ this device, by mentioning it in the way he does, he stands, ironically, guilty of using it himself. Nor can this be regarded as simply Socratic irony, for he goes on to make explicit use of it.

> The contrast may occur to his mind, and he may be set against me, and vote in anger because he is displeased at me on this account. Now if there be such a person among you—mind, I do not say there is—to him I may fairly reply: My friend, I am a man, and like other men, a creature of flesh and blood, and not "of wood or stone," as Homer says; and I have a family, yes, and sons, O Athenians, three in number, one almost a man, and two others who are still young; and yet I will not bring any of them hither in order to petition you for an acquittal.

This is, of course, a very subtle use of the appeal. A much more common example of it would be the following, taken from Clarence Darrow's defense of Thomas I. Kidd, who as general secretary of the Amalgamated Woodworkers International Union stood indicted on a charge of criminal conspiracy.

> I appeal to you not for Thomas Kidd, but I appeal to you for the long line—the long, long line reaching back through the ages and forward to the years to come—the long line of despoiled and downtrodden people of the earth. I appeal to you for those men who rise in the morning

before daylight comes and who go home at night when the light has faded from the sky and give their life, their strength, their toil to make others rich and great. I appeal to you in the name of those women who are offering up their lives to this modern god of gold, and I appeal to you in the name of those little children, the living and the unborn.

The trouble with appeals such as this is that, however moving they may be, they do not address themselves to the issues. They should not, therefore, carry any weight with us. Rather than attempt to convince, they attempt to play upon our sympathies.

Such appeals can often be very moving and very eloquent. And indeed where they are relevant they should be taken into account. Thus, while it would be a matter of committing the fallacy of Ad Misericordiam were a defense attorney to offer evidence about his client's unhappy and unfortunate childhood as a reason why the court should believe him innocent, it would be no fallacy for him to argue, and no sign of weakness for us to accept, this evidence (his miserable background) as a reason for treating him with leniency.

As with many of the devices and tactics we have been examining, this one, too, has been exploited by advertising. A particularly unfortunate example was the full-page advertisement placed by the television dealers in November 1950, when television was beginning to be mass-produced. It said:

THERE ARE SOME THINGS A SON OR DAUGHTER WON'T TELL YOU

"Aw gee, pop, why can't we get a television set?" You've heard that. But there's more you won't hear. Do you expect a seven-year-old to find words for the deep loneliness he's feeling?

He may complain — "The kids were mean and wouldn't play with me!" Do you expect him to blurt out the truth — that he's really ashamed to be with the gang — that he feels left out because he doesn't see the television shows they see, know the things they know?

You can tell someone about a bruised finger. How can a little girl describe a bruise deep inside? No, your daughter won't ever tell you the humiliation she's felt in begging those precious hours of television from a neighbor.

You give your child's body all the sunshine and fresh air and vitamins you can. How about sunshine for his morale? How about vitamins for his mind? Educators agree — television is all that and more for a growing child.

When television means so much more to a child than entertainment alone, can you deny it to your family any longer?

Many people found this advertisement offensive and in bad taste, which it was, and it was soon withdrawn. Present-day advertisements are somewhat more subtle.

Exercises

1. Advertisement for corn oil margarine: Should an 8-year old worry about cholesterol?

2. My client is the sole support of his aged parents. If he is sent to prison it will break their hearts, and they will be left homeless and penniless. You surely cannot find it in your heart to reach any other verdict than "not guilty."

3. Permitting increased immigration will actually strengthen this nation's economy. The unhappy peoples of other lands, the homeless of the world, children torn from their mother's arms, should be given a chance to find a new life among us.

4. News report: An attorney says a 62-year-old San Carlos man accused of bilking several members of the Seventh Day Adventist Church out of thousands of dollars could suffer a fatal attack if compelled to stand trial.

5. From Richard Nixon's Checkers Speech: "My family was one of modest circumstances and most of my early life was spent in a store out in East Whittier. It was a grocery store—one of those family enterprises. I worked my way through college and to a great extent through law school. The only reason we were able to make it go was because my mother and dad have five boys and we all worked in the store. Why do I feel so deeply? Why do I feel that in spite of the smears, the misunderstanding, the necessity for a man to come up here and bare his soul as I have? And I want to tell you why. Because you see, I love my country."

4. Argumentum ad verecundiam

This fallacy is sometimes called "misappeal to experts." It arises whenever we try to justify a proposal by quoting some "authority" in its support. If the idea lies within the authority's competence, then, of course, no fallacy is involved. We often find ourselves in need of expert opinion and we know where to get it. We do not, however, consult our barber regarding a tax problem, nor our accountant regarding a medical problem. Authorities remain authorities only within their areas of competence. Yet so charmed are some people by anyone possessing a skill or authority that they sometimes forget the simple truth that a man may know all there is to know about one subject and yet be a complete ignoramus about everything else.

John Locke gave this fallacy its Latin name. The name is appropriate, for "verecundia" means "modesty," the fallacy or appeal being an attempt to overawe or cow or shame an opponent into accepting something by playing on his natural reluctance, his sense of modesty or shame, to challenge noted or respected authorities — or even time-honored customs and traditions.

The fallacy of *ad verecundiam* can assume several forms, depending upon the kind of authority being appealed to. We have perhaps become somewhat hardened against the out-and-out appeal to numbers. The fact that millions of Americans use a particular product does not necessarily mean (we have all too often learned to our sorrow) that the product is any good. Yet the appeal is still widely used in advertising, so it is obviously still effective. Here is a small sample of this form of appeal as found in some recent advertisements:

1. Sony. Ask anyone.
2. You can take a White Horse anywhere.
3. Last year, over 5,000,000 cats switched to Tender Vittles.
4. The kind of car everyone's trying to build.
5. Cointreau. The world's largest selling liqueur specialité.

Nor is this form of the appeal absent from even the more serious kinds of discussion. The following is taken from *The Philosophy of the Practical*, by the famous philosopher, Benedetto Croce (1866–1952).

The Inquisition must have been justified and beneficial, if whole peoples invoked and defended it, if men of the loftiest souls founded and created it severally and impartially, and its very adversaries applied it on their own account, pyre answering pyre.

Obviously, the fact that many people endorsed the Inquisition did not make it right.

Exercises

1. There must be something to psychical research, since such famous physicists as Lodge and Jeans and Eddington took it seriously.

2. Advertisement: Eat Americam Lamb. Ten Million Coyotes Can't Be Wrong.

3. Everybody's wearing it.

4. People who have everything always smoke Richman cigars.

5. From *Points of Rebellion* by Justice William O. Douglas: "England's King George III was the symbol against which our founders made a revolution now considered bright and glorious. We must realize that today's Establishment is the new George III. Whether it will

continue to adhere to his tactics, we do not know. If it does, the redress, honored in tradition, is also revolution."

5. Argumentum ad ignorantiam

The *Argumentum ad ignorantiam* is an attempt to throw the burden of proof upon the other party. It is an attempt to use the other party's inability to disprove your proposition as proof of its correctness. The appeal, however, is irrelevant and fallacious, for one's ability to disprove a theory cannot by itself be regarded as proof of it. It must still be shown to be correct. It would, for example, be a case of trying to base an argument upon ignorance to argue that mental telepathy is true because no one has been able to prove that it is not true.

Similarly, it would be a case of trying to base an argument upon ignorance if we tried to argue that man has freedom of choice, for no one has been able to prove that he does not. If one believes that man has freedom of choice, it is up to him to establish this point. You can't shift that burden onto your opponent. We can easily turn this argument around and prove just the opposite thesis: that man has no freedom of choice because no one has proven that he has! To try to shift this burden of proof onto the other person by drawing upon his ignorance is simply to expose one's own. The absence of evidence against a claim cannot be counted as evidence for its truth.

A person making use of an Argumentum ad Ignorantiam will frequently try to strengthen his case by combining the appeal with Question-Begging Epithets. The following argument would be a typical example of this sort of double-barreled attack: "I have never come across any arguments for price control that any sensible man could accept. Therefore , price controls are obviously wrong." Not only is this argument objectionable because it bases its proof upon our ignorance of its refutation; it is also objectionable because by using the epithet "sensible" it condemns out of hand the disproof that we may be ready to offer, for it seems obvious, from the statement made, that it would be condemned as something no sensible man would accept.

It should be noted that this mode of argument is not fallacious in a court of law, where the defense can legitimately claim that if the prosecutor has not proved guilt, then this warrants a verdict of not guilty. Although this claim seems to commit the fallacy, we do not regard it as objectionable here because of the special legal principle we have adopted, that a person is presumed innocent until proven guilty. Notice that we do not say a person *is* innocent until proven guilty, but only that he is *presumed* to be so. Obviously, not every person who is presumed innocent, is innocent. Some are later proven to be guilty. But until this is done, they are regarded as legally innocent. So our practice in court is not really an exception to the rule. In addition, of course, after the man who had been presumed innocent has been tried and found to be innocent, we do not even then say he is innocent, but rather that he is legally innocent. He may, in fact, be guilty, but the law, having done all it can, cannot touch him.

Exercises

1. God exists because you cannot prove He doesn't.

2. Mental telepathy is true because no one has been able to prove that it isn't.

3. He did not make a mistake in his computation of his income tax, for I have never known him to make a mistake.

4. From *Psychic Discoveries behind the Iron Curtain* by Sheila Ostrander and Lynn Schroder (New York: Bantam Books, 1971, p. 102): Said the Soviet Academy of Sciences in March 1968, "the search for UFOs is anti-scientific." If they existed, scientists would know about them. The Academy stated, "None of our astronomers have ever seen a UFO. They've never been sighted by any of our ground scientists. Our defensive units, guarding the land day and night, have never seen a UFO." So, the Academy concluded, there can't be any UFOs.

5. If these writings are not Shakespeare's to whom do they belong?

6. Argumentum ad baculum

Let us now turn to our last fallacy — the *Argumentum ad Baculum*. This is an argument, if one may call it that, which some people (and countries) resort to when everything else fails. Although arguments involving threats of force or violence seldom settle matters, they are all the same very persuasive.

From a logical point of view, the Argumentum ad Baculum (or "swinging the big stick," as it is sometimes called) should be distinguished from the all-out threat. If someone should hold a gun to your back and say: "Your money or your life!" it would not do to reply: "Hey! That's a fallacy!" It is no fallacy at all, but a threat, and should be treated as such. It is not a fallacy because it is not an argument. The gunman is, of course, appealing to your sense of fear and even offering a reason why you should do what he tells you to. He is not, however, offering evidence in support of the truth of some statement, and therefore it is not, strictly speaking, an argument. To see more clearly the difference, we might compare this example with the case of the attorney who says to a jury: "If you do not convict this murderer, one of you may be his next victim." Here, too, the attorney is appealing to the jurors' fears, and he is also giving them a reason for doing as he instructs them to. But he is also doing something else. He is arguing a case and offering evidence in support of it. When expressed fully, his argument is as follows: you must believe with me that this man is guilty of the crime he is accused of committing, for if you do not find him guilty of it, he will be released and you may end up being his next victim. Put this way, we can see plainly that this is far from very solid proof that the man is in fact guilty of the crime of which he is charged. Obviously, what a defendant might do in the future is not relevant, and is in no way proof of his innocence or his guilt in the past. It is only fear put into our hearts by a clever prosecutor that may make us believe it is relevant. This is, then, a fairly good example of the Argumentum ad Baculum.

For an Argumentum ad Baculum to be considered as such, therefore, it must be an argument, and it must attempt to offer evidence. In some cases the evidence will be brief and implicit, as in the examples noted thus far; in other cases it may run to several pages. The following account of the Athenian appeal to Melos to join them, taken from Thucydides (460–400 B.C.), is perhaps a classic example of such an appeal to force. The Athenians wrote:

> You know as well as we do, that, in the logic of human nature, right only comes into question where there is a balance of power, while it is might that determines what the strong exhort and the weak concede . . . Your strongest weapons are hopes yet unrealized, while the weapons in your hands are somewhat inadequate for holding out against the forces already arranged against you . . . Reflect . . . that you are taking a decision for your country . . . a country whose fate hangs upon a single decision right or wrong.

Not all threats are expressed as elegantly as this. We are more likely to meet it in the following form: Desegregation of labor unions is not desirable, and any official who thinks it is — I want to tell him that he will discover his error at the next election.

Exercises

1. Without insurance, your life would be a deathtrap.

2. Advertisement: While you're thinking about going to an All American Tennis Camp, someone else might be booking your room.

3. You should vote for Democratic candidates. If the Republicans retain control of Congress, we are sure to have a depression.

4. From *The 12-Year Reich: A Social History of Nazi Germany 1933–1945* by Richard Grunberger (New York: Holt, Rinehart and Winston, 1971, p. 398): The Nazis used to send the following notice to German readers who let their subscription lapse: "Our paper certainly deserves the support of every German. We shall continue to forward copies to you, and hope that you will not want to expose yourself to unfortunate consequences in the case of cancellation.

5. One suggestion to those who don't care much for policemen is that the next time they get in trouble, they should call a hippie!

Summary

1. This chapter has been concerned with the common fallacies. Traditionally these fallacies have been divided into three groups: Fallacies of Ambiguity, Fallacies of Presumption, and Fallacies of Relevance.

2. Fallacies of Ambiguity were shown to be linguistic fallacies, in that they stem from the use of language having more than one meaning. We saw that the best way to unravel such fallacies is to clarify the language in question. The six fallacies of Ambiguity we looked at were: Amphiboly, Accent, Hypostatization, Equivocation, Composition, and Division.

    a. *Amphiboly* was shown to result from ambiguity in sentence structure as when Macbeth draws the wrong conclusion from the witch who prophecies that "none of woman born/ Shall harm Macbeth."

    b. *Accent* was shown to result from ambiguity of stress or tone, as in the case of Charlie Chaplin, who defends himself against the charge of having made a remark reflecting badly on the regime by pleading that after all, all he said was "This is a fine country to live in" — meaning, that it was a lovely, wonderful place.

    c. *Hypostatization* was shown to result when an abstract word or phrase is used as if it referred to something concrete. Such an abstraction was personified in the argument claiming that, because nature improves a race by eliminating the unfit, it is right for one group of people to eliminate another group.

    d. *Equivocation* was the name given to fallacies stemming from a shift in meaning of a key term during an argument. When we argue that "only man is rational" and that, because women are not men, it follows that "no woman is rational," we change the meaning of the word *man* during the course of the argument.

    e. *Composition* was shown to result from trying to apply what is true of the part or of the individual to the whole or group. But, as we saw, the whole or group is more than merely the sum of its parts or members.

    f. *Division* was shown to result from trying to apply what is true of the whole or the group what we therefore believe must be true of each part or member. But, as we saw, the Chicago Symphony Orchestra may be the best orchestra in the country but that does not necessarily mean that the first violinist in the orchestra is the best violinist in the country.

3. Fallacies of Presumption were shown to be arguments in which unfounded or unproven assumptions were smuggled in under the guise of valid argument forms. These fallacies were divided into three types: those in which the error lay in overlooking the facts, those in which the facts were evaded, and those in which they were distorted.

    Under *overlooking the facts* three fallacies were studied: Sweeping Generalization, Hasty Generalization, and Bifurcation.

    a. *Sweeping Generalization* was shown to result when a generalization is applied to a special case that properly falls outside of it, as when horseback riding is recommended for someone with a heart condition.

    b. *Hasty generalization* was shown to be the opposite of sweeping generalization. Here, an isolated or exceptional case is used erroneously to support a universal conclusion, as when a bad experience with a former husband is used to prove that all men are no good.

    c. *Bifurcation* overlooks a range of possibilities that lie between two polar alternatives, as in the assertion that something is either good or bad.

    Under *evading the facts* four fallacies were studied: Begging the Question, Question-Begging Epithets, Complex Question, and Special Pleading.

    a. *Begging the Question* was exposed as the result of assuming in the premises of an argument the very conclusion that the argument is supposed to prove. An example cited was the assertion that the belief in God was universal because everybody believes in God.

    b. *Question-Begging Epithets* were shown to be similar to fallacies of begging the question in that they too affirm something that is not yet proved. Question-begging epithets do so by means of slanted language, as in the use of the epithet "a heavily haired . . . wealthy post-adolescent" dissident to characterize a young author of a best-selling book.

    c. *Complex Question* was shown to assume a certain answer to a prior question that was never asked. An example cited was the complex question: Is Smith an unthinking conservative?

    d. *Special Pleading*, the last of the four fallacies that evade facts, was seen as an attempt to set up a double standard: a special standard for ourselves and another for others. This fallacy evades the facts by being prejudiced in favor of one's own side, as when we refer to our troops as "devoted" while those of our enemy are called "fanatical."

The third and last type of presumptive fallacy dealt with three fallacies that distort the facts.

a. *False analogy* was shown to distort by making the facts under discussion appear more similar to another set of facts than they really are. An example cited was King James I's comparison of cutting off the head of a body with removing the head of a state.

b. *False cause* was shown to distort facts by assuming that the two events are causally connected when in fact they may not be. The Egyptians' worship of birds that migrated to the Nile Valley just before a flood was cited as an illustration.

c. *Irrelevant thesis*, the last fallacy of presumption discussed here, was seen as a distortion of facts by means of the substitution of another issue for the one actually in dispute. We examined in this connection the argument that, since hunting gives a lot of pleasure to people, it cannot be cruel to animals.

4. Fallacies of Relevance were shown to be arguments in which the emotional appeal deceives us into believing that what is said is relevant to the conclusion being urged, when the real object of the appeal is to enlist support for the conclusion through an emotional rather than a logical response.

a. The *Argumentum ad Hominem* was shown to be an argument which attacks the person or persons associated with a question rather than attacking the question itself. An example was the argument dismissing a theory on the ground that its proposer is a man known for his communist sympathies. We saw that this fallacy, which plays on suspicions and prejudices, can take any of several forms: the abusive form, which insults the person; the genetic fallacy, which casts aspersions on the source of the argument; the circumstantial form, which suggests that vested interests are at stake; the tu quoque form, which charges inconsistency; and the form known as poisoning the well, which discredits all opposition in advance.

b. The *Argumentum ad Populum* was seen to result from various propagandist techniques used in combination to arouse people's emotions and to divert attention away from the real question. Westbrook Pegler's attack on Mayor LaGuardia was explored as a striking example.

c. The *Argumentum ad Misericordiam* was shown to result from trying to gain one's point by playing on people's sympathies. The advertisement beginning, "Aw gee, Pop. why can't we get a television set?" was cited as an illustration.

d. The *Argumentum ad Verecundiam* was seen as an attempt to intimidate us into accepting a conclusion because someone who is presented as an expert has endorsed it, although that person proves on examination not to be an expert on this subject. "Last year, over 5,000,000 cats switched to Tender Vittles" was one example given.

e. The *Argumentum ad Ignorantiam* was shown to be an argument that tries to intimidate us into believing that something must be so merely because we cannot prove it is not so. Just because no one has been able to prove that mental telepathy is not true does not prove that it is true.

f. The *Argumentum ad Baculum*, finally, was seen as the fallacy that arises when support for a conclusion is enlisted not by establishing that conclusion through logical inference but by the use of a threat of force or harm. The argument that "If you do not convict this murderer, one of you may be his next victim" was shown as exemplifying this fallacy.

For further study

1. Those wishing to pursue the study of fallacies further will find the following three texts extremely helpful: Lionel Ruby, *The Art of Making Sense: A Guide to Logical Thinking*, 3rd edition (Philadelphia: Lippincott, 1974). Howard Kahane, *Logic and Contemporary Rhetoric: The Use of Reason in Everyday Life*, 3rd edition, (Belmont, CA: Wadsworth, 1980). Michael Scriven, *Reasoning* (New York: McGraw-Hill, 1976).

2. For an account of the subject from the point of view of general semantics (which concerns itself with the way language orders our lives) see S.I. Hayakawa's classic work *Language in Thought and Action*, 3rd edition (New York: Harcourt Brace, 1972).

3. For a fictional account of many of the fallacies discussed in this chapter see Max Shulman's popular novel *The Many Loves of Dobie Gillis* (New York: Bantam, 1964). The story "Love Is A Fallacy" provides a delightful, if extreme, illustration of how fallacious reasoning can affect our everyday lives.

part three

ITS MAIN QUESTIONS

Augustus Saint-Gaudens, "Grief." The Bettmann Archive, Inc.

chapter 5

Ethics

What are we like and what should we do?

Introduction

The article was entitled "Doctor's Choice Causes Furor." Its subtitle let the reader know why: "Life or Death for Brain-Damaged Infant?"

Although its author probably did not intend it, his account of the hospital incident touched on almost every major ethical question all of us, at one time or another, in one context or another, have had to face.

> The baby was born with serious birth defects and, after five agonizing days, the doctor decided the best thing to do was to let him die "mercifully."
>
> Last Friday, after determining the infant was near death because of what appears to be a seriously defective brain, the doctor withdrew food from the baby.

Instead of following the standard practice of writing feeding orders the physician wrote nothing — in effect telling the staff the baby would be allowed to die.

The baby was not fed Saturday or Sunday but on Monday another physician in the hospital countermanded the orders and once more placed the infant on food.

Today the baby is still alive and apparently in no imminent danger of dying. He is taking some food by mouth but it is too early to tell whether he is growing. He has a good heart, lungs and kidneys — the essentials of physical life.

It is apparently not easy to determine how near to death anyone may be. On Friday one doctor thought the baby was at death's doorstep; by Monday the baby seemed to be doing quite well.

The case has become a *cause célèbre* among the staff at the hospital, which is in Southern California. Some of the nursing staff believe the decision to not feed the baby was tantamount to euthanasia. Some call it murder. Others, perhaps the majority, are in total agreement with the initial decision.

A rabbi who has learned of the case from a distraught nurse is shocked that physicians take it upon themselves to make decisions that he believes to be moral, not medical.

"The medical profession cannot presume to make moral judgments with impunity," the rabbi says.

"It may be that the decision not to feed the baby was morally correct, but I don't think any physician has the right to make such a decision exclusively."

Not an unimportant point. Whose decision should this be? All of us would probably agree that it should not be the doctor's exclusively. But should it be only the mother's? The church's? Society's?

A cross-section of medical school pediatricians queried by *The Times* — at least those willing to comment on such a sensitive issue — said they would never under any circumstances fail to feed a baby.

This sounds as if they would never fail to do so in the case of an infant. Would they feel the same concern if the patient was a decrepit old man? Should such questions be decided on the basis of the pity that was aroused?

It is not rare for doctors in a large population area like Los Angeles to be confronted with a decision as the one this physician was forced to make.

Not all of them — possibly not even the majority — would have made an identical decision.

But this case and the decision reached could have occurred in many hospitals.

Usually such cases involve persons with terminal diseases or head alive should be withdrawn, allowing the patient to die quietly.

Sometimes, as in this case, the patient is a baby born with severe impairments.

Often nature takes care of things by allowing the infant to die, no matter what the doctors may try.

In other cases, the defects may be such that the child will live for years, but with physical and mental defects that place him at an enormous disadvantage.

What should the doctor — and the parents if they are around — do?

But to return to the baby:

> The baby's doctor said Thursday that epileptic seizures which a week ago were occurring frequently have been controlled with drugs and that dosage is being diminished. He admits that he miscalculated in determining that death was imminent when he withdrew food and says he agrees that the baby should be fed.

The doctor now recognizes he had "miscalculated." I don't think we would want to stop feeding *him* because he had made a mistake, but such "mistakes" strengthen the case of those who argue that we have no right "to play God" and would be opposed to the action taken by this physician under *any* circumstances.

> He said he cannot say with 100% certainty that the baby is mentally retarded, but tests indicate his brain is structurally abnormal.
> The baby is believed to be blind. He has a double cleft palate and lip and his arms are tiny stubs.

This is getting even worse: it cannot, apparently, even be determined that the baby is mentally retarded, nor even whether he is blind! Some facts are, of course, not very easy to establish. He is obviously, however, not very pretty — but that is scarcely a good reason not to feed him. Nor has fortune smiled on him in other respects:

> The infant's mother is unwed. She did not share directly in the decision not to feed her baby. However, when the baby was admitted to the hospital, she told the doctor she wouldn't care if she did not see the baby again.
> "Some doctors believe that a 100% effort must be made on all babies to sustain life. To me this is reasonable, but it's a copout. It doesn't take into consideration the circumstances that surround a baby's life," the doctor said in an interview.
> "The mother has had a very tough time in life. She's unwed. She has three children at home. She said, "How can I help this baby through a tough life with all these defects laid on him?""

> "If she had showed some concern, some willingness to care for the baby, my decision would have been influenced."

The doctor's argument is stronger here, and his action, perhaps, more understandable, but why would his decision have been merely "influenced" had the mother shown more concern? Why would it not have proven decisive in keeping the baby alive? Shouldn't the mother's rights in such a case be absolute? And if not, why not?

> The physician said he does not think of his decision as being euthanasia, a practice against which his hospital has a strong policy.
>
> "I had a picture of euthanasia as doing something to kill someone — an overt action. For example, giving an overdose of drugs to a terminal cancer patient who is in deep pain.
>
> "In that case the doctor is doing an action. I was doing an inaction — I was refraining from writing feeding orders. I was saying I am not going to contribute to continuing this particular problem.
>
> "On the other hand, suppose I had a baby who was not responding to treatment for hyaline membrane disease, a potentially lethal lung disorder, and who was having seizures and heart arrests. If someone told me to turn off the respirator, I would have a hard time doing that."

This shows us how easy it is to deceive even ourselves: to fail to see, in this case, that "doing an inaction" and "doing an action" are both species of action. Some might even feel that of the two, the former was more culpable; the writer of the article in fact discovered just such a person:

> Of four pediatricians consulted by *The Times*, all indicated a strong aversion to withholding food from defective babies.
>
> But one of them — a woman physician — who was the most adamant against that course of action said that she would have far less inhibition against pulling the plug on a respirator if she thought the case was hopeless — the exact opposite of the situation with the physician in this story.

On the other hand we should not make light of this active–passive distinction invoked by the physician in charge. Like the woman physician consulted by *The Times*, many have argued that in some cases active euthanasia is preferable to passive. Although, for example, it is often the practice in cases of Downs Syndrome to allow the patients to die by dehydration and unchecked infection, some have argued that a lethal injection would be far more humane.

But to return to the baby:

> It is expected that the baby, whose care is being paid by the Medi-Cal program, soon will be moved from the hospital because he is not sick enough to stay and the cost — about $80 a day — is prohibitive.

He probably will be transferred to a nursing home.

What happens then will involve other difficult medical and possibly moral decisions.

(*Los Angeles Times*, Monday, March 17, 1972).

The basic moral decision is, of course, what is to be done? What *should* the doctor have done in this case?

If you had said, as is likely, that he should have done everything he could to keep the baby alive, for life is precious and must be preserved at all costs, it is also likely that he or someone else might have raised the question whether this applies to all life (including, say, livestock) or only to human life; and if only to human life, does this apply, you might have been asked, to all human life, even the most vicious of criminals? And if you were now tempted to begin to draw lines between those judged worthy of life and those who are not, it is more than likely that someone else might have reminded you that that indeed was how it began in Nazi Germany, where they went from mental defectives to political enemies to, finally, whole races of people whom they judged as "material" unworthy of life.

On the other hand it could be argued that, independent of the abuses people have made in judging life's quality, such issues as euthanasia, abortion, and capital punishment necessitate these judgments. One might add that in a society like our own, such judgments can be made rationally and held to firmly. To argue that to make any such judgments is to allow "the thin edge of the wedge" to enter is considered inapplicable by some people. This is still not to say that extreme caution is not to be taken on account of such historical disasters.

Whatever direction such a discussion might take, it is obvious that this question of life would be central to it. And once it is raised, you would very quickly find yourself embroiled in such related questions as, "What sort of life?" "What should matter most in life?" "How should one best conduct it?" and so on. To become concerned with such questions is to become concerned with the philosophical study of ethics.

The study of ethics during the course of the centuries has tended to take three different directions. It has occupied itself with the practical problem of what is to be done (with what we might call morality proper); it has gone on to consider the possible theoretical reasons for various lines of conduct (ethics proper); and last, it has become concerned with inquiry into the nature of those theories themselves (metaethics).

Although all great philosophers who have written on ethics have been concerned with all three types of investigation, it is characteristic of contemporary writers to be concerned with the third (questions of meaning); of writers of recent times to be occupied with the second (with ethical theories); and of ancient writers with the first (with what we ought to do, or what life is best to live).

One of the first philosophers to leave us a memorable account of the life he thought most worthy to live was Aristotle, whose name is already familiar to us.

Let us begin by examining his classic work, the *Nicomachean Ethics.*

Aristotle. Mary Evans Picture Library, London.

Aristotle's theory of ethics

Aristotle believed that all living things—from trees and shrubs to man—are endowed with certain capacities or potentialities, and that their well-being lies in realizing these potentialities. The acorn has the potentiality of becoming an oak tree, and its well-being lies in attaining that final state, which it is drawn to achieve by its nature. What is true of the rest of nature is true of man too, who has the added capacity of being conscious of the goals he tries to realize.

Ethics, which is the study of human conduct, must therefore begin with an investigation of the goals at which people aim. There is basically, however, only one goal people aim at, and this is happiness. But since nobody can be happy without being good, the investigation of happiness must entail an investigation of goodness. The ten books of the *Nicomachean Ethics* are therefore devoted to an exploration of these two major goals.

Aristotle begins by distinguishing between two types of ends: those that are good in themselves and that are desired for themselves alone; and those that are good as means toward such ends. There are ends which are, as we would now put it, "intrinsically good," and ends which are only "instrumentally good." Money, for example, is for most of us an example of an instrumental good, being desired not for itself but for the things it enables us to obtain; a miser, on the other hand, might turn it into an intrinsic good by desiring it for itself alone.

Yet even here we must be very clear, for the miser is typically someone who derives a great deal of pleasure from hoarding money. If he hoards the money *in order to* get this pleasure then it is still only an instrumental good — good only in its capacity to get something else — pleasure. If, on the other hand, he wants the money independent of anything it might gain him — material goods, security, or pleasure — then he is considering it an intrinsic good, something to be got purely for itself.

Not all goods, obviously, are desired only as means, for this would involve an infinite and meaningless progression — one thing desired only because of some other thing, desired only because of still some other thing, and so on. There must be some things that are desired for their own sake. And among these, there must be one that is valued more than the others.

There is, indeed, according to the common opinion of mankind, says Aristotle, such a final and supremely valued good. It is "happiness."

Since there are evidently more ends than one, and of these we choose some (e.g. wealth or musical instruments or tools generally) as means to something else, it is clear that not all of them are final ends, whereas the supreme good is obviously something final. So if there is only one final end, this will be the good of which we are in search; and if there are more than one, it will be the most final of these. Now we call an object pursued for its own sake more final than one pursued because of something else, and one which is never choosable because of another more final than those which are choosable because of it as well as for their own sakes; and that which is always choosable for its own sake and never because of something else we call final without qualifications.

Well, happiness more than anything else is thought to be just such an end, because we always choose it for itself, and never for any other reason. It is different with honor, pleasure, intelligence and good qualities generally. We do choose them partly for themselves (because we should choose each one of them irrespectively of any consequences); but we choose them also for the sake of our happiness, in the belief that they will be instrumental in promoting it. On the other hand nobody chooses happiness for *their* sake, or in general for any other reason. (Book I, vii)*

*The *Ethics of Aristotle* translated by J. A. K. Thomson (London: Allen and Unwin, 1953). Reproduced by permission.

Although everyone, as Aristotle notes, seems to be in agreement about this, not everyone has quite the same conception of happiness; and so further analysis is necessary.

Before proceeding to this deeper analysis, Aristotle cautions the reader not to expect that the results of such an investigation will have the neatness and precision found in a science like mathematics. We should demand absolutely certain proofs from a mathematician. But in complex and difficult matters such as this, we cannot expect hard-and-fast rigorous statements. We must look for precision in a subject to the degree that the subject admits. It is the mark of an educated man to do this. Such precision is not possible in ethics or human affairs generally.

Now we may note as a beginning that happiness is not some momentary, fleeting feeling or sensation. It is something more substantial and lasting. When we remark of someone that he has had a happy life, what we mean is that he has had a full life; that he has lived well; that he has realized his aims and ambitions as a man — in short, that he has been, as we might say, a success. The question is, What is it to live well, to be a success?

To answer this question Aristotle returns to his basic premise about the nature of living things. A living thing, he says, lives well, has a fortunate life, if it has attained its nature, if it has realized its potentialities. Since the potentialities of different things are different (the potentiality of an acorn being different from the potentiality of a cow, and that of a cow different from that of a human being), living well will be different for different things. In each case, however, the organism will "live well" only by attaining its highest potentialities, by attaining what is distinctive of *it*.

A human could not be said to live well if he or she only realized those capacities or potentialities shared with other living things; if, say, he or she lived a life of only eating and drinking. For a human to be happy the potentialities that are distinctive of a human being must be attained. In the case of humankind this is obviously reason, which is a human's instinctive capacity. The truly good life for a human being must therefore in some way involve the exercise, development, and perfection of reason.

If one were in a particularly critical or unsympathetic mood one might argue here against Aristotle, as others have in the past, that reason is not the only thing peculiar to humankind. What is peculiar to humans, in addition, is that they have a moral sense and a sense of anguish, and even that they are capable of laughter. Further, it seems more and more apparent that reason is not even itself peculiar to humankind, but is shared by a number of "lower" primates. Yet even if reason is not peculiar to humans, it is peculiar in the degree to which it is present, and further, although not the only distinguishing characteristic, it is nevertheless the chief one.

Aristotle stresses here that it is not enough to possess these higher potentialities or capacities, for happiness is not a state of being but a state of doing, of being involved, of achieving. The capacities we have must be exercised, not simply possessed, if we are to achieve happiness.

But although our happiness lies in the development, perfection, and exercise of these higher capacities, we must remember that our other needs must nevertheless also be satisifed. In fact they have to be satisfied first. For even if we do not live to eat, we have to eat to live. Nor is it only a matter of merely eating; a truly happy life requires the sunshine of prosperity.

> Happiness needs the addition of external goods, for it is difficult if not impossible to do fine deeds without any resources. Many can only be done by the help of friends, or wealth, or political influence. There are also certain advantages, such a good ancestry or good children, or personal beauty, the lack of which mars our felicity; for a man is scarcely happy if he is very ugly to look at, or of low birth, or solitary and childless; and presumably even less so if he had good ones who are now dead. So, as we said, happiness seems to require this sort of prosperity too. (Book I, viii)

Aristotle ends this passage by reminding us not to make the mistake of equating happiness with the possession of such external goods. Although they are necessary conditions for attaining happiness, they are not sufficient ones. All of us know many who have had them in abundance and yet have missed happiness.

One cannot help but admire Aristotle's level-headed and common-sense view on this matter. This can be seen best, perhaps, if we compare it with another view often popular in philosophy. Some have held that all we must do to attain happiness in this world is to have the right frame of mind, strength, and direction of will. Such was the view of the post-Aristotelian school of Stoicism. Let the world be as bad as you wish, they say, let your family die, your home burn, and your body be wracked with pain, but if your mind and will are in order you will be happy. Such, as we know only too well, is simply not the case with most of us. To be happy, we need life's amenities, we need family and security and love, and this is, of course, Aristotle's point.

To summarize Aristotle's argument: the supreme aim of life is happiness, and in the case of humankind this means living a life that is distinctive and can be lived only by humans. This cannot consist merely of a life of eating and drinking, for that can be lived equally well by all other creatures. It means the development and perfection of reason.

The perfection of our reason, Aristotle goes on to explain, enables us to develop two main kinds of desirable qualities (or virtues, as he calls them), whose exercise brings us happiness. The first set, tied to our intelligence and called the *intellectual virtues* by Aristotle, includes our ability to discover and recognize the rules of life we ought to follow; the second set, tied to our character and called the *moral virtues*, deals with our ability to check our appetites and passions so that they will obey the rules recognized as good.

Aristotle first takes up the moral virtues, which deal with our feelings, emotions, and impulses, whose training make possible the effective use of our intelligence. Unchecked, these emotions and passions may prevent us from recognizing what the right thing to do is, let alone from doing it.

Learning to check our emotions and passions, Aristotle says, is something we acquire slowly and gradually; it is not something we are born with. We are not, for example, born brave; we must learn to become so, and we learn by doing brave things. Furthermore, these passions of ours are in themselves neither good nor bad; they become so depending upon the degree of their expression. Dampening our sense of fear to such a degree that we become rash and foolhardy is just as bad as allowing this fear to overwhelm us so that we become timid and cowardly. Both extremes are equally bad. The man of good character is one who has learned to act bravely not by despising fear but by controlling it.

This is the case with the other moral qualities. They are, in the main, means or points of balance between two extremes, each extreme being a vice either of excess or defect. Modesty is thus the mean between pride (resulting from too much vanity) and humility (resulting from too little); ambition, between greed (the excess) and sloth (the defect); and so forth.

> It is in the nature of moral qualities that they are destroyed by deficiency and excess, just as we can see (since we have to use the evidence of visible facts to throw light on those that are invisible) in the case of bodily health and strength. For both excessive and insufficient exercise destroy one's strength, and both eating and drinking too much or too little destroy health, whereas the right quantity produces, increases and preserves it. So it is the same with temperance, courage and the other virtues. The man who shuns and fears everything and stands up to nothing becomes a coward; the man who is afraid of nothing at all, but marches up to every danger, becomes foolhardy. Similarly the man who indulges in every pleasure and refrains from none becomes licentious; but if a man behaves like a boor and turns his back on every pleasure, he is a case of insensibility. Thus temperance and courage are destroyed by excess and deficiency and preserved by the mean. (Book II, ii)

> We have now said enough to show that moral virtue is a mean, and in what sense it is so: that it is a mean between two vices, one of excess and the other of deficiency, and that it is such because it aims at hitting the mean point in feelings and actions. For this reason it is a difficult business to be good; because in any given case it is difficult to find the mid-point — for instance, not everyone can find the center of a circle; only the man who knows how. So too it is easy to get angry — anyone can do that — or to give and spend money; but to feel or act towards the right person to the right extent at the right time for the right reason in the right way — that is not easy, and it is not everyone that can do it. Hence to do these things well is a rare, laudable and fine achievement. (Book II, ix)

Although much of the *Nicomachean Ethics* is devoted to the analysis of this doctrine of the golden mean (as it has come to be called) his most memorable illustration of it is to be found not in the *Nicomachean Ethics* but in his *Rhetoric*, in the description of the three main stages of life as represented in the Youthful Man, the Elderly Man, and the Man in His Prime. In terms of the major virtues, the Youthful Man represents the excess, the Elderly Man the defect, and the man in His Prime the mean.

I will omit quoting here his sketch of the Youthful Man, since it contains the opposite of his description of the Elderly Man. Aristotle, however, finds the Youthful Man's innocence, ignorance, and inexperience engaging. The Youthful Man, he says, is also passionate, brave, noble, and disinterested, but only because he does not yet know life as it is. And this is precisely what the elderly do know, and that knowledge has a desolating effect.

> They have lived many years; they have often been taken in, and often made mistakes; and life on the whole is a bad business. The result is that they are sure about nothing and *under-do* everything. They "think" but they never "know"; and because of their hesitancy they always add a "possibly" or a "perhaps", putting everything this way and nothing positively.
>
> They are cynical; that is, they tend to put the worst construction on everything. Further, their experience makes them distrustful and therefore suspicious of evil. Consequently they neither love warmly nor hate bitterly, but following the hint of Bias they love as though they will some day hate and hate as though they will some day love.
>
> They are small-minded, because they have been humbled by life: their desires are set upon nothing more exalted or unusual than what will help them to keep alive. They are not generous, because money is one of the things they must have, and at the same time their experience has taught them how hard it is to get and how easy to lose. They are cowardly, and are always anticipating danger; unlike that of the young, who are warm-blooded, their temperament is chilly; old age has paved the way for cowardice; fear is, in fact, a form of chill. . . .
>
> They are too fond of themselves; this is one form that small-mindedness takes. Because of this, they guide their lives too much by consideration of what is useful and too little by what is noble — for the useful is what is good for oneself, and the noble what is good absolutely.
>
> They are not shy, but shameless rather; caring less for what is noble than for what is useful, they feel contempt for what people may think of them. . . . Old men may feel pity, as well as young men, but not for the same reason. Young men feel it out of kindness; old men out of weakness, imagining that anything that befalls anyone else might easily happen to them, which is a thought that excites pity. . . .
>
> Their fits of anger are sudden but feeble. Their sensual passions have altogether gone or have lost their vigor: consequently they do not feel their passions much, and their actions are inspired less by what they

do feel than by the love of gain. Hence men at this time of life are often supposed to have a self-controlled character; the fact is that their passions have slackened and they are slaves to the love of gain.

(*Rhetoric*, Book II, Chapter 13)*

Few current descriptions of the elderly are as impressive in their insights as this. He seems to know that life, we feel, and to have observed it closely. His sketch of the Man in His Prime is briefer:

As for Men in their Prime, clearly we shall find that they have a character between that of the young and that of the old, free from the extremes of either. They have neither that excess of confidence which amounts to rashness, nor too much timidity, but the right amount of each. They neither trust everybody nor distrust everybody, but judge people correctly. Their lives will be guided not by the sole consideration either of what is noble or what is useful, but by both; neither by parsimony nor by prodigality, but by what is fit and proper. So, too, in regard to anger and desire; they will be brave as well as temperate, and temperate as well as brave; these virtues are divided between the young and the old; the young are brave but intemperate, the old temperate but cowardly. To put it generally, all the valuable qualities that youth and age divide between them are united in the prime of life, while all their excesses or defects are replaced by moderation and fitness. The body is in its prime from thirty to five-and-thirty; the mind about forty-nine.

(*Rhetoric*, Book II, Chapter 14)

It is important to realize that the mean is not a rigid mathematical middle but a relative thing, differing for people of different temperaments and under different conditions. Finding your mean, therefore, requires experience and maturity: after a certain amount of practice in, say, generosity or courage, one comes to find the mean in any given case almost instinctively. But it is not instinct, although with practice it can become habitual.

Aristotle is also careful to point out that there are some moral virtues to which the doctrine of the mean does not apply, for their very nature already implies either their badness or goodness. Theft, envy, and spite would be typical examples. Here it is not a matter of too much or too little. They are simply bad. The same is true of such qualities as goodness and honesty.

There is one famous example in the Greek list of virtues that we would not regard as a virtue: it is what they called "high-mindedness" or "magnanimity." This is the quality of a person who, as Aristotle describes him, is superior in talents, who knows he is superior, and who takes good care to let you know it too. He claims honor and public respect, but great honor will only mildly please

---

*Aristotle's *Rhetoric*, translated by W. Rhys Roberts. In Richard McKeon (ed.), *The Basic Works of Aristotle*. New York: Random House, 1941. Reproduced by permission.

him because he deserves this and a lot more. He is quite ready to confer benefits on other people but is too lofty to accept benefits from others. He keeps aloof from public matters, unless there is important business that demands his talents. He is not petty; he loves beautiful and useless possessions. "His step," Aristotle says, "is slow, his voice deep, and his speech sedate" (Book IV, iii).

Needless to say, this is hardly our notion of the ideal man and we would tend to regard such a person as somewhat less than charming. One only hopes Aristotle is not describing himself in this sketch.

But if the mean is a relative thing that differs for different people (and even for the same people in different situations), so that no precise rules can be laid down as to what it might be at any one time, how does one go about determining it? Aristotle replies that it requires knowledge and wisdom, and this is why to attain happiness we need to attend not only to the moral virtues but also to the intellectual virtues.

However, what Aristotle now says about the attainment of these intellectual virtues is discouraging, for it soon becomes apparent that if he is right, only few of us can hope to achieve true happiness. For the perfection of the intellectual virtues, although indispensable in keeping the passions in check, is now described as having a value and purpose all its own. The goodness of intellect that makes possible the goodness of character, which brings happiness, is itself, we are now told, intrinsically finer and higher than anything else available to us.

What follows is not an elaborate account of the use of intelligence in the formation of character, but an eloquent defense and description of the contemplative life. Summarizing its values, he declares that this theoretic or contemplative life is superior to the merely practical life, because "the intellect is the highest thing in us, and the objects that it apprehends are the highest things than can be known"; it is more lasting than other activities; purer and more pleasurable than them; and as the highest human activity, it is most like that of the gods and tends to bring us closer to them.

> The man who exercises his intellect and cultivates it seems likely to be in the best state of mind and to be most loved by the gods. For if, as is generally supposed, the gods have some concern for human affairs, it would be reasonable to believe also that they take pleasure in that part of us which is best and most closely related to themselves (this being the intellect), and that they reward those who appreciate and honor it most highly; for they care for what is dear to them, and what they do is right and good. Now it is not hard to see that it is the wise man that possesses these qualities in the highest degree; therefore he is dearest to the gods. And it is natural that he should also be the happiest of men. So on this score too the wise man will be happy in the highest degree. (Book X, viii)

Aside from the irony that the highest activity a human is capable of, and which is most characteristic, turns out to be divine rather than human, this opinion must strike us as overintellectual and elitist. Also, we have gotten very far away from that severely afflicted infant with whom we began this chapter, who will obviously never achieve the kind of happiness, let alone blessedness, here described. Does this mean its life is of no value, or will be of no value, to itself or others?

But the position taken here by Aristotle not only excludes that unfortunate infant, but many others as well. For if Aristotle is correct, it means that the "good life" is possible only to a very few people, those who have the requisite degree of intellect, as well as the combination of all of those other qualities—health, wealth, family, and so on. One is tempted to ask, why should we believe that there is only one true road to happiness and that it is produced only by this single activity? Why should not a life devoted to service and good works, to the appreciation and production of beautiful things, lead to an equally happy and fulfilling life? Certainly most of us would be inclined to believe that composers, sculptors, painters, and so on, no less than scientists and philosophers, have it in their power to achieve the same heights of human perfection. And why draw the line at artists? The social activist, the reformer, the teacher, even the humble craftsman, why should we think that true happiness—assuming their work is satisfying to them—is eternally closed to them?

It is difficult to resist the thought that Aristotle's selection of the intellectual life as the supremely happy one displays an element of egocentrism. This does not mean that the view must therefore be mistaken; although biased, it may nevertheless be true.

But what seems even more revealing is that we seem to have in Aristotle's ethics an example of that very characteristic relation between a philosopher's thought and the cultural setting in which it arises, for it is difficult not to see in Aristotle's elaborate analysis and definition of virtue as a mean between extremes an attempt to provide a philosophical justification of the moral convictions of his own age and culture, as conveyed, for example, in the famous Delphic exhortation "Nothing in Excess."

Although living at a different time and place, we still find this commendable. But what a modern reader may find somewhat less commendable about Aristotle's ethical doctrine is not its cultural ethnocentrism but its egoism. Apparently, the happiness the virtuous man is to seek is not anyone else's but his own. I am obliged, says Aristotle, to look after only myself. We do indeed find Aristotle instructing us in such altruistic virtues as honesty, generosity, friendship, and so on, but their justification is not that they will increase the general happiness but that these things are desirable for me to have.

Yet on a more sympathetic note and in Aristotle's defense, we can see that if it is true that in order for happiness to be gotten we must cultivate and realize certain potentialities in us, then such happiness can only be gotten by attending to ourselves. And if such happiness was realized, the society could not help but benefit.

However, we might nevertheless ask, what happens when my good and the good of others come into conflict? What ought I to do then? It is one of the major limitations of Aristotle's ethics that this problem is hardly addressed by him — to say nothing of the way he would have been inclined to answer it.

The attempt to deal with this very sort of problem — Whose good ought I choose in case of conflict? — is what distinguishes the ethics of the modern period from that of the ancient period.

Kant's theory of ethics

Immanuel Kant (1724–1804) is without question the greatest figure in modern philosophy. He revolutionized practically every field of investigation he touched, including ethics, which is our present concern.

Kant was born in Königsberg, a seaport in East Prussia. He lived in or near this small city all his life, never traveling more than a few miles from it. His parents belonged to the lower middle class and were members of a devout Prot-

Immanuel Kant. Mary Evans Picture Library, London.

estant evangelical sect called Pietists. They were all deeply religious and Kant himself remained so all his life.

Kant entered the University of Königsberg at the age of 16, intending to embark upon a career in theology. By 22, however, both parents died and, along with his three sisters and one brother, he now had to make his own way as best he could. He supported himself for the next nine years by being a private tutor in several families of the East Prussian nobility.

At age 31 he returned to the University for further study. Upon completing his doctorate, he was appointed instructor, remaining in that position for 15 years. In 1770, at the age of 46, he was finally elevated to the position of professor, which he held to his retirement in 1797.

Although originally intending to embark upon a career in theology, Kant gradually found himself attracted to science, and then finally to philosophy.

Kant's first published work was not in theology nor philosophy but in physics. Its title was *Theory of the Heavens* and it was published in 1755. For 25 years after this work appeared, he published only occasional papers, using his time to formulate his own original and revolutionary philosophy.

Then in one decade he published five great works: *Critique of Pure Reason* (1781); *Prolegomena to Every Future System of Metaphysics* (1783); *Foundations of the Metaphysics of Morals* (1785); *Critique of Practical Reason* (1788); and *Critique of Judgment* (1790). Two of these five works deal with ethics, and the first of them, the *Foundations of the Metaphysics of Morals*, is considered one of the most important works ever written on the subject.

The regularity of Kant's life has become a byword: he rose, took his coffee, wrote, lectured, took his daily walk — always at precisely the same hour. His neighbors, it was said, would set their watches when he stepped out of his house each day at half past four to walk up and down his small avenue, now named after him. In the evening he abandoned himself to meditation, gazing abstractly at the tower of a neighboring church.

It may seem ironic in light of the retiring nature of his life, but nevertheless not uncharacteristic of his thought, that of the many social and political events of his day, those which most attracted his attention and with which he was in greatest sympathy, were the American and French Revolutions.

"Ethics," Kant says, putting himself with that remark in strict opposition to the view we have just discussed, "is not the doctrine of how to make ourselves happy, but of how we are to be worthy of happiness." To make happiness, as Aristotle does, the supreme principle of morality, is to miss what is central to it — the obligation we are all under to do what is right.

For there is nothing morally admirable (or for that matter moral) about a person seeking his own happiness; but there is something worthy of admiration about a person who, in the face of overwhelming dangers, does his duty and does it for no other reason than that it is his duty. The difference between the moral and immoral person, furthermore, is not that one is wise and the other foolish, that one knows what will lead to happiness and the other doesn't, but that one is good and the other is bad, one does what is right, whether it will bring him happiness or not, and the other is concerned only with his welfare.

But what makes a person good? Possession, Kant answers, of the only thing that is good without qualification, and this is a "good will."

What this "good will" is, and how we might come to recognize it, is the task Kant sets himself to explain in his little book which bears the imposing title *Foundations of the Metaphysics of Morals*. It opens with these remarks:

> Nothing in the world—indeed nothing even beyond the world—can possibly be conceived which could be called good without qualification except a *good will*. Intelligence, wit, judgment, and the other talents of the mind, however they may be named, or courage, resoluteness, and perseverance as qualities of temperament, are doubtless in many respects good and desirable. But they can become extremely bad and harmful if the will, which is to make use of these gifts of nature and which in its special constitution is called character, is not good. It is the same with the gifts of fortune. Power, riches, honor, even health, general well-being, and the contentment with one's condition which is called happiness, make for pride and even arrogance if there is not a good will to correct their influence on the mind and on its principles of action so as to make it universally conformable to its end. It need hardly be mentioned that the sight of a being adorned with no feature of a pure and good will, yet enjoying uninterrupted prosperity, can never give pleasure to a rational impartial observer. Thus the good will seems to constitute the indispensable condition even of worthiness to be happy. (p. 9)*

Kant does not deny, as we see from this opening statement, that there are many things in the world that may be regarded as good, and he lists a number of them for us, but he maintains that none of them are *absolutely* good. These things, he suggests, are morally good only if the will that directs them is good; and unless so directed they may in fact turn out to be bad (as in the case of great intelligence in a criminal).

A good will, then, does not derive its goodness, according to Kant, from being directed to the achievement of intelligence, courage, or wealth; for these things are good only when directed by a will that is already good. The goodness of the will is derived rather from the use of such faculties and gifts as intelligence, courage, and wealth in the service of duty.

What does this mean? A will to act from duty, Kant explains, follows the dictates not of desire or inclination, but of pure reason. It is the will of one who does the right thing not because that is what he wants to do, or because of the good consequences he sees will follow from it, but because it is what pure reason

*Translated by Louis White Beck (New York: Bobbs-Merrill,1969).

demands of him. And only actions springing from such a motive are, according to Kant, deserving of moral praise and respect.

Let us consider some examples. Suppose you were accosted by a beggar and you gave him money, but only because you wished to be rid of him. Kant would say of such an action that, although not morally bad, yet it does not deserve moral praise. You may have acted, he would say, in accordance *with* duty (you did what was right), but not *from* a sense of duty (*because* it was right).

The following example will make the meaning of this distinction clearer. Suppose you are playing chess and a child walks up to the table and without knowing the game, its rules, or even taking time to consider his action, moves your knight two squares up and one to the right (which is, as we know, the prescribed manner for the movement of a knight). Suppose further that not only was the move a permissable one but an excellent one. Now, we can say of the child that he has made a move, a good move, *in accordance with* the rules. However, to make a move *from* the rules (or duty) would require not only knowledge of the game, its permitted moves, and its goals, but also the will to follow its strictures.

To return now to our beggar example. Suppose now you were a completely warm-hearted person who delights in spreading joy around you, and you gave this beggar money for no other reason than simply because you wanted to. Kant would say of this action that it was the gratification of some desire. Certainly what you did, he would say, was not bad, but it is not morally praiseworthy either. You did it, he would say, merely for your own satisfaction. Such actions, he would add, may deserve encouragement, but not moral esteem.

But now suppose that you gave this beggar money not because you wanted to get rid of him, or because you felt kindly disposed toward him, but rather because you felt duty-bound to do so. Then and only then, says Kant, does your action have moral worth, for an action arising from that motive springs from a good will.

To make the meaning of such a will still clearer, Kant goes on to distinguish between two major types of "imperatives," as he calls them, that may direct our will.

There are first what we might call "technical" imperatives that command us to do certain things if we want to achieve certain ends. Thus, if it is our ambition to become a concert artist, such an imperative tells us that we must practice at least so many hours each day. However, we do not absolutely have to become concert artists, and should we decide not to, we are under no obligation to practice.

Similarly, there are certain "prudential" imperatives, which· tell us, for example, that if we want to enjoy ourselves we ought to go see the new play. But again, it is not absolutely necessary that we enjoy ourselves, and if we don't care to, we are under no obligation to do what we are inclined to.

These technical and prudential imperatives, Kant points out, are purely "hypothetical"; that is, they are conditional on certain wishes we may have, and, should we cease to have the wishes, they cease to bind us. The "oughts"which figure in them are therefore not *moral* oughts: if we don't care to become concert artists, or be entertained, we are not doing anything wrong in not practicing or not going to the new play.

But when *ought* is used in a distinctly moral sense, the imperative is not hypothetical but "categorical." For example, when we say to someone, "You ought to pay your debts" we mean that he ought to do so whether he wants to or not, or whether or not he will gain something by doing it. Such an "ought" is unconditional and is not preceded or followed by an "if." On the contrary, should we add an "if" to it (as in, "If you want people to trust you"), it immediately becomes a hypothetical, or conditional, imperative, and ceases to be moral. The person, Kant would say, who pays his debts for that reason is not acting from a pure motive, and therefore is not acting morally. That is not to say, of course, that he is acting immorally. It is merely that an act motivated in that way is not worthy of moral esteem.

But why, one might ask, should we be moral, honest, pay our debts, and so forth? Why should we do what these "categorical imperatives" command?

It is interesting that Kant's answer is not unlike that given by Aristotle although its elaboration is very different. It is that it would be unworthy of us as human beings to do otherwise. For to be human, as Kant explains, is to be rational, and to act as a human being, therefore, is to act rationally. It is, he explains — expanding on what he said earlier, to possess a will that is motivated to act, not by impulses or feeling, but by reason. Since the essence of reason (unlike impulse and feeling) is consistency, and the test of consistency is universal validity, an action in order to be rational must be motivated by a principle of conduct that is universally valid and binding. For just as it is characteristic of reason in the realm of science and mathematics to produce principles that are universally and necessarily true, so it must be characteristic of the principles issued by reason in the realm of human action and conduct to be universally valid and binding.

So to be rational in conduct, according to Kant, is to act on principles that can be willed to be universal; it is to act on principles that apply to every situation and to everyone equally. The person who is rational will not act on one principle in one situation and on another in a precisely similar situation, for that would be inconsistent and irrational. Nor will he try to make an exception in his own case, for that too would be inconsistent and irrational. For the rational (and therefore moral) person will realize that whatever is morally right for him, is right for all, and whatever is morally wrong for him, is also morally wrong for all. That, for Kant, is the essence of what it is to be moral.

Kant's basic and fundamental principle of morality thus becomes a philosophical version of the golden rule: do unto others what you would have them do unto you — or as Kant expressed it: "Act on that maxim and that maxim only, which you can at the same time will to be a universal law."

This, finally, is Kant's supreme principle of morality, his principle of universality, as it has come to be called. It is also, as we can now see more clearly, what he means when he says that to have a good will is to act out of respect for law — not out of respect for some particular law, but for law as such, respect for universality which is the form of law, respect for a law which has no exceptions and is the same for all. A person who succeeds in acting in this manner can be said to act from a sense of duty (he does what reason demands of him), and from a motive that is pure.

Kant offers the following example:

> A man finds himself forced by need to borrow money. He well knows that he will not be able to repay it, but he also sees that nothing will be loaned him if he does not firmly promise to repay it at a certain time. He desires to make such a promise, but he has enough conscience to ask himself whether it is not improper and opposed to duty to relieve his distress in such a way. Now, assuming he does decide to do so, the maxim of his action would be as follows: When I believe myself to be in need of money, I will borrow money and promise to repay it, although I know I shall never do so. Now this principle of self-love or of his own benefit may very well be compatible with his whole future welfare, but the question is whether it is right. He changes the pretension of self-love into a universal law and then puts the question: How would it be if my maxim became a universal law? He immediately sees that it could never hold as a universal law of nature and be consistent with itself; rather it must necessarily contradict itself. For the universality of a law which says that anyone who believes himself to be in need could promise what he pleased with the intention of not fulfilling it would make the promise itself and the end to be accomplished by it impossible; no one would believe what was promised to him but would only laugh at any such assertion as vain pretense (p. 40).

Just as Kant's principle of universality will be recognized as a philosophical version of the golden rule, so his question, "How would it be if my maxim became a universal law?" will be recognized as our ordinary question, "What if everybody behaved that way?"

Kant's formulation of this question, however, makes us see a good deal more clearly that what is wrong with everybody behaving that way is not that it would be unpleasant if they did, but rather that it would make lying, breaking promises, and so on self-defeating and pointless. For if everybody lied, nobody would believe anybody, and lying promises would defeat themselves. That is why, as Kant insists, willing such a thing is a contradiction, for obviously if there is to be any point to lying, it must occur as the exception, not as the rule.

And this is precisely what the immoral person does, in fact, want. He wants to make an exception in his own favor in respect to a rule which others must observe if he is to succeed in gaining his ends. It is not that he doesn't know the principle behind his action or the nature of the principle it would contradict. He knows all this but wishes to be treated differently. On the other hand the moral person does not try to make any exceptions for himself. He treats himself and others on the same basis. And for Kant that is ultimately the test of what is right and wrong, moral and immoral.

As inspiring and elevated an account of ethics as this may be, it is not without its difficulties. Let us consider here only those surrounding the ambiguity of the term "universal." Suppose one were to agree to act on Kant's principle of universality. One agreed, that is to say, to do only those things which can be universalized and not do anything that cannot. But by taking specific circumstances into account such a person could easily cheat: he could will that if anyone ever found himself in exactly the circumstances he now finds himself in, he may lie. In such a case the principle would not appear to forbid lying, yet by extending to anyone in this kind of situation the same privilege, it would continue to be "universal."

It is apparent, however, from Kant's writings that his intention was to forbid such a thing as lying entirely. But that would be possible only if his principle is taken in its most general sense (do not lie now, unless you are willing that anyone should lie at *any* time in *any* situation). But taken in such an unqualified sense, the principle suffers from the opposite difficulty — it is now too rigorous for most people. For suppose telling a lie will save an innocent life? Most of us would probably justify such a lie.

Kant's principle, therefore, seems either too restrictive or too permissive, and in cases of conflict between maxims (between telling the truth or saving an innocent life) it appears unhelpful.

In the case of the severely afflicted baby in the hospital, all parties could probably invoke Kant's principle in their support: the physician who stopped feeding orders and the mother of the baby could justify their decision by applying the principle narrowly; their critics could condemn their decision by applying Kant's principle rigorously.

But let us return to Kant's theory and note the way it deals with another type of objection. Suppose someone enquired of Kant's theory, "But why should we treat each other equally? Why indeed tell the truth, try to avoid the contradiction involved in making false promises, and so on? "To this sort of question Kant would answer that it is wrong to treat each other in this manner, because to do so is to turn each other into things when we are not things but persons, possessing absolute intrinsic worth. I am not, Kant would say, merely a-source-of-money-for-someone but a person, and being a person I am an end-in-myself, not a means or an instrument for someone else's end. When, however, we do such things as lie and cheat we treat each other as things, and this is both demeaning and unworthy of us.

The principle of universality instructs us, therefore, in Kant's new formulation of this principle: "Act so that you treat humanity, whether in your own person or in that of another, always as an end and never as a means only." The principle doesn't say never treat anyone "as a means"; it says never treat anyone "as a means only." There are times when we serve each other's needs. This is unavoidable. But we can avoid treating each other as mere means.

We hear a great deal nowadays about the "human condition," but what seems to have interested Kant most was not so much the human condition as the condition under which we are human. For him that condition was our reason.

To make it even clearer how the possession of reason endows man with absolute worth and places him in a unique position in the hierarchy of creation, Kant compares man's state, first with animals, and then with God. Central to his view and description are, again, the claims made on us by the emotional and rational sides of our nature.

As we saw, a good will does not derive its goodness from being directed to the achievement of intelligence, courage, wealth, and so on; its goodness comes rather from the use of these faculties in the service of duty. Reason, however, as we well know, does not always and infallibly determine the direction of our will, but does so only within limits. Not having full control over his will, man comes to experience the dictates of reason, Kant points out, as obligation — a feeling only he can experience, that comes to him in the form of a command or an imperative. Now when man follows the dictates of reason against the urges of desire and inclination and does what it demands, then his will can be said to be morally good.

Animals, not being subject to this conflict between duty and inclination, are incapable of that experience of obligation. An animal may indeed find itself torn between one want and another, but never between want and duty. An animal, therefore, being wholly determined by its natural inclinations, can be said to be innocent, and not, like man, either morally good or evil.

God, being perfect, has a will that is perfectly rational. His will and His reason coincide and there is never any tension between them. While an animal therefore is below the level of duty, God is above it. God, furthermore, may know the moral law, but He can have no desires that could possibly conflict with that law. God, that is, acts in conformity with the moral law, but He does so as a matter of course. God's will is therefore holy. Man, on the other hand, who never performs his duty as a matter of course but is always subject to desire, may be morally good but never holy.

Man, therefore, unlike animals or God, is a creature who belongs to two worlds at once — the world of sense and the world of reason — and unlike both is neither innocent nor holy but, depending on whether he does what reason commands, is either good or evil.

We are thus inevitably led to the question, the most fundamental of all, "Is man, however, free to do what reason demands?" Although Kant touches on this question here, he takes it up more fully in the *Critique of Practical Reason*, his second major work dealing with ethics. The conclusions he arrives at there are as follows: (1) we must be free, since the obligation to be moral (to do what reason demands) would make no sense were we not free to carry out such demands; (2) our souls must be immortal, for we are enjoined by reason to seek perfection, but this life alone is too brief to achieve it, hence we must survive this life to continue our striving toward that goal; and (3) God must exist, for reason tells us that a good man ought to be happy. But goodness and happiness do not go together in this world, hence there must be a Being who is all-knowing (and therefore can see through to our inner motives) and all-powerful (and therefore can reward us for them) and Who, being also all-good, will apportion happiness to goodness.

Kant is careful to point out that these are only postulates; he has no proof that what they assert is so. But if we cannot know that they are true, he urges, we also cannot know that they are not, hence belief in them is not irrational.

Whether true or not, however, these postulates are certainly not unfamiliar to us. They represent, obviously, some of the major tenets of Judaeo-Christian teaching about our earthly duties and future rewards. Kant's ethics, no less than Aristotle's, are, therefore, in good part a reflection of his age and culture.

But a philosophy is not merely a summary and reflection of the thought and experience of a particular period and people. Often it is groundbreaking, anticipating developments yet to take place or whose full impact has yet to be felt, and this is certainly the case with Kant's philosophy. If it is not difficult, therefore, to recognize in his postulates and in his principle of universality the influence of his religious heritage, so similarly it is not difficult for us to recognize in his further formulation of his fundamental principle (that we treat all men as ends and never merely as means) a philosophical expression of the equalitarian ideal represented by the two great social and political events of his age — the Industrial Revolution on the one hand, and the American and French Revolutions on the other.

Although the full impact of these vast social and political changes did not go unrecognized by Kant, their implications were not fully comprehended at Kant's writing. When this took place in the next century, it gave rise to ethical theories that were better suited than Kant's to take account of the new phenomena created by these events. A society of plenty with a growing awareness of its rights had arisen, and utilitarianism, as we will see, became its philosophical voice.

The utilitarian theory

Jeremy Bentham

Jeremy Bentham (1748–1832) was the founder of utilitarianism. The son of a well-to-do London lawyer, Bentham was sent to Oxford, destined for a legal career. But his temperament and his awareness of the plight of the working people of his time made him abandon the idea of a legal career. He decided instead to devote himself to the task of legal reform.

There was much to reform. The existing condition of England, soon to be so realistically described by Charles Dickens, with its workhouses, debtors' prisons,

Jeremy Bentham. Mary Evans Picture Library, London.

and slums, was shocking, and Bentham determined to correct them. He set about doing so not by taking to the streets but by working out a scientific system of law.

His father's generosity provided him with the financial independence to carry out the program he set himself. There now flowed from his pen a series of writings, the most famous of which was his *Principles of Morals and Legislation*, published in 1789. These works, and the ideas they proclaimed, gained him wide recognition, and there soon formed around him a group of like-minded intellectuals who, fired by his humanitarian ideals, pressed for social and political reforms.

Bentham died in 1832, aware that Parliament was about to pass its first reform bill—a landmark piece of legislation and a notable personal triumph for the man who, more than anyone else, had paved the way for its realization.

Bentham's main work, the *Principles of Morals and Legislation*, opens with this statement: "Nature has placed mankind under the governance of two sovereign masters, *pain* and *pleasure*. It is for them alone to point out what we ought to do, as well as to determine what we shall do."

Bentham's brief opening statement asserts two separate doctrines. One is descriptive, claiming that the motive which governs our actions is desire for pleasure; the other is ethical or normative, stating what our standard for action ought to be. One is a statement concerning the way things are, the other is a proposal concerning the way they ought to be.

This would seem to be an inauspicious way to open a work on ethics, for if pain and pleasure determine our decisions, there would seem to be no point, the matter having thus already been decided, to go on to say what we ought to do. The advice would seem to be either unnecessary or futile.

But Bentham embraces these two standpoints purposely, their contradiction being for him only apparent. Nature has indeed arranged things so that we are guided by our desire for happiness, but unfortunately we are burdened with mistaken notions of what happiness is, and an investigation to see how it might best be secured is therefore neither unnecessary nor doomed to failure.

The pleasure or happiness Bentham has in mind, as he very soon tells us, is not each person's *own* happiness or pleasure (as his predecessors, the ancient Greek hedonists, had maintained) but rather, in the words of his famous slogan, "the greatest happiness of the greatest number." In considering a course of action, what we have to be concerned with, he argues, is not merely our own pleasure but the amount of pleasure the action is likely to bring to all those whose interests are at stake.

This is Bentham's new principle. It maintains that there is only one way to determine whether something is right or wrong, good or bad, and this is by considering its usefulness or "utility" in bringing about pleasant results. An action is right, it says, if it brings about more happiness than any other possible action; it is wrong, if some other possible action could have produced more happiness.

Since, according to Bentham, what is right, good, and best is that which produces the most happiness, and happiness is simply a condition in which pain is outweighed by pleasure, it is obviously important to try to arrive at as clear an understanding of the nature of pleasure as possible. And this is what Bentham now proceeds to do. He proposes a kind of "hedonistic calculus," as he calls it, which we might use in evaluating pleasures, based on the seven ways in which, according to him, pleasures vary.

Before a particular course of action is adopted, to conform to the new principle of utility he is recommending, we should evaluate the pleasurable results anticipated by asking ourselves such questions as: (1) How intense are the pleasures? (2) How long can we expect them to last? (3) How certain are we they will occur? (4) How immediate or remote are they? (5) What is their chance of being followed by sensations of the same kind? (6) What is their chance of being followed by sensations of the opposite kind? and, finally, (7) How many other people will share in them? If after considering these seven different factors (the *intensity* of the pleasures, their *duration, certainty, propinquity, fecundity, purity,* and *extent*) it is discovered that the pleasures exceed the pains, then the action is right: if not, then it is wrong.

What strikes one most about Bentham's list is that an important ingredient of pleasure, namely its quality, seems to be missing, and that this omission must be an oversight. But this is not so. Desiring to keep his standard as simple and as practicable as possible, and being by nature suspicious of undue complexity, Bentham purposely omits it from the calculus. The only thing that matters as far as pleasures and pains are concerned, he asserts, is their quantity, not their quality. The quality of pleasure being equal, he was bold to remark, pushpin is as good as poetry — a remark that led his critics to call his new version of hedonism a "pig philosophy." But Bentham was undaunted: the source of pleasure, he felt, was irrelevant; what mattered was the amount of it after any unpleasantness or pain had been subtracted from it.

Bentham proposes, therefore, that we begin to measure and calculate our pleasures and pains in the same way and in the same spirit scientists measure and calculate the motion of bodies in space. Anticipating the question whether anyone ever has or would engage in this kind of calculation, Bentham replies (*Introduction to the Principles of Morals and Legislation*, p. 4):

> There are some who may look upon the nicety employed in the adjustment of such rules as so much labor lost: for gross ignorance, they will say, never troubles itself about laws, and passion does not calculate. But the evil of ignorance admits of cure: and when matters of such importance as pain and pleasure are at stake, and these in the highest degree, who is there that does not calculate? Men calculate, some with less exactness, indeed, and some with more: but all men calculate.

Although all men thus calculate, they do not unfortunately all do so in the right way, for they calculate their own pleasure or happiness, not, as they should, the greatest happiness of the greatest number.

It would be a simple matter to get them to calculate properly, says Bentham, if they were not by nature egoistic and selfish, but they are and we cannot change them.

What, then, is to be done? How are we to reconcile this ideal of universalism or altruism with the reality of egoism?

Seeing this as the main problem not only of ethics but of government as well, Bentham makes a proposal designed as a corrective for both. It is true, he says, we must leave men the way they are, for we cannot change them. Nevertheless we can get them to behave in a manner which will be for the good of all by making this course of action pay them personally. We can see to it, he says, that to deviate from the path of social good costs a man so much that he won't do so. By seeking his own good, such a person will then act in a way as to realize the maximum good for society.

Bentham did not need to look far to observe such a system of "sanctions," as he calls them, already at work. There were, first of all, the sanctions to be found in physical nature, operating to bring happiness to men who act in one way and pain (when they overeat for example) when they act in another; then there were the political and legal sanctions exacted by the law; the social sanctions of public opinion; and, finally, the sanctions of religion with its fear of divine punishment and promise of heavenly reward.

But the trouble is, Bentham argued, that in any existing society the sanctions applying to conduct are irrational. They have grown up in a haphazard manner and are now themselves the cause of much misery. They need to be made more reasonable by being brought into an orderly system on the basis of some first principle.

Take, for example, he said, our penal laws. Describing the shocking conditions in the prisons, Bentham pointed out how unnecessarily severe the punishments were. They inflicted more pain than was necessary in order to redirect conduct into socially desirable lines. Since pain is always evil, this was wrong. We need to inflict, he said, just that amount necessary to prevent a greater evil. To use more is unjustified and irrational.

The same is true, he urged, of the other areas of our life, arguing in the process, among other things, for a different sort of government (a democracy instead of a monarchy, for only where there is an identity between the rulers and the ruled will their interests be the same and the greatest happiness of the greatest number be assured) and less of it (since there is much the government tries to control that is really a matter of private morals and not its business at all).

Although we are here interested only in Bentham's moral theory, it becomes obvious when he comes to talk about problems of legislation, prison reform, theory of punishment, and so on, that everything until now has been preparatory and that the whole purpose of the analysis of pleasure, the calculus, and the nature of human motivation has been to expose the abuses of his day and by holding up a mirror to his age bring about a more humane and just society.

The reformist tendency and dual interest was characteristic of all the utilitarians who gathered around Bentham. Feeling compassion for the misery of the poor laboring long hours in the rising network of workhouses and factories; angered by the complacency of many of the owners of these factories; and offended by the injustice of the prevailing system of distribution of profits, they set out to change the social, legal, and economic organization of society that gave rise to these conditions and that, despite the cruelties, people generally continued to tolerate.

Like Bentham, however, they were convinced that reform could be achieved only if based on sound principles concerning the nature of human motivation, law, society, and government. They therefore set about to study such disciplines as psychology, ethics, education, and politics, making profound contributions to each. In all these investigations, their basic principle was and remained the same: the principle of utility — only those actions, practices, and codes of law are worthy that promote the greatest happiness of the greatest number.

If that principle seems obvious to us now, it was far from appearing so to Bentham's contemporaries. To make it more acceptable, Bentham's followers went about the task of refining it. The most famous of these was John Stuart Mill.

John Stuart Mill

Bentham's most important immediate disciple was James Mill (1773–1836), the father of John Stuart Mill. In addition to the first comprehensive history of India, a work that brought him fame and fortune and eventually the headship of the East India Company, James Mill also devoted his talents to studies in psychology and education, believing that education could change life and that the civil liberties and democratic ideals he shared with Bentham could be realized by properly conducted education.

The birth of his son, John Stuart Mill, in 1806 gave James Mill an opportunity to test his theories. He subjected the boy to a course of studies that still seems remarkable to us, and with remarkable results.

Sending him neither to school nor university, he set him to learn Greek at the age of 3; arithmetic and English grammar soon afterwards; and Latin not until the boy reached the ripe old age of 4. By 6½ he had him compose a work on the history of Rome, replete with footnotes. Some years later, at the age of 12, he set him to work on logic, economics, and philosophy. Much of this young Mill had to work on by himself, discussing what he had learned with his father during their walks. To master these subjects further he was assigned the task of teaching them to his younger brothers and sisters. Nor, of course, was he spared the systematic study of utilitarian principles: at the age of 18 we find him in jail for handing out birth-control pamphlets in a working-class slum.

So intense was this personal tutoring that Mill was later to say of it that it put him a quarter of a century ahead of his contemporaries. It also, however, took

John Stuart Mill. Mary Evans Picture Library, London.

its toll, for at the age of 20 he suffered a mental breakdown, which he attributed to the overemphasis upon analysis without a parallel development of the emotions. He tried to correct this imbalance by immersing himself in the writings of Coleridge, Carlyle, and Wordsworth — the English romantic poets and essayists.

Although he claimed this helped him, what undoubtedly helped him even more to achieve the balance — which enabled him to go on to hold down a full-time position at the East India Company (rising eventually, like his father before him, to become its chief administrative officer), becoming the founder and editor of the important and influential *Westminister Review,* a member of Parliament, and so on — was his long romance with Mrs. Harriet Taylor, which began when he was 25 and whom he married many years later when her husband died. Aside from Bentham, she was the most dominant influence in his life and, essentially, the coauthor of a number of his works.

Of Mill's works, apart from his groundbreaking and historically significant *System of Logic* (1843), his best known is his classic work on *Liberty* (1859), whose elaborately reasoned and passionately asserted defense of the right of the individual to think and act for himself has never been surpassed. The case for liberty, he argues here, is its utility — its power to create, maintain, and augment the greatest happiness of the greatest number. In striking and memorable words he says of this work:

> The object of this Essay is to assert one very simple principle as entitled to govern absolutely the dealings of society with the individual in the way of compulsion and control, whether the means used be physical force in the form of legal penalties, or the moral coercion of public opinion. That principle is, that the sole end for which mankind are warranted, individually or collectively, in interfering with the liberty of action of any of their number, is self-protection. That the only purpose for which power can be rightly exercised over any member of a civilized community, against his will, is to prevent harm to others. His own good, either physical or moral, is not a sufficient warrant. He cannot rightfully be compelled to do or forbear because it will be better for him to do so, because it will make him happier, because, in the opinions of others, to do so would be wise or even right. These are good reasons for remonstrating with him or reasoning with him, or persuading him, or entreating him, but not for compelling him, or visiting him with any evil in case he do otherwise. To justify that, the conduct from which it is desired to deter him must be calculated to produce evil to someone else. The only part of the conduct of anyone, for which he is amenable to society, is that which concerns others. In the part which merely concerns himself, his independence is, of right, absolute. Over himself, over his own body and mind, the individual is sovereign.

With this ideal of liberty still uppermost in his mind, Mill went on to defend it in a work written two years later entitled *Considerations on Representative*

Government (1861). Those who are to live under laws, he argues here, should choose those who are to make and administer the laws, for only a government of such elected representatives can assure the greatest happiness of the greatest number.

Finally, in another work, almost a century ahead of its time — *The Subjection of Women* (1869) — he went on to extend the argument of his treatise on *Liberty* to the position of women in the modern world. This work contains a protest against their political, economic, professional and social subjection, and an impassioned plea for their emancipation. In the long run and from an overall point of view, he argues here, women's subjection works against the greatest happiness of the greatest number, and their emancipation works for it.

Mill died in 1873 at the age of 67. A religious publication noted his death with these words: "His death is a loss to no one, for he was a crass infidel, however harmless he may have seemed, and a very dangerous person. The sooner those 'luminaries of thought' who hold the same views as his go where he is gone, the better it will be for the Church and the State."

His reading of Bentham's works and assimilation of the principle of utility made a profound impression on Mill. As he tells us in his *Autobiography*, which was published after his death:

> This principle gave unity to my conceptions of things. I now had opinions, a creed, a doctrine, a philosophy, in one among the best senses of the word a religion; the inculcation and diffusion of which could be made the principal outward purpose of a life. And I had a grand conception laid before me of changes to be effected in the condition of mankind through that doctrine. The vista of improvement which Bentham opened was sufficiently large and brilliant to light up my life as well as to give a definite shape to my aspirations (pp. 66–67).

But Bentham's version of the principle had stirred up many critics, and in his own work on *Utilitarianism* (1863), Mill set out to try to restate it in a way that would answer these critics and make it more convincing and appealing.

Mill proceeded to introduce two major modifications in Bentham's theory, one concerning Bentham's psychological hedonism (his view of the way we are), the other concerning his ethical hedonism (what ought to count with us).

Concerning the first Mill argued that we are not necessarily so made as to seek only our own happiness. Whereas Bentham tended to reduce our altruistic feelings, on those rare occasions when he even acknowledged their existence, to feelings of self-interest, Mill believed they were founded in a certain primitive, gregarious instinct characteristic of all of us. We are naturally, he says, altruistic and self-sacrificing, and find our individual happiness by promoting the happiness of the group. Human beings, in short, according to Mill, are capable of impartial action.

Nevertheless it takes all kinds of people to make a world, and the more room the world has in it for the self-development and expression of different individual characters, the better chance everyone has to be happy. The greatest happiness of the greatest number can thus be attained only under conditions of the greatest possible individual freedom. Hence his advocacy, as we have seen, of the freedom of the individual, his defense of civil liberties, and his abhorrence of any form of regimentation and paternalism.

Second, Mill asserted that pleasures do differ in quality, and this difference affects their value. Instead of Bentham's quantitative hedonism, Mill thus posited a qualitative hedonism. Some pleasures are intrinsically superior to others.

> It is quite compatible with the principle of utility to recognize the fact, that some *kinds* of pleasure are more desirable and more valuable than others. It would be absurd that while, in estimating all other things, quality is considered as well as quantity, the estimation of pleasures should be supposed to depend on quantity alone.
> (*Utilitarianism*, Chapter 2, Paragraph 4).

Human beings have vast capacities for enjoying pleasures of many kinds. They have animal appetites, to be sure, but they also have higher faculties. And the pleasure derived from the exercise of these higher faculties are better than the purely sensuous pleasures. (This distinction was actually already present much earlier in philosophy. Epicurus, a Greek philosopher of the third and fourth centuries B.C., distinguished between the "higher pleasures," the rational and the aesthetic, and the "lower pleasures," eating, drinking, and generally sensual pleasures.) Persons who have experienced, Mill went on to maintain, both of these kinds of pleasure know this to be so:

> Few human creatures would consent to be changed into any of the lower animals, for a promise of the fullest allowance of a beast's pleasures; no intelligent human being would consent to be a fool, no instructed person would be an ignoramus, no person of feeling and conscience would be selfish and base, even though they should be persuaded that the fool, the dunce, or the rascal is better satisfied with his lot than they are with theirs.

And so Mill comes to the conclusion which he expressed in the following famous words:

> It is better to be a human being dissatisfied than a pig satisfied; better to be Socrates dissatisfied than a fool satisfied. And if the fool, or the pig,

are of a different opinion, it is because they only know their own side of the question. The other party to the comparison knows both sides.

(Chapter 2, Paragraph 6).

This issue is, of course, of tremendous practical consequence. In distributing tax money, for example, how we decide such questions will determine whether to subsidize opera houses and art galleries, catering to very refined tastes and which few people enjoy, or use such monies to build sports arenas.

But aside from the obvious different practical consequences entailed, the modification would seem to constitute an abandonment of pure hedonism, for if pleasures are now to be graded not for their quantity but for their quality, then pleasure is no longer the standard or criterion determining our choices. If pleasure, in other words, has to be judged in the light of some quality or qualities these pleasures have or have not, pleasure as such then ceases to be the standard of value, and this quality or these qualities become the new standard by which pleasure and, therefore, human conduct, are to be judged.

It is strange that Mill does not appear to realize the difficulty he has placed himself in by introducing this modification, which in effect constitutes an abandonment of pleasure as the criterion of true happiness and therefore of human goodness.

This difficulty emerges again most clearly when Mill comes to deal with the question of what is the most "desirable" mode of conduct for man, and argues that it is happiness, as utilitarianism teaches. But how can we prove that happiness is indeed the true and desirable end of human life and conduct? To this Mill replies (in what has become one of the most quoted passages in modern philosophical literature for the remarkable error it contains):

The only proof capable of being given that an object is visible, is that people actually see it. The only proof that a sound is audible, is that people hear it: and so of the other sources of our experience. In like manner, I apprehend, the sole evidence it is possible to produce that anything is desirable, is that people do actually desire it.

Obviously, however, "desirable" and "visible" and "audible" do not run on all fours, since *desirable* is not related to *desired* in the same way that *visible* is to *seen*. One involves a moral distinction which the other does not, for whereas *visible* means simply that something is *capable of being seen*, *desirable* implies that something is *worthy of being desired*, that it *ought* to be desired. This being so, it may be quite true that a thing's being seen proves that it is visible, but it does not follow that because a thing is desired it is for that reason desirable. Many people may desire dope, but that does not prove that dope is therefore "desirable."

To establish that some pleasure is desirable, or more desirable than some other, involves therefore more than establishing the bare fact that many desire it, and if this is so, then pleasure as such ceases to be the standard of value and something else takes its place. And this is the surprising consequence of Mill's modification of Bentham's version of hedonism.

Hedonism, the view that the end of human activity is, or ought to be, pleasure or happiness, is probably the most widespread ethical theory we have, and so it might perhaps be well to spend a little longer on it.

Concerning its ancient form — conveyed in the well-known saying "Eat, drink and be merry, lest tomorrow we die" — little need be said except perhaps that we may be around tomorrow to suffer the consequences, and so perhaps we had better eat, drink, and be merry in moderation.

Concerning the pursuit of pleasure, it has often been pointed out that the best way "to get pleasure is to forget pleasure," that pleasure or happiness is like a butterfly, which when pursued is always just beyond our grasp. But this objection is really somewhat beside the point, for the question is not how we can best get pleasure but rather whether pleasure is worth getting or pursuing.

Of course, in Bentham's view, as we have seen, we would seem to have no choice in this matter, for we are so endowed by nature that we cannot help but pursue pleasure. On the contrary, it is, in his view, the goal of all our striving.

In the view of many people, however, this would appear to be an astounding generalization to make about human motivation. As many critics have pointed out, it is one thing to say that a person gets pleasure from accomplishing the end of his action, but quite another to say that the expectation of that pleasure is the *reason* for acting. For example, I frequently eat because I am hungry. I may get pleasure from the food, but that is not my reason for eating. Sometimes, however, I eat even though I am not hungry, because I like the food that is offered and hope to get pleasure from eating it. But it is obviously wrong to confuse these two cases and claim that I *always* eat in order to get pleasure.

Similarly, I help my friend when he is ill and go to a lot of trouble to do so. When he finally gets well, I derive a great deal of pleasure. Now obviously my reason for helping him is to see that *he* gets well, not I. Were an egoist to suggest that I went to all this trouble only because of the pleasure I knew I would get from seeing my friend get well, we might reply that if I am the kind of person who gets pleasure from that sort of thing — from making *other* people happy — then that is what is meant by saying that some people are capable of impartial action or altruism.

To disprove psychological hedonism all we need is find one case of a true altruistic act. Are there such acts? We must first note that as psychological hedonism and altruism refer to motives, our finding of such an act and labeling it "altruistic" will be inferential. That is to say, we do not see, feel, smell, or touch motives, we infer them from acts. Consider the case, for instance, of the happy easy-going soldier who though in the prime of his life, financially well off, and with a generally bright future, covers a hand-grenade with his body to save his fellow soldiers. Such cases have happened more than once and are well recorded. The psychological hedonist cannot say that he did it for any future pleasure, for not only will he not have any future pleasure, he will not even have a future, and he was well aware of that. Nor can the psychological hedonist say that he did it to escape a bleak future, or to end some great pain or sorrow, since neither is true. It would thus seem we can find at least one class of acts that are both altruistic and clearly count against psychological hedonism. These acts could be roughly described as those done for another's good and to the exclusion of our own. If this is so, which seems obvious, then the psychological hedonist is refuted. On this issue of psychological hedonism, therefore, Mill rather than Bentham would seem to be closer to the truth.

Ethical hedonism, to turn to this doctrine, maintains two main theses: one, that pleasure is always intrinsically good; and, two, that it is the only thing that is intrinsically good. But if the first thesis is correct, what shall we say of the sadist who derives his pleasure from torturing others? We would normally regard such pleasure as bad, derived as it is from pain. So pleasure is not always good. And if the second thesis is correct, that pleasure is the only thing which is intrinsically good, what shall we say about such things as the development of our intellectual or artistic capacities? Are these not good in themselves? Many would claim that they indeed are. And of those ethical hedonists who, like Bentham, equate happiness with pleasure, might we not ask whether happiness does not ordinarily include more than just pleasure. And if it includes *only* pleasure, would we call a world in which we could produce it medically and did so, one in which happiness had finally been achieved?

Utilitarianism, to turn to it finally, instructs us that our goal is to seek the happiness of all. But, we might ask, first, does anyone know what happiness is? Doesn't the diversity of individual interests hint at the multiplicity of human goals? In addition, may not Bentham's critics have touched on an important point in suggesting that in trying to achieve happiness for everybody, we may only succeed in achieving the lowest denomination of happiness and ultimately a "pig philosophy"?

Second, we might note that in fulfilling what we feel to be our obligation, the general welfare is not always what is uppermost in our minds. At such times what we are concerned about are such things as personal loyalty, the sanctity of promise-keeping, and so forth — things that have little or nothing to do with promoting the general good.

Third, according to utilitarianism we must take the total number of effects of our action into consideration before describing it as right. But the effects may be far-reaching, and we may have to wait infinitely long before we can describe an act as right. The principle of utility, therefore, would seem to lose its utility, its practical value, in such circumstances.

Fourth, the theory would also seem to lead to various logical contradictions: an action X looks as if it will have the best consequences, so you do it; but tomorrow you discover its consequences are really very bad. Does this mean the act was right when you did it, but wrong now?

Finally, can any teleological theory, such as utilitarianism, be ultimately adequate? For suppose we could somehow succeed in making everyone happy except one person who would be tortured in hell. Would anyone be satisfied to say this is right? Presumably not.

The emotive theory

We began our study of ethics by considering a recent hospital case in which the physician in charge had stopped feeding orders for a newly born defective infant on the verge of dying, and we asked ourselves whether the physician's action was right. We noted how some of the physician's colleagues responded to that decision; what a member of the clergy said of it; and how, on the whole, other members of society reacted to it.

Although many people tend to decide matters like this by asking themselves such questions as: Would my colleagues approve? Would the church approve? Would society? the ethical theorist does not ask these questions, nor does he engage in what we might call *moralizing*, in giving advice.

On the contrary, the ethical theorist, at one level, is concerned, like Aristotle, in deciding such wider and much more general questions (in terms of which these more particular moral questions could be answered more adequately) as, What is the good life for man? What sort of life is worth preserving or living? What ends or goals of life are worth seeking? As we saw, these were some of the issues with which Aristotle's *Nicomachean Ethics* was concerned.

In addition and at another level, the ethical theorist, as we have seen, is concerned in arriving at principles by which such further ethical problems as, How ought man, insofar as he is a moral being, to behave? What is a person responsible for, and what duties should we recognize and attempt to fulfill? When does a person have moral worth? What is the right thing to do (regardless what people say, believe, or approve)? Those occupied with investigations of this sort are considered to be studying ethics proper, and we took note, in this connection, of two such major ethical theories: a deontological one (Kant's theory of ethics); and a teleological one (the utilitarian theory of ethics).

Although these theories were designed to provide us with moral principles and rules we might use as guidelines, they proved to be, as we saw, far from satisfactory. Each tried to define what was right or wrong, good or evil, but did so in ways that ultimately could not be satisfactory. Each theory assumed that its definition of right or wrong was correct, but could not prove it.

The inability to do so (not only on the part of these two particular theories but also on the part of many others that have been proposed) has led recent writers on ethics to suspect that the very effort may be doomed to failure. Physical theories, such writers have said, can be proven because they can be dealt with experimentally, but ethics presumes to deal not with what is but with what ought to be, and there would seem to be no way in which such a question can be settled experimentally.

Therefore instead of trying to add to the number of ethical systems already proposed, these writers have turned their attention to an investigation (not of what is right or wrong, good or evil) but of the meaning of such terms as "right" and "wrong," "good" and "evil." This investigation has acquired the name of metaethics.

The shift of direction this represents is neither untypical of philosophy nor unprecedented. When two philosophical positions confront each other in a seemingly irreconcilable fashion (as we saw happen earlier, for example, between Heraclitus and Parmenides), subsequent philosophers have found it valuable to turn to an examination of the terms of the dispute to see whether it does not perhaps grow out of a conceptual confusion.

The result of this shift of interest here, however, turned out to be more severe and extreme than had been the case earlier in philosophy. Finding that they could not *solve* the controversy, these philosophers went on to *dissolve* it. Moral pronouncements, they said, were neither true nor false, for they were neither ordinary pronouncements or statements but merely expressions of emotion. Generalizing from this, they went on to assert that human reason had nothing to discover in the area of ethics, for ethical statements, appearances to the contrary, have no factual content and tell us nothing — at least nothing objective.

It is important to realize that those who began to maintain this position (and we will look at their view in a moment) were not simply questioning the answers their philosophic predecessors had proposed; on the contrary, what they were doing was much more extreme. They were repudiating the whole undertaking by questioning the very questions their predecessors had posed. There was no such thing as ethics, they were saying, to be investigated.

Many have seen this new development in contemporary ethics as a re-emergence of ancient skepticism, most succinctly conveyed by the famous remark of the ancient sophist philosopher Protagoras, who had maintained that "Man is the measure of all things," meaning by this that it was no use to try to discover truth, for there was no such thing as truth but only opinions of different individuals. This sort of ethical skepticism has become once again, they said, the special mark of our age, which has seen the rise of skepticism on a scale seldom paralleled before.

These critics have suggested that this widespread and wholesale skepticism is the result of disenchantment with science and its inability to solve the problems of modern life. But if it is a product of the disenchantment with science, it seems also to be the product of the attempt to apply science and its methods and presuppositions to the area of human values, which in this case "cures" the subject but only by eliminating it.

Moritz Schlick

The leading spirit of this contemporary movement in philosophy was Moritz Schlick (1882–1936). The group Schlick gathered around him in the late nineteen-twenties, which came to be called "the Vienna Circle," is in many ways reminiscent of the group that had formed a century earlier around Bentham. They were fired by the same revolutionary fervor but their goal was very differ-

Moritz Schlick. Austrian National Library.

ent. Schlick was a professor of philosophy at the University of Vienna, and the group, which met weekly, was composed of other academic people working in the areas of science, philosophy, and mathematics. Their goal was to make philosophy scientific and rigorous, and they were determined to accept only those parts of it that were able to pass the most rigid scrutiny.

The test was verifiability: was the statement in question capable of being empirically verified? If it was not, then, strictly speaking, the statement was not meaningful. It was a pseudo-statement lacking cognitive significance.

By using this "verification principle," Schlick and his colleagues discovered that many of the traditional problems of philosophy (especially those in the area of religion and ethics) were really pseudo-problems, as the theories in question, although purporting to convey knowledge about the world, were incapable of empirical verification. Since so much of philosophy falls into this category, they came to believe that traditional philosophy was simply nonsense and needed to be superseded by the kind of positive activity they were engaging in, namely, exposing the nonsense of the past and replacing it with the logical clarification of the concepts and achievements of science. As a result their movement came to be known as Logical Positivism.

Schlick was shot to death in 1936 by one of his graduate pupils whose doctoral thesis on some moral topic Schlick had rejected. Although the man had been in a mental hospital, he seems to have been encouraged by Schlick's enemies. In reporting the incident, the right-wing press, although not going so far as to condone the crime, suggested that if one persisted in teaching students positivism, this was not a wholly unnatural way for them to react. With the subsequent rise of Hitler to power, many members of the Vienna Circle, as well as other positivists from Germany, emigrated to England and the United States, making these two countries the centers of philosophy in the twentieth century.

A. J. Ayer

The person probably most responsible for helping make this movement so widely known was the Oxford philosopher A. J. Ayer (1910–   ), who attended the meetings of the Circle in 1932–1933, meeting many of the major figures and discussing their work with them.

While still quite young, before his twenty-fifth birthday, Ayer published a little book, *Language, Truth and Logic,* describing the ideas of the new philosophical movement. The book was published by Victor Gollancz in January 1936 in an edition of 500 copies. To the surprise of the publisher it sold out quickly. Not believing a relatively technical philosophical treatise would have much more demand, the publisher issued a second printing of only 250 copies. These too were soon sold out, and another printing was issued. The book continued to enjoy a brisk sale even though the publisher refused to issue it in a paperback edition. When, years later, the New York publisher, Dover, finally did so, it became a phenomenal success, selling nearly 300,000 copies—an unprecedented number for a technical work in philosophy.

Although Ayer has written many other books in the intervening years, they

Alfred Jules Ayer

are still overshadowed by the fame (or notoriety) of this brilliantly and pungently written little classic. It remains today the best exposition of the logical positivist view.

In order to understand the bases for our moral beliefs, according to the proponents of this new philosophical movement, we need to examine the grounds on which beliefs of any kind can ultimately be said to be either true or false. Statements or propositions may be true, they assert, only in two ways: they may be true by definition, or they may be true as a matter of fact.

For example, "All bachelors are unmarried" is an example of the first type, since the predicate "unmarried" merely states the meaning of the subject ("bachelors"). The proposition is thus true by definition. To say that bachelors are married would be inconsistent and false. Nor do we need to take a poll of bachelors to see whether the statement is true. We recognize that it is true simply as a result of the meaning of the terms that figure in it.

The statement, on the other hand, "All bachelors are unhappy" may or may not be true. It would not be inconsistent or contradictory to say that some are *not* unhappy. And to discover whether they are or are not cannot be decided merely by examining the meaning of the words but only by conducting a poll — by making an empirical inquiry of the matter.

If the truth of a statement cannot be determined either from the meaning of the words (if the statement is true by definition) or by employing scientific methods of inquiry (if it is true in fact), then the statement, proponents of this view maintained, is devoid of cognitive meaning and is, strictly speaking, nonsensical. This would be true of a statement such as "God exists," which can neither be confirmed nor disconfirmed by the test of either logical consistency (it can easily be denied without contradiction) or observation (there being no conceivable way to obtain such evidence).

And the same is true, they maintained, of ethical statements containing words such as "ought" and "should," as "You ought to pay your debts," "Stealing is wrong," and so on. Such statements are neither true by definition nor true as a matter of fact. Not capable of verification, they are therefore neither true nor false. They are not statements that impart knowledge and are consequently, they maintained, nonsensical.

But if moral concepts and the judgments in which they occur are not real concepts and real judgments, what are they, and what is our purpose in using them? To this question the logical positivists replied that moral concepts and judgments are used to express and excite feelings. Rather than being real proposition, moral pronouncements are simply, as Ayer put it, expressions of emotions.

> The presence of an ethical symbol in a proposition adds nothing to its factual content. Thus if I say to someone, "You acted wrongly in stealing that money," I am not stating anything more than if I had simply said, "You stole that money." In adding that this action is wrong I am not making any further statement about it. I am simply evincing my moral disapproval of it. It is as if I had said, "You stole that money," in a peculiar tone of horror, or written it with the addition of some special exclamation marks. The tone, or the exclamation marks, adds nothing to the literal meaning of the sentence. It merely serves to show that the expression of it is attended by certain feelings in the speaker.
>
> (*Language, Truth, and Logic*, p. 107).

Because such assertions are not descriptive but "emotive" they are unverifiable and factually nonsensical. "They are unverifiable," Ayer says, "for the same reason as a cry of pain, or a word command is unverifiable — because they do not express genuine propositions" (pp. 108–109). Such statements are no different from such ejaculations as "Hurrah!" or "Boo!"

A proposition, therefore, like "Stealing is wrong," according to Ayer, has no factual meaning and expresses nothing that is either true or false. It expresses only a person's moral sentiments, the word "wrong" having only an "emotive" use, expressing certain feelings about certain things, not making any assertions about them. The reason, therefore, why it has been impossible to find agreement upon criteria for determining the validity of ethical judgments (some saying it is "pleasure," others saying it is "duty," and still others "the greatest happiness of the greatest number," and so forth) is simply that ethical judgments have no objective validity.

But one problem remains: if this theory is right in maintaining that it is impossible to argue about purely ethical matters, that although in such confrontations there may be a clash of subjective attitudes, there can be no logical contradiction, why does it nevertheless seem to be otherwise? We do engage in ethical disputes, we do offer arguments, and do seem to believe they could make a difference in people's decisions and actions. How could we be so deceived about this?

To this question emotivists have two answers. The first is that ethical statements are designed not only to express our feelings of approval but also to induce like feelings in others. The expression "X is good" is similar to the more complex expression "I approve of X, do so also." Although, therefore, people do not contradict each other when they disagree as to whether X is good (each simply expressing different attitudes about X), each nevertheless attempts to induce the other to adopt *his* attitude to X. So such clashes are really attempts to change each other's feelings.

The second answer is that ethical disputes may really be rooted in disagreements concerning the facts of the case, without, however, the disputants being aware of this. When they come to realize that their dispute is really a factual one, it is quickly resolved and what remains, if disagreement still continues, is not a disagreement in belief (about what is or is not so) but rather of subjective attitudes to it.

Ethical assertions, according to the emotivists, are thus ultimately reducible to the basic contention that "I like so and so, you don't." To accept emotivism is to accept by implication that we could *never* truthfully utter the following line, "I know this act is right but I don't want it to happen." But does such a possibility really seem so outlandish? Consider the devoted wife of an admitted villain who is about to be put to death for his crimes. It seems very clear and indeed very plausible that she may in a very serious and somber mood say "I know he deserves it, and it is right for him to die, but I don't want it to happen." Yet if she can say this, or if anyone can say this, it means that "X is right" and "I like X or would like to see X happen" cannot mean the same thing, as emotivists would like us to believe they do.

Emotivism is a view that very few find convincing. The majority of people tend to believe that emotivism might be true in culinary matters, but not where right and wrong, good and evil, are concerned. In moral matters, they maintain, it is not simply a matter of getting others to like what we like, for no other reason than that we like it. If "Bah!" and "That is wrong" have the same import, the moral utterances, they would say, have no more significance than the utterances of cows who make use of similar expressions of delight or annoyance. We would like to think, however, that our expressions of annoyance or approval are somehow more deeply grounded.

Goodness and happiness

We began our investigation of ethics by noting that one of its major concerns was to define the nature of the good life, the sort of life that is worth living. In each of the major treatments of this problem we also noted that goodness (however differently each philosopher may have defined it) was regarded as somehow indispensable to the realization of such a life. But, curiously, we also noted that (with the possible exception of the emotivists) each philosopher seemed to have thought that happiness and goodness were somehow intimately connected, that it was not possible to achieve the one without the other. It is true, of course, that each major figure tended to define "goodness" differently: Aristotle defining it in the sense of becoming as knowledgeable and as wise as possible; Kant defining it in the sense of becoming worthy in God's eyes; Bentham and Mill defining it universally. What was common to each, however, was the view that happiness somehow involves the notion of approval, of being able to think well of oneself — of being able to applaud yourself.

It is interesting to note that in stressing this aspect of happiness these philosophers anticipated many of the discoveries and insights which have been achieved only in our own age and time. For practically all modern psychologists and psychotherapists have come to believe that a satisfying life is possible only in proportion to the esteem (to use a contemporary term) one feels for oneself. They regard this as a basic human need. Some call this sense of esteem for oneself self-love, others call it self-appreciation, and still others call it self-celebration. All, however, are agreed that without it the prospect of one's personality suffering a breakdown (let alone failing to achieve happiness) is very great.

They have come to believe, further, that many, if not all, our psychological problems, from the slightest neuroses to the deepest psychoses, are symptomatic of the frustration of this fundamental human need for a sense of personal worth. The depth and duration of the symptomatic problems engendered (whether these are phobias, guilt complexes, or feelings of paranoia) are indicative of the depth and duration of the deprivation of this sense of self-esteem.

These psychologists and psychotherapists also seem to be agreed that the main and fundamental source of this self-appreciation is the love of others. But this love, so essential to our sense of well-being, they say, is not something that can be banked and drawn on when needed. To maintain a state of well-being and be happy we need a steady flow of this reassurance and love from others. Without it we come to feel empty, bankrupt, and worthless.*

They have shown that those who fail to find this flow of love and approval from others, lapse into one of several well-defined and increasingly better understood mental states. The most common is depression — a feeling of morbid dejection and sadness, ranging from mild discouragement to despair. Depression, they say, is the organism's defense against the pain of rejection; it is an idling of the

---

*My account of these matters here follows that found in the very fine book by John Powell entitled *The Secret of Staying in Love* (Niles, Ill.: Angus Communications, 1974).

human organism that prevents the violent pain from tearing it completely apart. It is a substitute form of suffering, more tolerable than the one it masks.

Another response to our sense of worthlessness is anger and violence. Feeling unsuccessful as persons we vent our frustrations on others, making them pay for our sense of inadequacy and failure.

A third response, the most common of all, is physical illness. Here the psychological pain of failure is translated into physical symptoms that seem easier to bear. Many sicknesses, formerly regarded as organic, are really psychosomatic in origin, brought on by the severe judgments we pass on our secret selves.

Finally, a fourth common response to the failure to find love and a sense of worth in the public world is to escape to our own private world, a world of our own making, in which we no longer need to cope with our personal failure, having come to deny its very existence. This is a high price to pay for this liberation from failure, for unlike the retreat into fantasy by children when faced with disappointment, this escape is long-lasting, painful, and often permanent. Yet in desperation many choose it.

These alternatives to the admission of failure, although camouflaging and alleviating the original agony, do not do away with the pain we suffer. Still continuing to hurt, we try to kill the pain by resorting to such widely used but debilitating pain-killers as food, alcohol, and drugs. All are desperate attempts to dull the pain of a seemingly worthless existence and all are addictive and destructive.

The saddest aspect of this final attempt to solve our sense of failure as persons is that, if we succeed and remove the pain, we no longer feel the need to try to find our worth as persons, and withdraw from life, preferring our addiction to everything and everyone else.

Applauding ourselves

The final question that remains is therefore: What can we do to find this worth and with it a sense of peace with ourselves? This is what, in good part, the philosophers whose thought we have examined in this chapter have tried to deal with. It is also what a good deal of contemporary humanistic psychology is devoted to. And it has, of course, been a central theme of some of the great works of literature.

Probably the greatest and most memorable of these is Cervantes' masterpiece *Don Quixote* (1605)—a work revived in our day in a great stage musical, the *Man of La Mancha*.

The story, as reimagined and retold in the words and lyrics of the latter work,* is familiar but ever new and inspiring. Don Quixote lives a drab, poor, mean, and petty existence. To escape it, he immerses himself in books on chiv-

---

Man of La Mancha, written by Dale Wasserman, lyrics by Joe Darion. New York: Dell, 1968. Copyright © 1966 by Dale Wasserman. Reproduced by permission.

alry. Soon he imagines himself a dauntless knight living in the glorious days of chivalry. He will set out to do mighty deeds, redress great wrongs, risk great danger to win honor and fame — even if he has to do the impossible!

So he goes into the attic, finds a rusty old coat of armor and with his squire, potbellied Sancho Panza, riding a jackass, he sets off on his old scarecrow of a horse named Rocinante.

He sees an old windmill that he mistakes for a giant and does battle with it. Badly battered, he continues on his way. Of course he needs a lady-love for whom he will do these great deeds. He finally finds her when he stops at an inn, which he takes for a castle, and thinks the barmaid, who doubles as a trollop and whom he calls his "sweet lady . . . fair virgin . . .," is that lady-love.

He asks her name. "Aldonza," she growls. He thinks she must be joking, for that is the name of a kitchen scullion. No, he says, her name is Dulcinea. Smitten by her ("I have dreamt thee too long" he says) he sends Sancho Panza to ask her for a favor — some token of her esteem that he may carry as his standard into battle. Instead of a silken scarf she sends him a dirty dishrag. But he is not deterred by this. "Sheer gossamer" he exclaims on receiving it. He puts it on his head, covering it with a barber's shaving basin he had requisitioned, believing it to be the Golden Helmet of Mambrino, supposed to make the wearer, if noble of heart, invulnerable.

Having asked the innkeeper, whom he mistakes for the Lord of the Manor, to be knighted by him, he spends the evening on his knees in meditation and prayer: his eyes closed; head resting on the twisted, mangled sword, handle in the shape of the cross; the barber's shaving basin covering the dirty dish rag still resting on his head. Aldonza, stumbling upon him and hearing him mutter "Dulcinea," asks him:

Aldonza: Why do you call me by that name?

Quixote: Because it is thine.

Aldonza: My name is Aldonza!

Quixote: (Shakes his head respectfully) I know thee, lady.

Aldonza: My name is Aldonza and I think you know me *not.*

Quixote: All my years I have known thee. Thy virtue. Thy nobility of spirit.

Aldonza: (Laughs scornfully, whips the rebozo from her head) Take another look!

Quixote: (Gently) I have already seen thee in my heart.

Aldonza: Your heart doesn't know much about women!

Quixote: It knows all, my lady. They are the soul of man . . . the radiance that lights his way. A woman is . . . *glory!*

Aldonza: (Anger masking uncertainty) What do you want of me?

Quixote: Nothing.

Aldonza: Liar!

Quixote: (Bows his head) I deserved the rebuke. I ask of my lady —

Aldonza: Now we get to it.

Quixote: . . . that I may be allowed to serve her. That I may hold her in my heart. That I may dedicate each victory and call upon her in defeat. And if at last I give my life I give it in the sacred name of Dulcinea.

Aldonza: *(Draws her rebozo about her shoulders and backs away, shaken)* I must go . . . Pedro *(who has paid her in advance for services to be rendered)* is waiting. *(She pauses. Vehemently)* Why do you do these things?

Quixote: What things, my lady?

Aldonza: These . . . things you do!

Quixote: I hope to add some measure of grace to the world.

Aldonza: The world's a dungheap and we are maggots that crawl on it!

Quixote: My lady knows better in her heart.

Aldonza: What's in *my* heart will get me halfway to hell. And you, Señor Don Quixote — you're going to take such a beating!

Quixote: Whether I win or lose does not matter.

Aldonza: What does?

Quixote: Only that I follow the quest.

Aldonza: What does it mean — quest?

Quixote: The mission of each true knight . . . his duty — nay, his privilege!
To dream the impossible dream
To fight the unbeatable foe
To right the unrightable wrong
To try, when your arms are too weary
To reach the unreachable stars!

Aldonza: Once — just once — would you look at me as I really am?

Quixote: I see beauty. Purity. I see the woman each man holds secret within him. Dulcinea.

Although at first thinking him crazy, his faith in her soon transforms her into the person of beauty she held within herself in spite of the external ugliness of her life.

Not everyone can grasp the dream and force it to become the reality. For the others it is sheer madness. Don Quixote's physician, for example, tries to bring Quixote back to his senses by telling him there haven't been any knights for 300 years. When Don Quixote replies to this, "So learned, yet so misinformed," the doctor exclaims "But these are facts" — to which Don Quixote replies "Facts are the enemy of truth."

Even Sancho Panza remarks at one point "There's no use blaming my eye; it doesn't make the world, it only sees it." But to Don Quixote there is more to seeing than meets the eyeball.

But things are not fated to end well: Pedro, one of the gang of muleteers holed up in the inn, comes looking for Aldonza. Enraged that she has kept him waiting, he slaps her so that she goes spinning to the ground. Don Quixote, outraged, cries out "Monster." He goes to battle and, with the help of Aldonza and Sancho Panza, succeeds in sending the whole gang reeling to the floor, all of them badly battered.

Don Quixote celebrates the victory by having the innkeeper dub him a knight and then goes to minister to the wounds of the fallen muleteers, "as nobility demands." Aldonza, although thinking it crazy to bind the wounds of these thugs, insists on doing it for Don Quixote. Enraged at what had been done to them, the muleteers gather themselves up, beat and ravage her.

But that is the price we sometimes have to pay for our dreams and illusions, or, as Don Quixote puts it, for trying to add some measure of grace to the world.

But not to dream, not to have illusions, to try to fall in with the ways of the world in the hope of winning its applause, is to risk losing one's own. Certainly it is nice to be applauded by the world but we want to be able to applaud ourselves too.

And ultimately perhaps that is what happiness is.

Well, what about the baby? Did the physician do right or wrong in stopping feeding orders? As we have seen, the answer one is likely to give to this question will depend upon whether one takes a teleological, a deontological, or an emotivist attitude towards ethical questions.

If you are an emotivist the terms "right" and "wrong" have only emotive and not cognitive meaning for you, and the choice is in the end a personal one; if you are a teleologist, for whom the results of an action determine its rightness, you would tend to side with the physician; if you are a deontologist, you would no doubt see the physician's action as wrong and condemn it.

Is there, then, no way in which these three different attitudes and solutions can be reconciled? Are there no further arguments to offer? There does not seem to be an easy or very obvious way in which this can be done and no revolutionary arguments appear left to offer. Yet there is a consideration, already alluded to, which at least to this writer seems to offer hope of such a reconciliation.

Strangely enough, it consists in undertaking a form of argument made use of by Kant, for which he has been criticized.

Let us recall what Kant said in reply to the question "Why ought I to be moral?" Rather than giving a typically deontological answer Kant gives a teleological one. For example, he argues that it would be wrong to make a lying promise, because if everyone made promises without intending to fulfill them, promises would not be believed and there would be no point in making them. (This argument was criticized by Bertrand Russell, who said that Kant argued that it was wrong to borrow money, for if we all did so, there would be no money left to borrow.)

If, on the other hand, Kant goes on to argue, I find myself in prosperity, see all the wretchedness and poverty around me, but say "What concern is it of mine?" it would be immoral to act on that thought or even harbor it, for some day I might find myself in distress and wish I had not been so rash. On the same grounds it would be wrong, Kant says, for a man out of laziness to fail to develop talents he possesses, for such talents "serve him, and have been given him, for all sorts of possible purposes."

It is obvious what seems to have gone wrong here and why a Kantian must find himself embarrassed by these examples. For Kant's theory demands, of course, a *categorical* reason as to why we should be moral, but the reasons given are *hypothetical* and prudential — reasons in keeping with a teleological position and not a deontological one.

But while to hold this position might seem logically embarrassing, nevertheless there is something very persuasive and convincing about it. Another example that comes to mind may make it clearer what this is. Several years ago, Dr. Robert R. Wilson, director of the large Fermi Accelerator Laboratory, was repeatedly pressed before a Senate hearing to come up with some national security application of the research being conducted there. To the dismay of the supporters of the Laboratory, Dr. Wilson continued to insist that it had none. Finally Dr. Wilson told the senators: "The Accelerator Laboratory only has to do with the respect with which we regard one another. It has nothing to do with defending our country except to help make it worth defending." Similarly, perhaps, here. Perhaps the decision should have been to keep the baby alive, regardless of cost or its own prospects, not so much for its sake, as for our own.

Summary

1. Ethics is the study of human conduct. It asks itself questions such as: "What sort of life is most worth living?" "How should one best conduct it?" "What in it should matter most?"

2. The investigation of these questions has tended to take three distinct directions: (a) it has occupied itself with the strictly practical problems of how the most worthwhile life can best be achieved (*morality* proper); (b) it has gone on to consider the possible theoretical reasons for choosing various lines of conduct (*ethics* proper); and (c) it has become occupied with an inquiry into the nature and meaning of those theories *(metaethics)*.

3. Although in its typical form an ethical treatise consists of *moralizing* with the help of an *ethical* theory, defended on methodological or *metaethical* grounds, it is especially characteristic of ancient writers to be concerned with the question of what life is best to live (morality proper); of modern writers to be concerned with the question how such choices can best be justified (ethics proper); and of today's writers to be occupied with the question of the meaning and validity of the judgments proposed (metaethics).

4. Aristotle believed that the best thing to strive for in life was happiness; but happiness, he believed, could not be achieved without

realizing our highest capacities and potentialities, and in man's case this is reason. The happy life, therefore, according to Aristotle, was one devoted to the exercise, development, and perfection of reason, one guided by its dictates.

5. Unlike Aristotle, Kant argued that the basic question of ethics was not how to achieve happiness but rather how we might become worthy of it. To become so worthy, he argued, the rule to follow is not the Golden Mean (practising moderation in all things), as Aristotle had suggested, but rather the Golden Rule — doing unto others as we would have them do unto us. Kant therefore offered as his fundamental principle of morality the Categorical Imperative or the Principle of Universality: so act that the maxim of your action may be willed as a universal law. That alone is right which unconditionally permits everyone else to do it, one in which no exceptions are made for oneself. In another formulation, designed to bring out the notion that respect for each other as persons is central to ethical conduct, Kant stated his basic principle as follows: "Act so that you treat humanity, whether in your own person or in that of another, always as an end and never as a means only."

6. Utilitarianism, rejecting both personal happiness and the dictates of duty as the criterion of morality, argued that the only fit and proper standard was the principle of the greatest happiness of the greatest number, happiness being generally equated with pleasure. If an action, this Principle of Utility stated, produces the greatest balance of pleasure (considered quantitatively by Bentham but qualitatively by Mill) over pain for the greatest number of people concerned, then it is right and ought to be done; otherwise it is wrong and should be avoided.

7. Although utilitarians sought to arrive at a principle that would enable them to determine with scientific objectivity and accuracy whether an act was morally justifiable, the group of contemporary writers on ethics, known as Logical Positivists, by applying their Principle of Verification cast doubt on the validity and objective reality of the subject as a whole with its questionable notions of "right" and "wrong," "moral" and "immoral," and so forth. They concluded that these terms were cognitively meaningless and served only to express our feelings and emotions, or arouse similar feelings and emotions in others.

8. Although emotivists tried to resolve the traditional opposition between the deontological approach to ethical matters (as represented by Kant's theory) and the teleological approach (as represented by the Utilitarian theory) by suggesting there was really

nothing to resolve, the problems of ethics being essentially pseudo-problems, the subject and problems seem to resist this attempt to eliminate them. The problems remain and refuse to go away. And they remain because, of course, we remain, and the goals we set ourselves continue to elude us. We continue to believe with Aristotle that that goal is indeed happiness; we continue to believe both with him and many of the other great philosophers (as well as contemporary psychologists and psychotherapists) that it is somehow bound up with goodness. How and why are questions which still continue to intrigue and challenge us.

For further study

1. There are a number of translations of Aristotle's *Nicomachean Ethics*. The one used here is the Penguin edition of *The Ethics of Aristotle: The Nicomachean Ethics* (Harmondsworth, England, 1977). The student might wish to compare this translation with the Bobbs-Merrill edition, translated by Martin Ostwald (Indianapolis, Indiana: The Library of Liberal Arts, 1962).

2. For a brief and highly readable account of the life and thought of Aristotle, see A. E. Taylor's *Aristotle* (New York: Dover, 1955. Revised edition).

3. For recent discussions of Aristotle's philosophy, including his ethics, see *Aristotle: A Collection of Critical Essays* edited by J. M. E. Moravcsik (Garden City, New York: Doubleday, 1967). Pages 335–339 contain a selected bibliography of further recent literature, both of Aristotle's philosophy as a whole and of his ethics.

4. The translation of Kant's work on ethics (the *Grundlegung*) used here is by Lewis White Beck (New York: The Library of Liberal Arts Press, 1959). The student might wish to compare this translation with Thomas K. Abbott's *Fundamental Principles of the Metaphysics of Morals*, also published by the Liberal Arts Press, Inc. (Indianapolis, Indiana, 1949). This edition has a helpful Introduction by Marvin Fox.

5. Three other works of translation and commentary of the *Grundlegung* the advanced student might find interesting to explore are the following: (a) H. J. Paton: *The Moral Law or Kant's Groundwork of the Metaphysic of Morals: A New Translation with Analysis and Notes* (New York: Barnes & Noble, 1958). (b) Brendan E.A. Liddell: *Kant on the Foundation of Morality: A Modern Version of the Grundlegung. Translated with a Commentary* (Bloom-

ington: Indiana University Press, 1970). (c) Robert Paul Wolff: *The Autonomy of Reason: A Commentary on Kant's Groundwork of the Metaphysics of Morals* (New York: Harper Torchbooks, 1973).

6. For a series of recent critical essays on Kant's *Grundlegung* see: *Kant: Foundations of the Metaphysics of Morals: Text and Critical Essays* edited by Robert Paul Wolff (Indianapolis, Indiana: Bobbs-Merrill, 1969).

7. For Kant's ethics as developed in his second *Critique*, see *Immanuel Kant: Critique of Practical Reason* translated with an Introduction by Lewis White Beck (New York: The Liberal Arts Press, 1956). For a discussion of this Critique see: (a) Lewis White Beck: *A Commentary on Kant's Critique of Practical Reason* (Chicago: The University of Chicago Press, 1960). (b) H. J. Paton: *The Categorical Imperative: A Study in Kant's Moral Philosophy*, 6th edition (London: Hutchinson, 1967).

8. For Bentham's *Introduction to the Principles of Morals and Legislation* see the edition published by Hafner Publishing Co. (New York, 1948).

9. For extensive selections from John Stuart Mill's writings see *Selected Writings of John Stuart Mill*, edited with an Introduction by Maurice Cowling, (New York: Mentor, 1968). For the complete edition of his essay *On Liberty* see the Penguin Book edition (Harmondsworth, England, 1974). For his *The Subjection of Women* see the paperback edition published by the M.I.T. Press (Cambridge, Mass., 1970). For Mill's *Autobiography* see the Signet Classic edition, published by the New American Library (New York, 1964).

10. For a highly acclaimed recent biography of both Mill and his father see Bruce Mazlish: *James and John Stuart Mill: Father and Son in the 19th Century* (New York: Basic Books, 1975).

11. For an account of the history and meaning of utilitarianism, see:
    (a) David Baumgardt: *Bentham and the Ethics of Today* (Princeton: Princeton University Press, 1952).
    (b) Ernest Albee: *History of English Utilitarianism* (New York: Collier, 1962).

12. For an early expression of the emotive theory of ethics see C. Ogden and I. A. Richards, *The Meaning of Meaning* (London: Routledge, 1923).

13. In addition to Ayer's book *Language, Truth and Logic* (New York: Dover, 1952), the student will enjoy reading Ayer's recent auto-

biography *Part of My Life: The Memoirs of a Philosopher* (New York: Harcourt, 1977).

14. For Charles Stevenson's more fully developed version of the emotive theory see his *Ethics and Language* (New Haven: Yale University Press, 1943) and a later collection of his articles, *Facts and Values* (New Haven: Yale University Press, 1963).

15. For a detailed, critical discussion of the emotive theory see J. D. Urmson, *The Emotive Theory of Ethics* (London: Hutchinson, 1968).

Spiral Galaxy in Triangulum. Messier 33. Hale Observatories.

Metaphysics

Is the world such that we can do it?

Introduction

In August of A.D. 410 the Visigoths under Alaric finally broke through the defenses of Rome and took the city. Historians mark this date, the fall of the Eternal City, as the beginning of the Middle Ages. Man's history, of course, does not really fall into such neat divisions as those used by historians, but the periods themselves are real and distinct enough.

The Middle Ages differed from modern times in three fundamental ways: economically, politically, and religiously. Economically, the Middle Ages were mainly agricultural, while the modern world is primarily commercial and industrial. Politically, medieval states were feudal while most modern governments are bureaucratic, that is, run and controlled by a system of officials and bureaus. And religiously — which is most relevant for our story, the Christianity of the Middle

195

Saint Augustine. The Fitzwilliam Museum, Cambridge, England.

Ages was united under the authority of the Catholic Church, while Christianity in modern times is divided among many denominations.

The fall of Rome, although a great psychological shock, seeming to the people of the time to mark the end not only of civilization but to some, of the world itself, had the effect of strengthening and consolidating the power of the Church.

How could such a disaster have taken place? people wondered. Some traced the misfortune to the displeasure of the ancient deities, who had stood guard over the city during its long history before being displaced by the Chrisitan God. It had been scarcely a generation since the Emperor Theodosius I had proscribed the ancient cults and declared Christianity to be the Empire's official faith. The old gods, it was now said, were taking their revenge.

It fell to Augustine (354 – 430), Bishop of Hippo, one of the most penetrating thinkers of his age, to defend the Christian faith against these charges. The result was the *City of God*, which he began in 413 and took some 13 years to complete. It was the first important work of the Middle Ages, one largely responsible for shaping Christianity into the powerful force it became for over the next thousand years.

Augustine's argument was that history was a drama involving God and humanity. God created the earth for people, but Adam sinned against God, and he and Eve were driven out of the paradise God had created for them. But God gave humanity a second chance after flooding the world to destroy everyone in it except Noah and his family; and then a third chance by entering into a covenant with the Jews. But the Jews, Augustine argued, did not live up to the agreement they made with God and so God allowed them to be captured by their enemies. God then sought to redeem not only the Jews but all humankind by sending the Messiah Jesus to die as an atonement for the sinfulness of humanity. Those who have accepted the sacrifice make up the new community, the Church. The Church (the City of God) and those who do not accept the sacrifice of Jesus (the City of Man), now exist side by side and will do so until the Day of Judgment, when God will destroy those who have not accepted Jesus as their savior and will create a new earth for those who have.

Although the Church Fathers were at first divided on the use of coercion, Augustine's view that the state, like a benevolent father, was required to encourage heretics to return to orthodoxy and thus save their souls, in time became the dominant one. It was finally institutionalized in the Inquisition, with burning at the stake its innovative method of execution.

If Augustine marks the beginning of the Middle or Dark Ages, another Church Father, St. Thomas Aquinas (1225–1274), who is universally regarded as the greatest intellectual figure of this one thousand-year period, marks its height. Aquinas took it upon himself to reconcile the truths of revelation with the truths of reason. The teachings of St. Augustine, which by this time had dominated Western thought for more than 800 years, had insisted that in the search for truth man must depend upon inner thought rather than sensory experience. But the works of Aristotle, which were now becoming known once again, stressed the importance and value of experience and empirical knowledge in the search for truth. Aquinas set about to synthesize and harmonize Aristotelian science with Christian revelation. The truths of faith and those of sense experience, he argued, are not only compatible but even complementary: some truths, such as the mystery of the Incarnation, can be known only through revelation, while others, such

Saint Thomas Aquinas. Mary Evans Picture Library, London.

as knowledge of the composition of earthly things, can be known only through sense experience, and still others — such as man's awareness of God — require both revelation and sense experience for their perception.

Aquinas's main work (famous for its five proofs for the existence of God) was his *Summa Theologica* (1265), and its synthesis of philosophy and theology became in time the accepted teachings of the Roman Catholic Church. He was canonized in 1328 and declared a doctor of the Church in 1567. Pope Leo XIII made his teaching, called Thomism, the basis of instruction in all Roman Catholic schools, and Pius XII declared in an encyclical that all departure from it was to be condemned.

But if Augustine marks the beginning of the Middle Ages, and Aquinas its glory, Giordano Bruno (1548 — 1600), a Dominican monk who abandoned his calling to be claimed finally by the fires of the Inquisition (which in many ways were lit and sustained by those great predecessors of his) represents in essence its end — even though he came almost one hundred years after the close of the Middle Ages as officially demarcated by historians.

Before we go on to consider his tragic life and the enormously intriguing nature of his ideas (leading many to call him "the prophet of science"), we might ask: What has all this got to do with metaphysics, the subject of this chapter?

In the logical order of the material that forms the body of philosophy, metaphysics comes first. Unfortunately it also happens to be the most difficult part. As traditionally conceived metaphysics concerns itself with the question of the nature of the universe, asking itself what is there and what is it like? Is the world, it asks, rational and purposive, evolving toward some goal that is friendly to us and to our needs? Or is it essentially arational, goalless, and alien — dead matter conforming to immutable laws. In short, what metaphysics asks is: "How is it with the world?"

Metaphysics has also been interested in enquiring into the sort of beings we are. "What are we really like?" it asks. "Do we possess souls that survive the death of our bodies, and wills that are free; or are we determined by the same forces that govern other bodies in the universe, and like them are devoid of choice and freedom and perish in time?" Reactions to these kinds of questions have been mixed, to say the least. Here are some representative opinions:

C. S. Peirce: "Metaphysics is a subject the knowledge of which, like that of a sunken reef, serves chiefly to enable us to keep clear of it."

Kant: "Metaphysics is without a doubt the most difficult of all human studies; only no metaphysics has yet been written."

F. H. Bradley: "Metaphysics is the finding of bad reasons for what we believe on instinct — but the finding of these reasons is no less an instinct."

Bertrand Russell: "In Tibet the second official in the state is called the "metaphysician in chief." Elsewhere philosophy is no longer held in such high esteem."

The British philosopher J. E. McTaggart identified the nature of this discipline and the reason for its powerful hold on us, in these words: "The utility of metaphysics," he said, coming closer to describing it than any of the other writers, "is to be found in the comfort it can give us . . . in the chance that it may answer this supreme question (whether good or evil predominates in the universe) in a cheerful manner, that it may provide some solution which shall be a consolation and an encouragement."

We can perhaps see from these quotations why this part of philosophy, so reminiscent of what has traditionally been the goal of religion, has come to be identified with medieval thought — that period in man's history which more than any other was obsessed with religious speculation.

The subject, of course, has a longer history and is not confined merely to the question of salvation. The term itself was first used around 70 B.C. by one of the editors of Aristotle's manuscripts, Andronicus of Rhodes. Andronicus found a series of works among Aristotle's papers that followed his discussion of physics but bore no title. Not knowing what to call them, he simply gave them the label "meta-physics" — meaning works coming *after* physics. In time the word came to be used to describe any philosophical work treating the same material as Aristotle did in these writings — "What is being?" "How is it known?" and so on. Later the prefix *meta* was extended to cover not only discussions about the general nature of reality (what one would normally go on to consider *after* physics) but also discussions of matters lying *beyond* physics — the existence of God, freedom of the will, and the immortality of the soul.

It is not difficult to appreciate the development of the subject as first conceived by Aristotle and what others, including the Lamas of Tibet, later came to make of it. The most fundamental question we can ask, and we have a profound need to ask it, is the question of our existence. What are we and why are we here? What should — and what can — we do? And why must we die?

To reflect on our existence, on its approaching end, on the nature of the world in which it has been passed, and on whether one shall return to it or some other one, is to reflect on metaphysics. The religions of the world have arisen in response to our need to answer these questions.

Philosophy's answers differ from those offered by religion in that unlike the latter, their goal is not reassurance but understanding. But the questions are nevertheless the same, and over the centuries philosophers have devised special labels for each of the main questions that naturally arise in such discussions.

Thus, cosmology deals with the problem of what the universe as a whole is really like. "Why is there a universe?" it asks, and "Where did it come from?" Rational psychology deals with the nature of the soul and asks such questions as "Why we are here? and What is to become of us?" And rational theology, finally, is concerned with the question of God's existence. The study of nature, the soul, and God have thus traditionally formed the three main subdivisions of metaphysics.

Although these three topics, which formed the main preoccupation of the thought of the Middle Ages, were replaced in modern times with our own obsession with questions of knowledge (how and whether we can know any such matters, for example), these questions have by no means disappeared. The person who set them on a new course, allowing them to survive to be raised again and discussed in a new, secular context, was Giordano Bruno. For drawing the new implications for the teaching of religion of the new vision of the world as he came to see it, he was forced to pay with his life. That has been the fate, as history has taught us more than once, for all those whose disclosures threaten or undermine the comfort of others, even if the comfort in question is not, as in Socrates' case, political and economic, but, as in Bruno's case, spiritual.

Before examining and reflecting on these events, we ought perhaps to remind ourselves that although the questions posed by metaphysics seem esoteric and perhaps of interest only to occupants of ivory towers, this is not at all the case. Let us consider for a moment one of its main problems — "What is the uni-

Giordano Bruno. The Bettmann Archive, Inc.

verse made of?" — and see the profound effects the way this question has been answered (and of course the very asking of it) has had on our lives.

As we saw at the very beginning of this journey into philosophy, "What is the universe made of?" was in fact the first question the earliest philosophers posed: Thales saying it was water, Anaximenes that it was air, and Heraclitus that it was fire. Democritus and Leucippus finally resolved the problems raised by these conflicting answers by suggesting that the ultimate particles of reality were atoms. This metaphysical theory, first proposed by these ancient Greek philosophers, formed the foundation of scientific investigation into the ultimate building blocks of the universe well into the nineteenth and early twentieth century.

By the late nineteenth century physicists, of course, no longer supposed that these tiny particles had hooks on them, but they did assume that they were spherical in shape, resembling tiny billiard balls or marbles.

Later, in the twentieth century, however, a fundamental revision regarding the conception of the nature of these atoms took place, a change that resulted in a profound revolution in physics with vast implications for humanity as a whole. For later in that century it was discovered that the atom was not the ultimate particle but was constructed of still smaller particles — electrons, which revolve around a nucleus or "sun" much as the planets revolve about the sun. More recently still, it was discovered that the nucleus itself is composed of still tinier pieces of matter — neutrons and protons — and these of even smaller ones.

Of course, no physicist has ever claimed to have "seen" a neutron or a proton or any of the other particles. What one was able to observe was simply the *behavior* of these particles. This very fact itself had enormous implications, for it led investigators to the notion of a nuclear force as responsible for the observed motion, and this in turn led to the conception of atoms as points or poles of energy, and with it the motivation to release the energy within them — with results all too familiar to us.

It was this transformation of the conception of the atom from a tiny marble (harbored by Democritus and his successors) to the idea of it as "congealed energy" (essentially a change in metaphysical theory) that led to the creation of the atomic and thermonuclear bombs — those mighty symbols of modern man's supremacy over nature. None of this would have been possible on the old Democritean atomic theory; however, it would have been impossible without it either, for the old provided impetus for the new, and both were and are metaphysical theories.

But let us return to Giordano Bruno and consider some of the other concerns of metaphysics. As in the case of the discoveries of modern science, Giordano Bruno's search for the design of the outer world led him to discoveries of dismaying implications. And the same was the case with that much later thinker, Sigmund Freud, whose discoveries concerning the design of the inner world, the world of the mind, were also viewed with alarm.

In both worlds — as these two curious, sad, and unusual thinkers came to believe — we seem to be only pawns and playthings of fate, at the mercy of strange, alien forces. Should they be correct in these metaphysical speculations, as we will observe toward the end of this chapter, then the philosophical and human implications concerning our condition in this universe and our freedom will prove to be indeed profound.

Giordano Bruno: the design without

The series of events that led to Bruno's martyrdom began with a letter a gentleman of Venice by the name of Gioanni Mocenigo wrote on May 23, 1592, to the Father of the Venetian Inquisition. Some months earlier Mocenigo had invited Bruno to be his teacher, hoping to learn from him the arts of black magic, but this was not what Bruno taught.

Mocenigo wrote:*

> Very Reverend Father and Most-to-be-observed Sir:
>
> I, Gioanni Mocenigo, son of the Clarissimo Messer Marcoantonio, compelled by my conscience and ordered by my confessor, denounce to Your Very Reverend Paternity Giordano Bruno of Nola, whom I have heard say on various occasions when he was conversing with me in my own house, that Catholics do but blaspheme when they hold the Bread to be transubstantiated into the Flesh; that he is against the Mass; that no religion satisfies him; that Christ was a charlatan who, since he resorted to tricks to fool people, might well enough have foreseen that he would die a criminal's death; that there is no distinction of Persons in God; . . . that the world is eternal and that there are an infinite number of worlds, and that God is continually making an infinity of them because He wants as many as He can have; that Christ performed specious miracles; that he was a magician and the apostles were magicians too . . . (pp. 3–4).
>
> He has expressed the intention of making himself the founder of a new sect under the name of the new philosophy. He has said that the Virgin could not have brought a child into the world, and that our Catholic faith is full of blasphemies against the majesty of God; that it would be better to suppress the largesses of wrangling friars because they befoul the world; that they are all asses and that our common opinions are the teaching of asses; that we have no proof that our faith has merit with God; that the simple rule of not doing unto others what we would not have done unto us is sufficient for right living . . . (p. 5).

Having discovered this about Bruno, Mocenigo had locked him up in a room in his house, where he may now be found. "I had thought to learn from him," the letter goes on to explain: . . . not knowing him to be

---

*These quotations are from Edgar A. Singer, *Modern Thinkers and Present Problems* (New York: Holt, 1923).

the wicked man he is, and having noted all these things to lay before your Very Reverend Paternity, and fearing that he would take his departure as he said he wished to do, I have locked him in a room at your disposal. As I think him possessed of the devil, I hope you will decide quickly what is to be done with him . . . (pp. 5–6).

The next document of the trial is brief — the official entry of Bruno's arrest and imprisonment. It is dated Tuesday, May 26. It reads:

Clarissimo Dom Aloysius Fuscari presiding. Presented himself Dom Matheus de Avantio, Captain of the Constabulary, and reported as follows: Sabbath at three o'clock of the night, I arrested Giordano Bruno of Nola, whom I found in a house over against Saint Samuels, in which dwells the Clarissimo Ser Gioanni Mocenigo, and I have imprisoned him in the Prisons of the Holy Office, and this I have done by order of this Holy Tribunal (pp. 7–8).

Questioned the next day by the tribunal (composed of the Apostolic Nuncio, the Patriarch of Venice, and the Very Reverend Father Inquisitor), Bruno laid before it, as the clerk of the tribunal records it, the following account of his life:

My name is Giordano Bruno, of the family of the Bruni, of the city of Nola, twelve miles from Naples. In this place I was born and raised, and my profession was and is letters and the sciences. My father was named Gioanni, and my mother Fraulissa Savolina, and my father's calling was that of a soldier. He is dead since, and my mother too.

I am about forty-four years of age, and I was born, so far as I have heard from my people, in the year 1548. I remained in Naples learning the humanities, logic, and dialectics until fourteen years of age . . . and then I took the habit of St Dominic in the monastery or convent of St Dominic in Naples, and was invested by a padre who was then prior of that convent, called Maestro Ambrosio Pasqua. When the year of probation was passed, I was admitted by him to profession, which was solemnly made in the same convent. . . . Later I was promoted to holy orders and at the usual season to the priesthood. I sang my first Mass in Campagna, a city of the same state at a distance from Naples, residing the while in a convent of the Order, the San Bartolomeo, and continued in the religious habit of St Dominic, celebrating Masses and the divine offices, obedient to the superior of the Order and to the priors of the monasteries and convents where I was stationed until 1576 . . . (pp. 9–10).

But, as he tells his judges, he ran into trouble at the Order ("for giving away certain images of the saints, retaining only a crucifix," reading Erasmus and so on) and decided to flee. There followed, he recounts, 16 years of a life of restless wandering over the face of Europe, friendless and alone, living in poverty and supporting himself by tutoring young boys, and now and then lecturing at great universities on his new discoveries.

What were these discoveries? It may seem strange to us that the question of the relative motions of sun and earth should have been seen to have any religious implications. Nevertheless, the instincts of the princes of the Church, who saw in Copernicanism a threat to religion, were right. And the additions and extensions made to that theory by Bruno only succeeded in deepening these fears.

For what, for those of a religious turn of mind, lay at the heart of this issue was whether it was indeed the case, as Augustine had reassured the Church so many centuries earlier, that the whole of creation existed for the sake of man. How could this be so if man lives on a small, spinning planet, which far from being the center of the universe is not even the center of the solar system? And if Copernicus was right, furthermore, the fixed stars must lie at enormous distances from us—and God even farther.

Bruno poured salt on these wounds. He saw implications in Copernicus's theory that Copernicus himself had not noticed. Copernicus had given up the idea that the earth was the center of the universe, to substitute the sun for it. But Copernicus still supposed that the fixed stars were really fixed, and on a sphere that was the outermost boundary of the universe. Bruno, however, went much further. Abandoning the idea of a center to the universe as meaningless, he declared the so-called fixed stars to be suns like our own, scattered uniformly throughout infinite space. Revolving around each were planets like our own, with living creatures on them.

The implications for Christianity of such an infinite universe with as many inhabited globes as there were stars—globes inhabited by beings "perhaps better, perhaps worse than we are"—were staggering. Nor was Bruno fearful of spelling out these implications for his interrogators. Since these dwellers on distant planets are probably no better or no worse than we, and are like us the children of God, they must, like us, be in need of salvation and deserving of it. Are we then to suppose, he enquired, that the drama of Redemption is therefore being enacted over and over again throughout the infinity of the worlds? Is the Son of God being sacrificed over and over again for the sake of His other children? Is He at this moment perhaps redeeming with His life the dwellers on some star in the night yonder? No one before Bruno had asked these questions. And no one before him had made man seem so small, so diminished.

The end of Bruno's life is told in a letter written by one Gaspard Schopp, a recent convert to Catholicism, to his friend Rittershausen, Rector of the University of Altdorf:

> If I write to you now, it is because this very day Giordano Bruno was publicly burned for heresy in the Field of Flowers in front of the theatre of Pompey. . . .
>
> Now Bruno was that Nolan . . . a professed Dominican who some twenty-three years agone began to doubt of transubstantiation . . . then

forthright to deny it, and likewise the virginity of the Blessed Mary. He migrated to Geneva, . . . whence, not approving himself altogether sound in his Calvinism (than which, nevertheless, nothing leads straighter to atheism), he was driven to Lyons, whence to Toulouse, from whence he passed on to Paris, where he was a professor, but *extraordinarius*, as he found that the professor *ordinarius* was obliged to attend Mass. Thence to London, where he published a little book called *The Beast Trium-phant*, meaning thereby the Pope, whom your party is wont to honour with the name of beast. From here to Wittenberg, where, if I am not mistaken, he lectured publicly for two years. Having gone on to Prague, he published there the works *On the Boundless, On the Innumerable Worlds*, and yet one other, *On the Shadows of Ideas* in which he taught horrible and, moreover, most absurd things, as that there are innumerable worlds, that the soul passes from one body into another. . . .

From Prague he went on to Brunswick and Helmstadt, and there for a time is said to have taught. Then to Frankfort for the publishing of certain books, and later fell into the hands of the Inquisition at Venice, whence, when they had had enough of him, he was sent to Rome. Frequently examined by the Holy Office . . . of the Inquisition, convicted by the highest theologians, he now besought eighty days that he might consider, now promised recantation, now defended his point anew, now obtained another eighty days; but was really doing nothing but make a fool of the Pontiff and the Inquisition.

So that nearly eight years after he had come before the Inquisition here, on the ninth of February in the Palace of the Grand Inquisitor, there being present the Most Illustrious Cardinals of the Holy Office of the Inquisition. . . . theologians of counsel, and the secular magistrate, governer of the city, Bruno was brought in, and on bended knees heard sentence pronounced against him. And it was in this way: the story of his life was told, of his studies and teachings, and with what diligence and fraternal admonishment the Inquisition had sought to effect his conversion, and what obdurancy and impiety he had shown. Then they defrocked him, as we say, and straightway excommunicated him and handed him over to the secular arm to be punished, asking that this be done with clemency and without the shedding of blood.

While this was passing he answered nothing, except this word: "In greater fear, perhaps do you impose sentence upon me than I do receive it." So, taken away to prison by the governor's lictors, he was allowed a fortnight in case he should wish to recant his errors; but in vain. To-day he was led to the stake. When the image of our Saviour on the Cross was shown to him as he was about to die, he turned away his head and sullenly rejected it. In great misery he thus died, and is gone, I think, to tell in those other worlds of his imagining after what manner the men of Rome are wont to treat impious blasphemers . . . (pp. 31–34).

Having abandoned the doctrine of the crucifixion, Bruno replaced it with another one that seems to most of us every bit as mysterious, although those who uphold it claim it is deeply rational and scientific. It is the doctrine that the universe is one, immutable, inexorable. It is a unity, one from which all things spring and to which they all ultimately return.

This is a doctrine that has come to be identified with the name of the great Dutch philosopher of the following century, Baruch Spinoza. We will have a chance to look more closely at it in our next chapter, which is concerned with questions of knowledge. Both philosophers, as we will see, came to call this unity in which we all have our being and find our highest reality, God. And for both the secret of human happiness and blessedness lay in the love of this reality and our identification with it.

Although most often identified with Spinoza, this vision of the way things are is probably, as the American philosopher Richard Taylor has put it "the oldest philosophical and religious idea known to man." And it is simply that being is one and identical with God the creator. In his poem to his eloquent book, *With Heart and Mind* (New York: St. Martin's Press, 1973), Taylor adds these further words concerning this most fundamental of all metaphysical ideas:

Exactly the same picture is rediscovered in every age and in every corner of the world. It is at once terrifying and completely fulfilling. It will never perish, and nothing will ever finally replace it. Nothing possibly can; its endurance is that of the stars. Wise men, seers, philosophers, prophets, poets, hymnists, mystics, try again and again to paint this picture, in parable, declamation, psalm, poem, fable, dialectic, allegory and song, and I have added my own small effort. I have tried to express in various ways, some grave and some lighthearted, and some whimsical, what it is like to see at last, to penetrate the illusions that encompass us, to be in a certain state of heart and mind that can only be described, however prosaically, as an absolute love for God and the world, a love that banishes all arising and perishing, and reveals an identity of every spirit to the rest of a creation that is precious beyond any possibility of utterance.

Sigmund Freud: the design within

Freud needs no introduction to a contemporary reader. Along with Marx and Einstein, he ranks among the geniuses of the modern age. The world as we know it today is largely one that they have fashioned: the new insights we have gained, the awesome power at our command, and the things that divide us, are largely their work.

The discovery of the nature of the design without and the startling implications that design seemed to have for those of a religious turn of mind was, as we saw, the contribution of Giordano Bruno. For it he was despised, reviled, and martyred. It was left for Freud to discover the design within and to draw its implications. Although it was not his fate to be martyred for making these revelations, it is ironic that, at any rate initially, he met opposition almost as bitter as Bruno did.

Freud, the discoverer of psychoanalysis, was born on May 6, 1856, in Freiberg, Moravia, now a part of Czechoslovakia. Deciding on a medical career, he entered the University of Vienna and graduated with his M.D. degree in 1881. Although he was already at this point aware of his growing interest in psychology, he continued to do research on the physiology of the nervous system. However as a result of his work with Jean Martin Charcot (1825–1893) in Paris, and Joseph Breuer (1842–1925) in Vienna on the use of hypnosis in the treatment of hysteria, he turned his attention to mapping the geography of our mental life.

Using his "talking cure," his early term for the method he came to perfect, he was surprised to discover the influence that sexuality exerts on a person's development and how early that influence begins, revelations that earned him the scorn of both his medical colleagues and the general public. He was also astonished to discover how various memories stored in our subconscious mind continued to influence our mental life. This led him to believe, finally, that mental illness was largely the result of the continued pressure of such hidden memories and that a cure could be achieved by bringing these hidden memories out into consciousness.

A prolific writer, he published the results of his research in such works as *The Interpretation of Dreams* (1900), *Three Contributions to the Theory of Sex* (1905), *Wit and Its Relation to the Unconscious* (1905), *General Introduction to Psychoanalysis* (1920), *Beyond the Pleasure Principle* (1920), and *Civilization and Its Discontents* (1930).

His work attracted followers from many parts of the world, some of whom were highly gifted and creative psychologists and thinkers who contributed to making "psychoanalysis" a household word the world over, and Freud a legend in his own time.

Despite this world acclaim (combined, however, with scorn and revulsion on the part of many others offended by his revelations concerning our sexuality) his books were publicly burned in Berlin by the Nazis in 1933. Freud, however, continued to serve as professor of neuropathology at the University of Vienna until 1938. In that year, however, he finally had to flee to London to escape from the Nazis. He died there the following year of cancer, from which he had suffered for some 16 years, undergoing 33 operations.

In the introduction to one of his books, Freud remarks that man in the course of history has suffered three great blows to his self-esteem. The first of these occurred when Copernicus showed that the earth was not the center of the universe but was rather one of many planets revolving around the sun. Until then man had believed he occupied the central seat of the universe, placed there by

God himself. The second great blow to man's self-esteem occurred when Darwin showed that man did not have the genealogy he had supposed, having been fashioned by the hand of God himself, but had a somewhat more humble origin, having descended from the apes. The third and last great blow suffered by man Freud credits to himself, with his discovery of the Unconscious. For by this discovery he had shown, Freud says, that not only does man not occupy that central throne of the universe, nor was he fashioned by God himself, but man does not even enjoy the privilege of being master of his own life and destiny. Despite what he may believe, his thoughts, goals, and desires have their origins deep in his unconscious, and he is therefore very much like a leaf blown about by the wind, ignorant of the sources of his desires and victim to them.

That this situation is descriptive not only of those who have gone mad but of us all, Freud tried to show in a remarkable early book, written for the general public and entitled *The Psychopathology of Everyday Life* (1904), which we have had a chance to look at in Chapter 3. In this book Freud analyzes the unconscious sources of ordinary errors and lapses and tries to show that these "mistakes" are not accidents but rather stem from disturbances in our personalities, some of which are buried so deep in our unconscious that we are completely unaware of them.

Although such mishaps (or "symptomatic actions," as he calls them) are unknown to consciousness, they are nevertheless "intended" by us, and are in a very profound sense valid for us. In Chapter 3 we had occasion to observe a number of amusing examples of such mishaps. Freud's most striking examples, however, are his more serious ones. Of these the following two are especially noteworthy:

A young woman broke her leg below the knee in a carriage accident so that she was bedridden for weeks. The striking part of it was the lack of any manifestation of pain and the calmness with which she bore her misfortune. This calamity ushered in a long and serious neurotic illness, from which she was finally cured by psychotherapy. During the treatment I discovered the circumstances surrounding the accident. The young woman with her jealous husband spent some time on the farm of her married sister, in company with her numerous other brothers and sisters with their wives and husbands. One evening she gave an exhibition of one of her talents before this intimate circle: she danced artistically the "Cancan," to the great delight of her relatives, but to the great annoyance of her husband who afterward whispered to her, 'Again you have behaved like a prostitute'. The words took effect. That night she was restless in her sleep, and the next forenoon she decided to go out driving. She chose the horses herself, refusing one team and demanding another. Her youngest sister wished to have her baby with its nurse accompany her, but she opposed this vehemently. During the drive she was nervous; she reminded the coachman that the horses were getting skittish, and as the fidgety animals really produced a momentary difficulty she jumped from the carriage in fright and broke her leg, while those remaining in the carriage were uninjured. Although after the disclosure of these details we can hardly doubt that this accident was really contrived, we cannot fail to admire the skill which forced the accident to mete out a punishment so suitable to the crime. For as it happened "Cancan" dancing with her became impossible for a long time.*

Freud's other example is, perhaps, even more striking:

In one of Heijermans' (1914) sketches there occurs an example of a bungled action which the author uses as a dramatic *motif*.

The sketch is called "Tom and Teddie". They are a pair of divers who appear in a variety theatre; their act is given in an iron tank with glass walls, in which they stay under water for a considerable time and perform tricks. Recently the wife has started an affair with another man, an animal-trainer. Her diver-husband has caught them together in the dressing-room just before the performance. Dead silence, menacing looks, with the diver saying: "Afterwards!" — The act begins. The diver is about to perform his hardest trick: he will remain "two and a half minutes under water in a sealed trunk". — This is a trick they had performed often enough; the trunk was locked and "Teddie used to show the key to the audience, who checked the time by their watches". She also used purposely to drop the key once or twice into the tank and then dive hurriedly after it, so as not to be too late when the time came for the trunk to be opened.

This particular evening, January 31st, saw Tom locked up as usual by the neat fingers of his brisk and nimble wife. He smiled behind the peep-hole — she played with the key and waited for his warning sign. The trainer stood in the wings, in his impeccable evening dress, with his white tie and his horse-whip. Here was the "other man". To catch her attention, he gave a very short whistle. She looked at him, laughed, and with the clumsy gesture of someone whose attention is distracted she threw the key so wildly in the air that at exactly two minutes and twenty seconds, by an accurate reckoning, it fell by the side of the tank in the middle of the bunting covering the pedestal. No one had seen it. No one could see it. Viewed from the house, the optical illusion was such that everyone saw the key fall into the water — and none of the stage hands heard it since bunting muffled the sound.

Laughing, Teddie clambered without delay, over the edge of the tank. Laughing — Tom was holding out well — she came down the ladder. Laughing, she disappeared under the pedestal to look there and,

---

*The Psychopathology of Everyday Life, translated by A. A. Brill (New York: Random House, 1938), pp. 123–124.

when she did not find the key at once, she bowed in front of the bunting with a priceless gesture, and an expression on her face as if to say "Gracious me! what a nuisance this is!"

Meanwhile Tom was grimacing in his droll way behind the peep-hole, as if he too was becoming agitated. The audience saw the white of his false teeth, the champing of his lips under the flaxen moustache, the comical bubble-blowing that they had seen earlier, when he was eating the apple. They saw his pale knuckles as he grappled and clawed, and they laughed as they had laughed so often already that evening.

"Two minutes and fifty-eight seconds . . . "

"Three minutes and seven seconds . . . twelve seconds . . . "

"Bravo! Bravo! Bravo!"

Then consternation broke out in the house and there was a shuffling of feet, when the stage hands and the trainer began to search too, and the curtain came down before the lid had been raised.

Six English dancing-girls came on — then the man with the ponies, dog and monkeys. And so on.

It was not till the next morning that the public knew there had been an accident, that Teddie had been left a widow . . . "

"It is clear from this quotation," Freud says of this story, "what an excellent understanding the author must himself have had of the nature of a symptomatic act, seeing that he demonstrates to us so strikingly the deeper cause of the fatal clumsiness."*

Although Freud's work must be taken into account in any effort to settle the important philosophical problem of freedom of choice, its primary purpose was not to make a contribution to that problem but rather to help people find relief from their distress.

Before turning to consider this metaphysical problem of free choice (or the Free Will/ Determinism problem, as it is called) let us consider what light Freud's work throws on this.

Although much of what Freud has said has come under attack, much is still regarded as insightful and has been confirmed by other researchers. The fact seems to be that much of what happened to us at an early age, even as infants, continues to play a determining role later in our lives — in fact, in great part success in living consists in unlearning what we have learned and what has become such an integral part of our being.

A remark by a character in T. S. Eliot's play *The Cocktail Party* sums up a lot of what Freud, and many other recent psychotherapists, have been trying to teach us. "You are nothing but a bundle of obsolete responses," he says. What

---

The Psychopathology of Everyday Life, translated by Alan Tyson (New York: Norton, 1960) pp. 189–190.

this means is that we continue to try to deal with life's problems by methods which may have and probably were effective once but are no longer.

Take the example of little Johnny. He had the misfortune to be born into the wrong family at the wrong time. Daddy is having a hard time at work and Johnny has therefore learned to make himself unseen and unheard when he hears those footsteps approaching. He has been slapped and beaten enough to know that the better part of valor for him, when Daddy arrives from work, is to slip away and hide. Thus little Johnny had learned to survive: he moves about in this world of his, shoulders slightly stooped, neck stiff, eyes shifting nervously, his voice barely audible.

But little Johnny is 18 now and in the intervening years Daddy's situation had improved — so much so, in fact, that Johnny has been sent not to the state university but to a private, expensive, and prestigious college. He needs Professor Jones's signature so that he can take his course, and so he calls on him. The door to Professor Jones's office is open. Still stooped, eyes still shifting nervously, and with a voice still hardly audible, he says: "P . . . P . . . P . . . J . . . J . . . Jones, I'm . . . m . . . m . . . m . . . John Smith."

John Smith is 18 and not 5-year-old frightened-to-death little-Johnny, fearful that Daddy will give him another thrashing should he utter something inappropriate. The responses that enabled him to survive then are totally obsolete now. To survive now, to say nothing of thriving, he must throw them away. He must learn to acquire new responses; he must learn to change.

But is it possible to change habits that have become so ingrained, so much a part of one's whole make-up? Freud was often quite pessimistic about this. Certainly such habits are not easily given up, and they are not easily given up because in many cases they still carry an important "pay-off."

Mildred Newman and Bernard Berkowitz, in their book *How To Take Charge of Your Life*, give an interesting example:

> The young woman in the therapy group was complaining bitterly. Every time she was forced to have lunch with her mother, it was a horrible experience.
>
> No matter how hard she tried, her mother was a "bitch" who always got angry and did her best to make her daughter feel rotten.
>
> The young woman was very convincing.
>
> We were all in sympathy with the innocent, well-intentioned daughter.
>
> We could feel her pain as she described being relentlessly picked on and put down by her mother.
>
> But as the group listened and asked questions the picture began to blur and other images emerged.
>
> The mother valued good grooming. It appeared that the daughter made a point of dressing a little more sloppily than usual when she met her mother for lunch.

The daughter managed to be late for their appointments, even though she knew her mother also valued promptness.

It became clear, as she went into the details of the conversation, that the daughter consistently brought up those topics about which the two had long-standing disagreements.

As we listened we began to understand that the daughter baited her mother into losing her temper. That made it possible for the daughter to erupt with her own pent-up anger.

Somehow the group was able to help her see that she was provoking her mother to behave that way. It was not simply that her mother was mean, rotten, and terrible to her. There was some need on the part of the daughter to get her mother to behave in a destructive way.

The group was able to see that for her own reasons it was important to the daughter that the mother "mistreat" her.

She dreaded these lunches precisely because she knew how they had to end. It was a big step for her to be able to see that she really got what she wanted.*

It may be, then, that we find it difficult to change or cannot do so because we still have the deep need to get even, to settle old scores, to have revenge. It may well be — and this is where the hopes of psychotherapy lie — that in coming to realize the high price these pay-offs exact from us, we will give up the behavior in question and be freed of the obsessions which cause us so much misery.

But the question, more philosophical than psychological, which remains is: are we really free to do so? Can such knowledge in itself be effective in bringing about the necessary changes so that we will no longer provoke the responses which continue to torment us, or is this behavior, partly inherited, perhaps, and partly nurtured in us at an age when we had no choice in the matter, now so much a part of the way we are that we are simply doomed? So although the knowledge of our condition provided by psychotherapy may make that condition less oppressive it cannot remove it.

Considerations such as these lead directly to the ancient but still very much unsolved problem of freedom and determinism.

Freedom and necessity

As we saw in the last chapter, both main answers proposed to the question of the best life for man to follow rested finally on the assumption that man was free. For Kant man's goodness lay in fulfilling his duty and for Aristotle it lay in fulfilling himself, but the question left unresolved in each case was whether man was free to follow these recommendations for achieving the good life.

*New York: Harcourt, Brace, Jovanovich, 1976, pp. 39–41. Reproduced by permission.

From what we have seen so far in this chapter the hopes seem dim: matters appear very much decided for us. Whether in fact they are, is what the question of the freedom of the will, perhaps one of the oldest and certainly one of the most explored questions in philosophy, is all about. It is one of the central questions in metaphysics. Let us therefore conclude our account of this part of philosophy by looking at it in some detail.

First let us note the main terms generally used in the discussion of Freedom versus Determinism or Necessity.

Determinism, the basic postulate of science, is the view that the whole realm of nature, including man, is governed by the law of cause and effect. Given the cause, the effect necessarily follows and every event, it asserts, has causes. These produce the event, form it, and determine it. This is a necessary assumption of science, whose whole object is to seek order or law in nature, "law" simply entailing the discovery of causes (which specify that whenever A happens, B must follow).

Indeterminism is a denial of determinism. It is the belief that some events do not have causes but spring into being by pure chance without any relation to anything preceding.

The problem is that we find ourselves trying to hold onto two positions about human nature which seem incompatible. On the one hand, we assume in science — and to a large extent in practice — that human nature is determined. We do so, for example, when we pick the people we want as our friends, the neighborhood to live in, the schools to attend, and so on, believing that there is a certain stability in human nature and that the people in question are people we will be able to count on, the neighborhood will have the characteristics expected, and the schools will live up to their reputations.

But the consequences of this seem unfortunate, for if determinism is true, given the past, no one can help doing whatever they do, and the belief that they could have acted differently — the idea of freedom — must be a delusion.

On the other hand, in many of our practical and moral judgments we do assume that a person could have acted differently. Thus we say, for example, "You ought not to have done that!" implying that he could have acted otherwise. If we did not believe he could have acted differently, we would not blame him for what he did. Similarly, when we deliberate about a future course of action, we implicitly believe the future is not yet settled, that our present deliberation makes a difference. But if determinism were true, the future would have to be regarded as settled, for the future is determined by the present, the present is determined by the past, and everything is already settled and finished. But this seems difficult to accept.

We find ourselves therefore in the dilemma of either accepting determinism and being unable to justify basic moral and practical judgments, or rejecting determinism and being unable to justify some basic scientific principles. But we seem to be compelled to accept one or the other, with the result that we are either unable to justify some very basic moral and practical judgments, or some basic scientific judgments.

This is not a comfortable dilemma. No one wants to take up an antiscientific standpoint, nor does anyone want to give up some of these very basic moral and practical judgments. We do not want to become strict determinists and say that becoming, say, an alcoholic is like catching tuberculosis. We do want to say that while catching tuberculosis does not depend upon my choice and is unavoidable, becoming an alcoholic is avoidable and does depend on choice. And still we do want to be sufficiently scientific (and determinist) and say that there are reasons that turn some people to drink.

Is there any way, then, out of this dilemma? There is no easy solution to this problem, and the two most obvious ones are each very clearly unsatisfactory. These are either to give up determinism or to give up freedom.

Suppose we tried the first "solution" and just denied that all events are caused by past events and assumed instead that some events have no causes, that they spring into existence without any cause at all — just out of the blue, as we say. Scientifically, there seems to be some justification for such a view, since at the microcosmic level events of an uncaused nature do seem to take place, the regularity normally observed being merely the result of averaging out billions of these random events.

Now even if these suppositions regarding random, uncaused events were true, they would be useless as a solution to the problem of freedom, for the problem arises because, from the moral point of view, we need to fix responsibility for certain actions on certain people. But if an event happens for which there is no cause, no one can be held responsible. One could simply claim that the event sprung into being from nowhere, and being a freak occurrence, one should not be held responsible for it. Indeterminism therefore proves too much.

Nor could one act on such an assumption. All our predictions about the future are based on the assumption that the future will be like the past, that there are laws at work in nature, and that nature is orderly. But if an event could merely spring into being uncaused, one cannot be held responsible for it, having had no control over it. Such "free" actions, if granted, would bring chaos into nature and make it impossible to hold anyone responsible for anything. If responsibility cannot be saved by arguing that some events are uncaused, then this solution to the problem proves to be no solution at all.

But if we cannot solve the problem by denying determinism, let us see whether we can solve it by denying freedom.

When we deliberate about what we will do, we assume that the future is still open and not yet settled. If we believe things are settled we do not bother to deliberate, we merely wait for them to happen. But if determinism were true, the future would really be settled, and thinking would have to be regarded as merely useless. The future, we would have to say, is determined by the present, the present by the past, and the past by something that occurred at a point in time when, perhaps, one did not even exist. And how can one be held responsible for something that occurred before one was even born?

And we can apply the same thinking to "thinking" itself. Is that, we might ask, also determined? If it is, then in a sense the thought in question, having no other rationale, is false and we need pay no attention to it. And if it is not determined, then there is at least one thing which is not determined, and the statement that thinking (meaning *all* thinking) is determined must be false. So in either case determinism would be false.

Obviously, then, the dilemma cannot be resolved by either rejecting determinism or rejecting freedom. These "solutions" prove to be no solutions. Some people have thought the solution to this problem lies in the fact that human beings possess the power of reason. Even on a practical level, they have pointed out, one can see this criterion at work. Thus the law does not hold a person responsible for his actions until he is, as the saying goes, of the "age of reason." And if one becomes legally insane, if one "loses one's reason," one ceases to be held responsible for what one does.

Human freedom, they have said, is therefore somehow bound up with our possession of the ability to reason. We are not like animals or inanimate objects, who presumably behave as they do because of the force of instinct or the laws of nature. Our possession of reason and ability to deliberate give us a degree of power, of freedom, to select alternative courses of action. It is in this sense, therefore, that we can be said to have choice and be free.

Freedom, they have therefore said, can be made compatible with determinism. One's conduct is indeed determined, but it is determined by one's reason — that is, by oneself — and in this sense it can be said to be self-determined. Since each of us has reason, each of us is therefore free and can and should therefore be held responsible for what we do.

While, however, the possession of reason does obviously make a difference to our condition and distinguishes us from other beings and things in nature, it does not quite solve the problem. One could, for example, still ask: why are some people rational and others not? Or, if that does not seem entirely accurate, we might put the question in this form: why are some people more rational than others? Was this difference caused or not? If it was caused, then we are back to determinism, and if it was not caused, if it was due entirely to chance, then we are left in the equally unsatisfactory position of complete indeterminism, and this, as we saw, is no better than determinism. And so the problem remains.

In discussing ethics in the last chapter, we observed how the contemporary movement in philosophy, known as Logical Positivism, settled those questions by "dissolving" them; let us conclude this chapter by noting the use of the same method for the attempted "dissolution" of this problem.

Logical Positivism's attack on this problem, the attempt to dissolve it by an analysis that shows where there has been a confusion between the meanings of very similar terms used in different contexts, consists in the main of two parts.

The first is the attempt to show that there is no contradiction between freedom and causality, for the proper contrast is not between freedom and causality but between freedom and constraint. The second lies in showing that the concept of law, as it applies in the investigation of nature (as when we talk of laws of nature or natural laws) and the concept of law as it applies in other contexts (as when we talk of the laws of God or of man, implying the notion of power or lawful authority) are completely different and that nothing but confusion results from treating them as if they were the same, or had the same logic.

A man cannot be said to be acting freely if his action is causally determined. But it might be argued that freedom is properly to be contrasted not with causality but with constraint, so that while it may be true that if I am constrained to do something, I am therefore caused to do it, it perhaps does not follow that if I am caused to do something (as a result, say, of being the type of person I am) I am thereby constrained to do it.

For example, if someone holds a gun to my head to make me do something, then I am obviously constrained and not free. Similarly if I suffer from such a psychological condition as kleptomania, then I can similarly be said to be constrained and not free, because a kleptomaniac does not go through any process of deliberating whether to steal or not to steal. Whatever he resolved to do he would steal just the same.

But given that I am not a kleptomaniac or that no one has held a gun to my head forcing me to do what I did, then whatever I do, although causally determined by prior calculation and decision on my part, has to be regarded as voluntary and free. An action is voluntary, in short, according to this view, if one was not constrained to do it by threat or physical force or undue persuasion. If these conditions are fulfilled then this is what we mean by saying one acted freely — even though the choice and action was causally determined by the nature of person you are.

Linguistic analysts believe the point they are making here is not new; many of their British predecessors have asserted it. A case in point is the following comment from David Hume:

> It will not require many words to prove, that all mankind have ever agreed in the doctrine of liberty as well as in that of necessity, and that the whole dispute, has been hitherto merely verbal. For what is meant by liberty, when applied to voluntary actions? We cannot surely mean, that actions have so little connection with motives, inclinations, and circumstances, that one does not follow with a certain degree of uniformity from the other, and that one affords no inference by which we can conclude the existence of the other. For these are plain acknowledged matters of fact. By liberty, then, we can only mean *a power of acting, or not acting, according to the determination of the will:* that is, if we choose to remain at rest, we may; if we choose to move, we also may. Now this hypothetical liberty is universally allowed to belong to every one, who is not a prisoner and in chains. Here then is no subject of dispute.
> *(An Inquiry Concerning Human Understanding,* Section VIII, Part I).

The main point is therefore that liberty is not to be contrasted with causal determination but with external constraint.

Linguistic philosophers themselves, however, are aware that as reasonable and attractive as this view may be, it does not quite satisfy. Granted that our actions are causally determined by our own will (and are therefore free, not being compelled by external forces), but what about this will itself, this character of ours from which these actions are supposed to flow? Hasn't this character or will been somehow determined by factors in the natural and social environment over which we may have had little, if any, control?

In other words, one could still maintain, as we have already had occasion to observe, that our own psychological make-up and character in general are determined, without our really having anything to do with it, by natural laws of the same kind as those which operate in the physical and biological spheres. Many of the recent advances in behaviorist psychology would tend to support this view.

The crux of the problem coming to lie, as it appears, in the concept of *law*, linguistic philosophy has turned its attention to it. They have gone on to point out — and this constitutes the second part of their attack on the problem — that there is a logical muddle in the concept of *law* as applied in the context of the problem and as generally used in the context of science.

"Natural" laws, so-called, they have pointed out, are descriptive and not prescriptive: they describe what does happen or what has been observed to happen. They refer to observed uniformities. They do not prescribe what must happen, what has got to happen, nor, of course, what should happen. They are merely generalizations about observed regularities in nature. It is, of course, true that based upon them, predictions of high probability about the future can be made; but that still does not mean that they prescribe either what *must* or *ought* to happen.

Although we still have a strong tendency to speak of natural laws as if they were decrees (as when we speak, for example, of the natural laws *governing* the motions of the planets) it is very misleading to do so. Natural or scientific laws are not rules laid down by some authority that the planets have to obey. The so-called laws of nature, which are just metaphors or figures of speech, do not compel or command anything. They are simply descriptions of what, say, the planets, in common with other material bodies, in fact do. And similarly with so-called psychological laws that occur in the study of human behavior. These "laws" merely describe how people actually behave, they are not prescriptive and do not "order" or "force" people to behave as they do.

It is obvious that, being descriptions of observed regularity and not prescriptions, scientific laws are totally unlike laws of the state or laws of God. One can see more clearly how different these two types of "laws" are when we consider what happens when each of them are broken. If a law of the state is broken it still remains a law, and we continue to speak of it as such. But if what we call a law of nature is broken it ceases to be, or to be regarded, as a law, and is simply discarded as an exploded theory, or an inadequate hypothesis that no longer fits the facts.

It is therefore quite misleading, linguistic analysts have gone on to conclude, to speak as if scientific laws, whether in psychology or the behavioral sciences or anything else, ever could limit freedom of action. Laws of nature, which are generalizations from observation, do not, and, in the nature of the case, cannot "constrain" us. Therefore they cannot be spoken of as destroying human freedom. Human action, therefore, although in general predictable, is nevertheless free. So much, according to linguistic analysis, for the paradox of Freedom and Necessity.

As attractive as this reduction of the paradox may seem, others still find it difficult to set to rest the lingering suspicion that if, indeed, an action is in principle predictable, then it is not free. Although linguistic philosophers tend to reply to this that to say so is to reduce the problem to the purely verbal one as to what we mean by the term "free," others have tended to take the position that what we are to mean by "free" is, on the contrary, precisely what the problem is about.

Besides, as other critics have gone on to point out, linguistic philosophers have themselves been guilty here of a type of linguistic confusion. Certainly, as they have urged, a descriptive law does not say what ought to happen but if it is *really* a law it will tell us what has indeed got to happen.

For the word "law" can apply to what we may call "regularities," that is, recurrent events; it can apply to the *formulation* of these regularities; and it can apply to those forces in nature that underlie the observed regularities. Thus, "gravity" could refer to the equation applied to the set of regularities observed, but it could also stand for the real force itself. The former would clearly be a descriptive law, but the latter would be neither descriptive nor prescriptive but simply a "fact." The former could not be the sort of thing which could compel anything to happen, the latter easily could.

The solution to this ancient problem is thus obviously still beyond us.

Summary

1. The area of philosophy concerned with defining the nature of reality is called metaphysics. In addition to considering such questions as what the world as a whole is like, where it came from, and whether it has a goal towards which it is evolving (Rational Cosmology), it is also concerned with such further and related questions as what we are like and why we are here, whether we are free to do what we wish, and what happens to us after death (Rational Psychology). Finally, it is concerned with whether the world is ruled by a supreme Being, a God, who guides it on its course and metes out rewards and punishments (Rational Theology).

2. The attempt to unravel the design of the universe has always been fraught with danger for philosophers. Tending to challenge established religion and deeply held convictions, their discoveries about the nature of the universe have dismayed their contemporaries and

sometimes led to their deaths. In the history of astronomy one of the most tragic examples is the fate suffered by Giordano Bruno, whose speculations about other worlds and an infinite universe raised serious questions regarding the Crucifixion and God's mercy. For this "blasphemy" he was burnt at the stake.

3. It was left for Sigmund Freud to unravel the design within, and although he did not suffer Giordano Bruno's fate for doing so, his revelations were at first greeted with contempt and derision. Many of these relevations, however, have withstood the test of time, and much of what he discovered regarding our condition — especially the role that unconscious factors play in our lives — has come to be accepted by most psychologists today.

4. If we are part of a universe that is governed, as it appears, by immutable laws, and if, furthermore, we are compelled to live lives that are shaped by factors beyond our knowledge and control, then the question arises, to what degree can we be said to be free? This is the ancient problem of Freedom and Determinism, and on its resolution rests the question whether we are ever justified in holding anyone accountable for what he does.

5. The attempt to solve the problem by either denying freedom or denying determinism proves to be no solution, for the former, although succeeding in reaffirming the principles of science, tends to undermine those of morality, and the latter, although at first seeming to reaffirm the principles of morality, in the end tends to undermine both them and those of science as well.

6. The attempt on the part of linguistic analysts to dissolve the problem by showing that it has arisen from a false contrast (between freedom and causality rather than between freedom and restraint) as well as from confusion regarding the notion of causality (arising from the failure to differentiate between descriptive and prescriptive "laws"), although illuminating, does not prove entirely satisfactory either, and the solution to this ancient problem continues to elude us.

For further study

1. For an excellent collection of readings in metaphysics see *Introductory Readings in Metaphysics,* selected and edited by Richard Taylor (Englewood Cliffs, N.J.: Prentice Hall, 1978).

2. For a moving account of Bruno's life and a readable translation of his major work see Dorothea Waley Singer's *Giordano Bruno: His*

Life and Thought with an annotated translation of his work *On the Infinite Universe and Worlds* (New York: Henry Schuman, 1950).

3. For a recent and relatively brief account of Freud's thought see Richard Wollheim's *Sigmund Freud* (New York: Viking, 1971).

4. For a biographical novel about Freud see Irving Stone's *The Passions of the Mind* (Garden City: Doubleday, 1971).

5. The new and authoritative translation of Freud's *Psychopathology of Everyday Life* is the Norton edition by Alan Tyson, edited with an introduction by James Strachey (New York: 1965). The first English translation of this work by A. A. Brill, Freud's first American disciple, is still highly readable. It is available in the Mentor paperback edition (New York: New American Library, N.D.).

6. Among the many editions and collections of works on the problem of freedom and determinism the following three will be found especially helpful: (a) *Free Will and Determinism*, edited by Bernard Berofsky (New York: Harper, 1966). (b) *The Problem of Free Will: Selected Readings*, edited with an introduction by Willard F. Enteman (New York: Scribner's, 1967). (c) *Determinism, Free Will, and Moral Responsibility*, edited by Gerald Dworkin (Englewood Cliffs, N.J.: Prentice-Hall, 1970).

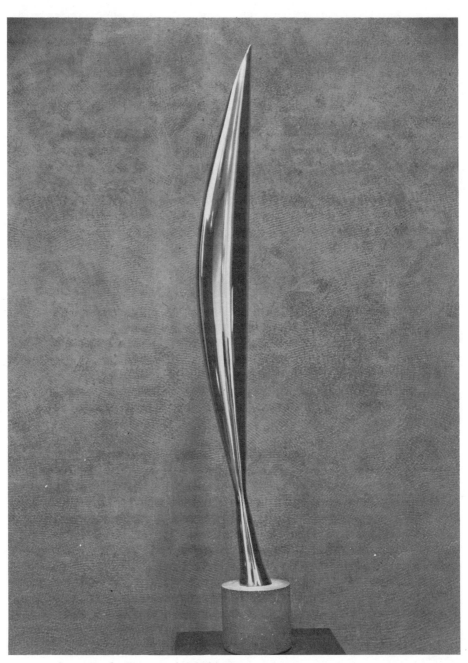

Constantin Brancusi, *Bird in Space.* The Museum of Modern Art.

chapter 7

Epistemology
How do we know all this?

Introduction

Dr. Wayne Dyer, in his popular book *Your Erroneous Zones*, relates the following story:

> A speaker stood before a group of alcoholics determined to demonstrate to them, once and for all, that alcohol was an evil beyond compare. On the platform he had what appeared to be two identical containers of clear fluid. He announced that one contained pure water and the other was filled with undiluted alcohol. He placed a small worm in the container while everyone watched as it swam around and headed for the side of the glass, whereupon it simply crawled to the top of the glass. He then took the same worm and placed it in the container with alcohol. The worm disintegrated right before their eyes. "There," said the speaker.

"What's the moral?" A voice from the rear of the room said quite clearly,
"I see that if you drink alcohol, you'll never have worms (p. 11)".

The moral of this story is, of course, what all of us know so well, that we see what we want to see. But we do not always recognize how pervasive and far-reaching that simple truth is. Let us consider some further examples.

In 1955 social psychologist Solomon Asch performed an experiment with college students that is still regarded as a classic. Asch told the students that they were going to be subjects in an experiment on visual judgment. Each subject was then put in a room, along with seven or eight other "subjects" who were really the experimenter's collaborators. Pairs of cards were then passed around and each "subject" (including, of course, the experimenter's planted subjects) was asked to pick out the line on Card B that matched in length the single line of Card A. The real subject was not aware, of course, that his fellow "subjects" were the experimenter's collaborators, and the idea was to see what influence, if any, group pressure would have on their decisions. The results were that the subjects — all of them intelligent, perceptive, alert students — almost uniformly went along with the group and picked out the wrong answer from the three lines on Card B, even when Asch made the wrong lines so wrong that nobody, seemingly, could possible miss (*Scientific American*, November, 1955).

A similar experiment devised to study the influence of sex prejudice on our attitudes and judgments produced the same results. Students were handed a brief essay on some difficult economic problem and were asked to give their opinions of the clarity and persuasiveness of the argument. Half the students were given copies identifying the author as "John Miller" and the other half were given copies with "Joan Miller" as the author. Even though the essays were identical in all copies, except for the name, the students with the copies signed "John Miller" rated the essay higher than those whose copy listed its author as "Joan Miller."

This latter experiment is perhaps more impressive than the former one, since it may be argued that the subjects in the former experiment really did see the lines were unequal but went along with the dominant opinion in order not to cause trouble; in the second experiment no such overt pressure was exerted and the subjects, apparently, actually believed they were judging the words fairly and objectively.

One last example: It might not perhaps seem too strange and surprising that teachers who are told the class they have been assigned (and only the teacher is told this, not the students nor their parents) is one of the brightest in the school and that the students in it are expected to make dramatic gains in their work, find this to be the case. But it surely would be surprising if *rats* performed better when the experimenters were falsely informed that the rats had been specially bred for intelligence. Yet this has proven to be the case.

The lesson these examples teach is obvious. There is no such thing as an "innocent eye." Our seeing is selective, filtered, and screened. What we receive is usually what we expect, or want, or believe, or are used to. What comes to be, in short, "seen" depends on experience, context, and interpretation; it is a joint product of the observer and the observed.

We have been considering so far the influence that psychological or cultural factors exert on our "seeing" or perceptions. There are in addition biological factors that limit us in even more striking and universal ways.

Sense awareness, first of all, varies profoundly among species. Some species have senses we lack, such as sensitivity to radio waves or to magnetic fields. Certain fish, for example, sense their surroundings by the deformation of electric fields, and some birds do so by changes in the barometric pressure.

The kind of information available to each creature, furthermore, is determined not only by its senses, but also by the range of stimuli. Human beings can hear sounds ranging from about 16 to 20,000 cycles per second, but some moths can hear up to 200,000 cycles; human sensitivity to odors is minimal, but salmon can smell their way home through countless miles of trackless water; we can see a spectrum of colors ranging from violet to red, but this relatively small range of visible light lies within a vast continuous range of similar electromagnetic waves not visible to us.

But not only are certain avenues of stimuli either completely closed to us or greatly limited, some are either highly ambiguous or downright deceptive. Grass is green, we say, but is it green on a cloudy day? Or under a microscope? Or to one who is color-blind? And what about dreams, illusions, and hallucinations — and phantom pain in amputated limbs? In these cases it is not a matter of something appearing other than it is (an oar appearing bent when submerged) but of having perceptions to which no physical objects correspond.

Our common-sense beliefs — that we perceive physical objects directly, that these objects exist independently of us, and that the character of these objects is as we perceive them to be — become highly suspect when these psychological, cultural, and biological phenomena are considered.

The truth seems to be that every organism lives in a world shaped for it by the nature of its sensory apparatus. Epistemology, or the study of the theory of knowledge, is that area of philosophy concerned with investigating the implications of this truth. It is the study of the ways in which the knower knows the known. The following are the main questions it has traditionally posed to itself:

What are the principal grounds of knowledge?
How certain can we properly be of what we think we know?
Are there limits beyond which we cannot reasonably hope to extend knowledge?

Sense and reason have traditionally been regarded as our two main sources of knowledge, and in modern times, when philosophic interest in epistemology reached a peak, replacing the medieval absorption with metaphysics, two schools tended to form round this issue. One, called rationalism, emphasized the role of reason in knowledge, the other, called empiricism, emphasized the role of sense or experience.

It is to the thought of these two schools, beginning with Descartes, the father of modern philosophy and the champion of rationalism, that we now turn.

The rationalists

Descartes

Descartes was born in 1596 in La Haye, a small town in Touraine, France, now called La Haye-Descartes, or simply Descartes.

The seventeenth century in which Descartes lived was a period of great intellectual activity and achievement, and among his contemporaries were such giants of the world of the intellect as Shakespeare, who had just finished *The Merchant of Venice*, and Galileo, who had just conducted his famous experiments.

Descartes's family belonged to the lesser nobility, with a long tradition of government service, his father being a councillor of the Parliament of Brittany. Upon his death Descartes inherited from him sufficient property to be financially independent for the rest of his life.

René Descartes. Mary Evans Picture Library, London.

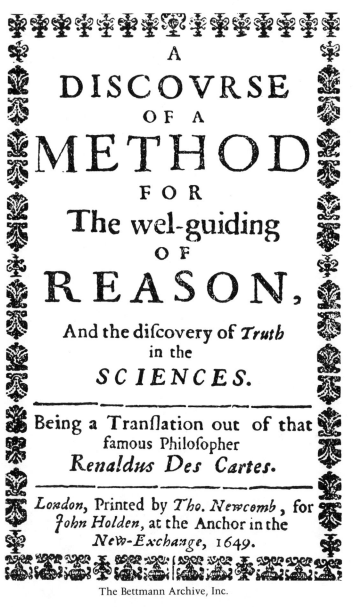

A
DISCOVRSE
OF A
METHOD
FOR
The wel-guiding
OF
REASON,
And the difcovery of *Truth*
in the
SCIENCES.

Being a Tranflation out of that
famous Philofopher
Renaldus Des Cartes.

London, Printed by *Tho. Newcomb*, for
John Holden, at the Anchor in the
New-Exchange, 1649.

The Bettmann Archive, Inc.

From 1604 to 1612 Descartes attended the Jesuit college of La Flèche, where he studied ancient languages, philosophy, and mathematics. He found himself deeply drawn to mathematics, to which he was later to make notable contributions, and deeply dissatisfied with the other studies, which he determined to abandon to seek only after such science "as he might discover in himself or in the great book of the world."

From La Flèche Descartes proceeded to the University of Poitiers, where in

1616 he graduated in law. Weary of study, he went to live in Paris, where for a period he led a life of indulgence: traveling, gambling, dueling. Tiring of this too, he enlisted as a soldier in the armies fighting the Thirty Years' War, eventually serving on both sides, the Protestant and the Catholic.

Leaving the army in 1621, he devoted himself to further study and travel. Feeling finally the need of solitude, he decided to settle down in Holland, the center then of culture and intellectual freedom. It was here that in the next 20 years (1629–1649) he wrote the works upon which his fame rests: *Discourse on Method* (1637), *Meditations on First Philosophy* (1641), *Principles of Philosophy* (1644), and *The Passions of the Soul* (1649).

By 1649 Descartes's fame was so great that Queen Christina of Sweden, just 22 years old, summoned him to teach her philosophy. He hesitated to go, but she was insistent, sent a ship to fetch him, and he came. The only time, however, she could spare for instruction in philosophy was 5 o'clock in the morning. Descartes—who, because of frail health, had been in the habit of staying in bed till noon—found the new regimen a great ordeal. In addition, the lessons were conducted in a cold library. Descartes caught pneumonia and died. He was 54 years old.

He had been educated, Descartes tells us, at one of the most celebrated schools in Europe, yet in thinking back on his studies he could not help but

Queen Christina of Sweden. Mary Evans Picture Library, London.

wonder about their value. The charming fables of ancient literature, although intellectually stimulating, were, after all, only fables that, portraying behavior of a superhuman kind, could obviously not be emulated by us. Nor was poetry any more helpful: certainly poets had the ability to make the truth "shine forth more brightly" than the philosophers, but their works were the product of inspiration, not the result of the application of a special method that we could adopt to further our knowledge. Nor could one find such a method in theology whose "revealed truths are quite above our intelligence." Finally, the philosophy taught him was not any more helpful, for he could not find a single thing it it that was "not subject to dispute." What he had been taught at school he found was therefore either unbelievable, incomprehensible, or doubtful.

He decided therefore, he tells us, to abandon books and learning for that "great book of the world," where, he thought, he might discover what he was seeking — a more exact type of reasoning and more certainty. But to his dismay, he found as much difference of opinion among practical men as among philosophers.

Not discouraged, he resolved to continue his search. Then on a memorable night, November 10, 1619, he had three dreams in which the key to the knowledge he was seeking was finally revealed to him.

The strange odyssey Descartes describes — which led him to break completely with the past, start afresh, and build a system of knowledge upon the powers of human reason alone — is highly reminiscent of the remarkably similar odyssey undertaken by Socrates many centuries earlier. But there are two interesting and significant differences: Descartes was searching for knowledge, not wisdom, and it led him to the discovery not of the soul but of the mind, conceived as a separate substance or entity distinct from the body. This was to prove to be a discovery of momentous importance in philosophy.

What Descartes had been vouchsafed that fateful night was a new method of securing knowledge. He had been enormously impressed with the success and achievements of mathematics and he suddenly saw that similar success might accompany his efforts were he to follow its procedure. What was therefore required was to abstract those rules that have been responsible for its success and use them in placing science and philosophy on a similarly sound foundation.

Analyzing the procedure used in mathematics, he discovered that what was characteristic of it was that it began with very simple and clear ideas, whose truth the mind was capable of apprehending directly and knowing with absolute certainty and distinctness. It then advanced step by step toward more complex truths, making sure that each step of the argument was indisputable. The mind achieved the first truths, Descartes saw, by way of *intuition* (a vision of such clarity that it left one in no doubt regarding the truth of what was apprehended) and the subsequent ones by way of *deduction* (a series of careful, clear, and certain inferences proceeding from what is obvious and simple to what is more complex and remote). Knowledge required both procedures.

Being certain he had found the proper method and wishing to make sure he would not forget or neglect it, he recorded the four principles it embraced:

The *first* was never to accept anything for true which I did not clearly know to be such . . . to comprise nothing more in my judgment than was presented to my mind so clearly and distinctly as to exclude all ground of doubt. The *second*, to divide each of the difficulties under examination into as many parts as possible, and as might be necessary for its adequate solution. The *third*, to conduct my thoughts in such order that by commencing with objects the simplest and easiest to know, I might ascend by little and little, and, as it were, step by step, to the knowledge of the more complex . . . And the *last*, in every case to make enumerations so complete, and reviews so general, that I might be assured that nothing was omitted.*

But is it possible to find in science and philosophy simple, clear, and obvious axioms on whose foundations we might construct this new system of knowledge, one that would be indubitable? Descartes was not certain of this but he was willing to try. In order to be faithful to his vision he decided that from now on he would accept nothing as true unless he clearly and distinctly perceived it to be so; even if it turned out that he would have to discard the most honored and cherished beliefs. How should he go about this? It occurred to him that he might accomplish it by turning himself into a radical skeptic and doubting everything that could possibly be doubted. As he put it: "Because I wished to give myself entirely to the search after truth, I thought it was necessary for me to reject as absolutely false everything concerning which I could imagine the least ground of doubt." He determined to sweep away all his former opinions "so that they might later on be replaced, either by others which were better, or by the same, when I had made them conform to the uniformity of a rational scheme."

Once he began to apply this method of doubt it quickly became apparent to him how uncertain indeed the knowledge he had been taught really was. He saw that he could without much difficulty doubt authorities; he could doubt common sense; he could doubt the testimony of the senses and memory; and he could doubt all the sciences based on these sources of knowledge. What could be clearer, as he reasoned to himself, than "that I am here, seated by the fire holding this paper in my hands?" But when I am asleep, I dream that I am sitting by the fire, and this makes me realize that "there are no conclusive indications by which waking life can be distinguished from sleep." But if the world and everything in it may thus simply be part of a dream, is it not similarly possible that this is true even of the sciences that deal with things? Although it is tempting to believe that mathematics and science are certain, for "whether I am awake or asleep, two and three together will always make the number five," yet it is possible to doubt that too, for this world may be the creation of an evil demon who leads me to be deceived even in matters of this sort as well.

If I can doubt whether there really are such things as an earth and a sky and external things, and whether two and three make five, can't I even doubt

*Discourse on Method, Part II.

whether I am now presently doubting? Having uttered this, Descartes caught himself and came to realize that that was one thing he could *not* doubt, for obviously it was impossible for him to doubt that he was doubting! Doubting being a form of thinking, Descartes came to express the indubitable truth he had finally discovered in the slogan, one of the most famous in all philosophy, "I think, therefore, I am."

This became Descartes's starting point — his Archimedean point of certainty on the basis of which he could now go on to construct a body of certain knowledge. "Remarking that this truth, *I think, therefore, I am* was so solid and so certain that all the most extravagant suppositions of the skeptics were incapable of upsetting it, I judged that I could receive it without scruple as the first priniciple of the philosophy that I sought."

Enquiring now what it was about this proposition that made it so certainly true, Descartes found it was the "clarity and distinctness" with which it forced itself upon him. He therefore decided to adopt this as his criterion of truth. If it would be absurd or nonsensical to deny a certain judgment as not being true, then that will constitute proof that the judgment in question is true. Any proposition will necessarily by true, in short, if it possesses this same extreme and peculiar kind of self-evidence.

But where is one to find other judgments as self-evident as the judgment "I exist"? In reflecting on this, it struck Descartes that the judgment "A perfect Being exists" had the same peculiar kind of clarity and distinctness. He thought that like the judgment "I exist" it too, once one understands what it conveys, cannot be logically doubted. For "by the name God," he reasoned, "I understand a substance which is infinite, independent, all knowing, all-powerful and by which I myself and everything else, if anything else exists, has been created." This being so, how can I, a finite, imperfect substance, produce the idea of an infinite and perfect substance? I obviously cannot. Therefore, since ideas have causes, and since the cause must have at least as much reality as the effect, God alone must be the cause of the idea I have of Him.

It is doubtful that many will be as convinced of the obviousness of this proof of God's existence as Descartes was, nor was this the only proof he offered in behalf of the judgment. Nevertheless he himself seems to have been convinced by it and proceeded to use it to establish his third and last major proposition — the existence of the external world. And his proof of this was simply that God, being good, would not deceive us. Although our ordinary judgments of perception are fallible and our senses at times deceive us, human knowledge, he came to conclude, is fundamentally reliable.

Although the existence of God is the second of Descartes's three major foundation stones of his system, having once set it in place he tended to neglect it in favor of the other two. And these two — mind and matter, distinct substances, existing independently of one another, each capable of being known and studied apart from the other — came to constitute the main ingredients of his philosophy.

Historically, one of the important consequences of this dualism of mind and matter, which came to constitute the philosophy of Descartes, was that it separated philosophy from science, allowing each to pursue its separate domains uninhibited by conflict with the other (philosophy taking charge of the mind and investigating it, and science being relegated to the study of matter and its laws of operation). Its major historical disadvantage, however, was that it bequeathed to philosophy a new and difficult problem, that of defining the relation between these two basic and utterly different realities. And this problem has continued to bedevil philosophy to this very day.

Nevertheless, this separation of the mind from the body or from matter came to be seen as Descartes's main contribution to philosophy. No philosopher before him had made the division as clearly and sharply as he had, And certainly no one before him had raised the mind to the level of matter, making it equal in importance. Mind and consciousness thus became, as they still are, the basic subject matter of philosophical investigation.

The immediate problem, however, was to define the relation between the two substances: if the two are as distinct as Descartes maintained, how do they come to interact with one another? Descartes himself believed the mind was "lodged" in the body ("as a pilot in a vessel") and was closely "united" with it. But how united?

All subsequent philosophy, up to the present day, has been concerned with defining this relation: European rationalists holding onto the division, and proposing ingenious methods of bridging it; the British empiricists trying to dissolve the division by reducing the one to the other (either by showing how mind is derived from matter, or matter is derived from mind).

The first major European thinker to pick things up where Descartes had left them was Spinoza.

Spinoza

Baruch Spinoza (1632–1677) was born in Holland, the son of a Portuguese Jewish family, refugees from the Spanish Inquisition. Sent to Hebrew school to study for the rabbinate, he was soon torn by doubts, unable to accept literally the teachings of the scriptures. He alarmed the Jewish community by expressing his doubts. Not at that time entitled to citizenship, and fearful of reprisals for permitting heresy in their midst, they formally excommunicated him, placing a curse on his head and forbidding on pain of excommunication anyone from seeing or communicating with him. He was then 24 years old.

Spinoza took the news calmly and for the rest of his life lived a lonely, quiet existence in various places in Holland, earning his living by grinding and polishing lenses. He died at 44, the victim of tuberculosis, exacerbated by the glass dust he had inhaled practicing his vocation.

Only two books by him appeared during his lifetime: one an exposition of Cartesianism entitled *The Principles of Descartes' Philosophy* (1663); the other, published anonymously, entitled *Treatise on Theology and Politics* (1670). This second work became a milestone in Biblical criticism, initiating the study of the

Baruch Spinoza. À La Vieille Russie Gallery, New York.

Bible as a historical document. It was also one of the first works to advocate the separation of church and state, to stress the value of individual liberty and religious toleration, and to argue for democracy as against the claims of monarchy and aristocracy.

But the dominant note of Spinoza's works was pantheism. This was not lost on his readers and during his lifetime and for at least two centuries after his death this aroused intense and almost universal indignation and led him to be despised as an atheist. It was only in the late nineteenth century that a change occurred and he became venerated, as he still is, as a "God-intoxicated man" and the model of what a philosopher should be.

Spinoza's crowning achievement was his masterpiece *The Ethics*, on which he began working in 1662 and into which he poured all his thought. It has come to be regarded as one of the most majestic of all philosophical works. It deals not only with ethics, as its title suggests, but with such diverse subject matters as physics, metaphysics, and psychology. He named it *Ethics* because he believed that the purpose of philosophical investigation and thought was not just speculation but moral action.

In common with Descartes, Spinoza thought that we could achieve exact knowledge of reality if we followed the methods which had proven so successful in geometry. And so, starting with simple, clear, and distinct first principles, he went on to deduce the whole of what he thought was knowable concerning reality by a process of deduction, using Euclid's geometry as his model. The result was a philosophical work consisting of a highly systematic arrangement of principles and axioms, all carefully and neatly demonstrated.

Spinoza chose as his starting point certain basic axioms, which, with Descartes, he believed were not arbitrarily hit upon but were vouchsafed by the mind as reflections of the true nature of things. And Spinoza's reasoning was the same here as Descartes's: since these ideas had the requisite properties of being both clear and distinct, and since every clear and distinct idea is true, a complete and systematic arrangement of them must give us a true picture of reality.

But sad to say, although Descartes and Spinoza claimed to rely upon the evidence of reason, and both claimed that evidence to be infallible, the reasoning of the one turned out to be different from the reasoning of the other. For in the system of Spinoza, Descartes's dualism became transformed into a monism, the two Cartesian substances — mind and body — definitive of reality, became aspects of only one substance, which he called "Nature" or "God."

Spinoza arrived at this by working out the logical implications of Descartes's basic ideas more rigorously and more consistently than Descartes had done. Descartes had started with the clear and distinct idea of his own existence and from it went on to deduce the existence of God and then the world. But Spinoza recognized that since God is obviously prior to everything else — being the only truly independent substance there can be — we must begin with him and by deduction try to discover whatever is true about us and the world. Furthermore, if "substance" is that which needs nothing other than itself in order to exist, then, strictly speaking, there can be only one substance, and everything else must be dependent on it. Consequently, thought and extension (Descartes's two other mutually independent substances) cannot really be separate substances but must be attributes of the one, single, independent substance, which is God.

God or Nature thus became for Spinoza the sole existent substance in the world. Whatever is, "is in God, and nothing can exist or be conceived without God." Everything in the universe is dependent on him and God is the cause of all things and the principle within which all things find their being. Thought and extension, which had been conceived by Descartes as attributes of mind and body, are really, Spinoza went on to explain, themselves attributes of that one single substance — mind and body being really "modes" or modifications of those two attributes. Attributes, he went on to explain, are ways in which our intellect perceives this one basic and infinite substance. We as human beings perceive God in terms of only these two attributes, but there are in reality an infinite number of ways in which this one infinite and eternal substance can manifest itself.

Thought and extension being attributes of God, and mind and body being modes of these attributes, it would not be correct to say that God is the creator of the world. God *is* the world. Similarly, since both thought and extension, or mind and body, are ultimately manifestations of this same basic substance, it would be incorrect to say that mind and body are separate and independent entities. They are really one, and what occurs in one finds its correlative occurrence in the other. Consciousness is thus not separate from body; it is simply "the idea of the body." The problem, therefore, of how mind can affect the body, or how the body can affect the mind, does not arise, for there is (as in the case, for example, of a concave and convex lense) a parallelism, not an inexplicable mysterious interaction between them.

These basic, and to Spinoza, simple and obvious metaphysical first principles, entailed certain important consequences of a moral and practical sort. And in the remaining portions of his major work, *The Ethics*, Spinoza went on to explain what these were. First, since everything is in God or is God, and everything therefore simply follows from the necessity of His nature, events must be seen as simply unfolding in the only possible way they can. It follows from this that being part of God we are not free to go our separate ways but are compelled to live lives whose destinies are fixed from eternity. And finally, this being so, nothing is in itself good or evil but only in relation to human interests. To God, and from "the aspect of eternity," all is fair.

The consequence of all this is, Spinoza argued, that such human emotions as hope and fear, humility and repentence, envy and hatred, with which we are burdened, are useless and futile, for the future is unalterably fixed. We can free ourselves, however, from our bondage to these emotions (for being the bodily equivalents of mental ideas they can be altered by knowledge) by striving through reason to achieve that identification with the order of the universe which will enable us to see how things must be the way they are. Spinoza calls this acceptance and love of our fate "the intellectual love of God." Its reward is "blessedness."

Leibniz

The last of the great rationalist philosophers on the continent to try to solve the basic problem raised by Descartes was Gottfried Wilhelm von Leibniz, born in Leipzig, Germany, in 1646. With Leibniz we have again that strange phenomenon — the boy genius. Not uncommon in the worlds of music and mathematics, it is rare elsewhere.

Mastering practically everything there was to master by the age of 20, Leibniz applied for the degree of Doctor of Laws at the University of Leipzig. The professors turned him down, partly because of his age, but partly also because they were jealous of his knowledge.

Incensed, he left his home town for Altdorf, where the University of Nuremberg offered him the degree as well as a professorship. He accepted the degree, declined the professorship, and set himself to master whatever still remained — leading Frederick the Great, one of his patrons, later to describe him as a "whole academy in himself."

At 21 Leibniz entered diplomatic service, serving in the capacity of librarian,

Baron Gottfried Wilhelm von Leibniz. Mary Evans Picture Library, London.

advisor, statesman, and international lawyer. Working every waking hour, he corresponded with scholars in 20 countries.

It was at this time that he invented a computing machine which was in many ways a remarkable anticipation of our modern computers. He also planned and partially worked out an international language modeled on mathematics. This was a forerunner of the system of symbolic logic, which was to come into its own some 200 years later.

In 1675 Leibniz discovered the differential calculus; and a year later, independently of Newton's slightly earlier work, he discovered the infinitesimal calculus. A long and bitter dispute arose as to who stole from whom, people taking sides along nationalistic lines: the French siding with Leibniz, the English with Newton. As a result of this, English mathematics fell behind for a century, because the Newtonian notation was not as flexible as the Leibnizian, which the French adopted.

It was also at this time that he took up the librarianship at Hanover, a position in which he remained until his death. When George of Hanover became King of England in 1714, Leibniz, because of the unfortunate repercussions of the controversy about the calculus, was not invited to follow the court to London. He stayed behind, embittered and neglected, and died two years later in 1716, at the age of seventy.

Although known as the best-of-all-possible-worlds philosopher, Leibniz's life, expecially toward the end, was hardly idyllic. Although acknowledged the greatest thinker of his time, he died friendless and alone — only one man attended the funeral. As one acquaintance wrote: "He was buried more like a robber than what he really was, the ornament of his country."

Although Leibniz was a prolific writer, his best known and still most widely read book is his *Monadology* (1714), which he wrote in response to a request by a royal patron for a short account of his philosophy.

Like Spinoza before him, Leibniz's work grows out of his reaction to the ideas of his predecessors. These include those of Spinoza as well as Descartes. What Leibniz found wanting in the systems of Descartes and Spinoza was their conception of substance. In his view it was not static but dynamic, and furthermore, it did not consist of a single entity (as Spinoza had maintained) nor of two (as Descartes had held) but of many. Spinoza's monism and Descartes's dualism was replaced in Leibniz's system with a type of pluralism.

Although what Leibniz says about the nature of this basic stuff of the universe is somewhat reminiscent of Democritus's atoms, his conception of it is in reality quite different. Calling these basic units "monads," he conceived them as unextended, endlessly diverse, throbbing centers of energy; each, furthermore, having the capacity of reflecting (some more clearly and more fully than others) the universe as a whole.

Our minds or souls, he suggested, are just such dynamic, immaterial monads, and what is true of our minds is true, in varying degrees, of all monads. They are all possessed of the same psychic, spiritual drives we find in ourselves and like us are endowed with powers of sensation and perception (or perhaps something analogous to what we know as "sensation" and "perception"), for the same principle, he argued, that expresses itself in the mind of man is active in all of nature.

Every monad, having these powers of perception, however inchoate, perceives and represents the whole of the universe in itself. Each monad is, in a way, the universe in miniature or, as Leibniz expressed it, a "living mirror of the universe." Each monad, however, mirrors or represents the universe only with its own particular degree of clarity. It represents it, that is to say, only in its own way and from its own unique point of view.

He argued that there is thus no absolute division, as Descartes had mistakenly believed, between mind and body, or thought and extension, but a continuity between them, for what we find in nature are not minds and bodies but forces. These forces are possessed of varying degrees of perceptions, differing in clearness and distinctness, very much in the same way in which our own minds differ in this regard. In the very lowest monads, those of plants, perception is of a very limited and primitive sort and everything is obscure and confused; on the other hand perception found among animals is of a much higher kind, one that we may call "consciousness"; and in the case of a man, "consciousness" becomes even more refined and clear, and turns into "self-consciousness."

But if monads are "mirrors of the universe" they are also "windowless." By this Leibniz means that each monad, being in a process of evolution, and busy realizing its nature by inner necessity, is neither determined nor influenced by anything outside it. Nor do they need to be, for being miniatures of the universe they are not dependent on anything from without but possess implicitly or potentially within themselves everything they need to and will come to be. There cannot, therefore, be any interaction between monads.

But if neither Descartes's interactionism nor Spinoza's parallelism is what governs the unity within or between substances, what does? Leibniz's reply was that the unity, or "harmony," that we find was "pre-established" by God when He first created the universe. Monads, Leibniz explained, are like clocks that have been wound up together to keep the same time. Having been made by a perfect maker, they keep perfect time. Or, as he explained it, they are like "several different bands of musicians and choirs, playing their parts separately, and so placed that they do not see or even hear one another, nevertheless they keep perfect time together, by each following their own notes, in such a way that he who hears them all finds in them a harmony that is wonderful, and much more surprising than if there had been any connection between them."

Despite the prescient notion of substance, or matter, as essentially force or energy, a notion which was to come into its own only in the twentieth century, this theory of monads, and the solution to the problem of mind and body it offered, although fascinating and intriguing, still continues to strike one as too fantastic to be believed.

Let us pause at this point and observe briefly what the three philosophers we have just looked at shared in common: a sublime confidence in the faculty of reason. The human mind, they believed, was so structured that by following the proper method it was capable of arriving at certain knowledge of reality. Unfortunately, although each claimed to use that same faculty in the same way, each arrived at a remarkably different answer. Each assumed that what they could think "clearly and distinctly" with their minds was a reflection of what existed in the world outside, but what they believed to so exist was impossibly contradictory. Depending on whom one chose to follow, it turned out to be one, two , or many. The different accounts arrived at, not surprisingly, led their successors, the English empiricist philosophers, to question the basic, underlying premise shared by these three major continental thinkers. How reliable an instrument of knowledge was our faculty of reason? they asked. The first to do so was John Locke.

The Empiricists

John Locke

John Locke (1632–1704) was born in Wrigton, Somerset, England. He was educated first at Westminster School, where he received a thorough grounding in the classics, and then at Oxford University, where he took his Master's degree in 1658. He remained at Oxford to teach and pursue his studies in chemistry and medicine, to which he was becoming more and more drawn.

He was not destined to stay at Oxford, for in 1666 he met Lord Ashley (later the first Earl of Shaftesbury) and became his personal physician, friend, and confidant. This meeting and friendship was to determine Locke's own later fortunes, for Shaftesbury's attempt to exclude James from the succession to the throne of England led to his dismissal and exile to Holland, and Locke followed him there.

In Holland Locke met Prince William and Princess Mary of Orange, and

John Locke. National Portrait Gallery, London.

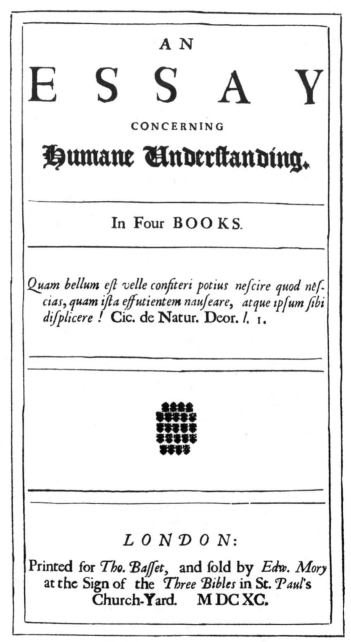

A N

E S S A Y

CONCERNING

Humane Understanding.

In Four BOOKS.

Quam bellum est velle confiteri potius nescire quod nescias, quam ista effutientem nauseare, atque ipsum sibi displicere ! Cic. de Natur. Deor. *l.* 1.

L O N D O N:

Printed for *Tho. Basset,* and sold by *Edw. Mory* at the Sign of the *Three Bibles* in St. *Paul's* Church-Yard. M DC XC.

when this couple ascended the throne of England after the bloodless revolution in 1688, Locke returned home with them.

Two years later saw the publication of the two works that were to make him famous as both a philosopher and a political theorist. The first was *An Essay Concerning Humane Understanding*, on which he had been working for some 20 years, and the second *Two Treatises of Government*. Both these works were to prove enormously influential: the former on the whole history of philosophy; the latter on political history, providing the philosophical justification not only for the English Revolution of 1668 but also for the American Revolution of 1776, profoundly affecting the language and ideas of both the Declaration of Independence and the Constitution.

Locke's impassioned appeal for peace (the "state of nature is one of peace, good will, mutual assistance and preservation"); his argument that civil government derives its power from the consent of its members; that its purpose is the defense of individual liberty and property, for men are "all equal and independent" and possess the natural rights to "life, health, liberty and possessions"; that in government the legislative branch is more important and authoritative than the executive; and that, in any case, there should be a strict separation between them, and between church and state; all were later to determine the course of the Western democracies.

What, no doubt, gave these ideas the attraction they had for him was the turbulent period through which he himself lived. The Thirty Years' War (1618–1648) overlapped the years of his own life (1632–1704); and during his lifetime he witnessed the execution of Charles I of England, the death of Cromwell, the Revolution of 1668, and the flight of James II. Elsewhere there occurred the rise of Louis XIV in France, Peter the Great in Russia, and Frederick I in Prussia. War and violence seemed everywhere, and in his political writings he explored alternatives to the tyrannical solutions the world seemed to be reverting to.

In 1691 Locke retired to an estate in Oates in Essex where he spent the remainder of his life, dying there in 1704 at the age of 72.

Locke himself has left us an account of how he came to undertake the book that was to occupy his thoughts for the next 20 years:

Were it fit to trouble thee with the history of this Essay, I should tell thee, that five or six friends meeting at my chamber, and discoursing on a subject very remote from this, found themselves quickly at a stand, by the difficulties that rose on every side. After we had a while puzzled ourselves, without coming any nearer a resolution of those doubts which perplexed us, it came into my thoughts that we took a wrong course: and that before we set ourselves upon inquiries of that nature, it was necessary to examine our own abilities, and see what objects our understandings were, or were not, fitted to deal with. This I proposed to the company, who all readily assented: and thereupon it was agreed that this should be our first inquiry. Some hasty and undigested thoughts on a subject I had never before considered, which I set down against our next meeting, gave the first entrance into this discourse; which having been thus begun by chance, was continued by entreaty; written by incoherent parcels; and after long intervals of neglect, resumed again, as my humor or occasion permitted; and at last, in a retirement, where an attendance on my health gave me leisure, it was brought into that order thou now seest it.*

But Locke's reason for undertaking this investigation "into the original, certainty, and extent of human knowledge, together with the grounds and degrees of belief, opinion, and assent" was not merely theoretical. Behind it lay the urgent desire to determine the sources and validity of the beliefs that brought people into such conflict with one another and caused so much bloodshed. He thought that if he could show how people's differing ideas resulted from their different experiences, this might make them more tolerant of each other and thus avoid the agony of conflict and war.

The Essay opens with an investigation of the rationalist doctrine of innate ideas, the belief that the mind is endowed from birth with certain ideas and principles. However, there is no idea, Locke argues, that all men have, and no principle that everyone accepts. Children and idiots, obviously, do not have such ideas or principles ready formed in their minds and so they cannot be born with them. To the objection that they are born with them but do not become aware of them until they reach the age of reason, he replies that there cannot by any ideas in the mind of which we are not aware. Besides, if reason is necessary to discover these ideas, there is no need for them to be innate. And with regard to morality, there is no single rule we can discover that is accepted by all societies, therefore there cannot be any moral principle that is innate. This does not mean moral principles could not be proved by reason. The point is they are not innate.

Instead of imagining that we have true beliefs from birth, let us see, he says, whether we cannot trace our ideas back to their source in experience:

Let us suppose the mind to be, as we say, white paper, void of all characters, without any ideas; how comes it to be furnished? Whence comes it by that vast store which the busy and boundless fancy of man has painted on it, with an almost endless variety? Whence has it all the materials of reason and knowledge? To this I answer, in one word, from experience; in that all our knowledge is founded, and from that it ultimately derives itself.*

That all knowledge comes from experience Locke now takes as his point of departure. The mind at birth, he says, is like a sheet of paper or blank tablet

---

*The Epistle to the Reader, preceding An Essay Concerning Humane Understanding.
*Essay, Book II, Chapter 1.

(tabula rasa) on which experience makes its marks. Experience furnishes us with sensations and the mind reflects upon them. Sensations and reflections are the only two sources of knowledge that we have; and we are incapable of having an idea that does not come from one or the other of these two sources. Ideas of sensation (yellow, cold, bitter, hard, and so on) come to us through our various senses when some external object stimulates our sense organs; ideas of reflection (doubting, believing, knowing, reasoning, remembering) are the ideas we get from observing the operation of our own mind as it is employed about the ideas it already has. For the mind not only receives ideas from without but also thinks about ideas, reasons, has doubts, and so on, and these operations of the mind can be perceived by us just as we can perceive and observe colors, tastes, sounds, and so on.

The ideas the mind gets directly from sensation and reflection are simple. Once the mind has a store of simple ideas it can repeat or compare or combine them in an infinite variety of ways to form new complex ideas. The number of simple ideas are very large and we have names for only some of them. But the mind is not able to invent one new simple idea. A blind man, for example, has no idea of color. These simple ideas come to us through one sense (color, for example); some through two senses (figure, motion); some simple ideas we get from both sensation and reflection (pleasure and pain); and some simple ideas we get from reflection only.

The power of an object to produce an idea in the mind Locke calls a quality of the object. Sugar, for example, has the power to produce in us such ideas as white, granular, solid, and sweet. Some of these qualities resemble the objects that produce them, and some do not. Those that do, Locke calls *primary qualities* and says they consist of solidity, extension, figure, motion or rest, and number. Those that do not resemble the objects that produce them, Locke calls *secondary qualities.* These consist of color, taste, sound, heat, and cold. These secondary qualities do not resemble any qualities of the object but are nothing more than powers to produce these ideas in us by means of the primary qualities in the object.

In the reception of simple ideas the mind is passive. The mind is concerned with the ideas it already has and is able to make new, complex ideas by combining, repeating, comparing, or abstracting from them. These complex ideas are made by the mind at will and it is in this way that the mind furnishes itself with many more ideas than it originally receives from sensation and reflection. These new complex ideas formed by the mind may or may not correspond to something in the outside world.

There are three kinds of complex ideas: modes, relations, and substances. A mode is a complex idea of something that is not thought of as existing by itself but as dependent on, or as being a property of, a thing or substance (triangle, gratitude, number, and so on). Relations involve a comparison of one idea with another. Locke distinguishes between particular substances and pure substance in general. Particular substances are such things as gold, house, man, or sugar. When we analyze our ideas of such particular substances we find that they are combinations of several, separate ideas plus something else. Our idea of gold, for example, initially is a combination of simple ideas of sensation — color, extension, solidity, and so on. Although we think of this combination of simple ideas as capable of existing by itself, at the same time we cannot conceive how they could do so except by supposing that there is some kind of support or bearer of ideas, which support or bearer we call substance. We think of this support as something besides the yellowness, the extension, the solidity. It is something that has all these or that supports all these, and is thought of as the substratum of yellowness, hardness, and so on. This idea of support or substratum is the idea of pure substance.

When I examine the idea of pure substance in general I find, Locke says, that I have no distinct idea of it at all. What then is it? In a famous phrase Locke replies to this question that it is a "something, I know not what."

We can now state what knowledge is: "Knowledge is the perception of the agreement or disagreement of our ideas." It is plain that the mind cannot know things directly or immediately; we can know them only through the intervention or mediation of our ideas. Knowledge, therefore, cannot extend further than our ideas do. We have certain knowledge when we actually do perceive the agreement or disagreement of our ideas; and we have real knowledge when there is a conformity or correspondence between our ideas and the reality of things.

The question which now inevitably arises in relation to Locke's theory of knowledge, is of course, this: if all we know are ideas and not the things themselves, how can we know that there is a conformity or correspondence between our ideas and reality? What justifies us in maintaining that there is a likeness between our perceptions and the things that produce them in us, if what we know are perceptions only? To prove such a correspondence, we would need to step outside our perceptions in order to compare them with the substances that cause them, and how can we do that? How can we step outside ourselves?

Locke's fatal error in his account of our situation was to posit a world we could know only through our ideas, one consisting of things held together by mysterious, unknowable substances. By doing so not only had he left himself open to the inevitable question as to how he could know what was unknowable, but also to the further question as to how he could know such a thing exists at all.

Berkeley

George Berkeley (1685–1753) was born in Kilkenney, Ireland, in 1685. At the age of 15 he entered Trinity College, Dublin, where he studied mathematics, logic, languages, and philosophy. In 1707 he received his master's degree and two years later was ordained as a minister in the Church of England. Elected a fellow of the College, he remained there until 1713.

It was during this period, while still in his twenties, that he composed the literary and philosophical works upon which his fame rests. The first was his *Essay Towards a New Theory of Vision*, concerned with the manner in which we perceive the distance, magnitude, and position of objects. It appeared in 1709 when he was only 24 years old. This was followed a year later by the publication

George Berkeley. Mary Evans Picture Library, London.

of his *Treatise Concerning the Principles of Human Knowledge* (1710), containing his main philosophical ideas. (A second volume of this work, which he lost in manuscript, was never rewritten.) Three years after the appearance of the *Treatise*, Berkeley published a more popular version of its main themes in a work entitled *Three Dialogues between Hylas and Philonus* (1713).

In 1713 Berkeley left the college for London. After spending several years there and several in touring Europe, he returned to Ireland, where he conceived a plan for building a college in Bermuda devoted to "the reformation of manners among the English in our western plantations, and the propagation of the Gospel among the American savages." In preparation, he wrote a poem *America, or the Muse's Refuge*, which gave expression to his almost messianic vision of this new land. The poem concluded with the following stanza:

> Westward the Course of Empire takes its Way,
>   The four first Acts already past.
> A fifth shall close the Drama with the Day,
>   The world's great Effort is the last.

Because of a navigation error, Berkeley's ship landed in Newport, Rhode Island, instead of Bermuda. Financial support for the planned college failing to materialize, Berkeley decided to remain in Newport, where during the next three years he succeeded in starting divinity schools both there and in Connecticut, as well as aiding the young universities of Yale and Harvard with donations of property and books.

Upon his return to England he was named Bishop of Cloyne. Moving to his diocese in southern Ireland, he remained here for the next eighteen years. In 1752 he settled with his wife and family in Oxford, where he died peacefully a year later at the age of sixty-eight.

Berkeley agreed with Locke that the materials of our knowledge are ideas — ideas of sensations and reflection, and ideas formed by the help of memory and imagination. In addition there is something that has the ideas and this is mind, soul, spirit, or simply oneself. The mind is not the same as an idea but is rather what has or perceives and knows ideas. Ideas exist in it.

In all this Berkeley agrees with Locke: ideas of reflection (thoughts, feelings, volitions) can obviously exist only in the mind for their very existence consists in being perceived by a mind; and the same is true of our ideas of sensation: they too, like thoughts and mental images, can exist only in the mind perceiving them. And it has been admitted by Locke that certain ideas of sensation — the secondary qualities — exist only in the mind and are not like anything existing apart from mind; while certain other ideas of sensation — the primary qualities — are copies of things or qualities existing outside the mind, and these things (extension, figure) actually do exist in external objects. External objects actually have extension, motion, and so on, and our ideas of these are more or less faithful copies of them.

But Berkeley now asks: how do we know that some of our ideas resemble qualities actually existing in external objects? On what ground can we say that the color of an object exists only in the mind, while shape really exists apart from mind? To be able to say that some qualities resemble the things in question and some do not, you would have to be able to compare your idea with the actual quality in the external object. But this is impossible, since what you can perceive immediately is only the sensation and not the real object. In short, if the secondary qualities are subjective, the same must be the case with the primary qualities. Furthermore, if what we know consists of ideas and ideas only, and if an idea cannot be compared with a "thing" but only with another idea, what evidence is there that physical objects exist at all?

The arguments with which Berkeley goes on to reinforce these questions seem irrefutable. Is the shape or other sensible quality that is supposed to exist in an external object, he asks, perceivable or not? If it is perceivable then it is an idea or sensation and exists in the mind; and if it is not perceivable, how can you say that the sensation or idea you perceive resembles it? Besides, how can a sensation or an idea be like something that is not a sensation or an idea? The qualities of external objects, furthermore, are supposed to be relatively stable, but our sensations are constantly changing with changes in our sense organs, and how can sensations that constantly change resemble qualities that are supposed to be fixed? If one of these resemblances of the quality in the object is the faithful one, which one is it? Which is the real shape of the coin that appears round from one angle and oval from another?

According to Locke, extension, shape, and so on actually exist in objects apart from our perception, while color exists only in the mind of the perceiver, but is it possible to see a shape without a color? It would seem not. On the contrary, we infer the very existence of the primary qualities from the secondary ones. We would not know that an object took up space except by *seeing* a colored patch, *touching* something hard, and so on. All arguments which can be produced to show that secondary qualities exist in the mind can be used to show that primary qualities do so too.

If there is nothing in an object except the qualities, and if the qualities are dependent upon experience, if follows, Berkeley concludes, that the object itself is dependent on experience. In short, if the "being of a color" means its being perceived, and the "being of a sound" means its being heard, and so on for the other qualities, then the complex of qualities we call an object must owe its being to the combined perception of its qualities. And if this is so then "to be is to be perceived" — *Esse est percipi*. This becomes Berkeley's famous thesis and summary of his philosophical position.

But, you will ask, doesn't matter exist? To this he replies that if by matter you mean some imperceptible and nonsensible entity, then as far as our senses are concerned it simply does not exist; and if by matter you mean some inert, unthinking substance that has extension, figure, solidity, mobility, and so forth, then the very notion is contradictory, since extension, figure, and so on, cannot exist outside the mind. Therefore matter in the usual sense of the word does not exist, and the belief that it is a "something, I know not what" is meaningless.

But if Locke was mistaken in believing in the existence of matter, he was not mistaken concerning the existence of mind or spirit. Mind, soul, or spirit (Berkeley uses these terms interchangeably) does exist. The mind or soul, he says, is simple, undivided, and active. It is what perceives ideas and operates about them. We do not and cannot have an idea of mind or spirit; we can, however, form a "notion" of it. We know that it exists because we know that in addition to ideas there must be something that perceives these ideas, and this something is what we call mind or spirit.

To return, however, to matter. If matter, you will say, does not exist then nothing in the physical world is real, and surely this is absurd. Surely, you will say, the tree I perceive is a real tree, and similarly with the other things I encounter all around me. Berkeley's reply to this is that he does not deny the reality of the physical world. Together with everyone else he believes his senses and believes that what he perceives by their means are the real things. His views are simply a combination of two views which used to be held separately — one by the common man, the other by the philosopher — and he has now brought these two views together. The common man has always believed that the things he immediately perceives are real; and the philosopher has always held that the things which are immediately perceived are in the mind. And what he is now saying is simply that what we perceive is real but obviously only mental.

One of the important advantages in seeing our situation in this light, says Berkeley, is that it removes all doubts concerning the possibility of knowledge. For so long as we suppose that there is a physical reality which can exist independently and unperceived, so long shall we remain in doubt whether our perception faithfully represents this reality to us. It is the belief in an independently existing reality that leads to doubt. But once we realize that the things we perceive are real and that these things exist in the mind, then we can once again trust our senses.

But one question still remains: if the real is what we perceive, then how can we know when we are perceiving a real object and when only an illusion? We can distinguish between the real and the imaginary, Berkeley replies, by noting such things as recurring patterns (when a perception is connected in a regular manner with previous and subsequent perceptions); when the perception does not depend on our will (in contradistinction to fantasies that do).

But, you may still wonder, if the reality of things depends upon our perception, does this mean that when I leave this room everything ceases to exist? Berkeley's reply to this is that the tree which is struck by lightning in a dense forest and crashes to the ground still makes a noise, and the distant stars still continue to exist in the daytime when we no longer see, because God is there to do so!

This strange turn of his argument, one of the strangest in all of philosophy, has led many to poke fun at it. Among the earliest examples is the following pair of limericks by Ronald Knox:

> There was a young man who said, "God
> Must think it exceedingly odd
>   That this little tree
>   Should continue to be
> When there is no one about in the quad."

> *Reply*
> "Dear Sir, it is not very odd;
> I am always about in the quad,
>   And that's why this tree
>   Will continue to be
> Since observed by
>   Yours faithfully,
>   God."

But however strange Berkeley's conclusion may appear, given the basic premise — that the only things we can know are ideas — the rest seems indeed to follow of necessity. For matter, as he has tried to show, is not the cause of ideas. Aside from the idea being meaningless, it is simply not conceivable how an unthinking substance could be the cause of ideas. And the ideas that we have must have some cause, for we ourselves are not their cause. And if matter is not their cause, nor we, then it must follow that some other spirit or mind is. And this *is* conceivable because we ourselves are the cause of our ideas (as when we daydream), and so we have experience of a mind causing ideas in a mind. Therefore it is conceivable that one mind may cause ideas in another, and this other mind or spirit must be God.

We can infer from the order of things, Berkeley adds, what sort of spirit this is. It is, he says, one that is all-wise, all-powerful, and all-good.

Starting from Locke's epistemological premises, Berkeley builds on them a view that is its diametrical opposite — Locke's realism or materialism transforming itself, almost magically, into a strict idealism.

And this is very much what Berkeley had hoped to achieve, for both skepticism and atheism, he believed, result from a belief in materialism, and by denying the existence of matter he had eliminated these twin evils.

Hume

The next and last of the three great British philosophers to rely upon sense experience alone for knowledge of reality was David Hume. Following the principle adopted by his immediate predecessors more rigorously than they did, he proceeded to draw, as we will see, some remarkable skeptical conclusions from them.

Born in 1711 in Edinburgh, Hume entered Edinburgh University at age 11, intending to pursue a career in law. But he abandoned all thoughts of a legal career when at the age of 18 he became convinced he had made a major philosophical discovery. He threw all his energies into its investigation with the result that a year later he suffered a severe nervous breakdown.

Recovering, he went on to pursue his studies in philosophy and to incorporate his findings in a book, *A Treatise of Human Nature*, which finally appeared in 1739, when he was still only in his twenties. To his great disappointment the book, as he put it, "fell deadborn from the press." He was more fortunate with his next: *Essays Moral and Political*, published in 1741–1742, which was an immediate success. This encouraged him to revise his *Treatise*, believing it was its style that originally held it back from achieving the success it deserved. Publishing it under the new title *An Enquiry Concerning Human Understanding* (1748), it drew more attention, although again failing to become the popular success he had hoped it would be. What, however, finally did bring him the fame and popularity he craved were his political and historical writings, especially his immensely popular and widely acclaimed *History of England* (1754–1762), which went through many editions during his lifetime.

His writings having won for him a wide reputation, he was offered and served in a number of public offices: Secretary to the British Ambassador to France in 1763 and Under-Secretary of State from 1767 to 1769.

In 1769 Hume returned to Edinburgh, where his house became the meeting place and center for the most distinguished members of society. He died there in 1776, widely mourned.

David Hume. National Galleries of Scotland.

Hume carried the tradition of Locke and Berkeley — that nothing should be accepted as knowledge unless it had been acquired through sense experience — to its logical conclusion. His predecessors, he argued, had not followed this principle rigorously; they had in fact, he believed, violated it.

Like Locke and Berkeley before him, Hume takes the primary data of human knowledge to be perceptions and reflections about perceptions. But he makes a distinction that they did not make, between "impressions" and "ideas." Impressions are the sensations, passions, emotions, desires, and so on we experience; ideas or thoughts are copies of impressions. Ideas differ from impressions only in that ideas are faint whereas impressions are vivid. We remember the impressions, which are the primary data of our knowledge, by way of these "faint images" of them, and we can have no idea that is not a copy of an antecedent impression.

Some of these "faint images" or ideas are simple and exactly resemble their antecedent impressions; other ideas are complex, which the mind forms by means of various operations, and these may not resemble anything of which we have ever had an impression — such as the idea of a unicorn.

Once we realize, says Hume, that each complex idea must be made up of simple ideas, every one of which must be copy of an antecedent impression, we are able to see that a good deal which has been said by philosophers is simply nonsense. For if a word is to mean anything, it must stand for an idea, which must be a copy of an antecedent impression, and you must be able to show from what impression this idea has been derived. If you cannot do this, then there is no idea and the word is meaningless. This means that a word such as "unicorn" has meaning because we can show the antecedent impressions of which this word is a complex representation. But there are some words that cannot be shown to have any such antecedent impressions. And this is the case, says Hume, with the word "substance."

Berkeley was quite correct, therefore, when he rejected the notion of a material substance. We have no sense impression, as Locke himself admitted, of such a thing, and therefore we should not say—as Locke, unfortunately, did— that our impressions are caused by such an external material substance (by that "something, I know not what"). But neither can we say with Berkeley that our impressions are caused by some spiritual substance (a "soul," a "self," or a "mind"), for we have no sense impressions of such a thing either. That notion, too, is therefore meaningless. What, then, is the soul or self?

> The soul, as far as we can conceive it, is nothing but a system or train of different perceptions, those of heat and cold, love and anger, thoughts and sensations; all united together, but without any perfect simplicity or identity. Everything that exists is particular: and therefore it must be our several particular perceptions, that compose the mind. I say, *compose* the mind, not *belong* to it. The mind is not a substance, in which the perceptions inhere. We have no idea of substance of any kind, since we have no idea but what is derived from some impression, and we have no impression of any substance either material or spiritual. We know nothing but particular qualities and perceptions.*

Since we know nothing of an external world, or of an internal self, we cannot, Hume concludes, know the origin of our impressions. The only things we can know are merely impressions and ideas. We believe, of course, in the existence of an external world and in the existence of a self, but no logical justification can be given for such beliefs. Metaphysics, therefore, which purports to investigate the nature of a reality independent of us, is thus impossible, for such an investigation is beyond us, requiring us to go, as it does, beyond our experience, and this we cannot do.

This being so, what kind of knowledge, according to Hume, are we capable of having? Two kinds, Hume replies: knowledge concerning "relations of ideas" and knowledge concerning "matters of fact." The first is arrived at by logical reasoning and issues in the kind of knowledge we have in a discipline such as

---

An Abstract of a Book Lately Published, Entitled "A Treatise of Human Nature." London, 1740. Reprinted in *A Treatise of Human Nature*, P. N. Nidditch, ed. Oxford University Press, 1978.

mathematics; the other is arrived at by observation, not by logical reasoning. This does not mean that reasoning is not involved in the latter; it is, but the reasoning, being grounded in empirical fact, cannot have the certainty of the former.

For example, I hear a sound at the door (a matter of fact) and I reason from this to the fact that a person is there; or I see a brick being thrown at a window and then I see the window shatter and reason that the one event is the cause of the other — meaning by this not merely that the one event preceded the other in time or was adjacent to it in space, but that there is some necessary connection between the two. Distinguishing between a sheer coincidence and real causation in terms of this notion, we say that the cause necessitates, or compels, the effect. And once having found such a causal connection between A and B, we feel that we can predict with complete confidence that the next time A happens, other things being equal, B will follow — that it must follow.

But, Hume asks, what is this causal relationship? What is this necessary connection? Has anyone ever observed it? All one ever observes is the constant, temporal conjunction of two events, one of which is prior to another. And since that is all, strictly speaking, we ever observe, that is all we ought to admit.

But, you may ask, says Hume, if sequence in time and contiguity in space is all we observe, how did we ever get the idea of a causal bond or connection? To this Hume replies that we got the idea from custom or habit: after observing the sequence A–B many times, we come by sheer habit, or psychological conditioning, to expect B after A. And this feeling of expectation is the only impression upon which the idea of cause rests. What is certain is that we do not find this necessary connection in experience, for all that experience ever provides us with are particular instances of associated facts and not general or universal necessary relations or connections between facts. Since therefore a large part of our investigation of matters of fact depends upon such causal relations, our knowledge must be considered both limited and uncertain.

The upshot of Hume's investigation is thus an extreme form of intellectual skepticism. By pushing Locke's and Berkeley's analysis of knowledge to its logical conclusion, he shows that we cannot be sure of the existence either of a self or of an external world, nor even of the law of cause and effect, the foundation of science.

Locke's realism, which in Berkeley's hands became transformed into idealism, has now in turn become transformed in Hume's hands into a full-blown skepticism.

The Kantian synthesis

The two philosophical traditions we have just outlined — continental rationalism and British empiricism — each reached, as we have seen, a kind of dead end.

The rationalists professed absolute confidence in reason but the reasoning of one differed profoundly from the reasoning of the other. Their neglect of experience led to the construction of ambitious systems of thought, which, for all their brilliance of speculation, struck those of a more scientific turn of mind as merely castles in the air, lacking solid foundation.

And the outcome of empiricism was similarly surprising and disappointing. Empiricism prided itself on its attachment to experimental science, yet when it faced the task of giving an intelligible account of some of the basic concepts underlying science itself — such as substance, mind, and cause — it proved unable to do so. Hume, by refusing to make any concessions to rationalism, came to assert, as we saw, that none of these concepts had any empirical meaning whatsoever: a "thing" was just a collection of sensations, the mind or self a "bundle of perceptions," and there was no such thing as a causal connection, only a series of "loose" or "separate" events.

Each system pursued in isolation thus came to an impasse: rationalism ending in dogmatism, and empiricism in skepticism. Each side, however, seemed on strong ground when it attacked the other and pointed out its weaknesses, although inadequate when it came to propose its own solutions. Each seemed strong, that is to say, precisely where the other was weak; human reason may not be sufficient to provide us with a knowledge of reality, as the empiricists emphasized, but it was certainly necessary in order to do so; and experience may not be the only source of our knowledge, as the rationalists argued, but it was certainly a major one. The one school seemed to have neglected the role of experience in knowledge and the other the role of reason.

What seemed to be required at this point in the investigation of the foundation and sources of knowledge was an attempt to synthesize the contributions of each of these two major movements, using the insights of one of these approaches to correct the errors of the other. The philosopher who undertook this task was Immanuel Kant.

We have already had occasion to meet Kant and to consider the revolutionary quality of his thinking in our discussion of ethics. We also had occasion then to consider certain aspects of his life and the strange and remarkable stages of his philosophical career — the revolutionary change in his philosophical outlook at a point in life when most people are beginning to think of retiring, publishing his most important work, the *Critique of Pure Reason* and gaining international fame with it at a stage in life (he was 57 years old when it appeared) when most people have already given up such hopes and ambitions.

But it is useful to remember that although this major work of his — some consider it the most important work in philosophy in modern times — was published in 1781 when he was 57 years old, it was not all written in his fifty-seventh year. Kant tells us he had been hard at work on this treatise for some 11 years. He did, however, "bring it to completion," to use his own puzzling phrase, in a very short time — within some four to five months. By this is probably meant that he put the final touches to it within that very brief period. Many readers since then have wished he had taken more time, and thus spared them the enormous labor of trying to make clear much that is and forever will remain very unclear indeed.

Kant himself attached great importance to the difference between the works he wrote before the *Critique of Pure Reason* and those that followed it. The former he regarded as devoid of interest. "Through this treatise," he wrote, referring to the *Critique of Pure Reason*, "the value of my earlier metaphysical works was totally destroyed." When a new edition of his complete works was projected, he wished it to begin with *On the Form and Principles of the Sensible and the Intelligible Worlds* (1770), which, though not yet an embodiment of the critical philosophy, represents an important step toward it.

Kant did not come to the new views contained in the *Critique of Pure Reason* suddenly. In the beginning of his career and for a long time afterwards the philosophy he taught and believed in was rationalism. This was the dominant school in German universities at that time. But Kant's interest in and knowledge of empirical science led him to see certain difficulties in this philosophy so that he gradually became more and more dissatisfied with it. And then, somewhere between 1756 and 1762, he came upon a translation of Hume's *Enquiry Concerning Human Understanding* (1739) and this made an enormous impact on him. This work of Hume's, as we have noted, "fell deadborn from the press," but not for Kant. He was the first major thinker to appreciate the full force of Hume's argument. It led him to break with rationalism.

In a famous paragraph in the *Prolegomena*,* Kant tells us of the effect this reading of Hume had on him:

> I openly confess that my remembering David Hume was the very thing which many years ago (he is writing this late in life, 1783) first interrupted my dogmatic slumber, and gave my investigations in the field of speculative philosophy a quite new direction. I was far from following him in the conclusions to which he arrived by considering, not the whole of his problem, but a part, which by itself can give us no information. If we start from a well-founded, but undeveloped thought which another has bequeathed to us, we may well hope by continued reflection to advance farther than the acute man to whom we owe the first spark of light.

Hume, Kant tells us here, not only started him thinking but gave him a clue to follow. What this clue was we will soon see. What is interesting here is that he apparently will try to out-Hume Hume. Hume, he believes, did not go far enough, stopping at skepticism; by continuing Hume's line of thought, he suggests here, we should be able to arrive at a more satisfactory solution.

Before beginning to look at the *Critique*, it is interesting to note that Kant dedicated it to Baron von Zedlitz, who was Minister of Education to Frederick the

---

Prolegomena to Any Future Metaphysics, a work that Kant wrote in 1783 to clarify and explain the ideas of the *Critique of Pure Reason* (1781). The passage quoted is from the Preface to the *Prolegomena.* A recent edition is the Paul Carus translation, extensively revised by James W. Ellington (Indianapolis: Hackett, 1977, p. 5).

Great. Kant held him in very high esteem. Why he did so is perhaps made clear from a letter (quoted by Norman Kemp Smith, one of the greatest twentieth-century Kantian scholars and commentators)† that Zedlitz wrote to Kant, which reads in part:

> Should your inventive power extend so far, suggest to me the means of holding back the students in the universities from bread and butter studies, and of making them understand that their modicum of law, even their theology and medicine, will be immensely more easily acquired and safely applied, if they are in possession of more philosophical knowledge. They can be judges, advocates, preachers and physicians only for a few hours each day; but in these and all the remainder of the day they are men, and have need of other sciences. In short, you must instruct me how this is to be brought home to students. Printed injunctions, laws, regulations — these are even worse than bread and butter study itself.*

This passage, Norman Kemp Smith says, may perhaps have suggested to Kant the appropriateness of dedicating his *Critique* to so wise and discerning a patron of true philosophy. "A Minister of Education," Norman Kemp Smith adds, who "ranks philosophy above professional studies, and both as more important than all academic machinery, holds his office by divine right."

The word "critique" in the title of Kant's work is borrowed from English literature and means "a critical examination" — in this case of the nature and operation of "reason." The work opens with these words of the preface.

> Human reason has this peculiar fate that in one species of its knowledge it is burdened by questions which, as prescribed by the very nature of reason itself, it is not able to ignore, but which, as transcending all its powers, it is not able to answer.†

Human reason, or understanding, Kant is saying here, is doomed to ask questions it is apparently fated not to be able to answer. This is the human predicament as he sees it, and his attempt at a critical examination of human reason is designed to throw light on this predicament.

The attempt, however, is also very much within the spirit of his age, as he goes on to point out. This was the eighteenth century, the period of the Enlightenment, a period that prided itself on its critical spirit and whose watchword was Reason.

Commentary to the Critique (New York: Humanities Press, 1962, p. 7).

†*Emmanuel Kant's Critique of Pure Reason*, translated by Norman Kemp Smith (New York: St. Martin's, 1965).

> Our age is, in especial degree, the age of criticism, and to criticism every-thing must submit. Religion through its sanctity, and law-giving through its majesty, may seek to exempt themselves from it. But they then awaken just suspicion, and cannot claim the sincere respect which reason accords only to that which has been able to sustain the test of free and open examination.

This was an attitude inspired by admiration for the achievements of reason in natural science, especially in Newtonian physics.

But, Kant goes on to say, when we look more carefully into this praise of reason, when we inquire into its foundations, we find a sorry state of affairs. Metaphysics, the supreme work of reason, lies in ruins and in disrepute. At one time she was regarded as the Queen of the Sciences, but now she is met with scorn: a matron outcast and forsaken, she mourns like Hecuba. Her government under the administration of the dogmatists (rationalists), was at first despotic. Gradually, through internecine wars (rationalists competing among themselves) her empire gave way to complete anarchy, and so the skeptics (the empiricists), "a species of nomads, despising all settled modes of life, broke up from time to time all civil society." Happily, he says, they were few in number and could not completely destroy the empire, although they did a great deal of damage. In more recent times the "celebrated Locke" tried to put an end to all these controversies by proposing a "physiology of the human understanding." This attempt to cast doubt upon the pretensions of the Queen of all the Sciences, by tracing her lineage to vulgar origins in common experience, failed to accomplish its task. This has been recognized as a fictitiously invented genealogy and metaphysics has con-tinued to uphold her claims. And so now we have a return to dogmatism but one that is greeted with complete indifference.

But indifference to such matters, he says in a striking passage, is not com-patible with being human. We should not therefore abandon our attempts to achieve this knowledge we so deeply desire. Although it is thought that all meth-ods have been tried and found wanting, there is still one remaining at our disposal which has yet to be tested. This is the method of criticism of pure reason.

> I do not mean by this a critique of books and systems, but of the faculty of reason in general, in respect of all knowledge after which it may strive *independently of all experience*. It will therefore decide as to the possi-bility or impossibility of metaphysics in general, and determine its sources, its extent, and its limits — all in accordance with principles. The subject of the present enquiry is the question, how much we can hope to achieve by reason, when all the materials and assistance of experience are taken away. (Kant's italics.)

And so Kant will now once again undertake to reconsider and reconstruct the foundations of knowledge to see what it is we can or cannot be certain about.

In this preface to the first edition of his work he expresses some doubts, as he will continue to do, here and in other works, about his powers of expression. He might have made, he says, the work clearer and easier to comprehend had he used more examples and illustrations, but this would have made the work too bulky and it is that already. In any case, such examples and illustrations are necessary only from a popular point of view and "this work can never be made suitable for popular consumption"—a view from which he never wavered and to which in the *Prolegomena* he added the remark that not everyone is bound to study metaphysics. Such assistance, he here further explains, is not required by genuine students of the science, and, though always pleasing, might very well in this case have been self-defeating in its effects. In this connection he quotes a French author who remarked that if the size of a volume were to be measured not by the number of its pages but by the time required to master it, it could be said of many a book, "that it would be much shorter if it were not so short." To this, however, he adds that "many a book would have been much clearer if it had not made such an effort to be clear." For the aids to clearness, though they may be of assistance in regard to details, often interfere with our grasp of the whole. He ends the preface by making the bold claim that he had solved forever the main questions of philosophy.

In his preface to the second edition of the *Critique*, Kant returns to this note of what it is or is not possible for us to know. How can we put any faith in human reason, he asks, if in one of the very things that we most desire to know, reason not merely forsakes us, but lures us on by false hopes only to cheat us in the end? But are there, perhaps, any indications that the true path has still to be found, and that by starting afresh we may yet succeed where others failed?

Obviously, if we are going to succeed, a thorough reconstruction will be necessary. And he goes on to refer to the examples of scientific discovery, in geometry and in physics, and the point he makes about these examples is that scientific discovery comes, not from passive observation, but from an activity on our part. Galileo, he says, did not just watch balls rolling down an inclined plane: he conceived a theory of what was happening and then devised an experiment to confirm or reject his theory. He approached nature with certain definite ideas of his own, with certain hypotheses, and forced nature to answer his questions. This teaches us that "reason has insight only into that which it produces after a plan of its own."

Kant goes on to show how this moral can be of benefit in reconstructing philosophy. All previous philosophies—and this includes both rationalism and empiricism—have started from a common view about the nature of mind and its relation to the world of objects. They have assumed that the human mind is set over against a world of objects, which it tries to know, but to the nature of which it has contributed nothing. The object has been thought of as merely given to the mind; mind has had nothing to do with the making of the object. Beginning with this point of view, it is no wonder that both rationalism and empiricism ran into difficulties: rationalism unable to explain how its innate principles were capable of giving us knowledge of this independent reality (for how could we be certain there was a conformity between the ways of the mind and the ways of things?

and empiricism (with the belief that the mind was a passive observer) unable to explain how we could ever attain anything more than collections of past observations lacking all predictive power.

It is this basic assumption, underlying both modes of philosophy, that, Kant says, must be questioned. For if the human mind is to succeed in achieving a knowledge of objects, then these objects cannot be independent of the mind. The mind cannot be simply a spectator; it must itself contribute actively to the nature of the objects that confront it in experience. For again, the mind can only know that which it itself makes.

Now this is certainly clear in the case of the mathematical sciences. The objects of mathematics (yards, feet, inches, and so on) are objects we have made and hence they are entirely knowable and also, consequently, certain. But what Kant is going to try to show in his *Critique* is that the mind, instead of being a passive spectator, also contributes something to the nature of *all* objects, including physical objects, and this fact is the key to their intelligibility.

This reversal of point of view — of making objects depend on the mind, instead of vice versa — is compared by Kant to the revolution in astronomy brought about by Copernicus.

> Hitherto it has been assumed that all our knowledge must conform to objects. But all attempts to extend our knowledge of objects by establishing something in regard to them a priori, by means of concepts, have, on this assumption, ended in failure. We must therefore make trial whether we may not have more success in the tasks of metaphysics, if we suppose that objects must conform to our knowledge. This would agree better with what is desired, namely, that it should be possible to have knowledge of objects a priori, determining something in regard to them prior to their being given. We should then be proceeding precisely on the lines of Copernicus's primary hypothesis. Failing of satisfactory progress in explaining the movements of the heavenly bodies on the supposition that they all revolved round the spectator, he tried whether he might not have better success if he made the spectator to revolve and the stars to remain at rest.*

And if we try this same sort of thing in metaphysics, or philosophy, we shall find, says Kant, that just as some of the motions the stars were thought to have were not really due to them but to us, to our motion, so similarly certain of the characteristics objects have will be seen as not due to some external reality but to us, to the work of the mind.

In a series of articles, beginning in the year 1883, which the great German poet Heinrich Heine wrote on German philosophy for the Parisian journal *European Literature* he explained this major Kantian point in the following memorable way:

*Preface to the second edition of the *Critique* (Norman Kemp Smith translation), p. 22.

With the appearance of Kant former systems of philosophy, which had merely sniffed about the external aspect of things, assembling and classifying their characteristics, ceased to exist. Kant led investigation back to the human intellect, and inquired what the latter had to reveal. Not without reason, therefore did he compare his philosophy to the method of Copernicus. Formerly, when men conceived the world as standing still, and the sun as revolving round it, astronomical calculations failed to agree accurately. But when Copernicus made the sun stand still and the earth revolve round it, behold! everything accorded admirably. So formerly reason, like the sun, moved round the universe of phenomena, and sought to throw light upon it. But Kant bade reason, the sun, stand still, and the universe of phenomena now turns round, and is illuminated the moment it comes within the region of the intellectual orb.*

In the concluding portions of this preface to the second edition of his work, Kant goes on to share with his readers some of the results he expects to achieve. If we accept the standpoint of the Copernican Revolution, he points out, then we shall be able to prove rigorously that certain knowledge of reality is possible, and thus be in a position to reply to Hume's skepticism. But the only reality we will discover we can truly know is that which is given to us in sense experience. We will see that we cannot have knowledge, in the proper sense of that word, of anything lying beyond experience. In particular, we will come to see that we cannot and never will be able to establish three points which have been important to traditional philosophy: the existence of God, freedom, and immortality.

But although this is fatal to the usual claims of rationalism, which professes to be able to prove such ideas, Kant insists that we can find any meaning and any value in these ideas only if knowledge of them is *not* possible. And this would seem to follow from our basic premise, for if knowledge is restricted to things we can experience, then if God were knowable, he would have to be a thing of a physical sort, bound by the limitations characteristic of human beings: Such a God would lose all meaning for us. And similarly with the notions of freedom and immortality. If these ideas are to have any meaning for us they must refer to a sort of reality lying beyond our empirical, phenomenal world.

And so Kant, toward the end of the preface, makes a remarkable assertion: "I have therefore found it necessary to deny knowledge of God, freedom, and immortality in order to find a place for faith."

If it thus appears that in the end Kant does come after all to agree with Hume that we really cannot have knowledge of the things we so desperately wish we did, we shall also see that he will show that we are in possession of a good deal more knowledge than Hume believed.

Kant begins his introduction to the *Critique* by summarizing what he takes to be the correct insights of both empiricism and rationalism. He says "there can

*Heinrich Heine, *Religion and Philosophy in Germany*. Translated by John Snodgrass (Boston: Beacon, 1959, p. 114).

be no doubt whatever that all our knowledge begins with experience," for in no other way could our faculty of knowledge get any material to work upon. It is experience, he says, that gives us "the raw material of our sense impressions." In the order of time, therefore, we have no knowledge prior to experience, and with experience all our knowledge begins.

To think that we can have knowledge without experience (as the rationalists contended) would be the same — making use of a remarkable and memorable analogy — as if a dove were to imagine that since it can easily fly through air, it could with equal, if not more, ease fly through empty space.

The fact, however, that all our knowledge begins *with* experience (which is the essential truth in empiricism) does not mean that it all originates *from* experience. The contribution the mind itself makes to its knowledge of things must be taken into account as well, for the mind is not a passive observer but takes an active role (and this is the essential truth in rationalism) in organizing and imposing form on the material that comes to it in experience.

If we could somehow combine these two basic insights we might be able to achieve a solution to the problem of what it is we can or cannot know and what it is we can or cannot be certain about. And what Kant does here is to translate these basic insights into strictly logical terms and by their means go on to pose as clearly as possible the really significant question, doing so in a way which will make it amenable to a logical solution.

This question first suggested itself to him as a result of his reflections on Hume. We will soon look at the passages in Hume that occasioned it. Hume, he thought, almost stumbled on it himself; he probably would have had he continued further and not stopped short at skepticism.

To fix the question more clearly both for himself and the reader Kant resorts to some technical terminology. Any knowledge that we might possess or wish to convey to others would, first of all, need to be expressed or conveyed in the form of statements, statements that could then be judged to be either true or false. Although it is customary now to call such statements "propositions," the term Kant uses is "judgments."

Some judgments we make, Kant points out, are *a priori*, that is, they are ones we can know to be true apart from experience — such as the judgment or proposition that 7 plus 5 equals 12. Such judgments have two distinguishing marks: universality and necessity — they are true everywhere and with certainty. In contrast are judgments that are *a posteriori*, ones that are derivable with the help, at some point, of sense experience. "The grass is green" would be an example of such a judgment.

There are, in addition, two other significant features about judgments. Some are *analytic*: they are propositions where the predicate is contained in the subject, as in "A bachelor is an unmarried male." In making such a judgment we are simply drawing out, or analyzing, the nature of the subject term of the proposition. This being so, the predicate term in such propositions adds nothing to the subject and the propositions therefore do not provide us with any new knowledge.

In contrast, there are judgments, such as "The house is burning," that are *synthetic*. In synthetic judgments the predicate is not identical with the subject. You may analyze the subject term of such a judgment ad infinitum and never elicit from it the knowledge contained in the predicate term. And you cannot do so in the case of such judgments because the predicate is not part of the subject and therefore cannot be found there. Synthetic judgments, unlike analytic ones, do therefore tell us something new and are informative.

These distinctions overlap, giving rise to two types of propositions; those that are *analytic a priori* and those that are *synthetic a posteriori*. An analytic a priori proposition would be any truism: "*A is A*"; "A bald-headed man is one who has no hair on his head," and so on. These propositions are necessarily and universally true, but they are also empty and uninformative, the predicate term merely explicating the subject term. A synthetic a posteriori proposition, on the other hand, is a proposition in which we record an empirical observation ("The grass is green"). These are informative but lack universality and necessity.

According to Hume (although he did not use these terms to describe them) these were the only kinds of propositions we could have. The following is the famous passage in the *Enquiry* (which proved so suggestive to Kant) where Hume enunciates his view:

> All the objects of human reason or inquiry may naturally be divided into two kinds, to wit, "Relations of Ideas" and "Matters of Fact". Of the first kind are the sciences of Geometry, Algebra, and Arithmetic, and, in short, every affirmation which is either intuitively or demonstratively certain. That the square of the hypotenuse is equal to the square of the two sides is a proposition which expresses a relation between these figures. That three times five is equal to the half of thirty expresses a relation between these numbers. Propositions of this kind are discoverable by the mere operation of thought, without dependence on what is anywhere existent in the universe. Though there never were a circle or triangle in nature, the truths demonstrated by Euclid would forever retain their certainty and evidence. Matters of fact, which are the second objects of human reason, are not ascertained in the same manner, nor is our evidence of their truth, however great, of a like nature with the foregoing. The contrary of every matter of fact is still possible, because it can never imply a contradiction and is conceived by the mind with the same facility and distinctness as if ever so conformable to reality. That the sun will not rise tomorrow is no less intelligible a proposition and implies no more contradiction than the affirmation that it will rise. We should in vain, therefore, attempt to demonstrate its falsehood. Were it demonstratively false, it would imply a contradiction and could never be distinctly conceived by the mind.

Hume was fully aware of the vast implications of the position he was here adumbrating. So that they would not entirely escape his readers he himself points out what these are in the devastating passage with which he brings his book to a close:

> When we run over libraries, persuaded of these principles, what havoc must we make? If we take in our hand any volume; of divinity or school metaphysics, for instance; let us ask, Does it contain any abstract reasoning concerning quantity or number? No. Does it contain any experimental reasoning concerning matters of fact and existence? No. Commit it then to the flames: for it can contain nothing but sophistry and illusion.

We thus possess, according to Hume, only two kinds of propositions: a priori truths (his "relations of ideas"), which are really only *analytic* — meaning that they do not extend our knowledge about the world but tell us only about the interconnections of our ideas; and a posteriori truths (his "matters of fact"), which are really only *synthetic* — meaning that they merely summarize what we have observed and cannot serve therefore as predictions of future experience. A priori propositions, according to Hume, are indeed universally true but they say nothing, for they are empty of content; and a posteriori propositions may be true, but because they cannot be universalized they are useless. Hence Hume's skepticism.

But once having seen the dichotomy presented by Hume in his terms, Kant wondered whether we might not have within our reach still a third type of proposition, one that possessed the best features of the two admitted by Hume, namely a proposition that was *synthetic* and *a priori*. So he asked himself that momentous question: How are synthetic a priori propositions possible? This would be a most valuable kind of proposition to have — to say the least — for as a priori it would be universally true, and as synthetic it would have an important content to it and could serve as a premise for valuable inferences and predictions about areas of natural events not yet observed or observable.

It might be thought that Hume must have considered the possibility of the existence of such a third type of proposition but simply dismissed it as either meaningless or impossible. Once we realize, however, how strange the very idea of the possibility of such a proposition is, the occurrence of the idea does not seem so inevitable. For the possession of such a proposition, or this type of knowledge, would be a most remarkable thing indeed, and one's first inclination, assuming the idea of it did occur to one, would be to reject it as a piece of pure fiction. For, we might ask, how could it be possible for us, or our minds, to attain to a kind of knowledge that is significant or important (not trivial as in the case of analytic propositions) and yet that is certain and universal in scope by way of pure thought alone?

The difficulty is that if these are synthetic propositions, the subject and the predicate are two distinct notions. By what right can we say that nevertheless they are necessarily connected in some way, so that the proposition "*S* is *P*" is always true? This problem does not arise for analytic propostitions, for here *P* is just part of *S*. It does not arise for synthetic propositions, for these do not assert any necessary connection. But it does arise for synthetic a priori propositions.

Hume saw this as a problem limited to causation and solved it by denying its existence. The causal axiom is synthetic; every synthetic proposition rests on experience (or is a posteriori); and therefore we cannot be sure of its universality or necessity (as we would were it a priori).

Kant was certain, however, that the causal axiom was not an a posteriori but an a priori truth, and that therefore all events are subject to it. But Kant also realized that the problem Hume was raising was not limited to causation; he realized that the question was much wider, although the causal axiom was an important example of it. The question was really whether it was possible for us to have this type of knowledge at all. And this was the form in which Kant decided to tackle the question.

The general question (How are synthetic a priori propositions possible?), if solved, would answer, he realized, three special problems, each again much wider than the question about causation originally posed by Hume: how such a discipline as mathematics is possible; how such a discipline as physics is possible; and, in the light of these, whether such a discipline as metaphysics is possible.

The three main sections of Kant's work — the Transcendental Aesthetic, the Transcendental Analytic, and the Transcendental Dialectic — are devoted to an exploration of these three main questions. His attack consisted in carrying through the Copernican revolution, the reversal of that common point of view, discussed earlier, which had been responsible for the previous impasses. If the mind were merely a passive spectator of objects, a priori knowledge of a synthetic kind would be impossible. But on the assumption that the mind is active, that it does and must contribute something to the nature of objects of experience, we can see how such synthetic a priori knowledge is indeed possible.

Our cognitive situation, he argued, is similar to what it would be were we compelled (to make use of a well-worn analogy) to wear blue spectacles we could not remove. We would then be able to predict something about every object we saw, namely, that it would be colored some shade of blue. Nothing could be perceived by us without having this blue color imposed on it. We would consequently have some a priori information about any possible future object of experience. There would, of course, be differences between objects we could not predict (for example, red things would appear darker than pink things). But on one point we would be certain: whatever we experienced would be experienced as colored some shade of blue.

Now suppose that the mind imposes, by laws of its own, certain conditions upon what comes to it in experience. The resulting objects of experience — called *phenomena* by Kant — would bear upon themselves the stamp of the mind's activity. This would make possible synthetic a priori assertions. If the mind legislates in part for the nature of phenomena, then we can know in advance something about their nature: that part of their nature which would be due to mind.

These a priori elements contributed by the mind to the nature of phenomena fall into two main groups: the a priori elements relating to the way we sense objects and the a priori elements relating to the way we think about objects. The mind, that is to say, senses the material which comes to it in experience in certain ways (imposes certain forms of sensuous intuition on it); and it comes to understand it in certain characteristic ways (organizes it by way of certain conceptual patterns or "categories"). These are the two separate modes of organization, or structuring, imposed by the mind upon the raw material supplied it in experience. The finished products are the objects or phenomena of experience, but since certain elements in the finished product are due to the mind, they are therefore predictable ("the mind has insight into that which it produces after a plan of its own"). It is thus possible for us to have a priori knowledge of a synthetic kind.

According to Kant it is our faculty of Sensibility that imposes the forms of sensuous intuition on the material that comes to it in experience; and it is our faculty of Understanding that imposes its conceptual categories on the objects it thinks about. The task of investigating the a priori forms imposed by the mind by the former faculty is undertaken in the first of the three main divisions of the *Critique* (the Transcendental Aesthetic); the a priori elements imposed by the mind through its faculty of Understanding is undertaken in the second of these three main divisions (the Transcendental Analytic); in the last and third of these three divisions (the Transcendental Dialectic) Kant investigates the intellectual elements offered by "reason" (in the narrow sense of the word) and shows that unlike the contributions made by Sensibility and Understanding, what Reason offers is not valid of experience.

"Transcendental Aesthetic," the title of the section in the *Critique* to which we are now turning, is a technical way of identifying a discussion concerned with sense-perception. By "transcendental," however, Kant means to isolate the factors that make possible the kind of sense-perception we as human beings are subject to. It is concerned, to put it a little more technically, with the analysis of the condition (or preconditions) presupposed by knowledge. It is a method of investigation that starts with some facts about our experience and then asks: what are the conditions that make this fact possible, that explains this fact?

Kant himself gives the following definition of "transcendental knowledge": it is, he says, "all knowledge that is concerned, not with objects, but with the way in which a knowledge of objects may be gained, so far as that is possible a priori." In a sense, of course, this is what all of Kant's philosophy is about: an investigation of the conditions under which knowledge is possible.

But here we are concerned with the investigation of the conditions (or the a priori elements) involved in perception. Is perception merely a matter of opening our eyes and our other senses to what may be inscribed or imprinted on them by things external to them, or is the situation somewhat more complicated? Are there, perhaps, certain universal and necessary conditions imposed by the mind in order for objects to be perceived by us the way they are? Kant, of course, will argue that we do impose such features on phenomena. He will argue that when we consider phenomena and abstract from our perception of such objects all conceptual and perceptual differences (for example, the fact that the thing in question is a kitchen table and not a dining-room table, and that it is brown in color rather than yellow) and anything else we might be capable of so abstracting or removing, we shall find remaining two factors we will not be able to remove: spatiality, the notion of this bare something as having extension and figure, and temporality, the notion of it as existing now. Space and time remain, it is Kant's argument, because they are due to our mind and this is why we cannot think them away.

This will undoubtedly strike the reader as very curious. Does this mean that, according to Kant, space and time are not real but subjective — a kind of phantasm of the mind? The answer to this is yes and no. Kant himself had gone from an absolute theory of space, as embraced by Newton (the notion of it as being a kind of box or receptacle, more fundamental than matter, in which things are located), to a relational theory, as embraced by Leibniz (that it is nothing apart from the relations among objects and arises from their manner of organization), to, finally, his own theory that it is a form of perception, belonging to the subjective constitution of our own mind, "apart from which it cannot be predicated of anything whatever."

Kant goes on to produce a number of highly condensed arguments in support of this new view of the nature of space and time. Of these probably the most convincing and illuminating is the suggestion that our experience of externality is, on the level of bare sensation, nonspatial. We have sensations of this object or that object, and the sensations in question, although they differ in quality, do not, as bare sensations, differ in terms of their different spatial locations. The spatiality they come to possess, therefore, is something that we give to them. The representation of space, therefore, far from being derived from external experience, as we might be inclined to believe, is what first makes it possible. As a subjective form that lies ready in the mind, if precedes experience and cooperates in producing it. Were the representation of space not within us, the sensation of external objects would not be capable of being experienced by us as spatial.

It may still seem like a remarkable and unbelievable view to maintain. Are not things simply "out there"? Why should we believe that anything more is needed than simply to open our eyes and observe things located where in fact we find them?

The fact is we have long forgotten how things really were when we first opened our eyes to the world, and what a struggle it was to generate the space in which we came to locate these so-called external objects. Recent experiences with patients recovering from blindness tend to confirm this.*

When surgical techniques allowed for the safe removal of cataracts, people who had been afflicted with this condition since birth were able to see for the first time. It is tempting to think that upon opening their eyes, they experienced the beautiful and familiar world of vision — a

---

*Arthur J. Minton. *Philosophy: Paradox and Discovery* (New York: McGraw-Hill, 1976, pp. xix–xxi). Quotations in the passage are taken from Marius Von Senden, *Space and Sight* (New York: The Free Press, 1960). This remarkable book is a collection of case histories of persons who acquired sight for the first time through surgery or by spontaneous remission.

world of form and color, of public objects in a public space. But this does not occur. The patient is immediately confronted with a wall of brightness containing color patches that blend indistinguishably into one another. The flood of sensations is absolutely meaningless. There is no awareness of shape or size, nor any idea of distance. In fact, some patients report the impression that the swirl of color is touching their eyes. Familiar shapes, such as squares and triangles, which are easily identified by touch, are unrecognized in the visual array. One investigator writes:

> The newly-operated patients do not localize their visual impressions: they do not relate them to any point, either to the eye or to any surface, even a spherical one; they see colors much as we smell an odor of peat or varnish, which enfolds and intrudes upon us, but without occupying any specific form of extension in a more exactly definable way.

Gradually, the newly sighted learn that the color patches represent objects at a distance. They discover that they can move through the field of color, that the colors move to the edge of the visual field as they walk, and that no matter how they turn their bodies, the visual swirl surrounds them. Slowly, they begin to apprehend that there are things behind them and in front of them, but their conception of the spatial world is woefully inadequate. About his patient, one doctor wrote:

> I have found in her no notion of size, for example, not even within the narrow limits she might have encompassed with the aid of touch. Thus when I asked her to show me how big her mother was, she did not stretch out her hands, but set her two index fingers apart.

Another physician reported similar effects in his patients:

> Those who are blind from birth have no real conception of distance. A house that is a mile away is thought of as nearby, but requiring the taking of a lot of steps.

Only after long and painful experience do the patients come to have an idea of objective space. At first, only things extremely close are seen in depth, while objects at a distance remain parts of a flat wall of sensation where everything ends. Here one object moving in front of another is seen as two color patches melding into one another. When a newly sighted girl first saw photographs and paintings, she asked: "Why do they put those dark marks all over them?" "Those aren't dark marks," her mother responded, "those are shadows . . . if it were not for shadows, many things would look flat." The girl answered: "Well, that's how things do look. Everything looks flat with dark patches." With time, however, the world begins to assume depth and the flat curtain of color recedes into the background.

The mental effort involved in learning to see is enormous. Without mental exertion, experimentation, and training, the bright wall of sensation remains a dazzling, incoherent barrier. Sometimes the task proves too much for adults who have spent their lifetime relying on other senses, and they relapse into their old habits. A doctor writes about his twenty-one-year-old patient:

> Her unfortunate father, who had hoped for so much from this operation, wrote that his daughter carefully shuts her eyes whenever she wishes to go about the house, especially when she comes to a staircase, and that she is never happier and more at ease than when, by closing her eyelids, she relapses into her former state of total blindness.

For the first time these people are struck by the tremendous size of the world, and they are oppressed by their own insignificance. They become aware of the fact that they have been visible to others all along, and they feel it as an intrusion into their privacy. Their emotional and mental lives are shaken to the very core.

The newly sighted undergo experiences which those of us born with vision toiled through in infancy and have long since forgotten. Long ago the flat wall of sensation fragmented into objects that zoomed away into space, and now it is almost impossible for us to regard our visual field as a blur of color patches. Our perceptual skills have become so routine and automatic that they give the illusion of naturalness, like the technique of an accomplished musician. We tend to forget that what is now easy was once painfully difficult. The experience of the blind in coping with their newfound sense of vision illustrates that even in the most elementary perception, reason and judgment are at work, albeit in dim and forgotten ways. The world that presents itself to our eyes—the world of three-dimensional objects in a public space—is as much a result of thought as of pure sensation.

Now that Kant has shown what the nature of space is, he can go on to show how this view of it (and *only* this view of it) renders comprehensible the possibility of a certain body of synthetic a priori knowledge based on space.

But what body of knowledge is based on the phenomenon of space? The answer, of course, is geometry, which is the study of space. What is interesting and relevant here about geometry is that it gives us new truths which do not seem to rest on an analysis of mere concepts alone. It is not, in other words, a body of purely analytic propositions. Let us consider Kant's own example: the proposition that a straight line is the shortest distance between two points. This is very much *like* the proposition that a bachelor is an unmarried male, for here too we do not find it necessary to verify the proposition. We *know* it is true. Yet, unlike the example of the bachelor, we do not know it to be true because of the meaning of the term "straight." For nothing in that term tells us about "shortest." The concept of "straight" only defines direction or quality of line; it says nothing about quantity. So it is not analytic, albeit a priori. It must therefore be an example of that strange hybrid proposition — the synthetic a priori.

We have here then an example of a piece of knowledge that has the characteristics of universality and necessity that, were space not as defined by Kant, would be completely inexplicable.

Let us consider other "facts" about space (and time), otherwise similarly inexplicable, such as the knowledge that there is and can be only one space or that time is irreversible. We are certain about all these things. They are not simply brute facts we happen to have discovered about our universe. We *know* this is the way our universe is and we cannot conceive that it could be otherwise. We know this to be so without our having any evidence in support of it — or even thinking that such evidence is necessary. (As in the similar case of our bachelor: we haven't interviewed every bachelor in the world to see whether it is indeed the case that all bachelors are unmarried males, nor do we feel we need to; we know it for a certainty). But in the case of space this seems strange. This is not our ordinary reaction to ordinary facts of the world, and the certainty in question seems more appropriate to analytic than to synthetic propositions.

But it ceases to be strange, Kant argues, once we come to realize that we are dealing with a very peculiar phenomenon — a space we carry around with us, which conditions everything experienced in its terms. And this is why we do not have to worry about running into a triangle (say, one on Mars) to which Euclid's theorems may not apply. As long as we continue to experience, we will continue to do so in terms of the kind of space illuminated by Euclid's geometry.

This is indeed what gives this particular discipline its peculiar certainty. The knowledge provided by that science is certain, because it is based on a space whose properties are not descriptive of some independent, external reality, but of an inner, subjective, mind-dependent one.

Does this mean, then, that space and everything in it is unreal? Kant's answer to this is that if by *things* you mean things as they are in themselves, then space does not define them and is not real. But if you mean things as we experience them, then it is both true of them and real enough. For space is only the way in which we, as human beings, possessed of the kind of nature and cognitions descriptive of us, happen to experience the world presented to us. This is not the only way it can be experienced; certainly this is not the way a tiny insect experiences it, nor it it the way angels, if they exist, experience it. Doubtlessly, there are aspects and ways of viewing reality that are completely closed to us. But for human beings space and time are the only ways in which that reality can be perceived by us.

This does not mean we live in a world of illusion; it does mean the world of man is a human world and the knowledge we have of it is a human knowledge. If it is an illusion, it is a universal one. This is both fortunate and unfortunate: unfortunate since what we obviously know about this reality is infected by that human viewpoint; fortunate in that, although that knowledge is therefore necessarily limited we need not doubt its certainty. And that is our ultimate dilemma or predicament: the very thing which enables us to know certain things is the very thing which makes it impossible to know other things. If I am compelled to wear blue spectacles all my life, to return to that useful analogy, I can know in advance and with certainty the color of any object of my experience, but I also know that I cannot ever know what its real color is, assuming it is colored.

But the deeper truth of all this is that we are part of the fabric of this universe. We have been fashioned for it and it has been fashioned to fit us. We are very much like that little dove, or that little fish in the ocean — if I may stretch Kant's analogy somewhat — who, noticing the way the air or the water fits so nicely around its wings or fins so that they seem to belong together, is led to believe that those wings or fins are not really part of its body but of the air or water which surrounds and envelops it. And it is the same with us. Space and time are our wings and fins, and despite the perfect fit between them and the things they embrace, we must recognize that they belong to us and are part of us, and are not of the things or events they so perfectly match.

Space and time, Kant would therefore say, are real enough. But because they have been fashioned for us and define our particular being, they do not define the life of other possible beings and therefore cannot be said to be real in themselves.

And this is what Kant means when he speaks of a world of phenomena or appearances and a world of noumena or things-in-themselves. The world of appearances is not a world of illusion; it is the world as it must appear to creatures constituted as we are. How the world is in itself we cannot know. But to know that much — that it must appear the way it does because of the way we are — and really know it, is to know a great deal.

As the great German pessimist philosopher, Arthur Schopenhauer, who regarded himself as the only true successor to Kant, expressed it:

> Kant's teaching produces in the mind of every one who has comprehended it a fundamental change which is so great that it may be regarded as an intellectual new-birth. It alone is able really to remove the inborn realism which proceeds from the original character of the intellect, which neither Berkeley nor Malebranche succeed in doing, for they remain too much in the universal, while Kant goes into the particular, and indeed in a way that is quite unexplained both before and after him, and which has quite a peculiar, and, we might say, immediate effect upon the mind in consequence of which it undergoes a complete undeception, and forthwith looks at all things in another light. Only in this way can any one become susceptible to the more positive expositions which I have to give. On the other hand, he who has not mastered the Kantian philosophy, whatever else he may have studied, is, as it were, in a state of innocence; that is to say, he remains in the grasp of that natural and childish realism in which we are all born, and which fits us

for everything possible, with the single exception of philosophy. Such a man then stands to the man who knows the Kantian philosophy as a minor to a man of full age.*

(*The World as Will and Idea*, pp. xxv–vi).

The rest of Kant's argument, as it is set out in the Transcendental Analytic and Transcendental Dialectic, we may discuss more briefly, since it takes almost a lifetime to master Kant's thought and all we wish to do here is simply understand the idea behind it.

Just as Kant has shown that the a priori forms of sensibility (space and time) are the necessary conditions of objects being objects of perception to us, so he now goes on to show how certain forms of the understanding (he calls them "categories") are necessary conditions of perceived objects being objects of thought for us. Knowing what the necessary conditions are (and they turn out to be simply the laws of thought) we can know a priori those truths about the world that are functions of these conditions.

For example, one of the ways we as human beings form judgments about the things in this world is by way of the "if–then," or hypothetical, relationship. Thus we say such things as, "If it rains then the party is called off," "If you drop this glass, it will break," and so on. These all have the same form: "If P then Q." P is the ground, Q is the consequent.

It is typical for my understanding to function in this way: it always must find "reasons" or grounds for things. If I could be sure that this tendency to organize my thought in this manner is matched by the way things are themselves organized, then I could be certain that in the phenomenal world there must be things corresponding to P and Q such that P is the explanation of Q. Such things, or events, are what we call causes and effects. What Kant does in the Transcendental Analytic is to prove that not only is there such a correspondence but that there must be.

The proof extends over quite a number of chapters, to say nothing of pages; cost him, as he put it, "the most pains"; and in the words of one of the great Kantian scholars, H. J. Paton, "The crossing of the Great Arabian Desert can scarcely be a more exhausting task."

But if its elaboration is complicated, its key idea, like the idea of space and time being our air and water, is basically simple. Just as nothing is capable of being perceived by us except through the forms or by means of space and time, so similarly his argument here is that nothing is capable of being experienced by us unless organized in certain ways. If something is to be an object of experience for me, it must be put in a form absorbable by me, one capable of being understood by me. What are the ways in which we understand, apprehend, or absorb things? One of them is by way of the ground–consequent relation, and its corresponding, analogous relation in the world of things is the principle of causation. If, therefore, we are going to continue to think, we will do so by way of such

---

*Translated by R. B. Haldane and J. Kemp (London: Kegan Paul, 1950, Volume I).

logical relations, and if our experience will continue to be meaningful, we need never fear that the principles which make them meaningful will cease to apply. Should they do so such a world would be inconceivable and inexperienceable by us, and would simply cease to exist — just as a world not perceived in terms of space and time is impossible for us.

So as we can see, Kant bases his case on the necessity we have to experience the world and the things in it in ways familiar to us. That need tells us something ultimate about ourselves, and since we are part of the fabric of this world, it tells us something objectively valid about it.

The clue to this basic truth Kant owed to Hume. And it had to do with Hume's questioning of the principle of causality — although, as we have pointed out, Kant came to see it as not limited to the problem of causality. Hume had noticed that the causal relationship was a synthetic one. He then had, as a strict empiricist, contended that all synthetic judgments have to be established through experience. But experience only tells us what is, not what must be, and so the principle could not be justified and could not be proven.

But why do we nevertheless believe in it? We do so, Hume replied, as a result of custom and habit. The curious thing about this explanation is that it presupposes causes. There is no reason, Hume is saying (without realizing the irony), for believing in the existence of causal connections; but the reason he assigns for our having a belief in the existence of causal connections presupposes the existence of causal connections. It is caused by habit. So Hume, as Kant observed, had to presuppose the existence of causation to account for its nonexistence!

Kant's attempt to understand this curious fact led him to the development of the *Critique* with its doctrine of subjective forms and categories, which because they define our experience are therefore objectively valid of our world.

But we have other determinations as well — those that issue from reason — and in the last division of the *Critique* Kant takes these up.

Unlike the forms of sensibility and the categories of the understanding, the ideals of reason have no objective validity. They may define us but they do not define the world they try to penetrate.

It is natural, for example, for our understanding to seek causes, and causes of those causes, and so on, as far back as one can seek them out. Reason, wearying of a seemingly endless regression but deeply committed to the search for causes and assured of their nearness, reaches for them and asserts them. An end to the series of causes, it thinks, must necessarily exist, absolutely necessary as it is, to think it. And so reason goes on to posit it — meaning by this, of course, that it posits God, the originator of the series of causes and its first cause. Thus it is that, as Kant says towards the end of the *Critique*, "In all peoples, there shine amidst the most benighted polytheism some gleams of monotheism, to which they have been led, not by reflection and profound speculation, but simply by the natural bent of the common understanding; as step by step it has come to apprehend its own requirements." Kant means that we are led to this search for God (and freedom and immortality) by deep tendencies in our nature. But this determination to define a reality lying beyond our world, through forms (causal series as in this example) applicable only to this world, must always remain suspect.

And so we are brought back here to two images struck at the very beginning of this intricate journey Kant has taken us on. The first are the opening words to the *Critique* regarding our human predicament of being doomed to ask questions which we cannot answer (Is there a God? Are we free? Is our soul immortal?); and the second is that of the dove, who, cleaving the air in its flight and feeling its resistance, might imagine it would do so much better in empty space. But, like it, we have to remind ourselves that our wings (forms, categories, ideals) are made for this world; they are not made for worlds which are alien to them and for which they are not fitted.

We must therefore settle for this world; we have after all, no other choice.

Conclusion

Where do things stand now?

Let us observe first that philosophic problems, even when they appear to be resolved, have a tendency to become manifest again in another age as a result of its own peculiar concern and dilemmas.

We certainly see this in the case of the dispute between rationalism and empiricism in our own time. The question whether it all comes from reason or from experience has surfaced once again in our own questions concerning genetics and education. Is human behavior a learned response based on social *nurture*, as Skinner and Pettigrew, our contemporary "empiricists," contend, or is it based, as contemporary "rationalists" such as Chomsky and Jensen contend, on innate human *nature?*

A great deal of the drive toward equal education in the past several decades has come from the belief that differences in intelligence and school performance were due more to environmental than to hereditary factors. More recently, however, some geneticists have argued that heredity is more decisive. Undoubtedly both play a role, but the question is their relative importance and its degree. No one needs to be reminded of the profound social and political implications of this current issue. No Kantian has yet emerged to synthesize the findings of these two schools of thought, and the solution continues to elude us.

The second thing we might observe is that even a philosophical position which may have proven successful in resolving the issues of its age in terms meaningful to that age but not to ours, does not become completely obsolete. A residue tends to remain and continues to exert its influence on its successors. And this has been the case with the thought of Immanuel Kant. Very few today may still agree with his overall solutions, yet his philosophizing, especially his terminology, continues to exert its influence even on those who completely disagree with him. Very few now draw the line between the analytic and synthetic where he did, yet the analytic–synthetic distinction, bequeathed by him, continues to be one of the most intensely investigated issues in philosophy.

But it is not only individual problems, or the language in which a philosopher has dealt with them, that continue to survive in the work of successive generations. There is also a certain general thrust to a philosophy, which leaves its imprint on successive generations of philosophers who try to reinterpret its insights in terms meaningful to it and its new understanding of the way things are. And this too has been the case with the philosophy of Kant.

His work has tended to divide the world of contemporary philosophy into two camps: those who have refused to abide by the limits of reason as set by him and have gone on to describe what lies beyond them; and those who have confined their activities to further inquiries concerning those limits and what lies within them. The former, beginning in the nineteenth century with the so-called post-Kantian idealists, who include such popular twentieth-century philosophers as Camus and Sartre, have mainly been absorbed with describing the full range and scope of man's *experience* — political, historical, religious, and moral. The latter have restricted the scope of their inquiries to *reason* itself, investigating the nature of those limits that, as Kant showed, serve as a kind of prison of the human mind.

One of the great twentieth-century figures to pursue this latter investigation — succeeding profoundly in advancing our understanding of our prison — was Ludwig Wittgenstein, to whom we shall later turn.

Summary

1. Epistemology studies the nature, sources, limitations, and validity of knowledge. The questions it asks itself are: how do we know, and how certain can we be of it?

2. There are two main sources of knowledge: reason and experience.

3. Although both sources would seem to be intimately involved in knowledge, historically the question has tended to divide philosophers into two camps: those who placed their stress on reason and those who placed it on experience.

4. Philosophers who chose reason as our only trustworthy source of knowledge came to be called rationalists. These thinkers — Descartes, Spinoza, and Leibniz — shared a number of characteristics: they all lived on the Continent; all believed that reason by itself was capable of arriving at a true knowledge of reality; all believed in the doctrine of innate ideas; their model of the perfect science was mathematics; and their test of whether our ideas were true or not was intuition: "the absence of doubt in the unclouded and attentive mind."

5. Philosophers who chose experience as our prime source of knowledge came to be called empiricists. These thinkers — Locke, Berkeley, and Hume — also shared a number of characteristics in common: they all lived in Britain; all put their faith in experience as our main source of knowledge, doubting whether human reason was capable by itself of arriving at anything more than a few basic propositions about reality; all believed that the mind at birth was a *tabula rasa,* utterly blank of ideas; and their test of truth was exeternal, not internal: ideas are true if they correspond with what we can find in the outside world.

6. Each school, by proceeding on its assumption, arrived at a dead end. Rationalism professed absolute confidence in reason's ability to arrive at a perfect knowledge of reality, yet the results each rationalist achieved differed markedly from those achieved by the others: Descartes's reasoning leading him to dualism, Spinoza's to monism, and Leibniz's to pluralism. And empiricism prided itself on its attachment to experimental science, yet in the end none of the major empiricists were able to give an intelligible account of some of the basic concepts underlying science itself: Locke having to admit that substance was "a something, I know not what"; Berkeley that if we do not have an "idea" of the self we nevertheless have a "notion" of it; and Hume that what we call causes are only a series of "loose" or "separate" events.

7. Immanuel Kant tried to rescue what was valuable in these two schools of thought, rationalism and empiricism, by means of a new attack on the problem of knowledge. He came to realize that each school had arrived at an impasse because of a wrong assumption about the mind's relation to the world. If we are to understand how knowledge is possible we must come to see, Kant argued, that the mind is not, as both rationalism and empiricism assumed, totally independent of the world of objects it tries to know, but rather that it contributes something to that world. What this is Kant tries to identify in the *Critique.*

8. The *Critique* is divided into three main parts: the Transcendental Aesthetic, the Transcendental Analytic, and the Transcendental Dialectic. The first deals with the faculty of sensibility and shows how synthetic a priori propositions are possible in mathematics; the second deals with the faculty of understanding and shows how synthetic a priori propositions are possible in natural science; the third deals with the faculty of reason and shows how and why the a priori elements offered by it and the claims made on their behalf by traditional metaphysics are not possible.

9.   Although Kant's contribution to our understanding of these matters was profound, much still remains unsettled and in doubt. As a result of these philosophic labors, however, we now see more clearly that the source of an idea cannot guarantee its validity (as rationalism had mistakenly believed); that the importance of empirical evidence lies not so much in being the source of ideas (as empiricism also mistakenly thought) as in being a means of testing and confirming them; that the process of information-gathering, in order to be fruitful, must be guided (and Kant was right about this) by leading questions or hypotheses; but (and here is where he was probably mistaken) that the dream of an absolutely certain science built of synthetic a priori propositions is impossible.

For further study

Descartes

1.   For Descartes's collected major works see *The Philosophical Works of Descartes*, 2 volumes, translated by Elizabeth S. Haldane and G. R. T. Ross. (New York: Cambridge University Press, 1967).

2.   Anthony Kenny's *Descartes: A Study of His Philosophy* (New York: Random House, 1968) is a helpful introduction to Descartes's philosophy for the beginning student.

3.   For a collection of recent important discussions of Descartes's thought see Willis Doney's *Descartes: A Collection of Critical Essays* (Garden City: Doubleday, 1967).

4.   For an influential contemporary critique of Descartes's position see Gilbert Ryle's important work *The Concept of Mind* (New York: Barnes & Noble, 1949).

Spinoza

1.   For Spinoza's collected major works see *The Chief Works of Benedict De Spinoza*, 2 volumes, translated from the Latin, with an Introduction by R. H. M. Elwes, (New York: Dover, 1962).

2.   For a helpful full-length study of Spinoza's work by a leading contemporary philosopher see Stuart Hampshire, *Spinoza* (Baltimore: Penguin Books, 1962).

3.   For some recent collections of critical essays on some of the major themes of Spinoza's philosophy see Marjorie Grene (Ed.), *Spinoza:*

A Collection of Critical Essays (Garden City: Doubleday, 1973); and Maurice Mandelbaum and Eugene Freeman (Eds.), *Spinoza: Essays in Interpretation* (LaSalle, Illinois: Open Court, 1975).

4. Still highly regarded as the classic study of Spinoza's *Ethics*, exploring in immense detail its historical sources and antecedents, is Harry Austryn Wolfson, *The Philosophy of Spinoza*, first published in 1934 (reprinted, Cleveland: World, 1958).

Leibniz

1. For selections from the writings of Leibniz see P. P. Wiener (Ed.), *Leibniz: Selections* (New York: Scribner's, 1959).

2. For a general treatment of his philosophy as a whole see R. L. Saw, *Leibniz* (Baltimore: Penguin Books, 1954): and the more recent study by C. D. Broad (New York: Cambridge Unversity Press, 1975).

3. For a selection of recent papers on various aspects of Leibniz's philosophy see Harry Frankfurt (Ed.), *Leibniz: A Collection of Critical Essays* (Garden City: Doubleday, 1972).

Locke

1. A reprint of Locke's *Essay*, complete in two volumes, is available in the Dover series (New York, 1959); and an inexpensive paperback abridgement of the *Essay* is available in the Gateway series (Chicago: Henry Regnery, 1956).

2. For a general introduction to Locke's philosophy see either R. I. Aaron, *John Locke* (New York: Oxford University Press, 1965); or D. J. O'Connor, *John Locke* (New York: Dover, 1967).

3. For a recent collection of essays on both Locke and Berkeley see C. B. Martin and D. M. Armstrong (Eds.), *Locke and Berkeley: A Collection of Critical Essays* (Garden City: Doubleday, 1968).

4. For a recent reexamination of some of Locke's political ideas see Robert Nozick, *Anarchy, State, and Utopia* (New York: Basic Books, 1974).

Berkeley

1. For a general account of Berkeley's philosophy see G. J. Warnock, *Berkeley* (Baltimore: Penguin Books, 1953); and, more recently, Harry M. Bracken, *Berkeley* (New York: St. Martin's, 1974).

2. For the text of Berkeley's *Principles* together with a critical discussion of it, see C. M. Turbayne, (Ed.), *Berkeley's Treatise Concerning the Principles of Human Knowledge: With Critical Essays* (Indianapolis: Bobbs-Merrill, 1970).

3. For a comparison of Berkeley's theories with those of both Locke and Hume see Jonathan Bennett, *Locke, Berkeley, Hume: Central Themes* (Oxford; Clarendon, 1971).

Hume

1. A paperback edition of Hume's *Enquiry* has been published by Hackett Publishing (Indianapolis, 1977), edited by Eric Steinberg.

2. For a short general introduction to Hume's philosophy see John Passmore, *Hume's Intentions* (London: Duckworth, 1968).

3. For recent discussions of various aspects of Hume's philosophy see V. C. Chappell (Ed.), *Hume: A Collection of Critical Essays* (Garden City: Doubleday, 1966).

4. For an account of the development of the problem of induction from Hume to the present day see Wesley C. Salmon, *The Foundations of Scientific Inference* (Pittsburgh: University of Pittsburgh Press, 1966).

Kant

1. The most widely used translation of Kant's *Critique of Pure Reason* is Norman Kemp Smith's, published in a paperback edition by St. Martin's Press (New York, 1965).

2. Norman Kemp Smith is also the author of one of the most frequently consulted commentaries on the *Critique* (New York: Humanities Press, 1962).

3. For a recently revised translation of Kant's *Prolegomena* see the edition published by Hackett (Indianapolis, 1977).

4. For a selection of recent papers on various aspects of Kant's thought see Robert Paul Wolff's *Kant: A Collection of Critical Essays* (Garden City: Doubleday, 1968).

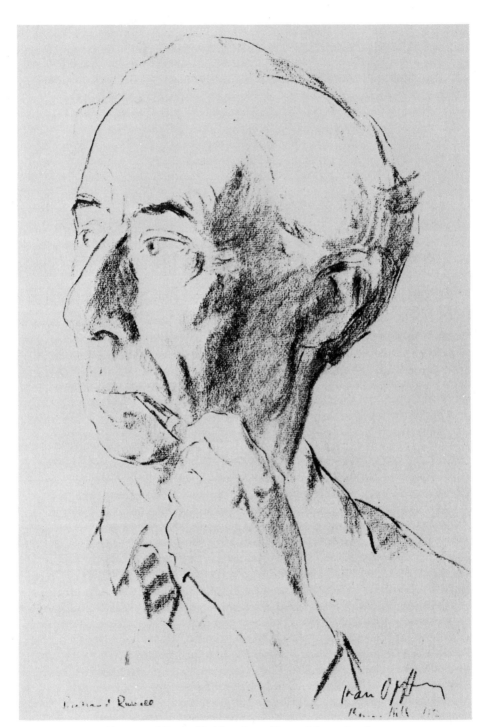

Bertrand Russell. Mary Evans Picture Library, London.

> *Tweedledum:* I know what you're thinking about;
> but it isn't so, nohow.
> *Tweedledee:* Contrariwise. If it were so, it might
> be; and if it were so, it would be;
> but as it isn't, it ain't. That's logic.
> *Through the Looking Glass*

> Thinking consists of journeys through the mazes
> of our linguistic forms, and logic is the study of
> the relations that obtain in and among these
> forms.
> *Source unknown*

> There is nothing — and even if there were, we
> couldn't know it; and if we knew it, we couldn't
> communicate it.
> *Ancient Greek philosopher Gorgias*

Logic

How much faith can we place in this knowledge?

Introduction: Bertrand Russell

When one thinks of a philosopher in our modern age, the name likely to come to mind is Bertrand Russell.

Early in this account of philosophy we discussed the life and thought of Socrates, one of the greatest philosophers of all time, and it is perhaps appropriate to end our account, or begin to end it, with Russell, who resembles him in so many respects.

Russell was born in 1872 and died in 1970. His life was rich and fruitful, eventful and turbulent, filled with both much despair and many triumphs.

Russell's parents, who were close friends of John Stuart Mill (whose life and thought we discussed in a former chapter), died when Russell was a child, and he, together with an older brother, was raised in the house of his paternal grandfather, the first Earl Russell. The family had been eminent in British politics and society for centuries, especially noted for their strong liberal leanings, although members of the peerage. It was this same grandfather (who died at the age of 86 when Russell was 6) who introduced in Parliament the Reform Bill of 1832.

These strong liberal tendencies seemed to have been passed on to Russell, but in his case they did not lead to the position of Prime Minister (as it had in the case of his grandfather and great-grandfather) but to jail — once during World War I for "pacifism" and again, more briefly, in the early 1960s for taking part in nuclear disarmament demonstrations.

They also led, however, to the Order of Merit, Britain's highest honor, and the Nobel Prize, awarded him in 1950.

But always along with the acclaim there was public hostility — including the outcry in 1940 against his appointment to teach philosophy in the City College of New York. The judge who upheld the suit brought against the Board of Education, which made the appointment, declared at the time that in offering the position to Russell the College was "in effect establishing a chair in indecency."

Russell was to record the event on the title page of his book *An Inquiry into Meaning and Truth*, reproduced here. It was his fiftieth publication.

Long before the appearance of this book, Russell succeeded in securing a place for himself in the history of philosophy with the publication, in collaboration with philosopher-mathematician Alfred North Whitehead (1861–1947), of *Principia Mathematica* (1910–1913) — a work described by the American philosopher W. V. O. Quine as "one of the great intellectual monuments of all time."

This was a groundbreaking work whose impact on twentieth-century thought and technology has been immense. The technological revolution we have experienced, and continue to experience especially as a result of various advances in computer science, owes much of its impetus to this pioneering work.

But not only does the technological revolution owe much to these early contributions of Russell's; the social revolution we have experienced in the West, especially in America, with its more enlightened and liberated (or perhaps overly "permissive," as its critics would say) views and attitudes towards childrearing, marriage, women, work, and so on also owes much to him. No doubt in time it will be seen that the new social world we now inhabit was in good part also fashioned by him — in the series of nontechnical social and political works which came from his pen, works such as *Marriage and Morals, In Praise of Idleness*, and *Has Man a Future?*

In light of their actual impact it may seem ironic to us now that he should have wondered, as he sometimes did, whether these works, and the enormous energies he expended on them, could or would ever bear fruit. The following passage, written in a reflective moment, captures not only this mood but much of the sort of person he was:

> When I come to what I myself can do or ought to do about the world situation I find myself in two minds. A perpetual argument goes on within me between two different points of view which I will call that

AN INQUIRY

INTO

MEANING AND

TRUTH

BY

BERTRAND RUSSELL

M.A., F.R.S.

Holder of the Nicholas Murray Butler Medal of Columbia University (1915), the Sylvester Medal of the Royal Society (1932) and the de Morgan Medal of the London Mathematical Society (1933). Honorary Member of the Reale Accademia dei Lincei. Fellow (1895–1901) and Lecturer (1910–1916) of Trinity College, Cambridge. Herbert Spencer Lecturer at Oxford (1914). Visiting Professor of Philosophy at Harvard University (1914) and at The Chinese Government University of Peking (1920–1921). Tarner Lecturer at Cambridge (1926). Special Lecturer at the London School of Economics and Political Science (1937) and at The University of Oxford (1938). Visiting Professor of Philosophy at the University of Chicago (1938–1939). Professor of Philosophy at the University of California at Los Angeles (1939–1940). Occasional Lecturer at the Universities of Uppsala, Copenhagen, Barcelona, the Sorbonne, etc., etc.

Judicially pronounced unworthy to be Professor of Philosophy at the College of the City of New York (1940)

LONDON
GEORGE ALLEN AND UNWIN LTD

of the Devil's Advocate and that of the Earnest Publicist. . . . The voice of the Devil's Advocate is, at least in part, the voice of reason. "Can't you see," says this cynical character, "that what happens in the world does not depend upon you? Whether the populations of the world are to live or die rests with the decisions of Khrushchev, Mao Tse-tung and Mr. John Foster Dulles, not with ordinary mortals like ourselves. If they say 'die,' we shall die. If they say 'live,' we shall live. They do not read your books, and would think them very silly if they did. You forget that you are not living in 1688, when your family and a few others gave the king notice and hired another. It is only a failure to move with the times that makes you bother your head with public affairs." Perhaps the Devil's Advocate is right — but perhaps he is wrong. Perhaps dictators are not so all-powerful as they seem; perhaps public opinion can still sway them, at any rate in some degree; and perhaps books can help to create public opinion. And so I persist, regardless of his taunts. There are limits to his severities. "Well, at any rate," he says, "writing books is an innocent occupation and it keeps you out of mischief." And so I go on writing books, though whether any good will come of doing so, I do not know.

This passage is taken from a book published in 1956 (hence the reference to the political figures of the day, all dead now) entitled *Portraits from Memory* (New York: Simon and Schuster, pp. 48–49).

But it is Russell's technical works in philosophy — his *Principles of Mathematics* (1903), *Principia Mathematica* (1910–1913), and *Philosophy of Logical Atomism* (1918), and not these other social and political writings, which are of concern to us here. They prepared the ground, as we will see, for the philosophy of Wittgenstein, whose theme, that we are prisoners of language, was to dominated the world of philosophy in this century.

It had been recognized since the beginning of philosophy that in some way logic and mathematics are connected — for example, the two disciplines, and only they, proceed by way of necessary inference — but the nature of this connection had never been made clear.

Russell and Whitehead, building on some earlier work, undertook to do this. They came to the conclusion, demonstrated in *Principia Mathematica*, that the fundamental principles of mathematics are really a development of some quite simple, elementary, logical notions. The various fields of mathematics itself had already been shown to be reducible essentially to arithmetic ("the arithmatization of mathematics") and what Russell and Whitehead now did was to show that the fundamental ideas of arithmetic itself (numbers, addition, and so on) could be developed from some purely logical concepts. This program of the unification of mathematics and logic was carried out by Russell and Whitehead with the aid of a new type of symbolism, and the resulting work came to be designated symbolic or mathematical logic.

The immediate impetus for undertaking this task was the emergence of certain perplexing contradictions (called logical paradoxes) in the branch of mathematics known as set theory. Unless these could be resolved, mathematics was in danger of losing its claims to certainty. By showing that classical mathematics is to a large degree a subdivision or an extension of logic, and possessing therefore its rigor and exactness, Russell and Whitehead succeeded in confirming the essential correctness of classical mathematics, and thus dispelling the dismay which mathematicians were beginning to experience.

Although this was a notable achievement in itself, no less notable was the effect its findings had on the emergence of a new conception of the nature of philosophy. For *Principia Mathematica* gave rise to the belief that what it had uncovered or discovered was a kind of *ideal* language, one which correctly *pictured* or *mirrored* reality, a reality unfortunately distorted by ordinary, natural languages, arisen, as these have, in a haphazard manner over centuries. This being so, the job of the philosopher, in describing as accurately as possible what there is, is to trace philosophical problems and confusions to their true sources in language, and thus solve or resolve them, aided in this task by the use of the precise symbolism of *Principia Mathematica*.

These seemingly revolutionary theses, first enunciated in *Principia Mathematica* and explored further in some of Russell's subsequent works—the theses that what we are immediately and directly acquainted with is language, that language mirrors reality, and that the job of philosophy is to correct the distortions created by the languages in use—came to acquire the force and thrust they did in the hands of Russell's pupil and colleague, Ludwig Wittgenstein, who combined them in such a way as to form a powerful and explosive mixture.

Ludwig Wittgenstein

Ludwig Wittgenstein (1889–1951) was born into a wealthy, gifted, and cultured Viennese family. He was educated at home until he was 14 and then was sent to technical schools.

He first came to England in 1908 at the age of 19 as a research student in the department of aeronautical engineering in the University of Manchester, where he was occupied in the design of a jet engine. He left Manchester for Cambridge in 1912 to study with Russell, whose *Principia Mathematica* made him realize

Ludwig Wittgenstein

that his true interests lay in pure mathematics and logic rather than in engineering. Russell recognized his extraordinary gifts at once and tried to encourage him in his work in logic and mathematics. But Wittgenstein, never really at ease in the company of others, spent less than two years at Cambridge before retiring to complete seclusion in Norway.

At the outbreak of World War I in 1914 he returned to Austria and joined the army, using his leisure time to compose the *Tractatus*. He was taken prisoner by the Italians in 1918 and spent some months as a prisoner of war. From his prison camp he sent the manuscript of this remarkable little book (containing only some 80 pages) to Russell, who recognized its importance but did not manage to secure its publication until 1921, and then only in a learned journal, which, as it happened, ceased publication after that issue.

Russell's influence is evident throughout the work, which opens with the following statement to the reader:

> The book deals with the problems of philosophy, and shows, I believe, that the reason why these problems are posed is that the logic of our language is misunderstood. The whole sense of the book might be summed up in the following words: what can be said at all can be said clearly, and what we cannot talk about we must pass over in silence.
>
> Thus the aim of the book is to set a limit to thought, or rather — not to thought, but to the expression of thoughts: for in order to be able to set a limit to thought, we should have to find both sides of the limit thinkable (i.e., we should have to be able to think what cannot be thought).
>
> It will therefore only be in language that the limit can be set, and what lies on the other side of the limit will simply be nonsense.

The book then goes on to state — in a cryptic, elegant, and aphoristic style — that "the world is everything that is the case": that it consists of "facts, not things"; that we "picture" these facts to ourselves in propositions or sentences; and that, therefore, how such sentences come to be significant is the big mystery of both language and philosophy. All this is explored in seven main propositions, which are numbered 1 to 7, and everything else is either a comment on one of these seven propositions (and given a number with one decimal place — for example 1.1., 2.1), or it is a comment on one of these comments (and therefore given a number with two decimal places — for instance, 1.11, 2.11), or it is a comment on one of the comments on a comment, and so forth.

This neatness stands in stark contrast with the inner turmoil of his life, one troubled by several suicides in his immediate family, constant fear of impending insanity, and tragedy.

Wittgenstein ended this first book of his, the only one to be published in his lifetime, with the following propositions — very much in the style of the entire book:

6.53   The right method of philosophy would be this. To say nothing except what can be said, i.e., the propositions of natural science, i.e., something that has nothing to do with philosophy: and then always, when someone else wished to say something metaphysical, to demonstrate to him that he had given no meaning to certain signs in his propositions. This method would be unsatisfying to the other — he would not have the feeling that we were teaching him philosophy — but it would be the only strictly correct method.

6.54   My propositions are elucidatory in this way: he who understands me finally recognizes them as senseless, when he has climbed out through them, on them, over them. (He must so to speak throw away the ladder, after he has climbed up on it). He must surmount these propositions; then he sees the world rightly.

7.   Whereof one cannot speak, thereof one must remain silent.

Thinking that he had thus solved all philosophical problems, Wittgenstein followed his own advice and gave up philosophy. For the next ten years he occupied himself with working as a gardener, teaching school, and designing a house for his sister in Vienna.

Then in 1928, after hearing a lecture given in Vienna by the famous Dutch mathematician L. J. Brouwer, he found himself interested once again in philosophy and decided to return to Cambridge. His *Tractatus*, published some eight years earlier and already famous, was accepted as his doctoral dissertation, and with Russell acting as one of the members of his "thesis" committee, he was awarded the Ph.D. in June 1929. He had given away the considerable fortune he had inherited from his father and now lived in great simplicty on the stipend from his position as philosophy tutor at Cambridge.

Although working feverishly at philosophy once again, he published nothing during these years. However he dictated notes to his pupils and these achieved a wide underground circulation. Although they proved mystifying to most of their readers — because of the novelty of both their themes and their manner of exposition — their impact and influence in Britain and the United States was enormous. These notes (composed between 1933 and 1935) came to be known as the *Blue* and *Brown Books*, titles deriving from the color of the covers on the original copies.

In 1949 Wittgenstein completed a lengthy manuscript, originally begun in 1936, which was published posthumously as *Philosophical Investigations*. This has come to be regarded as the chief work of his later period. It is also thought to represent a sharp break with the philosophy of the *Tractatus*, although, as we will see, there is much in common between it and the earlier work.

What has also not changed is the manner of presentation. Although the discussion is not nearly as cryptic and aphoristic as in the *Tractatus*, much else remains the same. In his Preface to this later work, Wittgenstein describes its style and contents in these words:

> The thoughts which I publish in what follows are the precipitate of philosophical investigations which have occupied me for the last sixteen years. They concern many subjects: the concepts of meaning, of understanding, of a proposition, of logic, the foundations of mathematics, states of consciousness, and other things. I have written down all these thoughts as remarks, short paragraphs, of which there is sometimes a fairly long chain about the same subject, while I sometimes make a sudden change, jumping from one topic to another. It was my intention at first to bring all this together in a book whose form I pictured differently at different times. But the essential thing was that the thoughts should proceed from one subject to another in a natural order and without breaks.
>
> After several unsuccessful attempts to weld my results together into such a whole, I realized that I should never succeed. The best that I could write would never be more than philosophical remarks; my thoughts were soon crippled if I tried to force them on in any single direction against their natural inclination. And this was, of course, connected with the very nature of the investigation. For this compels us to travel over a wide field of thought criss-cross in every direction. The philosophical remarks in this book are, as it were, a number of sketches of landscapes which were made in the course of these long and involved journeyings.

Wittgenstein lectured off and on at Cambridge from 1930 to 1947, when ill health forced him to resign his post. For three years during World War II he served as hospital orderly and laboratory assistant. And both before and after the war, his restlessness forced him to seek solace, as it had done in earlier years, in living in seclusion for extended periods of time in Norway, and sometimes in Ireland. He finally returned to Cambridge from Ireland when he discovered he was suffering from cancer. He died from the disease on April 29, 1951.

Pictures

One of the difficulties in trying to describe Wittgenstein's philosophy is that he does not really have a "philosophy," as we usually understand that term, to describe. As we have noted, his books are essentially collections of remarks on diverse and seemingly unrelated topics.

This, however, does not mean that there are no philosophical theories to be found in Wittgenstein's writings, or to be abstracted from them. Among these the fundamental one has to do with the way language holds us captive by generating certain "pictures" in our minds of the way things are or must be.

Although this doctrine tends to undergo various changes as we move from the work of his early period (which deals with the philosophy of logic) to that of the middle period (which deals with the philosophy of imagery), to the work of the late period (which deals with the philosophy of language), it is without doubt the closest thing to a unifying thread in his writings. It would be best, therefore, to concentrate our attention on it.

Wittgenstein's interest in "pictures" begins very early. In a brief passage in the *Notebooks* (dated November 15, 1914) he says: "That shadow which the picture as it were casts upon the world: How am I to get an exact grasp of it? Here is a deep mystery."

The mystery Wittgenstein is here referring to — How is it that language can refer to reality? — has occupied philosophers from the beginning. It has not always been posed in these terms, and it is perhaps part of Wittgenstein's greatness and ingenuity that he was able to do so. However, neither the problem nor even some of Wittgenstein's proposed solutions to it are without precedent.

Nor is the problem merely an academic one. For how indeed is it that two things which are as different from each other as words and things are yet able to stand for one another? From one point of view nothing perhaps could be simpler, for, after all, as we might be tempted to argue, by convention certain sounds have come to stand for and be associated with certain objects in our experience, and on the occasion of their use, these sounds simply bring these objects to our minds. But to say this does not, of course, solve our problem, for this leaves unclear the very point at issue: how it is that such things as sounds — which are, again, so different from such things as tables and chairs — are yet able to recall them to our minds and stand for them? And if it should be said that it is not the sounds themselves, of course, that do so, but rather the images these sounds generate in our minds that manage it, then not only does this, again, leave unclear how it is possible for such unlike things as images (which are mental) and chairs and tables (which are not) to stand for one another, but raises the related and equally difficult problem of how it is possible for such things as words to arouse in our minds such things as images, seeing that words are words and images are images.

Kant struggled with this problem. Having arrived in his chapter in the *Critique of Pure Reason* on the "Schematism of the Categories," at the point where, in order to bring his argument to completion, he was compelled to show how it was that the categories applied to reality, he was faced with the problem of trying to relate things which were completely conceptual in nature (the Categories) to things which were completely perceptual or sensuous in nature (objects). Related they obviously were, but how? What Kant believed he needed (naively, as we now see it) was some "third thing" — something that being both "intellectual" and "sensuous" would mediate between the two and show how one was or could be an exemplification of the other. Kant thought he found what he wanted in the "transcendental schema." But precisely what this "transcendental schema" is, and what there was about it that made him believe it could perform this miracle, no one has ever properly been able to say. For after all, even if such a third thing was indeed involved here, being a separate entity, two further "third things" would be required to connect *it* to each of the two things it is to connect, and so on *ad infinitum*. And if we were to suggest that it is not some separate entity that brought these two together, but something inherent in the two things themselves, what reason is there to suppose that the two are indeed separate? Either, therefore, as we are now tempted to say, the two are separate and nothing can conceivably bring them together, or they are not separate and require nothing to do so.

It would be a mistake to think that these logical objections, however disturbing they may be to Kant's formulation and solution of the problem, are irrelevant to Wittgenstein's statement of it. As we will see soon, this is not at all so. As everywhere else in the *Critique of Pure Reason*, Kant's object in this chapter, like Wittgenstein's in the *Tractatus*, is to define the conditions of significance and intelligibility. Kant's argument is that in itself and as such, the world is alien to the mind and therefore unknowable to it. For it to become knowable, it must in some way be mindlike. It must contain within it elements of rationality — something, that is, which our concepts can take up and absorb. This something Kant finds in its structure and order. This is what is rational about the world and that is what the mind can absorb. It is also, he tries to show in this chapter on schematism, what the mind knows when it comes to know the world.

If that is indeed Kant's argument, then we are obviously only a short step away from the position of the *Tractatus*. For if the mind, according to Kant, can absorb only that which is like itself, then in a sense even more fundamental than Wittgenstein intended it, "the limits of my language" are indeed "the limits of my world," and language becomes the only reality with which we need concern ourselves.

The picture theory of Wittgenstein's *Tractatus*, like Kant's parallel theory of the transcendental schema, has caused endless trouble to those who have tried to grapple with it. "We picture facts to ourselves," he says enigmatically at 2.1. "A picture," he adds at 2.12, "is a model of reality." How is this possible? It is possible because, as he puts it, "In a picture objects have the elements of the picture corresponding to them" (2.13); or, put otherwise, "In a picture the elements of the picture are the representatives of objects" (2.131). A picture, he says, "is attached to reality; it reaches right out to it" (2.1511); "it is laid against reality like a ruler" (2.1512).

But the important question here, of course, is, how do "pictures" manage to "reach out" in this way and become such "models" of reality? Not unlike Kant, he replies that "pictures" are able to do this in virtue of possessing "something in common" with what they depict (2.16 and 2.161), and what they have in common with reality is "logical form" (2.18). Thus, a picture can depict any reality whose form it has. It is this that enables a "proposition," for example, to *picture* reality, for a proposition is in fact a picture or a model of reality (4.01).

Wittgenstein is quite aware that a proposition (one "set out on the printed page, for example") does not at first sight "seem to be a picture of the reality with which it is concerned." "But no more," he adds, "does musical notation at first sight seem to be a picture of music, nor our phonetic notation (the alphabet) to be a picture of our speech. And yet these sign-languages prove to be pictures, even in the ordinary sense, of what they represent" (4.01).

One might object that neither music nor the phonetic system even remotely resembles musical sound or speech, but again what he obviously has in mind here is their common formal or logical patterns and not anything strictly pictorial. This seems at least to be indicated by such further remarks as: "It is obvious that a proposition of the form a R b strikes us as a picture. In this case the sign is obviously a likeness of what is signified" (4.012). "They are all constructed," he remarks again at 4.014, "according to a common logical plan." "That is what constitutes the inner similarity between these things which seem to be constructed in such entirely different ways" (4.0141).

He notes further, in a manner remarkably reminiscent of what Kant had said, that this is what, as a matter of fact, lies behind the possibility "of all imagery, of all our pictorial modes of expression," for logical form is more fundamental and prior to the imagery and the strictly pictorial characteristics. These are, he suggests, a later product and, in a sense, even unnecessary. For, as he says at 4.016, "in order to understand the essential nature of a proposition we should consider hieroglyphic script, which depicts the facts that it describes. And alphabetic script developed out of it without losing what was essential to depiction." In other words, alphabetic script stands for Wittgenstein to hieroglyphic script in the same relation in which schemata stand to images for Kant. In both cases what enables the hieroglyphics or images to function in the way they do is not anything pictorial or iconic about them but rather the logical patterns they inscribe for us.

Interpreting Wittgenstein's account in this way tends to remove some of the objections that have frequently been raised against it. Thus, for example, it has sometimes been objected that while it may be true that propositions may "refer" to reality, "state" things about it, "describe" it, and so on, it cannot, strictly speaking, be said, as Wittgenstein seems to be saying, that they *represent* or *picture* it. To criticize Wittgenstein in this way, however, is to misunderstand his point here. What obviously, according to him, permits the proposition to "picture" the facts it describes is simply, as in Kant, the logical structure it shares with them, and not anything sensual, which it obviously does not possess in common with them. Propositions, that is to say, can picture facts not because they are identical or homomorphic with them but rather because they are structurally similar or isomorphic with them.

What perhaps has tended to mislead readers is that they have thought Wittgenstein was speaking here about the way ordinary sentences picture ordinary, everyday objects, whereas what Wittgenstein seems to be concerned with are not ordinary sentences and ordinary, everyday objects, but rather unordinary, primitive or elementary *propositions* and the way these depict what he calls *states of affairs*.

If it is indeed true that what is involved here are not ordinary sentences but something bordering on the conceptual (that is, "states of affairs"), then to say the one "pictures" the other is not any longer to say anything very startling. For the "picturing" here, far from representing or applying anything like a mirror image, obviously implies something far different from it. That this must be so seems to be clear from his reference to hieroglyphic script. For, after all, even hieroglyphic script does not in any ordinary sense "depict the facts that it describes." If it did even a child would be able to decipher it. Yet he describes this as a "depiction."

In other words, like Kant, Wittgenstein is obviously still dealing here with matters that are far removed from ordinary or familiar events, and the mirror images in which we tend on that plane occasionally to conceive them. Not that these "pictures," as we might say with Kant again, are always "completely congruent with the concept" they are designed to depict. On the contrary, that is precisely how confusions arise. For they arise from the fact, according to Wittgenstein, "that the apparent logical form of a proposition," as already pointed out by Russell, "need not be its real one" (4.0031). Although this diagnosis has also given rise to a good many objections and has often struck readers as superficial, in view of the simple and primitive nature of the linguistic or conceptual structures dealt with here, it is not perhaps, after all, entirely unconvincing. For if successful communication is, theoretically, a matter of using sentences that logically match or are congruent with the states of affairs they describe, then obviously any incongruence in the match will tend to lead to confusion. And on that level of discourse, where we are dealing with such bare and abstract possibilities, a simple failure in our ideography is all that is needed to bring this about.

Although viewing Wittgenstein's *Tractatus* picture theory in the light of Kant's parallel theory enables us to meet some of the objections that have been raised against it, there remains one objection this comparison cannot succeed in removing: if what enables the proposition to function in the way it does is the common logical structure it shares with that which it depicts, then the question immediately arises: how can we ever be certain that it does indeed so depict it? Can we step out of language in order to compare the two? It would seem that we could not.

Unfortunately, Wittgenstein's answer to this question is not only less satisfactory than Kant's but a good deal more mysterious. "In order to be able to represent logical form," he points out, "we should have to be able to station ourselves with propositions somewhere outside logic, that is to say outside the world" (4.12), and, of course, we cannot do that. And we cannot do that, for, again, "what finds its reflection in language, language cannot represent. What expresses *itself* in language, *we* cannot express by means of language" (4.121). But this, he says, does not mean that we are entirely trapped in language. What cannot be *said*, can yet be *shown*. Thus it is that while it is true that a picture cannot depict its pictorial form, it can yet display it (2.172). And similarly with propositions: while it is true that they cannot represent logical form, this does not prevent them from mirroring it (4.121). "There are, indeed," as he reassures the reader towards the end of the *Tractatus*, "things that cannot be put into words" (6.522). "They *make themselves manifest*"; they are, he ends by saying, "what is mystical."

It is interesting that when Wittgenstein returned to philosophy some ten years later, it was precisely this question of how language comes to signify, "solved" so mysteriously here in the *Tractatus*, to which he once again directed his attention. In this new period of his thought he came to see that his old conception of language as being a mirror of reality was somehow mistaken. He decided therefore to make a fresh start — or what at first sight appeared to him to be a fresh start.

Briefly, he came to see that far from being a mirror whose sole object was to reflect reality, language was a tool capable of many uses. Since the failure to take note of this peculiar feature of language was something he shared with other philosophers, he came to regard this as not only responsible for his own former impasses but also what was at the root of the impasses of his fellow philosophers. And thus was born what he regarded as his new mission: to show others how they too have been misled by language.

In carrying out this mission, Wittgenstein seems to have been caught between two opposite drives. He realized that he had discovered what he called a "new method" of doing philosophy. Anxious to test it, he proceeded to apply it to all kinds of situations and problems, sometimes with startling results. In fact, so startling did these results appear to him that their elaboration tended to absorb him in their own right and to overshadow his prime object — the articulation of his new theory of language.

The picture theory that gradually emerges in these new works is, like the one found in the *Tractatus*, designed to show us how it is that we become trapped in language. Unlike the *Tractatus* theory, however, the trap here is not an ontological one but a phenomenological one: that is, it is one we can free ourselves from, given the proper insights. All involve becoming aware of certain peculiarities of language. The first of these has to do with the nature of words; the second, with the nature of sentences; and the third, with certain aspects of our psychology.

What particularly struck him about words was that despite the numerous and diverse roles they play, the mental images they generate do not always keep up with the new usages but tend to lag behind them. And it is the same with the sentences we form with these words: while the facts of our experience are unlimited and enormously varied, the forms of language, or sentence structures with which we are compelled to describe and record them are few in number. The dangers of misdescribing and misrecording these facts are thus unlimited. What, finally, feeds and is in turn fed by these tendencies towards economy in language is our own mental attitudes, which strive always towards unity, simplicity, and economy. And this too tends to do violence to the multifarious nature of our experience.

Mainly, however, what he came to see at this point in his thinking was that a different, more literal, sort of "picturing" seems to take place in language, one which, more than anything else, seems to be responsible for our philosophic puzzlement and confusion. What this is may be gathered from a rather striking example recounted by Professor Norman Malcolm in his *Memoir* of Wittgenstein:

> At one of the at-homes, Wittgenstein related a riddle for the purpose of throwing some light on the nature of philosophy. It went as follows: Suppose that a cord was stretched tightly around the earth at the equator. Now suppose that a piece one yard long was added to the cord. If the cord was kept taut and circular in form, how much above the surface of the earth would it be? Without stopping to work it out, everyone present was inclined to say that the distance of the cord from the surface of the earth would be so *minute* that it would be imperceptible. But this is wrong. The actual distance would be nearly six inches. Wittgenstein declared that this is the *kind* of mistake that occurs in philosophy. It consists in being *misled by a picture.* In the riddle the picture that misleads us is the comparison of the length of the additioanl piece with the length of the whole cord. The picture itself is correct enough: for a piece one yard long would be an insignificant fraction of the length of the whole cord. But we are misled by it to draw a wrong conclusion. A similar thing happens in philosophy: we are constantly deceived by mental pictures which are in themselves correct" (pp. 53–4).

According to Wittgenstein these "pictures" generated by the way we speak have an especially strong tendency to mislead the nonprofessional and the philosopher anxious to understand the work and contributions of the various new discoveries and inventions — the nonmathematicians, for example, whose interest in the work of the mathematician stems, initially, not from anything internal or directly relevant to these investigations but rather from the associations these expressions tend to arouse in their minds. What fascinates them are the pictures the mathematician's talk about his work tends to conjure up. And these pictures are misleading: they tend to make his work seem more important and more glamorous than it would otherwise seem to be. This may not be a bad thing, for without such glamor no one might have become interested in these problems to begin with; they are, however, not what the problems, once begun, are really about.

In order to understand a word, says Wittgenstein, we must know its use. With a great many words a certain picture represents for us both its meaning and its use. This is the case, for example, with the word "chair." One of the great benefits this tendency of words to arouse pictures of what they represent has, is that it guarantees that we will all use these words in the same way. In other cases, however, these pictures are very misleading. An example here is the word "particle," which, unfortunately, is no longer used in such a way that the picture has any use. For rather than guaranteeing that we will use the word in similar ways, such new uses to which old words are put tend rather to have the reverse effect. And this will be so whenever the words in question no longer continue to be used by us in their ordinary and familiar ways. Then the words are misleading — and understandably so, for the pictures they create lead us to expect the wrong things — and with obvious results.

But that is not all. For a curious by-product of this tendency to continue to apply standard pictures in situations where they are no longer really appropriate is the sense of amazement this often generates. Thus, for example, thinking of the formula "the cardinal number of all cardinal numbers" in term of, say, "chairs" has a kind of dizzying effect on the mind, for the number involved is truly staggering. It conjures up, he says, "a picture of an *enormous colossal* number. And this picture has a charm." But the imagery here, although a natural and understandable consequence of our tendency to assimilate and correlate various expressions in our language, is entirely inappropriate. For in fact, we have as yet, as he puts it, "no right to have an image. The imagery is connected with a different calculus: $30 \times 30 = 900$." It is the same in many other cases: the sense of amazement and puzzlement experienced at such occasions is simply a product of a misapplied image.

On the contrary, we may go even further than that. If something about a certain subject or problem "charms or astounds" us, we may conclude from this that it is because we have been captivated by "the wrong imagery." Imagery of that sort is a function of metaphors and such metaphors remain "fishy" as long as they are "exciting." When we begin to see these things in their true light, the amazement and excitement simply vanishes. Thus, for example, certain parts of mathematics are regarded as "deep." "But the apparent depth comes from a wrong imagery. It is pedestrian as any calculus." Yet that is precisely the way people were misled about the infinitesimal calculus when they mistakenly believed that it treated of infinitely small quantities. It is because we think of such things in terms of such misleading images (in terms, for example, of sizes, as here) that we go wrong. The amazement and excitement such things inspire in us should be taken as a sign that we have simply been misled.

Wittgenstein speaks in these mathematical writings of "charm," "excitement," "amazement," and so on, but it is easy to see how these expressions give way in the other works to such more familiar ones as "puzzlement," "wonder," and "confusion." That transition is to be found, in fact, in these writings themselves. He remarks, for example:

There is one kind of misunderstanding which has a kind of charm . . . we say that the line intersects at an imaginary point. This sets the mind in a whirl, and gives a pleasant feeling of paradox, e.g. saying that there are numbers bigger than infinity. . . . He has employed a sensational way of expressing what he has discovered, so that it looks like a different *kind* of discovery. . . . he describes a new state of affairs in old words, and so we don't understand him. The picture he makes does not lead us on. By the words of ordinary language we conjure up a familiar picture — but we need more than the right picture, we need to know the correct use. (*Math Notes*. San Francisco, Calif. 1954, p.6).*

And this is precisely where such new notations, he emphasizes here, fail us so badly. The fact is that "in an overwhelming number of cases people do have the same sort of images suggested by words. This is a mere matter of fact about what happens in our minds, but a fact of enormous importance." In view of this, it is not difficult to see why and how confusions arise. For all that is really necessary for this to happen is for us to use familiar words in unfamiliar ways. The pictures aroused will be correct enough but, of course, they will be misleading. And it is in such misleading pictures, he concludes here as well, "that most of the problems of philosophy arise."

Not only, obviously, are these remarks related to those quoted above from Norman Malcolm's *Memoir* of Wittgenstein but they are also obviously closely related to those to be found in the *Tractatus*. "A sign," he says there, "is what can be perceived of a symbol" (3.32). But one and the same sign can be common to two different symbols, as is so often the case in our language. No harm is done by this as long as we realize they are signifying two quite different things, and really therefore belong to two different symbols. But this is not always the case. "In the proposition, 'Green is green,'" for example, "where the first word is the proper name of a person and the last an adjective — these words do not merely have different meanings: they are *different* symbols" (3.323). This is, of course, an obvious example and not likely to mislead anyone. It is, however, in this way that "the most fundamental confusions are easily produced (the whole of philosophy is full of them)" (3.324). " In order to avoid such errors we must make use of a sign-language that excludes them by not using the same sign for symbols and by not using in a superficially similar way signs that have different modes of signification: that is to say, a sign-language that is governed by *logical* grammar — by logical syntax" (3.325). We need here only replace sign by "image," and symbol by "word" to see the close correspondence between the two picture theories and how little indeed Wittgenstein needed to change in his original theory as he moved from a strictly ontological investigation to a more phenomenological one in the later works.

This second attempt to describe the way language "pictures" reality was not Wittgenstein's last. He went on to explore still a third view of language, built on this second one, one more detailed and more fully developed, yet just as intriguing. This third view is not so much concerned with the genesis of confusion arising from the "pictures" generated by words as with the confusions stemming from our misunderstanding of what he now calls the "grammar" of words.

*An anonymous publication, based — without his authorization — on Malcolm's notes of Wittgenstein's lectures.

A good example is the ancient problem regarding the nature of time. Trying to solve this problem in the way we might try to solve the problem regarding, say, the ultimate constituents of matter and not succeeding very well has tended to make us think that these philosophical entities are very queer things, and very difficult to get at: "That here are," as he puts it, "things hidden, something we can see from the outside but which we can't look into." "And yet nothing of the sort is the case. It is not new facts about time which we want to know. All the facts that concern us lie open before us" (*Blue Book*, p. 6). But it is the use of the noun "time" and the form in which we pose this question that misleads us into dealing with it in an impossible way. If we would look into the "grammar" of that word we would no longer be puzzled and would know quite well how to use it. And that is all we mean by it.

But unfortunately the question, "What is Time?" which so puzzled Saint Augustine, like ordinary scientific questions, appears to ask for something else — for some factual information — and this leads us to deal with it as if it were indeed an ordinary scientific or empirical question. But this is obviously wrong and not what is wanted here. We do not see this because the puzzlement expresses itself here in a misleading way by means of the form of the question "What is . . . ?" But this is simply, in this case, an utterance of "unclarity, of mental discomfort . . . comparable with the question "Why?" as children so often ask it" — a question that like "What is . . . ?" "doesn't necessarily ask for either a cause or a reason," but is simply an expression of puzzlement (*Blue Book*, p. 26).

It is little wonder, therefore, that such questions cannot be answered by providing information but only by coming to recognize their cause, which lies in certain "contradictions" in the grammar of the words used. "Augustine, we might say, thinks of the process of measuring a *length:* say, the distance between two marks on a travelling band which passes us, and of which we can only see a tiny bit (the present) in front of us" (*Blue Book*, p. 26). Thinking of time in terms of such an analogy — of such a picture embedded in the notion of "measuring" common to the two cases — he naturally became puzzled as to how it could be done; how, that is, it should be possible for one to be able to measure it. For the past, as he himself put it, can't be measured, as it is gone by; and the future can't be measured because it has not yet come; and, finally, the present can't be measured, for it has no extension. What, then, *is* time?

If time were indeed like such a passing band (the part that is to be measured not having arrived yet and the other part already gone by) we would certainly not be able to measure it by laying, say, a ruler alongside it. To solve this puzzle, obviously what we must therefore do is to come to see that we mean quite a different thing by "measurement" when applied to a band continuously passing by us and when applied to such a thing as time. It is because we try to apply such words rigidly and consistently and find that we cannot, that we run into difficulties and become bewildered. We fail to see that we are really victims here of a kind of equivocation, that the same word may have quite different meanings when used in different contexts. "The problem may seem simple, but its extreme difficulty is due to the fascination which the analogy between two similar structures in our language can exert on us" (*Blue Book*, p. 26). Like children, we find it hard to believe that one word can have two meanings.

Wittgenstein goes on to generalize this point. "Philosophy, as we use the word, is a fight," he says, "against the fascination which forms of expression exert upon us" (*Blue Book*, p. 27). It is an attempt "to counteract the misleading effect of certain analogies" (*Blue Book*, p. 28). "The man who is philosophically puzzled sees a law in the way a word is used, and, trying to apply this law consistently, comes up against cases where it leads to paradoxical results" (*Blue Book*, p. 27). What we must try to do is to undermine and loosen this rigidity of mind and counteract the effect these misleading analogies have upon us.

Two aspects of Wittgenstein's analysis here are important. The first is his view, apparently, that what makes us particularly prone to these pitfalls in language is a certain mental laziness or lack of alertness. If we have come to understand a term in a certain way, we have a tendency to continue to understand it that way, come what may. Mentally, it is easier and requires less energy to do this than to be constantly alert to changing circumstances. Unfortunately for us (and here we come to Wittgenstein's second point), certain features of language tend to collaborate to sustain this mental laziness. This feature is the highly analogical character of language, which tends to lull us into thinking that there is more unity and uniformity in the facts recorded than there really is. Wittgenstein never tires of emphasizing the hypnotic effect this feature of language has on us. "We aren't able to rid ourselves of the implications of our symbolism" (*Brown Book*, p. 108), he says at one place. "We are led into puzzlement by an analogy which irresistibly drags us on" (ibid.). Or again: "A picture held us captive. We could not get outside it, for it lay in our language and language seemed to repeat it to us inexorably" (*Philosophical Investigations* I, 115).

Wittgenstein doesn't want to claim that all analogies necessarily lead to the kind of confusion he describes here, nor that all analogical thinking is bad. There are no doubt many analogies that are, from this point of view, entirely harmless, and many of them are extremely useful. "When we say that by our method we try to counteract the misleading effect of certain analogies," he qualifies his remaks here, "it is important that you should understand that the idea of an analogy being misleading is nothing sharply defined. No sharp boundary can be drawn round the cases in which we should say that a man was misled by an analogy. The use of expressions constructed on analogical patterns stresses analogies between cases often far apart. And by doing this these expressions may be extremely useful. It is, in most cases, impossible to show an exact point where an analogy begins to mislead us. Every particular notation stresses some particular point of view" (*Blue Book*, p. 28).

"The cases," however, "in which particularly we wish to say that someone is misled by a form of expression are those in which we would say: 'He wouldn't talk as he does if he were aware of this difference in the grammar of such-and-such words, or if he were aware of this other possibility of expression' and so on" (ibid.).

To make this point clearer Wittgenstein draws our attention to a host of different examples. "It might be found practical," he points out, "to call a certain state of decay in a tooth, not accompanied by what we commonly call toothache, 'unconscious toothache' and to use in such a case the expression that we have toothache, but don't know it. It is just in this sense that psychoanalysis talks of unconscious thoughts, acts of volition, etc. Now is it wrong in this sense to say that I have toothache but don't know it? There is nothing wrong about it, as it is just a new terminology and can at any time be translated into ordinary language. On the other hand it obviously makes use of the word "to know" in a new way (ibid., pp. 22–23).

But unfortunately the new expression not only leads us to think that we have done more than we actually have but it also calls up for us "pictures and analogies which make it extremely difficult for us to go through with our conventions" (ibid., p. 25). And this in turn creates puzzlement and gives rise to bad philosophy.

Thus, by the expression "unconscious toothache," for example, we are "misled into thinking that a stupendous discovery has been made, a discovery which in a sense altogether bewilders our understanding; or else you may be extremely puzzled by the expression (the puzzlement of philosophy) and perhaps ask such a question as 'How is unconscious toothache possible?' You may then be tempted to deny the possibility of unconscious toothache; but the scientist will tell you that it is a proved fact that there is such a thing, and will say it like a man who is destroying a common prejudice. He will say: 'Surely it's quite simple; there are other things which you don't know of and there can also be toothache which you don't know of. It is just a new discovery.' You won't be satisfied, but you won't know what to answer" (ibid.). But obviously what has been overlooked by these disputants is, inter alia, the fact that these other things we "don't know of" are things which, unlike having a toothache, we "don't have." And what puzzles us is the fact that since a toothache is something "we have," we ought, normally speaking, "know of it." The new notation, although not unintelligible, does not seem to provide room for this, and thus runs into conflict with the old. This generates confusion and puzzlement.

It is the same with the so-called "discoveries" of psychoanalysis and all the disputes and confusion this has caused. "'Can we have unconscious thoughts, unconscious feelings, etc?' The idea that we can has revolted many people. Others again have said that these were wrong in supposing that there could only be conscious thoughts, and that psychoanalysis had discovered unconscious ones." Both, however, were confused about what had really happened. "The objectors to unconscious thought," for example, "did not see that they were not objecting to the newly discovered psychological reactions, but to the way in which they were described. The psychoanalysts on the other hand were misled by their own way of expression into thinking that they had done more than discover new psychological reactions; that they had, in a sense, discovered conscious thoughts which were unconscious. The first could have stated their objection by saying 'We don't wish to use the phrase "unconscious thoughts"; we wish to reserve the word "thought" for what you call "conscious thought."' They state their case wrongly when they say: 'There can only be conscious thoughts and no unconscious ones.' For if they don't wish to talk of 'unconscious thought' they should not use the phrase 'conscious thought, either" (*Blue Book*, p. 57–58).

These disputes and difficulties can be cleared up by recognizing that they are essentially verbal, that what is being disputed are not the facts of the case — whatever they may be — but simply their description. It is this confusion of the grammatical with the experiential that has led philosophers to say typically metaphysical (that is, paradoxical) things. This is also what has led them to believe that they have somehow stumbled upon some very striking scientific or empirical discoveries when as a matter of fact they have merely used words in consistently and therefore systematically misleading ways. If there is anything actually new that they have accomplished here it is to forge some new conventions regarding the uses of words, and speaking about them. To do this, however, is not to discover anything new or startling about any of the things described by these expressions. In the end it is simply a matter of making new notations. Philosophers, however, have not as a rule been aware that that is all it is.

That this third, more generalized view of the way we are misled by language is intimately connected with the second view concerning the image-generating capacity of language, is clear from numerous other passages scattered throughout his writings, where both views seem to exist side by side. Let me illustrate this with one or two examples.

"The new expression misleads us," he says in the *Blue Book*, "by calling up pictures and analogies which make it difficult for us to go through with our conventions. And it is extremely difficult to discard these pictures unless we are constantly watchful" (p. 23). Now we can be so watchful, he goes on, by asking ourselves at such times *"How far does the analogy between these uses go:"* We can also try to construct "new notations, in order to break the spell of those which we are accustomed to." In view of what we have seen Wittgenstein say about "pictures," we can perhaps now understand, much better than was possible before, the deeper implications of these remarks: why, for example, he should say that it is extremely difficult to discard these pictures; how being watchful in the way he suggests will enable us to do so; and why he should speak of the whole process in the terms he does ("go through with our conventions," "spell," "notation," and so forth). The same may be said of a good many other passages in the *Blue Book*.

Although such discussions tend to be more puzzling without these further aids, occasionally they are, as we now see, surprisingly explicit and clear. His remark on page 43 of the *Blue Book* is a case in point. "The scrutiny of the grammar of a word," he says there, summarizing his results, "weakens the position of certain fixed standards of our expression which had prevented us from seeing facts with unbiased eyes. Our investigation tried to remove this bias, which forces us to think that the facts *must* conform to certain pictures embedded in our language."

To see, however, how Wittgenstein came to connect his thoughts about this picture-generating capacity of language with his later thoughts on the nature and sources of philosophical confusion, we need to turn to the *Philosophical Investigations*.

The trouble with our failure "to get away from the idea that using a sentence involves imagining something for every word" is, he argues there, that we do not realize that we do all sorts of things with words — turning "them sometimes into one picture, sometimes into another" (*Philosophical Investigations* I, 449). Furthermore, such pictures are often "only like an illustration to a story" and from it alone it is mostly impossible "to conclude anything at all" — for only "when one knows the story does one know the significance of the picture" (*Philosophical Investigations* I, 663). But mainly, of course, the trouble with such pictures is that they seem "to fix the sense *unambiguously*" when this is not at all the case. On the contrary, "the actual use, compared with that suggested by the picture," is "muddied" (*Philosophical Investigations* I, 426).

Certainly language has this effect on us — "the picture is there"; nor need we necessarily dispute its "validity in any particular case." But we do "want to understand the application of the picture" (*Philosophical Investigations* I, 423). And not only is this often lacking, but other pernicious effects result as well. Or, as he puts it later, "what this language primarily describes is a picture. What is to be done with the picture, how it is to be used, is still obscure. Quite clearly, however, it must be explored if we want to understand the sense of what we are saying. But the picture seems to spare us this work: it already points to a particular use. This is how it takes us in" (*Philosophical Investigations* II, vii).

In order to save ourselves from being taken in, we ought always to ask: does reality accord with such pictures? (*Philosophical Investigations* I, 352). These pictures seem "to determine what we have to do, what to look for, and how," but they do not really do so. They seem "to make the sense of the expressions unmistakable" but in fact prove to be utterly misleading (*Philosophical Investigations* I, 352). For example, "what am I believing in when I believe that men have souls? What am I believing in, when I believe that this substance contains two carbon rings? In both cases there is a picture in the foreground, but the sense lies far in the background; that is, the application of the picture is not easy to survey" (*Philosophical Investigations* I, 422). In ordinary circumstances such words and the pictures they generate "have an application with which we are familiar. — But if we suppose a case in which this application is absent we become as it were conscious for the first time of the nakedness of the words and the picture" (*Philosophical Investigations* I, 349), of how "idle" such pictures are (*Philosophical Investigations* I, 291). In the end we must simply regard them as "illustrated turns of speech" (*Philosophical Investigations* I, 295), which stand "in the way of our seeing the use of the word as it is" (*Philosophical Investigations* I, 305).

In restating, as I have tried to do here, Wittgenstein's position in terms of this new idea and emphasis, I have, of course, taken some liberties with the order of his own exposition. This has been necessary in order to make it possible for us to look at such remarks in the *Philosophical Investigations* as, for example, "philosophy is a battle against the bewitchment of our intelligence by means of language" (I, 109); "a simile that has been absorbed into the forms of our language produces a false appearance" (I, 112); " a *picture* held us captive" (I, 115); and so on, in the way in which we ought now, perhaps, to look at all Wittgenstein's remarks regarding the genesis of philosophical confusion.

One of the values to be derived, it seems to me, from doing so is that it enables us to meet an objection that must strike every reader who tries to come to terms with Wittgenstein's attack upon philosophy. One is often tempted to object that it seems preposterous to attribute the rise of various metaphysical theories, complex as they often are and supported by such subtle and intricate arguments, to such seemingly absurd and unbelievable causes. Surely, one is inclined to say at such times, it is pure fancy to suggest that Augustine's puzzlement about Time arose in this way. On the contrary, to try to dismiss it in such a high-handed manner is itself simply absurd. For, after all, what proof is there that such an analogy even occurred to him during his deliberations on this problem?

But from what has been said here, it could perhaps be argued that it is really not Wittgenstein's intention to try to base his case, here or elsewhere, on any such claims. His point seems rather to be that our questions (about Time or anything else) are often products of our tendency to look at these things through misleading pictures (whatever these may be at any one occasion or for any one particular philosopher). On the other hand, should it be argued that he did indeed intend to be a good deal more specific than this, then the whole question simply becomes an empirical one. To settle it we would need to ask people whether, for example, in thinking about the flow of Time they had in their minds, however dimly (as he seems to suggest in the *Brown Book* that they apparently do — see pp. 107–108), some notion of the flow of logs down a river. We might by investigating it in this way discover that either they had something else in the back of their minds (must it be *logs?* could it not be, perhaps, clouds floating across the sky?) or, more probably, nothing at all. But this is probably not what Wittgenstein has in mind here. His point seems rather to be that the general tendency of language is to generate pictures in our minds (this is a fact of language and is essential to his case) and that this being so, it simply cannot fail to have an adverse effect upon thinking. Such pictures, being often incongruent with the facts which they are designed to explain, must prove misleading.

It is perhaps this general fact about language (and not any one particular picture he need necessarily defend) upon which he seems mainly to base his case. This is what, for example, his remarks about "symbolism" in his later works seem to entail. "Thus it can come about," he says, "that we aren't able to rid ourselves of the implications of our symbolism." We become "obsessed" with it — an analogy which "irresistibly drags us on" leads us into confusion (*Brown Book*, p. 108).

The "symbolism" or ideography of which he speaks here is obviously of a much more complicated kind than the one discussed in the *Tractatus*. But like it, it is designed to show how language, by failing to be congruent with the states of affairs it is designed to depict, gives rise to difficulties. Both doctrines, that is to say, are designed to be descriptive of certain very general and universal aspects of the operation of language.

Wittgenstein and our philosophic tradition

In being concerned with these questions and in exploring them the way he does, it might appear as if Wittgenstein, and the contemporary analytic and linguistic philosophy he influenced so profoundly, are very remote from the central concerns of philosophy. Although many have believed this to be so, in an important sense, what Wittgenstein has tried to achieve can be seen as lying very much in the direct line of development of philosophy, and that he has been occupied with what has always been central to it.

Let me begin with a remark found in Wittgenstein's *Notebooks:* "The great problem round which everything that I write turns is: Is there an order in the world *a priori*, and if so what does it consist in?" (p. 53). This attempt to find the true structure or order of the world and make sense of it, is what philosophy, as we have seen, has traditionally been conceived to be mainly concerned with.

Like all great philosophers before him, Wittgenstein has tried to show that the world as it appears to us appears so as a result of the conceptual system we use in organizing it, and since this system is essentially a human (or "man-made") one, we are in a fundamental sense our own prisoners. How to break free of this prison, how to come to see the way things really are — this is the theme round which all philosophy turns.

Some of philosophy's most memorable passages have been devoted to describing this condition in which we find ourselves. Among the greatest of these is Plato's Parable of the Cave in his most famous work, the *Republic.*

As an illustration of the degree to which our nature may be enlightened or unenlightened, Plato says, imagine the condition of men imprisoned in a dark and deep underground cave. They are chained to their seats and are able to move neither to the right nor to the left. They have been there from birth and sit facing the wall of the cave. It is a deep cave and the long winding entrance behind them permits no light to enter. Somewhat farther behind them there is a wall or partition, and behind this wall, a path or track. Farther back still a fire is burning. Along this track people walk to and fro, carrying all sorts of objects (figures of men, animals, and so on) which project above the partition. As they walk by, some talking, some silent, the fire casts shadows of these figures onto the wall of the cave facing the prisoners. But the prisoners, like their modern counterparts in movie theaters, see neither the fire nor, of course, the men who carry these objects whose shadows are reflected on the wall of the cave. They see only the shadows; they are aware of nothing else. But from these shadows that they see, and that they take to be real things, and the echoes they hear, they form, after perhaps much trial and error, various theories, some, as we might suppose, highly ingenious — perhaps that these activities of which they are spectators generally last for periods of some eight hours a day, and only five days of the week. To this knowledge they add, in the course of time, further bits of insight, and thus they pass their existence: the only one they know.

But now suppose, says Plato, we released one of these prisoners and brought him to the rear. He sees the wall and the track . . . the fire burning in the distance . . . the people and the objects which they carry . . . and he sees the prisoners sitting below watching the shadows.

Not accustomed to such intense light he shuts his eyes, in pain and disbelief. He is seized with fear and is overcome by an urge to return to the more familiar and comfortable condition of the darkness of the cave. In time, however, his eyes become accustomed to the light and he comes to see that what he once took to be real things were indeed only shadows, and an intense desire possesses him to return to the cave to tell the others what he has seen.

Suppose we now follow him there. The other prisoners have seen neither the wall, nor the men, nor the fire. They see him descending into the cave, falling and stumbling, for the cave is dark and it is difficult for him to find his way about. They laugh and jeer at him, for his movements are absurd. "He has gone up," they say, "only to come back with his sight ruined." He begins, however, to tell them about the great fire burning and about the partition and the statues and the other things he has seen, but it sounds absurd to them. Obviously it is not worth one's while, they say, even to attempt the ascent. But he is undaunted and persists in enlightening them. They become annoyed and their laughter now turns to anger. They instruct him to keep his peace and not disturb them, or else they themselves will silence him. And that, concludes Plato, with obvious allusions to Socrates, is what they will do should an opportunity present itself.

This parable is Plato's way of expressing his belief that the world may, for all we know, be quite other than what it appears to be — that with regard to it we are or may be in a state of human and universal deception.

Ever since Plato, philosophers have tried to come to understand more clearly the source and nature of this universal deception. Spinoza, another philosopher whom we have already encountered, believed a good deal of it originated from our belief in the purposiveness of nature. Why, he asked himself, in his *Ethics*, are people so prone to believe this about nature? What is it that stands in their way of seeing that the facts are quite the contrary, namely, that "nature has no particular goal in view" and that everything in it "proceeds from a sort of necessity, and with the utmost perfection" (p. 75).

Partly, he answers, it is due to ignorance of natural causes, and partly to the human propensity to seek and believe only that which is useful to us. "Herefrom it follows, first, that men think themselves free inasmuch as they are conscious of their volitions and desires, and never even dream, in their ignorance, of the causes which have disposed them so to wish and desire. Secondly, that men do all things for an end, namely for that which is useful to them, and which they seek" and that nature too behaves similarly.

Thus it comes to pass that they only look for a knowledge of the final causes of events, and when these are learned, they are content, as having no cause for further doubt. If they cannot learn such causes from external sources, they are compelled to turn to considering themselves, and reflecting what end would have induced them personally to bring about the given event, and thus they necessarily judge other natures by their own. Further, as they find in themselves and outside themselves many means which assist them not a little in their search for what is useful, for instance, eyes for seeing, teeth for chewing, herbs and animals for yielding food, the sun for giving light, the sea for breeding fish, etc., they come to look on the whole of nature as a means for obtaining such conveniences. Now as they are aware, that they found these conveniences and did not make them, they think they have cause for believing, that some other being has made them for their use. As they look upon things as means, they cannot believe them to be self-created; but, judging from the means they are accustomed to prepare for themselves, they are bound to believe in some ruler or rulers of the universe endowed with human freedom, who have arranged and adapted everything for human use. They are bound to estimate the nature of such rulers (having no information on the subject) in accordance with their own nature, and therefore they assert that the gods ordained everything for the use of man, in order to bind man to themselves and obtain from him the highest honor. Hence also it follows, that everyone thought out for himself, according to his abilities, a different way of worshipping God, so that God might love him more than his fellows, and direct the whole course of nature for the satisfaction of his blind cupidity and insatiable avarice.*

"Thus the prejudice," Spinoza concludes this brief history of natural religion, "developed into superstition, and took deep root in the human mind; and for this reason everyone strove zealously to understand and explain the final causes of things; but in their endeavour to show that nature does nothing in vain, i.e., nothing which is useless to man, they only seem to have demonstrated that nature, the gods, and men are all mad together" (pp. 75–76). Consider, he urges, the result:

Among the many helps of nature they were bound to find hindrances, such as storms, earthquakes, diseases, etc.: so they declared that such things happen, because the gods are angry at some wrong done them by men, or at some fault committed in their worship. Experience day by day protested and showed by infinite examples, that good and evil fortunes fall to the lot of pious and impious alike; still they would not abandon their inveterate prejudice, for it was more easy for them to class such

* The Chief Works of Benedict De Spinoza, translated by R. H. M. Elwes (N.Y.: Dover, 1951). Volume II, pp. 75–76.

contradictions among other unknown things of whose use they were ignorant, and thus retain their actual and innate condition of ignorance, than to destroy the whole fabric of their reasoning and start afresh. They therefore laid down as an axiom [deserting in the process the very principle with which they began] that God's judgment far transcends human understanding.

Spinoza goes on to try to correct these misconceptions, asserting the doctrines for which he is noted, that "final causes are mere human figments," "that everyone judges of things according to the state of his brain," that names may be names of nothing at all, and so on.

Spinoza's account is interesting not only because of the nature of its doctrines (important as these are) but also because of the effect their exposition is designed to have upon the mind of the reader. And this is of deflation and disillusionment. Like Plato before him, and, as we will see in a moment, Wittgenstein after him, the task Spinoza has here set himself is to free the mind from the pictures and illusions that have captivated it and held it in bondage. It is an attempt to show that the world as we tend to experience it is very much a product of our own making, that as such and in itself, stripped of the illusions and deceptions prone to our ways of comprehending it, it is absurdly different from what we are inclined to take it to be.

When we turn to Wittgenstein, we find that he too has taken this, the unmasking of the illusions and deceptions to which we are so prone, as his main object. The passages I should like to quote here are directly concerned with our belief in "essences" — our tendency to think that there must be something in common among all the members of a class of things called by the same name. It is the kind of tendency to which, for example, Socrates apparently was especially liable. In the *Meno*, for example, he asks: "What is this thing which is called 'shape'? ... Don't you see that I am looking for what is the same in all of them? ... What is it that is common to roundness and straightness and the other things which you call shapes?" Clear and as natural as that kind of question must once have appeared, Wittgenstein would have us see that that is really a "complex question." For why should we assume, as he would ask, that there is such one common property or essence which runs through all such things? Surely, he would say, until we have settled that things share such common properties it makes no sense to ask for them. Such questions are impossible to answer and produce puzzlement because they are often impossible questions. They keep the mind, as he puts it in his *Blue* and *Brown Books*, "pressing against a blank wall, thereby preventing it from ever finding the outlet. To show a man how to get out you have first of all to free him from the misleading influence of the question" (p. 169).

"Instead of producing something common," Wittgenstein explains in the *Philosophical Investigations*, "I am saying that these phenomena have no one thing in common which makes us use the same word for all, — but that they are *related* to one another in many different ways. And it is because of this relationship, or these relationships, that we call them all [by the same name]. I will try to explain this" (italics added).

> Consider for example the proceeding that we call 'games'. I mean board-games, card-games, ball-games, Olympic games, and so on. What is common to them all?—Don't say: There *must* be something common, or they would not be called 'games'—but *look and see* whether there is anything common to all. For if you look at them you will not see something that is common to *all*, but similarities, relationships, and a whole series of them at that. To repeat: Don't think, but look!—Look for example at board-games, with their multifarious relationships. Now pass to card-games; here you find many correspondences with the first group, but many common features drop out, and others appear. When we pass next to ball-games, much that is common is retained, but much is lost.—Are they all 'amusing'? Compare chess with noughts and crosses. Or is there always winning and losing, or competition between players? Think of patience . . . we can go through the many, many other groups of games in the same way; we can see how similarities crop up and disappear.

> I can think of no better expression to characterize these similarities than 'family resemblance'; for the various resemblances between members of a family: build, features, colour of eyes, gait, temperament, etc. etc. overlap and criss-cross in the same way.—. . . 'games' form a family.

> The kinds of number form a family in the same way. Why do we call something a 'number'? Well, perhaps because it has a—direct—relationship with several things that have hitherto been called number; and this can be said to give it an indirect relationship to other things we call the same name. And we extend our concept of number as in spinning a thread we twist fibre on fibre. And the strength of the thread does not reside in the fact that some one fibre runs through its whole length, but in the overlapping of many fibres.

> But if someone wished to say: "There is something common to all these constructions—namely the disjunction of all their common properties"—I should reply: Now you are only playing with words. One might as well say: "Something runs through the whole thread—namely the continuous overlapping of those fibres."

> I *can* give the concept 'number' rigid limits . . . but I can also use it so that the extension of the concept is *not* closed by a frontier. And this is how we do use the word 'game'. For how is the concept of a game bounded? What still counts as a game and what no longer does? Can you

give the boundary? No. You can *draw* one; for none has so far been drawn.

"But then the use of the word is unregulated, the 'game' we play with it is unregulated." — It is not everywhere circumscribed by rules; but no more are there rules for how high one throws the ball in tennis, or how hard; yet tennis is a game for all that and has rules too. (*Philosophical Investigations* I, pp. 65–68).

It would be a mistake to think that Wittgenstein is interested here in merely unseating or unmasking "essentialism" — the belief in the existence of essences. Nor is he merely trying to point out that such questions as, for example, What are games? What is beauty? Justice? and so on, are really "loaded" questions, which need themselves to be questioned before they are answered. What he is interested in showing us is not that there are no such essences to be found, but rather what this search for them, invited as it is by such questions, tends to do to us. For this desire for unity and this will to system, which such questions illustrate and invite, blunts and blinds our perceptions and sensitivities. It does violence to the multifarious nature of our experience, makes it easy for us to ignore what is exceptional in that experience, and leads us to take a contemptuous attitude to what is unique and individual in it.

In other words, this approach to the world tends to produce the illusion that the world really is as we have parceled it out by means of our concepts; that our conceptual net has really caught all there is to catch and nothing has gotten away. But how can we be sure of this? Perhaps some fish have not been caught, and those that have are not at all representative of what there is to catch.

I said earlier that I thought the leading idea round which all philosophy turns is this insight regarding the existence of two worlds — the world of reality and the world of appearance, the world as it is in itself and the world as it appears to us. Although only the passages I quoted from Plato seem to deal directly with this question, I think we can see that in dealing with our conceptual frameworks in the way Wittgenstein and the other philosophers do, they too are very much involved in the same endeavor. For like Plato before them, what they are saying is that the sort of world we are able to experience depends very much on the conceptual system we use in organizing it for ourselves, and that in regard to it, therefore, we must consider ourselves under a kind of human and universal deception. And that, I believe, is the moral that Plato's parable, as well as the rest of Western philosophy, has as its main object.

I do not wish to imply that all the great philosophers are unanimous on this question. They are not. But what divides them are not goals but means. In these goals they are remarkably at one. They do not, however, always agree as to what constitutes the best methods of arriving at these goals. Another way of putting this would be to say that they agree in their conclusions but not in the proofs that have been provided for them. And on these proofs philosophers are still at work.

Summary

1. The person who set the course contemporary philosophy in the English-speaking world was to follow was Bertrand Russell (1872–1970).

2. Through his contributions to mathematical logic and his social and political activism, Russell was not only one of the major forces responsible for the revolution which has taken place in philosophy, but was also one of the major figures responsible for the social and technological revolutions that have taken place in this century.

3. Although Russell was the catalyst of the revolution in contemporary philosophy, it was his pupil Ludwig Wittgenstein (1889–1951) who charted its course and gave it the tone and character that still marks it.

4. Taking his cue from Whitehead and Russell's *Principia Mathematica* (1910–1913), Wittgenstein went on to show in his first work, the *Tractatus*, composed in 1918, that language, far from being a jungle as might at first be thought, had a definite structure and order to it, one which mirrored or pictured the structure of reality, and that the new job of philosophy was to describe as accurately as possible what this structure is, and in this way solve or dissolve, as the case may be, whatever philosophical problems might still remain.

5. Believing that he had solved all the problems of philosophy, Wittgenstein gave up its study for other occupations. By 1929, however, he returned to philosophy. Although he did not this time seek to publish the results of his new investigations, he did, around 1933, begin to circulate his new ideas in the form of two sets of lecture notes, one in a blue folder (the *Blue Book*), the other in brown (the *Brown Book*).

6. Although their ideas were at first regarded as representing a complete break with those contained in the *Tractatus*, as well as being wholly unprecedented in the history of philosophy, neither of these views is now considered entirely accurate.

7. In retrospect, we can now see that Wittgenstein, like his predecessors in philosophy, is concerned in these later works with describing the conceptual systems we use, or are compelled to use, in our effort to arrive at a knowledge of reality — conceptual systems (language in his case) which, because of their very nature, must represent a veil between us and the reality they seek to glimpse. Philosophical theories, Wittgenstein therefore concluded, as he had in the *Tractatus*, being products of the distorting mirror of language, are necessarily confusions.

8. The theme common to Wittgenstein's early and late works is that language is the prison house of the mind. With appropriate modifications or alterations, this is a theme which is common to almost the whole of the history of western philosophy.

For further study

1. For a brief and insightful overview of this period in contemporary English philosophy, written with much charm and elegance, see G. J. Warnock's *English Philosophy Since 1900* (New York: Oxford University Press, 1966).

2. Those interested in Bertrand Russell the man as well as the philosopher might wish to read his *Autobiography* (Boston: Little, Brown, 1968–1969, three volumes). Aside from the purely technical works, most of Russell's other writings are both easy and a joy to read.

3. The key works of Wittgenstein's three periods — early, middle, and late — are the following:
   a. *Tractatus Logico-Philosophicus*, translated by D. F. Pears and B. F. McGuiness and with an introduction by Bertrand Russell (London: Routledge & Kegan Paul, 1961).
   b. *The Blue and Brown Books* (New York: Harper & Row, 1965).
   c. *Philosophical Investigations*, translated by G. E. M. Anscombe (2nd ed.) (Oxford: Blackwell, 1963).

4. For a brief and beautiful account of Wittgenstein's life see Norman Malcolm's *Ludwig Wittgenstein: A Memoir*, with a biographical sketch by Georg Henrik von Wright (New York: Oxford University Press, 1958).

5. For an extremely helpful and perceptive exposition of Wittgenstein's works see K. T. Fann's *Wittgenstein's Conception of Philosophy* (Berkeley: University of California Press, 1971).

6. For an excellent collection of essays on Wittgenstein see K. T. Fann (Ed.), *Ludwig Wittgenstein: The Man and His Philosophy* (New York: Dell, 1967).

7. For a collection of somewhat more technical essays concerned with Wittgenstein's late period see George Pitcher (Ed.), *Wittgenstein: The Philosophical Investigations* (Garden City: Doubleday, 1966).

part four:
OTHER QUESTIONS

Honoré Daumier, *Le drame.* The Bettmann Archive, Inc.

chapter **9**

Tragedy and the mystery of human suffering

Philosophy's other questions

As we have seen, to be a philosopher is to be interested in four basic questions: What is there? Who are we? What can we know? and How so? The four main areas of philosophy in which these questions are taken up are, as we saw, metaphysics, ethics, epistemology, and logic. These four areas have traditionally constituted the field of philosophy proper.

These four areas, however, although representing the core of philosophy and what is intrinsic to it, do not exhaust its interests. For philosophers have traditionally not only been interested in investigating the foundations of their own specific concerns; they have also been interested in exploring the foundations of the concerns of other thinkers — artists, scientists, historians, educators, theologians, and so on. What is it that these people do, they have enquired, and what is its meaning?

What is art, what do artists hope to achieve by their creations, and why do their works have the kind of impact on us that they do? What is education, why do we devote ourselves to it, what do we hope to achieve by it, and why? What is history, what is important in it, can we learn anything from its study and how so?

When we engage in these reflective activities we are not engaging in the creation of works of art, in the process of educating people, recording what took place, and so on, but rather in trying to arrive at the meaning of these activities and to make deeper sense of them.

It is important to observe that the artist as artist, or the educator as educator, and historian as historian, is not concerned with raising and pursuing these sorts of questions. The writer of a tragedy, for example, knows quite well that if he truly succeeds in writing a great tragedy it will move those who read it or come to see it in the ways with which we are all familiar. But he is not interested in exploring why such productions leave the spectator in a state of enchantment. He hopes he has sufficient gifts and skill to bring it off and all his energies are directed to doing so. Similarly with the historian, the educator, the scientist, the minister. They are not concerned with what we might call the intellectual aspects of these activities but only in the activities themselves.

Of course they might be interested in investigating these intellectual aspects, but if that is the case then they too are then involved in a very different sort of activity than the one which is their true calling. They then become philosophers and their activity philosophical. And this is obvious, for the results of one's *reflection* concerning, say, the nature of music would not be another piece of music but a dissertation *about* music; and similarly with one's reflection about dramatic tragedy.

These reflective, critical investigations of activities of other thinkers, writers, and artists have given rise to wholly new areas of philosophical inquiry bearing such titles as the philosophy of art, the philosophy of religion, philosophy of history, philosophy of education, science, and so on. Some of these areas are very ancient, some relatively new. In the older branches well-defined problems have emerged, which in turn have given rise to a series of alternative suggested solutions.

In order to get a clearer idea of the nature of this aspect of philosophy, in what follows we will explore one specific problem within one of the more ancient branches. It happens to be a problem closely connected with what we might call the meaning of life and so is not remote from the central concern of philosophy as pursued in its core disciplines, and in investigating it here what we will want to do is not only observe the solutions that various philosophers have proposed but go on and be philosophers in our own right and evaluate these solutions to see what viewpoint we ourselves might arrive at.

The problem chosen is one that emerges from one of the arts — tragedy — and concerns the question why tragedy has the effect on us that it does; a state in which, as Plato put it, we seem to enjoy our very weeping.

How, indeed, can we leave the theater, having viewed scenes of intense suffering and misery, feeling good about things, feeling elated, as if in a state of enchantment? This is the problem and paradox of tragedy.

Six theories of tragedy

Aristotle

The first person to deal with this problem in detail, as well as to inspire a vast literature on the subject, was Aristotle, some of whose other contributions to philosophy we have already explored.

There is a famous passage in Aristotle's *Poetics* that summarizes beautifully what he has to say on the question. Tragedy, he says there, is "an imitation of an action that is serious, complete, and of a certain magnitude, by means of language made pleasing for each part separately; it relies in its various elements not on narrative but on acting; through pity and fear it achieves the purgation of such emotions."

Almost every word in this passage has been the occasion of detailed and seemingly endless analysis and discussion. Writers have explored such questions as Aristotle's meaning of "imitation," "pity and fear," and "purgation." What is "complete" and what "magnitude" (or length) is right? What are the other elements and their combination that best lead to the desired effects?

Although there has been endless dispute over these questions, Aristotle's main view seems clear enough. Tragedy, according to him, by exciting — or, as we would now say, by helping us get in touch — with such feelings as pity and fear, purges us of them and leaves us with a sense of pleasurable relief. This, in his view, is the main function and end of tragedy and it can best be achieved, he says, surprisingly, by a happy ending.

The best tragic drama, according to him, is therefore one that brings before us a noble character who out of ignorance is about to commit a horrible deed but is saved at the eleventh hour when his ignorance turns to knowledge. This sudden and unexpected reprieve relaxes the tension before the play is over and stimulates the flow of tears.

This is Aristotle's solution to the problem. It is a solution, one is tempted to say here, characteristic of the man — proud rationalist, scientist, physician. This is reflected in his view that the best type of hero for tragedy is someone of aristocratic birth, the best type of plot one scientifically based on the universal principle of causality, and the best type of flaw leading to the disaster one that is intellectual in nature — a flaw of judgment. It is also reflected in his rejection of the good, the evil, and the mediocre as unsuitable tragic heroes, the kind of flaw which might morally justify the disaster, and those dramatic effects that are arbitrarily achieved. But perhaps above all it is reflected in his conception of the final tragic effect, which he takes to be medicinal in nature.

Hegel

Skipping some centuries, we find the great nineteenth-century German philosopher Georg Wilhelm Friedrich Hegel (1770–1831) taking a different view of tragedy.

Some people have regarded Hegel as the most profound thinker of all time.

Georg Wilhelm Friedrich Hegel. Berlin State Museum.

Few would doubt that he has been one of the most important in modern times, responsible for shaping the events and the kind of world we now inhabit.

It is strange that Hegel should have had such an impact. He is the most obscure of writers, even for a philosopher, and his ideas — at least, as expressed by him — are not of the sort that would be of much interest to the person in the street.

The key idea in his writings is "the Absolute," conceived as a kind of living, rational, dynamic, evolving Being or Organism. Its entire career, from beginning to end, is open to our direct inspection, for thought and being are one. Both function dialectically: a procedure in which the end (the achievement of the higher, richer, more embracing truth) justifies the means (the subordination and suppression of the particular, limited truth). The evolution of thought thus entails contradictions, oppositions, and negations. But this is not a bad thing, for in the struggle to rise to loftier levels of organization, complexity, and unity, evolving reason and nature — the Absolute — is motivated by one controlling passion: the realization of the final truth, the Absolute Idea. This is a state of affairs in which all contradictions are resolved, all oppositions reconciled, and everything of value conserved. Translated into human terms this means struggle, suffering, and death. But this too is justified, for struggle is the law of growth and the end of life is achievement, not happiness.

In this evolutionary scheme, "beauty" is the emergence of the Absolute Idea through the veils of the world of the senses. Since, however, there is much in nature that is unaesthetic, it is the job of the artist to correct and amend nature, resolve its contradictions, and give the Idea its proper sensuous form. The tragedian shows how the Absolute, by disintegrating and entering the world of particularity, runs into contradiction with itself and labors to become whole again. In the denouement of his drama, this contradiction or division, exemplified by the collision of such eternal ethical principles as "love" and "loyalty" (to one of which alone the tragic hero uncompromisingly commits himself) is resolved.

The hero must, of course, perish in this tragic issue. But his death, rather than shocking us, gives us pleasure, for we realize that it is only his physical life which has come to an end. The ethical principle, which he represented in its false, one-sided particularity, has not been abrogated. It lives on in the Absolute, as do indeed the other particular and equally legitimate and justifiable ethical forces he attempted to deny and negate. We rejoice in this final reconciliation, knowing full well that nothing of real value has been lost in this process of ingathering, and that the Absolute, in whom all things move and have their being, has triumphed once again.

Comedy, Hegel adds, has the same subject matter as tragedy. The goal of comedy is to justify the Absolute, but it achieves this result in a manner different from tragedy. Comedy justifies ethical values by exposing and putting to ridicule whatever is superficial, hollow, and worthless. It does this in one of two ways: by showing the comic character in pursuit of some empty and worthless goal, one which we know can give him no comfort, or by showing him pretentiously aiming at some substantial goal, which, however, eludes his feeble grasp. In either case he fails, to the great amusement of the audience, and the dignity of the Absolute remains unimpaired. Greek comedy, Hegel says, is not funny.

None of this may, perhaps, make much sense to the reader. With patience and some guidance, however, one can extract from it ideas about tragedy that are enormously illuminating.

Put in very simple terms, what Hegel claims tragedy is about is the following: in a tragic work we have the portrayal of a struggle not between heroes and villains or good and bad (melodramas may be about that) but rather between two forces or protagonists, each of whom has right on his side. But although they come to destroy each other in this inevitable conflict, their death does not depress us, for we realize that what each stood for survives their individual, particular deaths and cannot die. There is much in this that seems wise.

Schopenhauer

If it is true that in his account of tragedy Hegel projected upon the stage a budding German moralist, then one might say that Schopenhauer, the next philosopher whose theory of tragedy we consider here, projects upon the stage a budding Oriental pessimist. And a pessimist he might well be, for the force in the universe that bedevils him is irrational. Its name is Will.

The Will, according to Schopenhauer (who lived at the same time as Hegel), is a blind, aimless, irrational force that eternally erupts in an infinite number of living forms. Being blind, it has no goal; being irrational, it has no plan. But it creates with great fecundity all manner of species and, infecting them with its own insatiable desires and demands, sends them out into the world to engage in a pointless and meaningless struggle for mere survival. Man is at the mercy of this purposeless will and his life is a series of endless futile attempts, accompanied by pain, suffering, and sorrow, to satisfy insatiable desires and to overcome the essential tedium of his existence. In this frantic pursuit of happiness man invariably fails, and he continues to fail, till death finally puts an end to his vain hopes and empty dreams.

Arthur Schopenhauer. Mary Evans Picture Library, London.

But salvation from the tyranny and oppression of the will can be achieved, Schopenhauer tells us, by giving up our one inborn error — that we exist in order to be happy. In this task art proves to be a marvelous aid, for art is like the stage upon the stage in *Hamlet*: it objectifies and elevates life's experiences to a higher plane and, in the process, raises both the artist and man in general on to a higher stage of perception. From this elevation we see, at last, life as it is. This produces a quieting effect on the will and gives us the strength and courage to turn away from life as from a bad dream. Joyfully, we renounce the will and, momentarily, enter the peaceful, restful state of Nirvana.

Tragedy, which presents, in a great and striking example, the vanity of human effort and the nothingness of the whole of existence, achieves this result in a direct way. In tragedy the wretchedness of life and the strife of the will with itself is completely unfolded before us. The sorrows and misfortunes of the tragic hero drive home to us the misery and uncertainty of life and we rejoice in his death, realizing in addition that it is not his individual sins that the tragic hero atones for in his death, but original sin, the crime of existence itself. And it is upon this "deeper insight," Schopenhauer contends, that the entire sense of tragedy depends.

Since the object of the tragic drama is to teach the gospel of renunciation, it is clear, Schopenhauer argues, that modern Christian tragedy is greater and superior to ancient tragedy. Unlike Christian tragedy, which portrays the surrender of the whole will to live and the joyful forsaking of the world in the consciousness of its worthlessness and vanity, the ancients show only submission. This is not enough. In fact, he observes, the ancients had really not yet attained the summit and goal of tragedy, nor that view of life itself upon which the true, tragic impression depends. Still, even though the ancients display little of the spirit of resignation in their tragic heroes, the peculiar tendency and effect of tragedy remains, for it awakens that spirit in the spectator. The Greek poet presents, so to speak, the premises and leaves the conclusion to us.

Schopenhauer dismisses the comic drama with a short, incisive comment. Like every representation of human life, comedy, he says, must bring before our eyes suffering and adversity. It cannot escape that. But unlike tragedy it presents it to us as passing and resolving itself into joy, so that if the tendency and ultimate intention of tragedy lies in turning to resignation, in a denial of the will to live, the tendency in comedy lies in the ultimate assertion of the will to live. But comedy is based upon an error in the judgment of life: it declares that life as a whole is thoroughly good and is always amusing. It is just as well that the curtain is brought down in time, for there is still another act to be played.

Nietzsche (1844–1900)

The difference between the theories of tragedy of Hegel and Schopenhauer is that whereas the audience at a Hegelian spectacle delights in seeing the Absolute triumph, at a Schopenhauerian spectacle it delights in seeing it defeated. The Absolute of Hegel and the Will of Schopenhauer reappear on the Nietzschean

Friedrich Nietzsche. Mary Evans Picture Library, London.

stage as Dionysus. And Dionysus differs from the Absolute in the sense that while the Absolute enters the drama dismembered and departs whole, Dionysus enters the drama whole and departs dismembered; and he differs from the Will in the sense that while the Will's performance tends to disenchant us, performance of Dionysus delights and enchants us and makes life desirable.

Nietzsche's aesthetics is formally expounded in his first published book, *The Birth of Tragedy* (1871). It is the function of tragedy, says Nietzsche, to express the Dionysian world view. This is a philosophy of life which recognizes that the world, with all its terror and absurdity, is neither moral nor rational but only beautiful; that this world is nothing more than an aesthetic phenomenon, a product of a suffering, delirious god—Dionysus—who finds peace and the justification for his suffering in the contemplation of his hallucinations. He is the supreme artist, the supreme sufferer, and the world and all that is in it is a product of his state of delirium, a product of his suffering. But while the world is Dionysus's Apollonian artwork and his tragic comfort, our consolation and the justification for our suffering must be sought in our own healing visions and illusions. We are both artworks and artists, and as artists we justify life and make it possible.

In art, then, we must seek our salvation. But, as Schopenhauer failed to see, there are two kinds of art: Romantic and Dionysian. Romantic art is primarily concerned with the *excitation of emotion* and is thus decadent, morbid, sickly; Dionysian art is concerned with the *discharge of emotion* and is strong, healthy, powerful. These two kinds of art appeal to two different kinds of sufferers. Romantic art appeals to those who suffer from reduced vitality and thus crave repose and intoxication; Dionysian art appeals to those who, like Dionysus himself, experience an overflowing vitality and a plethora of health.

Tragedy speaks to the Dionysian sufferer. It speaks to him primarily through music, which is the melodious, plaintive lament of suffering Dionysus. From this music and the state of enchantment it produces there arises the tragic Appollonian myth, which now speaks to those who, in addition to communicating directly with the "Primordial One," wish to *hear* him.

Although there appear to be many myths and legends, they are all variations on one theme: a theme embodied by the Hellenic world in the myth of Prometheus and in the Semitic world in the myth of the Fall of Man. Both myths teach that the best and highest that man can acquire must be obtained by crime (at the expense of God in the Promethean myth) or sin (in the face of God in the Semitic myth) and that he must, in his turn, take upon himself the inevitable consequences: the flood of suffering and sorrow that the offended celestials must inflict upon him. In the tragic myth human evil is shown to be justified and to be a virtue — but a virtue for which we must atone. The tragic myth teaches us to accept this fate with tragic cheerfulness and acquiescence.

The dramatic representation of this myth, in various guises, is the tragic play. In tragedy, Dionysian knowledge is communicated to the audience. But this is a kind of knowledge that finds a response only in those who listen with their hearts and not with their minds. It is a knowledge that can be achieved only by those who "join in" and surrender themselves to the mood and mystery of existence. It says nothing to those who adopt a questioning, rationalistic attitude and who wish, not only to *hear* Dionysus speak but also to *understand* him. It says nothing to those who apply a moral or scientific, instead of an aesthetic, standard to life. But those who do surrender themselves to the mystery of existence become one with Dionysus and experience a tragic delight at the annihilation of the tragic hero. They perceive that in spite of the perpetual flow of phenomena life is at bottom indestructibly powerful and beautiful. The hero dies but life itself goes on, eternally re-creating itself in beautiful illusions, which are the product of delirium and suffering. Dionysus, through the medium of the tragic drama, declares: "Be like me — a creator and destroyer — and rejoice!"

Neitzsche regards his theory of tragedy as the only truly aesthetic theory and thus the only one that can unlock the mystery. And it is from this aesthetic point of view that he levels his criticism at Aristotle, Hegel, and Schopenhauer. His criticism of Hegel's theory of tragedy is that it is founded on the mistaken belief that the world can be justified on moral grounds, whereas, in truth, only a purely aesthetic meaning can be attributed to all process. His criticism of Aristotle is that the essence of the tragic could not lie in the depressing emotions of fear and pity. Had Aristotle been right, he argues, tragedy would be an art harmful and unfriendly to life, for it is a misconception to think that by exercising the emotions of pity and fear we purge ourselves of them. Art is the great tonic of life, the great intoxicant; but something that habitually excites fear and pity only disorganizes and weakens the very will to life. If Schopenhauer, on the other hand, were right in thinking that tragedy taught resignation, then this would presuppose an art in which art itself was denied. Tragedy would constitute a process of dissolution in which the instinct of life would destroy itself in the instinct of art. Tragedy would be a symbol of decline, which it is not.

Hume

In Hume we find a new approach and a different emphasis. Hume's solution to the problem of tragedy consists in making what he calls an "addition" to the current theory — that the peculiar pleasure of tragedy is at bottom nothing more that "sorrow softened by fiction" (criticized by Hume because it cannot account for the factual, historical tragedy) — which is itself, Hume points out, an emendation of the popular view that one enjoys tragic spectacles because it is better to be distressed than bored (rejected by Hume, again, on the ground that it fails to explain why real-life tragedies do not "afford any entertainment").

In tragedy, according to Hume, there are two movements at work: the terror that rouses our passions and the eloquence that charms and enchants us. Since the latter is the prevailing movement in tragedy it overpowers and annuls the depressing effect the lesser movement would ordinarily have upon us. This, and not the fictional nature of dramatic productions, is the principle of softening that takes the edge off the pain to which the representation of the melancholy scenes of life give rise, while at the same time morbidly feeding on our agitated passions. The end result is a kind of bitter-sweet emotion, which is "altogether delightful."

This principle is not confined to tragedy. Hume observes it at work in many of the affairs of daily life. He singles out such phenomena as the love of parents for that child who has given them most concern; the grief at the death of a friend that endears his memory to us; the jealousy that feeds love; the absence that makes the heart grow fonder, and so on. In these phenomena, as in tragedy, the subordinate movement is given a new direction by the predominant, while continuing to nourish and stimulate it.

If, on the other hand, the predominant movement (love, eloquence) for some reason fails to prevail, a contrary effect takes place: the subordinate converts the predominant and the end result is heightened pain and distress, not pleasure. Thus, too much jealousy extinguishes love; long absences prove fatal; and great infirmities disgust. In dramatic productions the effects produced by the inversion of this principle are felt when the theme is too painful for the "beauties of eloquence" to subdue, or when we find ourselves too close to it, or, again, when our sense of justice is outraged. In these circumstances the tragic representation can give us no pleasure.

Jaspers

In Hume, tragedy is brought down from the high position it occupies in Hegel, Schopenhauer, and Nietzsche by his emphasis upon the decorative aspect of the art; in existentialist philosopher Karl Jaspers, it is brought down because (as the title of his book tells us) *Tragedy Is Not Enough.*

Jaspers (1883–1969) approaches tragedy with a seriousness reminiscent of Schopenhauer. But this is a kind of seriousness that no longer finds its consummation within tragedy. Tragedy, to Jaspers, is put to the test and is found wanting.

The truly tragic, according to Jaspers, presents in vast perspectives the whole

Karl Jaspers. The Bettman Archive, Inc.

of existence. It shows man foundering at the edge of doom in search of truth, liberation, and the realization of his higher self. In its "climax of silence" it suggests man's infinite possibilities: dignity, greatness, and courage. But tragedy, as we know it, tends to bring this search to a premature end and to turn this "climax of silence" into a vociferous missionizing.

Using as his measuring stick such key notions as the eternal search for truth, the vision of higher horizons, and the liberation of the human spirit, Jaspers runs through the history and development of tragedy and makes the following observations: that in mythical tragedy man merely endures his suffering, does not as yet yearn for deliverance, and that his questions stop too soon; that in Greek tragedy there is defiance and a yearning for deliverance but also a premature solution in the acceptance of the idea of justice and the reality of good and evil; that Shakespearian tragedy suffers from a similar naiveté; and finally, that Christian tragedy, the tragedy of Calderon and Racine, with its "built-in" deliverances, is no longer tragedy. Here the chance of being saved destroys the tragic sense of being trapped without any possibility of escape.

Although the tragic drama has failed to respond to the challenge of facing the abyss of "universal shipwreck," it has not failed to produce two tragic heroes who have. These are Oedipus and Hamlet. In both men the will to know (exemplified in *Oedipus* in his search for truth about the oracle's prophecy, and in *Hamlet* the truth about his uncle) is without limit. Their unrelenting thirst for knowledge and unconditional acceptance of its consequences create a new value in the universe. They rise in worth and so do we. With Oedipus "his tomb becomes a shrine."

But it is not enough for tragedy, Jaspers points out, to tell the story of human misery, grief, suffering, and misfortune. In themselves these are not tragic. But, by revealing our potentialities and possibilities in the face of human misery and disaster, tragedy prepares us for the encounter with "essential reality," with the "bottomless." In this encounter, a new kind of solidarity among humans develops. A bond of mutual trust, love, and openness is created which entirely conquers the tragic. In the drama, this has been depicted only once: in Lessing's *Nathan the Wise*. And *Nathan the Wise*, Jaspers adds, is not tragedy.

Summary remarks

These six theories do not, by any means, exhaust the multitude of proposals put forward in the literature of tragedy. But the solutions offered are either variations on one or more of these philosophic theories or, more often, attempts to tackle the problem from the point of view of psychology.

Of these six philosophical theories themselves, when considered individually none seems to satisfy entirely. Yet it seems equally clear that all have isolated some factor in the total tragic experience which is both important and integral to it. There is little doubt, for example, that there is in tragedy a certain *inevitability* (Aristotle) of process, some kind of *reconciliation* (Hegel) and *harmony* (Hume) of parts, and that its subject matter is human *misery* (Schopenhauer); nor can there be any question that there is something *illusory* (Nietzsche) about tragedy and, consequently, that tragedy is, in some sense, *inadequate* (Jaspers). These categories are fundamental to tragedy. Any theory that purports to account for its paradoxical effect upon us must take these central notions into consideration. It must try to understand the kind of inevitability involved in tragedy, what in it is reconciled and harmonized, how human misery can be the occasion of pleasure, and why the end product is illusory and thus inadequate.

In what follows let us try to put these various elements together in our own attempt to unravel the mystery that is tragedy.

The anatomy of enchantment

The consolation of tragedy

Few will argue with Schopenhauer that the subject matter of tragedy is human misery in all its expressions: its heartaches, emptiness, pains, and false promises. Tragedy faces the facts of life. But tragedy also thinks it can explain them: that it can explain the triumph of evil, the suffering of the innocent, the emptiness at the pit of the stomach, and the lump in the throat; that it can explain the despair of Job, the predicament of Oedipus, the doubts of Hamlet, and the madness of Lear.

In the drama there is always an attempt to account for human misery and the particular lot of the tragic hero. This is not always immediately apparent, for the dramatist's first task is to arouse our passions, not to appeal to our understanding. But if he hopes to achieve the proper tragic effect upon his audience he must not fail to do both. He must not (and he cannot even if he sometimes pretends to do so) fail to embody in his dramatic works a certain philosophy of life that in some way tries to make intelligible the scene of suffering he brings before our eyes. Even those tragedies in which the fall of the hero is shown to be brought about by pure mischance and that appear to contain no reasoned intellectual scheme of things presuppose a certain philosophic point of view about our human condition, for in the affairs of life to decide negatively is still to decide for *something*.

The dramatist's decision, embodied in the intellectual scheme of the drama, produces a certain state of mind in the spectator — that of understanding. The spectator is made to feel that he "understands" what the suffering of the hero was all about and why it was inevitable. Tragedy, to put it briefly, confronts us with the mystery of human suffering and tries to explain it. We respond to the mystery and are elevated by the explanation. The consolation of tragedy is the consolation of attaining some insight into one's grief or distress, and the greater the insight the greater the sense of elation. This seems to be a universal feature of all tragic dramas and seems to lie at the very foundation of the tragic experience.

Question and answer

Regarded from within, every tragedy consists of two parts: a question and an answer. These two parts cannot always be separated and often neither the question nor the answer is explicitly formulated. But sometimes the question is asked by the tragic hero who also supplies the answer. An extreme and early example of this process is the tragedy of Hosea.

He married, Hosea relates, in a book of the prophets in the Old Testament that bears his name, a woman by the name of Gomer who, he later discovered, had become unfaithful to him. But although her infidelity bore down heavily upon him, he could neither change her ways nor stop loving her. And so he continued to keep her in his house and to care for the children from her licentious unions until, one day, she left him completely for a life of sin and vice, which eventually found her the slave concubine of another man. But his love for her — a love that degrades as well as elevates — was so overpowering that he sought her out, redeemed her from slavery, and reclaimed her as his lawful wife. Seeking some reason for this madness and passion, which filled and tortured his soul, and finding none, Hosea turned to see who else in this vast universe loved so deeply and suffered so much, and discovered God. He came to see, he tells us, that his agony was preordained and that his own tragic life was symbolic of the story of the relationship between God and His people Israel. This discovery made his suffering, at last, appear intelligible — even desirable — to him, and was the beginning of his ministry in the service of God. He proclaimed throughout the land that infidelity is the root of all evil and the chief sin of which the people of Israel, the adulterous wife, is guilty against Yahweh, her loving husband, but that in spite of this infidelity, God's infinite love for his people will not allow Him to cast Israel away, just as he — Hosea — could not cast his wife Gomer from his heart. And so from hilltop to hilltop, Hosea, "the prophet of the sorrowful heart," told the intimate story of his life and pleaded with the people to repent.

The tragic art

Not all tragic heroes find an answer to their suffering and some do not even ask the question. The majority go down with a cry of revenge and a curse on their lips. But in the intellectual scheme of his drama, the tragedian poses the question for them and takes account of even these last signs of rebellion. This is not to say that the spectator who views the entire scene in its totality can, as a result of the dramatist's efforts, put into words just why suffering and misery are now intelligible to him. That he cannot is, indeed, a rather good sign. But in his state of enchantment and elevation, which such understanding and insight produces in him and which is the peculiar pleasure of tragedy, he feels reconciled to the scene depicted on stage, and that is sufficient for him.

That tragedy can do this to him, that it can make him feel that he understands without being able to say what he understands, and in this spirit induce him to make his peace with life, is largely due to the fact that the theatergoer is both a participant and a spectator, who follows the events on stage with a sense of personal involvement and yet at the same time with a certain amount of detachment. To reconcile himself to the scene of suffering, to life, means to achieve a harmony between the participant and the spectator in him. The dramatist takes great pains to maintain this delicate balance, for he knows that such harmony is essential, if tragedy is not to be sacrificed either to melodrama or to comedy. But the intellectual scheme of the drama, designed as it is to make the scene of suffering acceptable and intelligible to the spectator, has such an overpowering effect upon him that he experiences this sense of reconciliation even in those dramas, considered nontragic by both Hegel and Schopenhauer, where the heroes themselves do not achieve it, or where a reconciliation of divergent and conflicting interests does not appear to take place.

Every theatergoer, nevertheless, must at some point in his life ask himself the question: what, in fact, is he reconciled to? The tragic drama has, by means of its intellectual scheme, "solved" for him the mystery of human suffering, and he is delighted. But what is he delighted with? Is he delighted with the fact that there is a God in Heaven who knows what he does? Or is he delighted with the fact that there is no God and no Heaven and that men know not what they do? Is he delighted with the fact that we are all brothers in guilt? Or is he delighted with the fact that we are all innocent but that there is something heroic in suffering for no reason at all? To ask these questions of him is to force him to examine the metaphysical scheme of the drama and to destroy his delight.

This is not a difficult thing to do, for although it is in the nature and interests of art to veil the methods by which it achieves its effects, it is not in the interests of tragedy to hide completely the intellectual scheme that attempts to make human suffering meaningful for the spectator. The dramatist takes, of course, great pains to tie the two strands of his drama tightly together, but by means of a number of subtle dramatic devices (the Greek Chorus, the Shakespearian fool, the subplot that illuminates the major plot, the soliloquy) he takes his audience into his confidence and helps them find their way through the drama. Occasionally he even allows his tragic heroes to question the intellectual scheme of the drama of which they are part. Job's questioning of God's mercy, Orestes's accusation of Apollo, Lear's denunciation of Nature are some notable examples. This kind of inner tension, however, tends to loosen the knots the dramatist has taken such great pains to secure and to weaken the intellectual structure of the drama. Momentarily, it also tends to destroy the illusion that the drama has labored to build up and that is the life of any tragedy. The inadequacy of the artwork is in these tense moments glaringly exposed, and one's apprehensions regarding the tragic art are at such times completely confirmed.

The intellectual scheme

But it would be a mistake to think that the intellectual scheme of the drama is a simple affair. In some tragedies a number of conflicting schemes, each intent upon solving the problem of human suffering and each resting upon an elaborate metaphysical or cosmological system of beliefs, vie for supremacy. The Bible supplies us here with another simple and extreme case — the *Book of Job*.

The *Book of Job* is a product of many hands. This makes it all the more interesting, since it permits us to see the ways in which different minds have approached and struggled with its central issue — the suffering of man. The first and oldest version of the legend is contained in the Prologue and Epilogue and represents the ancient folk saga as it existed long before it was written down. This ancient legend told the story of a man in the land of Uz, named Job, who was perfect and upright, and who feared God and eschewed evil. He possessed every mark of divine favor and was blessed with a large family, great wealth, and many friends. But one day in the Council of Heaven Job's integrity, having been praised by God, is questioned by Satan. Remove the divine Grace from Job, Satan declared, and Job will curse God. The challenge is accepted and Satan is permitted to test the extent of Job's piety. In a series of quick, merciless blows Job is deprived of his wealth, his family, and his friends, and is stricken with an ugly and painful disease. But nothing can shake his trust and faith and he continues to bear his lot piously and patiently, for which he is, in the end, blessed again with wealth, honor, many sons and daughters, and a long, happy life.

The intellectual scheme of the legend in this form is naive and primitive. Human suffering is envisaged as the accidental product of a conflict among supernatural forces over an issue that is almost childish and the outcome of which is never really in doubt. This is tragedy at the lowest level. Too many questions are left unanswered and the problem of human suffering is never really faced. The tragedy of Job is here entirely overshadowed by the drama taking place in Heaven and, although the life of a man hangs in the balance, this fact holds no terror for us since human life as a whole is conceived as a mere pawn in a heavenly game.

Some such dissatisfaction with the legend, no doubt, compelled the author of the *Book of Job* to reconsider its intellectual superstructure. And so, breaking in upon the story at the point where Job is sitting on the refuse heap outside the walls of the town, he sends three friends to Job to condole with him. For seven days and seven nights they sit in silence and mourn. Finally the silence is broken and the debate begins.

The problem before them is unambiguous: why has this lot befallen Job? "Job's comforters," having searched their own minds for some light and finding none, fall back in desperation upon the ancient, traditional conception of the distribution of divine favor in this world. They first gently hint, then affirm, that God is just and that man inhabits a moral universe in which the righteous and the wicked receive their just deserts. If, therefore, an apparently righteous man suffers he cannot be as righteous as he seems. Some kind of sin, they insist, must lie at the root of Job's troubles, and they urge him to commit himself to God.

But this solution to the mystery of human suffering makes no sense at all to Job, who rejects the thesis that sin is the only cause of suffering. It is all too evident, he argues, that human conduct is *not* justly rewarded or punished on earth, and he cites his own innocence, which he defends passionately and eloquently, in support of his convictions. Desperate and bewildered, Job now points an accusing finger at an unjust and heartless God and demands a better account of the facts. But although Job's eloquence and passion silence his friends, it does not convince them: only a solution to human suffering as clear-cut as theirs could do that, and Job has no such solution or intellectual scheme to offer. And so although he wins the debate, the issue remains.

A later reader of the *Book of Job*, following closely the debate on the justice of God in His dealings with human beings, grew progressively impatient with the way in which the drama was proceeding and offered in the person of Elihu his own answer to the problem of human suffering. Elihu first takes Job's friends to task for their poor defense of their position and then condemns Job for his self-justification. Human suffering, he submits, purifies the soul and is a divine warning against evil.

But the last and final attempt to meet the problem is made by God Himself, who confronts Job with a series of unanswerable questions on the mysteries of the universe, the wonders of creation, and the government of nature. Job, who comes to sense man's insignificance in this vast scheme of things, is silenced and his complaints cease. The humbling knowledge, which he receives at the hand of God, perhaps does not make his suffering any more intelligible to him, but its personal revelation makes it at least acceptable — and who can hope for more?

The mystery of human suffering

Although the prevailing theme of all tragedy seems to be the mystery of human suffering, the conception of that mystery has in the course of the history of the drama undergone profound changes. These changes have been largely determined by the attitude to suffering prevalent in a certain age and the intellectual tools at that age's disposal. In Biblical tragedy man stands speechless before his suffering and only God's personal revelation can make that suffering intelligible to him. In the secular drama, however, the belief that the mystery of human suffering can be "solved," if solved at all, in terms of some inscrutable divine purpose has almost entirely vanished. The question that the secular drama poses to itself is not, What purpose is there in human suffering? but, Why does man suffer? And together with the emergence of this new question there is a growing realization (especially strong in Euripides and Shakespeare) that the problem of human suffering is a problem concerning man's *response* to his situation or condition in the universe and not a problem concerning God's design for man.

But ultimately even this new kind of tragedy containing this deeper question fails too. And it fails because its tragic heroes tend to question the *cause* of their suffering — the inordinate penalty for small faults and slight failures — and not the *effect*, their inordinate response. In its attempts to make intelligible this effect in this way, the tragic drama is doomed to failure, for in matters of this kind to explain the cause is not to account for the effect. And this effect, this response, cannot be explained.

There are two movements at work in every tragedy: the drama as the tragic hero sees it and the drama as it takes place in his soul. And although it is in the nature of the art of tragedy to induce the belief that these two movements meet, they never really do. This division is particularly severe in *Hamlet* and the play is wrecked on it. But this is a failure peculiar to all tragedy and the chief source of its illusion — an illusion further fortified by the impression that the two movements stand in some causal relation to one another. It is obvious, however, that there is as great a disparity and incommensurability between the *pain* inflicted upon the tragic hero and the *suffering* he experiences as there is, for example, between the particles of light that strike the retina and the image we see. The particle of light is not the image, although the "cause" of it, and the pain is not the human suffering, although, again, in some sense the cause of it. The particles of light and the pain can be explained, but not the image and the suffering that result and that are not reducible to their causes. These remain a mystery. If the tragic drama induces the belief that it can explain this mystery, and if the state of enchantment experienced at the conclusion of a tragedy is based upon this belief, both are illusions.

The failure of tragedy

The inadequacy of causality

The view that the peculiar pleasure of tragedy arises from the insight we think we now have into the mystery of human suffering is new only in its conclusions. The premises, on the other hand, are ones that the critic (whose entire effort is directed to explaining why tragedy affects us the way it does) has all along assumed. But the conclusion, that since the mystery cannot be explained the state of enchantment induced is founded upon an illusion, is unavoidable and will become evident to anyone who will take the trouble to isolate the intellectual scheme of a tragedy and see what it does and does not explain.

But the tragic drama would not have the powerful effect it has upon us and the illusion it produces would not be difficult to expose if it explained nothing at all. Neither of these two propositions is true, for the tragic drama does, in fact, explain something, although it is not that which it appears to explain — witness the world of Greek tragedy.

When one considers the bare patterns of Greek tragedy one comes to see why Nietzsche was led to characterize the Hellenic mind as troubled and obsessed with the notion of crime. A chain of crime and guilt does indeed seem to hang over the web of Greek myth, a web the Greek tragedian charges with fresh emotion and a new logic. But the sensitive reader cannot fail to perceive that if Biblical tragedy fails to explain the mystery of human suffering in terms of sin, Greek tragedy cannot do it in terms of crime.

But why does it appear to do so? Or, to put it otherwise, how was such suffering and such perversity, as embodied, for example, in Aeschylus' *Prometheus* (where the good not only suffer but suffer *because* of their goodness), made acceptable and intelligible to the Greek audience? The answer to this question is to be found in Aristotle, who selected the plot as the soul of tragedy. And Aristotle elevated the plot to this high function because no other part of the drama can induce the impression of causal sequence and necessity so effectively as the plot. The spectator who exposes himself to its series of causally determined actions finds not only a kind of imaginative satisfaction in the inevitability of the chain of crimes — each requiring a vengeance (which he understands) and which is the beginning of a fresh crime (which he also understands) — but is led to believe, mistakenly, that he now understands the cause of the whole series itself. But although each link in this series is adequately accounted for, the beginning of the series, the first cause, the first crime, the basic presupposition (ancestral guilt, the inheritance of evil, and so forth), which alone can, or is supposed to, unravel the mystery of human suffering, is silently glossed over and is never come to terms with at all. The belief that Greek tragedy has explained these other things — a belief that induces the feeling of elevation and enchantment that is the paradox of tragedy — is simply a case of transference or false association. Judged on its own merits, science or causality is no more an answer to the mystery of human suffering than is revelation.

But, interestingly enough, there are unmistakable signs within Greek tragedy of a rising dissatisfaction with the *causal* "solution" to the problem. This dissatisfaction expresses itself in the rejection of the traditional conclusion to the causal series and the substitution of the kind of conclusion which we find in such tragedies as the *Oresteia* trilogy of Aeschylus and the *Oedipus Coloneus* of Sophocles. In the *Oedipus Coloneus*, Oedipus, who in life was cast down by the gods and his body declared a *curse* and a source of contamination, is in death shown to be exalted by the gods and the possession of that body declared a *blessing* on the land and a source of strength. The *Oresteia*, where a similar transformation mysteriously takes place, is even more instructive.

Orestes's murder of his mother Clytemnestra is clearly a deed that is forced upon him by the mounting and cumulative guilt of past generations, for Orestes is the son of Agamemnon, who in the course of the Trojan adventure had sacrificed his daughter Iphigenia and thus earned his death at the hands of his wife Clytemnestra and her paramour Aegisthus. But the deed can be traced back a generation more, for Aegisthus is the son of Thyestes, who seduced his brother's, Atreus's, wife and suffered the penalty of having his young children served up to him at a banquet by the avenging Atreus, the father of Agamemnon. Orestes's crime lay thus in the line of causation and was, in a sense, preordained. In the ordinary run of things he too would now be called upon to pay for his crime in the usual way. And had he been made to pay the usual violent penalty the Greeks would have "understood" and been delighted. But although Orestes's hands are unclean he escapes from this net, which for generations has been tightening around the house of Tantalus, and breaks the causal chain. A new note is now heard in the world of Greek tragedy.

This new note is struck in the third play of the trilogy, the *Eumenides*, where Orestes, maddened and pursued by the Furies who seek to avenge his crime, flees to Athens and throws himself upon the protection of the Goddess Athena. He reminds Athena that in committing the crime for which the Furies now demand payment he was merely fulfilling the will of God, as that will was revealed to him through Apollo. If he is guilty, so is Zeus.

If Orestes is to be saved and Zeus reconciled with himself, the Furies must be persuaded to moderate their claims upon Orestes. Athena hopes to achieve this by means of reason and the due process of law. She summons a jury and hears the case. And in this new light of reason the question of Orestes' guilt is carefully shown to resolve itself into the question as to which of the two crimes — Clytemnestra's murder of her husband or Orestes's murder of his mother — is the more heinous. On this legal issue the Furies take the stand that, while those who kill a parent are guilty of shedding kindred blood, the crime of a wife who kills a husband is not of the same odious nature. Apollo, however, contends in Orestes's defense that this attitude not only dishonors Aphrodite and the institution of marriage, but is baseless from the point of view of the science of biology, for the real parent of a child is the father, the woman being only the seedbed in which the child grows. Since the relation between a child and its mother is not, therefore, any closer than that between a husband and wife, Orestes's deed was no more foul that Clytemnestra's. If the Furies felt no necessity to pursue Clytemnestra, there is no good reason to think they should feel this necessity with Orestes.

When a vote is taken, it is found to be evenly divided. Athena casts her vote and Orestes is acquitted. But although reason and logic (and the science of biology) liberate Orestes and lay the curse on the house of Tantalus to rest, the Furies still thirst for vengeance. It is apparent that the rational has failed to achieve complete victory over the irrational. It continues to fail in other tragedies as well. But Athena's powers of persuasion are unlimited and she pleads with the Furies to yield, promising them an honored place in Athens and in the hearts of men: from *cursing* deities and the afflictors of men they will become *blessing* deities and the benefactors of men. The Furies bend to Athena's persuasion and like Jacob are given a new name indicative of their new role in the cosmos: the Eumenides, "the Kindly Ones."

Although this approach to the mystery of human suffering is, like the causal approach, imaginatively satisfying, from the point of view of intelligibility it succeeds no better in unraveling that mystery than causality or revelation. One mystery is here confronted with another and both remain essentially unintelligible.

If it should be thought, however, that the causal approach (which fails in the world of Greek tragedy and is ultimately replaced) is confined only to that world, then a glance at Shakespearian tragedy will soon dispel this notion. For even the tragedy of Shakespeare still labors under the illusion that it can explain these ultimate mysteries by the use of causal principles. And so in *King Lear*, to take his greatest work, we find Glouster's suffering explicitly connected with his adultery, and Lear the victim of the principle of the inheritance of acquired characteristics. With a great subtlety, Shakespeare shows how Cordelia, Goneril, and Regan have all inherited some of their father's traits: Cordelia his pride which prevents her from saying (and why should she not have said it?) that she loves her father dearly, and Goneril and Regan his businesslike approach to matters of the heart (evidenced, particularly, in their haggling over the 100 retainers), and the former episode is made to appear as the logical cause of the latter. With Shakespeare, as with the Greek tragedians, biology and causality go hand in hand.

The Failure of Tragedy

Whatever the precise nature of the religious ritual or practice which gave birth to tragedy (a point on which there is still much disagreement) it is obvious that tragedy has not forgotten its origins and has never, not even in the strictly secular drama, entirely severed its links with religion.

Both tragedy and religion attempt in their respective ways to build a wall around man, tame the irrational in his nature, and give meaning and importance to his life. Religion achieves this goal by providing man with a system of essentially incomprehensible rituals, which it claims are God-given but which are guaranteed to secure holiness and eternal bliss for their performer. Tragedy makes no such high claims, but it replaces the rituals of religion with its own system of controls, a system whose distinguishing feature is its intelligibility, but whose only reward is that temporary kind of bliss which is the paradox of tragedy.

In the eyes of religion, to continue this comparison, the greatest tragedy that can befall man is to lose faith in this wall God has built around him; in tragedy the height of despair is reached when the system of controls, the intellectual scheme (the wall the dramatist has built around *his* hero) fails and collapses. When such a collapse takes place within the framework of religion only revelation can heal the wound in man's soul and save him for life. When it happens in the drama, as it inevitably must (for the mystery of human suffering cannot be explained in any rational way), there is only one solution open, and this is to suggest, as in fact tragedy does, a *higher rationality*.

This is the failure of tragedy — not indeed an ignoble failure, but a failure nevertheless and a tragic one. The spectator cannot be unaware of this failure. It does not affect his tragic response, for he senses that out of the ashes of the rubble from the wall the dramatist has built around his tragic hero, there rises a higher rationality which he also thinks he 'understands.'

Conclusion

Tragedy tells the story of a human being alone and a stranger in the universe, confronted by forces he does not understand, at the mercy of passions he is unable to control, and destined to a doom he cannot avoid — a mystery to himself and to others. He fights his friends and embraces his enemies; he misreads the signs and works for his own destruction. But his desire for life is overpowering, and his departure is difficult.

This is not, surely, the kind of story that fills one with joy, yet the tragedian's telling of it warms the heart, delights the mind, and elevates the soul. The reflections upon life and death, deftly interwoven into the tale, appeal strongly to our will to wisdom and desire for light. That will and that desire the tragedian satisfies as best he can, and the passion aroused in us by the scene of suffering ceases to be a passion as it gives way to understanding.

But what are these reflections, and how much light do they shed? Let us isolate them, and see whether they will bear inspection.

It is true, of course, that to be affected aesthetically by tragedy you do not have to share the philosophy of life upon which it is built, for in responding to a dramatic presentation, one does not respond to the intellectual scheme in which it has been conceived — a thing that differs in different cultures and even in the different ages of the same culture — but to the mystery of human suffering it describes. And this mystery remains constant in all cultures and in all ages. But the intellectual scheme, designed as it is to make that mystery intelligible to us, is essential to the total tragic experience; and tragedy, as we know it, must stand or fall with it.

In this analysis of tragedy we have not tried to dispute the fact that one comes away from tragedy feeling wiser and happier. Tragedy's mystic way of looking at our world seems to tell us something about it, which, we feel, we can learn nowhere else — least of all in science. This experience is too common and universal to be doubted. But the question that nevertheless forces itself upon us is: if tragedy, which stands first in the hierarchy of the arts, expresses truths not to be found elsewhere, by virtue of what special method is it enabled to do so?

An investigation of the art of tragedy shows that it has no special method. On the contrary, tragedy seems to approach the mystery of human suffering with an intellectual scheme that reflects the critical thought and philosophical ambitions of its own age. In a highly religious climate, as we can see, if we reflect upon some of the broad lines that tragedy has taken in its handling of its theme, the mystery has been reduced to a problem of evil; in a critical age, to a question of cause and effect; and in an age of sophistication, to a matter of depth psychology. Yet running throughout all tragedy, of whatever age, is the ambition to reveal the *reason* in the *unreason*. And on this success depends the so-called "paradox" of tragedy, a paradox that disappears as soon as the illusion upon which it rests is exposed.

This illusion is created in a number of different ways. We have examined in some detail only one way, and a rather obvious one at that. But it was certainly not obvious to Aristotle nor to the countless number of theatergoers since the time of Aristotle who have been enchanted by the *logic* of the drama. And so captivating is this logic, and so appealing to our human understanding, that it gains our assent to matters which lie beyond that understanding. And thus it happens that we come away from tragedy feeling that we "know," for example, why Prometheus stole fire from Heaven and suffered the penalty of being nailed to a desolate crag; why Io refused Zeus and was metamorphosed into a cow, doomed to roam aimlessly over the earth pursued and tormented by a gadfly; why Antigone defied Creon and was immured in a rocky chamber to die from starvation; and why Cordelia was silent. Although the cause is as absurd as the effect, by placing them in a line of causation the dramatist succeeds in making us believe that he has unraveled the mystery and dissolved the absurdity. Yet he has brought us not a whit closer to the mysteries of the human soul that are expressed in the pity that would save a wretched race of men against the will of their creator, the chastity that refuses to yield even to a god, the loyalty that knows no bounds, and the love that has no voice. The fabric of causes and effects, which the dramatist weaves around this mystery of human suffering, nevertheless succeeds in drawing our attention away as we become consumed in the fascinating and imaginatively satisfying play of forces. The fabric itself he never permits us to penetrate — obviously with good reason.

What has been said illustrates sufficiently how empty and disenchanting the victory is that is won in tragedy. This is not to imply, of course, that to become aware of these illusions — illusions which make us think we are led to the inside of things when, in reality, we are only taken around the outside — is to cease to be enchanted by tragedy. The human mind is enchanted by failure no less than by success. For the awareness of failure is itself a piece of knowledge — and in tragedy, the only *real* piece of knowledge.

Tragedy does not succeed in solving the problem. Its failure to do so is everywhere apparent, perhaps not to the audience of its time but certainly to one of a succeeding age; for who can reflect upon Hosea, for example, and not wonder whether his compulsion to share his domestic sorrows with others reveals not so much a divine call as a human — very human — need? Or who can resist smiling at the kind of science that regards the father as the sole parent of the child? But to judge tragedy in this way is to look at it, so to speak, *von Oben herab* (from the point of view of another intellectual scheme), and there is no need to do this. Tragedy does not attempt to conceal its failure. In fact, the failure of tragedy to show the reason in the unreason is itself tragic, and tragedy tends, as I have suggested, to turn this failure to good account.

But is this *recovery* of tragedy (this sudden and unexpected appeal to a higher rationality) a symptom of its strength and health, or is it a symptom of its weakness and failure? Although philosophic writing on tragedy celebrates this gratuitous victory in the name of Dionysus, Will, the Absolute, and so forth, it is all too obvious that this ghost of tragedy (not properly part of the action at all and appearing, as it does, only when all else fails and the curtain falls) is like all ghosts, simply a sign of death.

The death and failure of reason in tragedy forces the spectator to make a decision. These are trying moments for both spectator and tragedy. The spectator knows that the entire value of tragedy and whether or not he will leave the theatre enchanted or depressed depends upon this decision, and he makes it in silence. It hardly needs to be said that this experience is an irrational one.

But if it is true, as has been argued here, that the theme of tragedy is the mystery of human suffering; that the intellectual scheme which tries to make the mystery intelligible to us merely reflects the hopes, visions, and intellectual pretensions of its own age; that such an attempt is, in any case, doomed to failure; what is left of tragedy? I think simply the story: the story of a human being alone and a stranger in the universe, confronted by forces he does not understand, at the mercy of passions he is unable to control, and destined to a doom he cannot avoid — a mystery to himself and to others.

Summary

1. Metaphysics, ethics, epistemology, and logic are the four areas that have traditionally constituted the field of philosophy. In addition, philosophers have investigated the foundations of such other fields as art, science, and history. In the field of art and art criticism one of the classic questions it has tackled is the paradox of tragedy.

2. Among the many solutions proposed in the course of the investigation of this problem, the most widely admired have been those by Aristotle, Hegel, Schopenhauer, Nietzsche, Hume, and Jaspers. Although none of these seems able to satisfy the requirements of the total tragic experience, nevertheless each isolates at least some factor in this experience that is integral to it.

3. There seems, indeed, to be in tragedy a certain *inevitability* (Aristotle) of process, some kind of *reconciliation* (Hegel) and *harmony* (Hume) of parts, and apparently its subject matter is human *misery*

(Schopenhauer); nor can there by any question that there is something *illusory* (Nietzsche) about tragedy, and, consequently, that tragedy is, in some sense, *inadequate* (Jaspers).

4.   But tragedy's attempt to explain the mystery of human suffering must be judged a failure. This failure springs in part from the fact that its intellectual scheme tends merely to reflect the philosophical assumptions of the age which created the tragic work and cannot therefore exceed that available to philosophy and religion.

5.   For its effects tragedy comes finally to depend upon illusion, and in this illusion (of having discovered the reason in the unreason) is to be found both its aesthetic appeal and its real failure.

For further study

1.   For a classic text in aesthetics, beautifully written and covering in some detail the problem of tragedy, see Jerome Stolnitz's *Aesthetics and Philosophy of Art Criticism: A Critical Introduction* (Boston: Houghton Mifflin, 1960).

2.   For a work devoted entirely to this problem see Walter Kaufmann's *Tragedy and Philosophy* (Garden City: Doubleday, 1969).

3.   Those who may wish to read the six philosophers whose theories have been reviewed and summarized will find them in the following works and editions: (a) For Aristotle see S. H. Butcher's *Aristotle's Theory of Poetry and Fine Art, With a Critical Text and Translation of The Poetics* (New York: Dover, 1951). (b) For Hegel's theory see G. W. F. Hegel, *The Philosophy of Fine Arts*, translated by F. P. R. Osmaston (London: Bell, 1920). The relevant passages on tragedy will be found reprinted in Melvin Rader's *A Modern Book of Esthetics: An Anthology* (New York: Holt, Rinehart and Winston, 1979, pp. 234–240). (c) For Schopenhauer's theory see his major opus, *The World as Will and Representation*, translated by E. F. J. Payne (Indian Hill, Colorado: Falcon's Wing Press, 1958). (d) For Nietzsche's theory see his *The Birth of Tragedy*, translated, with commentary, by Walter Kaufmann (New York: Random House, 1967). (e) For Hume's theory see his essay "Of Tragedy" in *Of the Standard of Taste And Other Essays*, edited with an Introduction by John W. Lenz (Indianapolis, Indiana: Bobbs-Merrill, 1965). (f) For Jasper's theory see his book *Tragedy Is Not Enough*, translated by A. T. Reiche, H. T. Moore, and K. W. Deutsch (London: Gollancz, 1953).